A GUIDE FOR THE ELEMENTARY SOCIAL STUDIES TEACHER

A GUIDE FOR THE ELEMENTARY SOCIAL STUDIES TEACHER

Third Edition

W. LINWOOD CHASE

Emeritus Professor, Boston University

MARTHA TYLER JOHN

Professor, Mid-America Nazarene College

Allyn and Bacon, Inc.
Boston London Sydney Toronto

LIBRARY OF CONGRESS CATALOGING IN PUBLICATION DATA

Chase, Willard Linwood
A guide for the elementary social studies teacher.

Includes bibliographies and index.
1. Social sciences—Study and teaching (Elementary)
I. John, Martha Tyler, joint author. II. Title.
LB1584.C48 1978 372.8'3'043 77-21606

ISBN 0-205-05938-4

Second printing . . . August, 1979

CONTENTS

PREFACE

The third edition of *A Guide for the Elementary Social Studies Teacher* has been designed to include many of the current topics of concern in social studies education. It also presents methodologies that are more workable in the flexible, mobile elementary curriculum that we see in operation everywhere. We deleted with a vengeance, added with pleasure, and reorganized with careful, thoughtful consideration.

The second edition of the Guide was viewed by a critical reader as ". . . a much needed practical guide to teaching elementary school social studies . . ." In this third edition, we have kept this foremost in our thoughts and have endeavored to retain the integrity of the first and second editions as a *practical* aid to teachers. We acknowledge that the development of theoretical statements, models, and curricular schemes are essential to the production of quality teaching. We also believe that both students in training and experienced teachers seek help in translating these structures into a workable program.

Our concern for the improvement of classroom teaching and learning has determined our choice and treatment of the material in this third edition of the *Guide*.

W. Linwood Chase
Martha Tyler John

SOCIAL STUDIES FOR THE PRESENT AND THE FUTURE

Chapter one

Social studies is concerned with knowledge of the past, but we must teach children in the present, real world and prepare these children for the future. It is not possible to tell exactly what the world will be like when today's elementary children are adults, but what it becomes will undoubtedly stem from the changes going on now. Present events and recent shifts and improvements can be assessed. Extrapolations and predictions based on these shifts can be made, and they are being made already by many experts in different fields.

Technology has been largely responsible for the rapid changes that have taken place during the past century. However, technology has not been a totally munificent mother. It has demanded a toll that is now being collected. The price for overuse of resources and rapid growth is becoming more and more evident, and the students we are teaching today will be forced to deal with this problem.

The questions we, as social studies educators, must consider very seriously are these: Is the social studies curriculum preparing children to live in a world that reflects gross technological change? Are we preparing children to deal with the accumulated problems of the past and the present as thoughtful, positive individuals who can also plan for a better future?

A major objective in education is the development of the thinking citizen who is aware of his responsibility to society, yet at the same time is able to fulfill his own needs as an individual in a changing world. Social studies has a special role in this development.

The classroom teacher is the key person who conveys the contribution that the social studies make to the education of children in a democracy. Curriculum guides do not become class lessons until the teacher implements them, and the objectives of curricula cannot be realized except through involvement of the children. Changes in curriculum are necessary if our youth are to understand the world in which they live and become knowledgeable participants in a society that will be very different from that of today. Since 1960, re-assessment of social studies programs has been underway in an increasing number of special studies and projects. It seems evident that changing content will not in itself improve the quality of teaching. There must be improvement of teaching and learning in the classroom. First, however, there must be a commitment to action on the part of the teachers and their supervisors. That such a willingness exists is more evident than it has been in the past, but a continuing effort—a commitment—is more difficult to maintain.

School systems cannot simply wait for *the* book to give them an exact pattern of what to do and how and when to do it. Social scientists as a group are not in agreement regarding what changes are needed. Many social scientists, for example, would like their own discipline to be the focus of an elementary social studies curriculum. Who, then, are to be the architects of change? In the final analysis, it is each school system by its own decision, each elementary school by its own decision, each classroom teacher by his own decision, encouraged by administration, that will make social studies for the children better in content and better in method of developing understanding of their own country and the world about them. Yet, while individual and group decisions provide the impetus for change, the social sciences must serve as the base for scholarly improvement of the content.

CONCEPTUAL APPROACH TO LEARNING

In the recent past the development of sophisticated technology has increased the quantity of information available in all disciplines. Students cannot possibly cover all the information available in the various social sciences. What, then, shall they learn? Can students be expected to remember the date of a given encounter in Viet Nam? Should they know the specific amount of grain grown in a certain state last year? These facts may be of utmost importance to a particular individual or group but not all students can be expected to learn them. What facts must all the students know? How many discrete facts shall they learn? Would it not be a more efficient use of learning time for students to acquire some analytical thinking strategies, some skills in working with social science content, and some positive feelings about learning that will have a more long-range use? Analytical skills and strategies have more transfer potential for new content and other disciplines.

Conceptual learning does not depend entirely on rote memorization. Such learning is based on the development and clarification of broad concepts. Concepts are mental constructs based on a process involving delineating specific elements, organizing the related elements, analyzing the results, and then reorganizing and redefining the construct. The process of concept formation is a complex one and is based on both the experiences the student has had and the time provided for the reorganizing of these experiences as they relate to the concept.

There are concepts in each of the social science disciplines that can help provide guidelines and a focus for instruction. It is important that the major ideas within the disciplines be sorted out and used as a base for a carefully planned curriculum where concepts and skills are developed with increasing sophistication each year. This approach is referred to by Taba et al. as the *spiral curriculum.*[1] It is one in which concepts such as *cultural change* are introduced and reintroduced each successive year using broader content. For example, *cultural change* might be examined in first grade as it relates to the family. Bringing a new baby home or moving to a new house can provide a base for examining cultural change at this grade level. By the time a student is in the fifth grade he may be examining the same concept in terms of the changes involved for the people who came to the New World on the Mayflower, the problems presented when large numbers of Oriental immigrants began to arrive in western United States in the late nineteenth century, or the cultural change factor for a community in which Viet Nam refugees have taken up residence. All of these projects—at both grade levels—have more inherent challenge than just simple memorization. It is interesting to note, however, that the student will need many facts before he can deal with the content in a satisfactory manner. Which facts and how many resources must be used will be a part of the decision-making process for the student. This is an important part of the conceptual approach to learning and helps prepare the student for real-life situations in which many decisions must be made.

The following section presents all of the social science disciplines and provides a practical lesson application for each one. In addition, some concepts and generalizations from each discipline will be given as typical exemplars.

THE SOCIAL SCIENCES

The social sciences study human beings and their interactions with each other and the environment. Social scientists have made valuable contributions in developing scholarly information systems for their separate disciplines. While there is considerable

1. Hilda Taba, et al., *A Teacher's Handbook to Elementary Social Studies,* 2nd. ed. (Reading, Mass.: Addison-Wesley, 1971).

overlap, there are some concepts and generalizations that pertain more specifically to one discipline of the social sciences than another. A concept is an abstract idea that collects and codifies or systematizes a number of items—it is a *pattern label* for some class of objects. For instance, *transportation* is a pattern label—it refers to a large collection of objects that have a common function or are based on a pattern that one can detect and examine. A generalization is the relationship of two or more concepts. For example: In this country technology [concept] has greatly affected the development of transportation systems [concept].

Anthropology

Anthropology is "the study of man and his works"—an all-encompassing definition to be sure. It has also been defined as "the study of man embracing woman"—a provocative definition indeed. Actually, it is the study of people and their customs both past and present. It has potential for futuristic projections because it provides data about the primary needs of human beings. One of the key concepts of anthropology is culture, that is, the system of beliefs, artifacts, and behaviors peculiar to a specific group of people, or a society.

Anthropologists are interested in different aspects of the study of man. Physical anthropologists are intrigued by the fossil remains of man and other primates. They study the bones of ancient people, and they also study people of the present day to see how and why they differ in physical appearance. The physical anthropologist is also interested in primates such as baboons and chimpanzees and in the similarities and differences in behavior and physical development between them and man.

Archaeologists, another group of specialists, dig in ancient ruins to find out about the cultures of long-vanished societies. They search for artifacts that will give them information about the people who lived in the past.

Linguists study systems of human communication and look for comparisons between languages and coding systems. They may be concerned with the development of language in a particular culture. Linguistic anthropologists hope to discover the common ancestors of words, expressions, or phrases.

Ethnologists or cultural anthropologists seek to discover commonalities between groups of people by making systematic comparisons of folklore, music, economic systems, or other cultural patterns. They are interested in the changes in culture and the reasons for change.

The research methods of the anthropologist are of interest to the teacher. "Fieldwork is undoubtedly the favorite activity of the anthropologist, for research in all the subfields of anthropology is frequently pursued in out-of-the-way places, distant lands—in Africa, the Arctic, or the South Pacific. An anthropologist's first field trip, particularly if it deals with a primitive society, far from cities and civilization, is regarded as an initiation rite after which he is 'never the same again'."[2] While this idea is frequently joked about, it is in a very real sense the truth. The anthropologist's research method is one of participant observation. He lives in the culture he is studying and tries to observe behavior in a scholarly, objective way. He collects a great deal of data from which he sorts out recurring themes that can be translated into generalizations about the culture. Anthropological generalizations are often based on interpretive judgments rather than on objective, hard facts. The anthropologist's attention to detail and care in examining evidence are strategies that have universal application for the researcher.

Considerable use of anthropological concepts is currently evident in classrooms. Many units of work now examine a cross-cultural comparison of people, such as between the Plains Indians and the Desert Indians of the United States. Young children enjoy studying about different homes, food, and ways of learning, and can use their own mores as a basis for comparison. Subcultural groups within the United States, especially Black Americans, Native Americans, and Spanish Americans, are a frequent basis for study in the elementary grades.

Let us imagine that you want to study a unit with an anthropological emphasis. The concept of *culture* might be a good one to emphasize, and the main idea involved could be that culture is a complex system of beliefs, behaviors, and man-made objects. Here is a partner role-playing vignette that you might use to stimulate the students' interest and to provide a concrete base for studying their own and other cultures:

> *U.S. student:* You are just meeting a Japanese student in your classroom in Japan. It is the first time you have ever been in Japan, and you feel a little shy and unsure of yourself, but a Japanese student who seems friendly has just asked you to tell him what Americans are like. You say . . . .
>
> *Japanese student:* You have wanted to go to the United States for a long time because you have heard a lot about it. A new student from the United States has just been placed in your class. You can hardly wait to ask, "What are Americans really like?" So as soon as you get the chance you turn to whisper your question. You say, "Hello, it's nice to have you in the class. Can you tell me something about America? What are Americans really like?"

Let the students discuss this in teams simultaneously. Collect the summaries of their discussions on the board and you are ready to begin a study of one culture, which can branch to comparisons across time and space.

2. Perrti J. Pelto, *The Study of Anthropology* (Columbus, Ohio: Charles E. Merrill, 1965), p. 33.

CONCEPTS IN ANTHROPOLOGY: customs culture artifacts primitive society

GENERALIZATION: Culture is a complex system of beliefs, behaviors, and man-made objects.

FOR FURTHER READING

Anthropology in Today's World. Columbus, Ohio: American Education Publications, Inc. A 64-page paperback. Case studies of people and cultures.

Bailey, Wilfred, and Marion J. Rice. *Development of a Sequential Curriculum in Anthropology for Grades 1-7.* Anthropology Curriculum Project, Fain Hall, University of Georgia, Athens, Georgia 30601.

Banks, James A., and Ambrose A. Clegg, Jr. *Teaching Strategies for the Social Studies.* 2nd ed. Reading, Mass.: Addison-Wesley Publishing Company, 1977. Chapter 9.

"Focus on Anthropology." *Social Education,* March 1968. Five articles on anthropology in the elementary school.

Joyce, Bruce R. *New Strategies for Social Education.* 2nd ed. Chicago: Science Research Associates, 1972. Chapter 3.

Muessig, Raymond H., and Vincent R. Rogers, eds. *Social Science Seminar Series.* Columbus, Ohio: Charles E. Merrill, 1965. The editors have written a concluding chapter (thirty-five to sixty pages) for each volume suggesting many activities. All these volumes will give the reader excellent capsules of the social science and provide some stimulating ideas for elementary social studies classes:

Henry Steele Commager, *The Nature and Study of History;* Jan O.M. Broek, *Geography: Its Scope and Spirit;* Pertti J. Pelto, *The Study of Anthropology;* Caroline B. Rose, *Sociology, The Study of Man in Society;* Francis J. Sorauf, *Political Science: An Informed Overview;* Richard S. Martin and Reuben G. Miller, *Economics and Its Significance.*

Spindler, George D., and Louise S. Spindler, eds. *Case Studies in Cultural Anthropology.* New York: Holt, Rinehart and Winston. Paperback series, including such titles as *The Eskimos of North America, The Mexican Americans of South Texas.*

"Teaching about American Indians." *Social Education,* May 1972, pp. 481-534.

Sociology

Sociology is the study of human relationship, of the individual as a social being. It involves people in a variety of group settings, such as families, schools, tribes, labor groups, prisons, or nations. Any collection of people in which there is some interaction is the basis for sociological investigation.

There are several specialized divisions of sociology that provide focus for the social researcher. Some sociologists study institutions and relatively permanent groups, such as the army or the family. Other experts concern themselves with more flexible groups, such as crowds, delinquent gangs or audiences. Still another group of sociologists are interested in the way society affects a person's behavior and personality. These social psychologists investigate the processes by which a person learns to behave in groups, the roles an individual performs in society, and the model the individual chooses to imitate in achieving selected behaviors.

The case study and the survey are two sociological procedures. Other methods of gathering and assessing information, such as questionnaires, opinionnaires, and interviews, are used to ferret out unconscious attitudes and motives. Projective tests consisting of verbal and nonverbal components are designed and administered to get the individual to respond honestly with his true feelings about a group or a situation.

One method of investigation that is shared with the anthropologist is the participant observation technique. This is a strategy in which the researcher becomes a member of the group and records the behaviors in the group as objectively as possible. Sociologists have even had themselves imprisoned to study groups in penal institutions.

Many sociological concepts are already a part of the social studies curriculum. For example, the family and the community are a part of nearly every primary program. Institutions like the school are explored at a beginning level and can be developed in more detail to provide depth and challenge. The comparative community is a beginning emphasis that has promise for further sociological research in the elementary school.

Let us assume that you wish to begin a unit or sequence of lessons with a sociological base. Following is an exemplar of a beginning lesson.

CONCEPT. . . . . .COOPERATION

1. Have students list examples of "ways in which people cooperate."
2. Collect the statements.
3. Arrange the students in small groups.
4. Hand out the statements to the students. Each group will have a different sample of statements. Have them sort the statements into categories (statements that belong together) and name the categories.
5. Collect their groupings of statements from all the groups.
6. Anticipated categories: long/short statements; helping others / doing as you are told; children helping / adults helping.
7. Now, through a series of lessons, examine the ways in which people cooperate, and check the application of the students' groupings to the lesson being developed. Use a variety of materials, media, and direct experience exercises in explaining the advantages and disadvantages of cooperation. Students could work in production lines or watch a movie (e.g., on the reclamation of a swamp) in which cooperation is emphasized.

CONCEPTS IN SOCIOLOGY: norm socialization role value

GENERALIZATION: Population growth is one of the most challenging problems of modern times.

FOR FURTHER READING

Banks, James A., and Ambrose A. Clegg, Jr. *Teaching Strategies for the Social Studies*. 2nd ed. Reading, Mass.: Addison-Wesley Publishing Company, 1977. Chapter 8.

Joyce, Bruce R. *New Strategies for Social Education*. Chicago: Science Research Associates, Inc., 1972, pp. 66-77.

Michaelis, John U., and A. Montgomery Johnston. *The Social Sciences: Foundations of the Social Studies*. Boston: Allyn and Bacon, 1965.

Rose, Caroline B., *Sociology, The Study of Man in Society*. Social Science Seminar Series. Columbus, Ohio: Charles E. Merrill, 1965.

Economics

Economics is the study of the production, distribution, and consumption of goods and services. It is concerned with the ordinary individual's income and expenditures as well as with the giant economic systems and problems of finance of nations. Economics is important to the man who earns $3.00 an hour and to the senator who is considering a bill for several billion dollars of revenue.

The economist is interested in the process of exchange of goods and in the flow of money payments from consumers to business and back to the public. He is aware that a scarcity of goods or services will force choices and that the choices made will be based on needs and values combined. Some economists have specialized in the history of economic systems and how they have developed and changed. Another group of specialists are concerned with a particular modern economic system. They may study unemployment, federal highway programs, or the impact of the tariff on oil imports. Some experts narrow their range of interests to a small specialty and examine history, present findings, and make predictions about the future of this special interest. "In economics, forecasting is generally systematic, explicit, and data-based, although not always accurate, partly because the forecasts themselves lead to intervention in the economic system."[3] It is clear from Toffler's point of view that economic predictors make an honest effort to be objective, but that their very predictions may influence and alter the system so that the predictions go awry.

3. Alvin Toffler, ed., *Learning for Tomorrow* (New York: Vintage, 1974), p.88.

The research and investigation in economics is becoming increasingly scientific. Computers are frequently used to store the data collected from a large sample. Statistical comparisons can then be made with relative ease. Modern economic research relies on mathematical and/or statistical analysis, and the typical economist develops skills in these areas. The interpretation of statistics has become an important part of economics.

Much of the content of elementary social studies programs can be related directly to the economics discipline. For example, the family is a typical subject in the early grades. How members of the family earn a living and how the income is spent are matters of concern for every student. Students should be encouraged to examine career opportunities in their community. The services of banks and savings plans are also of interest. Recreational facilities and their initial cost and maintenance should be part of the student's education. The field of economics is a rich one for students and, in fact, is already an operating part of most curricula.

Let us assume that a teacher wishes to begin a series of lessons with a strong economic emphasis. Table 1.1 is an example of a matrix that might stimulate the

TABLE 1-1. MATRIX FOR PEOPLE AND THE EVERYDAY BUSINESS OF LIFE

	LIVING IN A COMMUNITY	INDUSTRIAL WORK	OBLIGATION TO THE GOVERNMENT
Social Skills	Use of transportation: subway, bus Asking directions—police Recreation, parks, museums	Job preparation and safety Interview skills Use of leisure	Army obligations Social Security obligations Tax forms
Information-processing Skills *listening* *locating* *collecting* *organizing*	Phone directory Newspaper ads Banking facilities	Job application Map skills Following directions Banking paychecks	News interpretation Banking facilities Knowledge of benefits from army Social Security claims
Decision-making Skills *comparing* *analyzing*	Apartment choice Reporting problems to proper authority	Choice of factory or industrial complex Consumer competency	Voting Serving on jury

development of activities about "People and the Every-day Business of Life." These suggested variables deal with the academic skills that are needed for the areas indicated. Students can explore the economic implications of each. Training required to carry out the obligations to government, time involved, benefits derived, and suggestions for other areas of involvement can be part of the follow-up lessons.

CONCEPTS IN ECONOMICS: consumers producers choices specialization

GENERALIZATION: Within the home all members of the family are consumers, but only some are producers.

FOR FURTHER READING

Coon, Anne. "Introducing the Economic World to Primary Grade Pupils." *Social Education* 30 (April 1966): 253-256.

"Focus on Economics." *Social Education,* January 1968. Five articles on economics in the elementary school.

Jarolimek, John, and Huber M. Walsh, eds. *Readings for Social Studies in Elementary Education*. New York: Macmillan, 1974.

Joint Council on Economic Education, 1212 Avenue of the Americas, New York, N.Y. 10036. A clearinghouse for economic education. A newsletter provides continuing references to classroom resources. Write for its checklist, which lists such publications as "Learning Economics Through Children's Stories"; "Economics and Our Community: A Research Unit for Grades 4,5, and 6."; and "The Child's World of Choices."

Martin, Richard S., and Reuben G. Miller. *Economics and Its Significance*. Social Science Seminar Series. Columbus, Ohio: Charles E. Merrill, 1965.

Morrissett, Irving, and W. Williams, eds. *Social Science in the Schools: A Search for Rationale*. New York: Holt, Rinehart and Winston, 1971. Chapter 9, "Economics in the Curriculum."

Senesh, Lawrance. *Our Working World*. Books for pupils, teacher's resource units, and phonograph records are published by Science Research Associates, Chicago, Ill. 60611.

Walsh, Huber M., ed. *An Anthology of Readings in Elementary Social Studies*. Washington, D.C.: National Council for the Social Studies, 1971. Read "The Pattern of the Economic Curriculum" by Lawrence Senesh and "Economic Education in the Middle Grades" by Ardis Gustafson.

Political science

Political science is the body of knowledge that describes, explores, and analyzes political systems, power groups, and institutions of government. It is a science that examines the individuals who make up a particular system and the decision-making process of which they are a part. Political science as a discipline is concerned with theories of government and research in a number of specialties.

Political scientists study political parties, elections, the influence of interest groups, people's voting habits, and the effects of news media on political events. They are interested in political socialization, that is, how an individual develops in a particular society as a political person. What makes people participate in the political workings of their country? Political scientists are interested in the ways in which governments in different countries relate to each other and in the changes that take place in governmental policies as a result of these interactions.

The methods the political scientists use to gather information are of interest to the social studies teacher. Perhaps of all the social scientists, political scientists have been most futuristic in their research procedures. They study election trends and polls and on the basis of this information extrapolate. ". . . . In a modest way they [political scientists] have engaged in trend analysis and formulated images of both the immediate and remote future."[4]

While this is true, there is a division of thinking among political scientists about the bases on which predictions or extrapolations should be made. One group of experts feels strongly that political science studies (futuristic as well as past and present investigations) should be based on the objective facts of the particular situation. Such scientists have designed computer programs for codifying data and recording facts. This process produces a dependable accumulation of data, but carries with it an obvious problem. The human element, the unpredictable event or action, is difficult to take into account in a computer program. The second group of specialists at the other end of the objective/subjective continuum is interested in the decisions that have been reached and in the effect the values of the people involved have had on the final decision. This group tends to study people in situations in a more personalized prediction technique. The problem inherent in this approach is clear. The degree of generalizing ability is severely limited, and therefore, in extreme application, each particular person and/or event may need to be explored separately—a time-consuming task.

With either group of experts the skills of charting, graphing, and sequencing of events are crucial. The careful accumulation of data and the derivation of generalizations based on the data are important. Prediction is based on information, and scholarly effort is involved in the organization of facts that are behind the predictions.

Some of the emphases of political science can be found in the elementary school at the present time. Children study about their own government, the revolutionary action that brought it into being, the internal war that threatened its survival, and even the recent threat to its credibility based on the actions of persons in respon-

4. Ibid., p. 88.

sible roles in our government. Children study about community government when they visit the mayor's office and the fire station. It is even possible for them to learn the ways of democracy through actual practice of such procedures in the classroom. Indeed, a considerable amount of political science content is available to the elementary teacher.

Let us imagine a good beginning for a sequence of lessons that have strong political science flavor. The following questions could form part of a questionnaire to be used to introduce the topic of government to the children.

1. What are the three branches of federal government? Place an X over the list that names all three.

____	____	____
Congress	President	Congress
Governors	Mayors	President
Supreme Court	Governors	Supreme Court

2. Can you list the title of our government leaders?

   a. Name the head of the federal government.

   ______________________________.

   b. Name the head of a city or town government.

   ______________________________.

   c. Name the head of a state goverment.

   ______________________________.

3. How many years is the President elected to office?

   a. Four years____

   b. Three years____

   c. Six years____

   d. None of the above____

4. Can you name one U.S. Senator?

   ______________________________.

Other questions might be added. With the students' help, tally and graph the results. (The tallying and graphing exercises are a valuable part of learning how to handle a questionnaire.) Determine the topic with which the students need the most help. In a joint planning session design a procedure for finding out about the topic.

POLITICAL SCIENCE CONCEPTS: role political party political behavior power government

GENERALIZATION: In countries around the world man has developed various forms of government.

FOR FURTHER READING

Casteel, Doyle. "Current Events and Political Science: Seeking a Functional Relationship." In *Political Science in the Social Studies,* 36th Yearbook of the National Council for the Social Studies, Chap. 20. Arlington, Va.: National Council for the Social Studies, 1966.

Cleary, Robert E. *Political Education in the American Democracy.* Scranton, Pa.: Intext Educational Publishers, 1971. Paperback.

Easton, David, and Jack Dennis. "Political Socialization of the Elementary School Child." In *Political Science,* pp. 216-235.

Greenstein, Fred. *Children and Politics.* New Haven: Yale Univ. Press, 1965.

Jarolimek, John. "Political Science in the Elementary and Junior High School." In *Political Science,* pp. 236-253.

Niemeyer, John H. "Education for Citizenship." In *Social Studies in the Elementary School,* 56th Yearbook of the National Society for the Study of Education, part II, Chap. 9. Chicago: Univ. of Chicago Press, 1957. A classic in its field.

Payne, Rebecca S. "Focus on Primary Grades: Practicing Citizenship." *Childhood Education* 42 (March 1966): 423.

Sorauf, Francis J. *Political Science: An Informed Overview.* Social Science Seminar Series. Columbus, Ohio: Charles E. Merrill, 1965.

Geography

Geography is a study of the land and the interrelationships of man. While geography deals primarily with the spatial arrangements of the earth's physical and cultural features, it is more than a study of places. It is concerned as much with the people who live in these places as with the places themselves.

1. Each individual place or area on earth is related to all other places on the earth in terms of size, direction, distance, and time.
2. Maps represent different ways to view the earth. There are many kinds of maps. They are useful to geographers, travelers, statesmen, economists, planners, businessmen, and citizens in general.
3. A *region* is a mental concept useful in organizing knowledge about the earth and its people. It is an area which in one or more ways has relatively homogeneous characteristics such as physical features, cultural features, occupations, or political affiliation, and is in one or more of these respects different from surrounding areas.

4. A human settlement, whether a single residence or business or metropolis, is related to other places that supply it or receive from it goods and services in a form of geographic linkage.
5. The natural materials and conditions of the earth influence the ways in which people live and work, but because of their cultural achievements and their ability to think, people can evaluate and use geographical elements in different ways. They can modify their environments to suit their purposes. As people's ideas and technologies change, their ways of living and their use of the geographic elements may change.

In research in the field, geographers usually specialize. Physical geographers are concerned with the physical features of the earth, which include climate, water, soils, and landforms—what is on, in, and above the earth. Regional geographers explore areas with somewhat similar physical characteristics (polar lands, dry lands, etc.). They may also be interested in culture regions (the Orient, the Middle East, the Corn Belt). Cultural geographers examine the relationships between man and the modification of the natural environment—what might be called human geography. Historical geographers have been described by Phillip Bacon as those "primarily interested in the past geographies of a region in order [to] better understand its contemporary geography. The physical patterns are relatively durable and only slowly changing, but the cultural patterns are always in process of rapid change."[5] Many professional geographers consider themselves spatial geographers. They study the location of places and are able to explain why cities, mountains, or human populations are arranged as they are. These geographers work in cartography, the production of maps.

> Much of the drive in contemporary American geography stems from the "spatial tradition." It is here that one finds concern for a whole gamut of generalizations related to spatial distributions, spatial associations, and spatial interactions. It is an understanding of these spatial relations and processes, along with an understanding of their significance to human activities, that encourages the student to analyze why things are where they are. Much of the work being done on the frontier of the discipline today falls into this tradition. . . . Elementary school geographers can find a sustaining bond of fellowship with the research geographer in even the most rudimentary work that they might undertake in problems concerned with direction, distance, and location. These are spatial problems and, as such, are tied directly to the spatial tradition in the discipline of geography.[6]

The following geographic exercises can be used at an intermediate level:

5. Phillip Bacon, "Changing Aspects of Geography and the Elementary Curriculum," *Social Education* 31 (November 1967): 609-611, 624.
6. Ibid.

1. Ask the students to think of the place they have traveled furthest from their present home. Then ask them to tell what they saw that would not be found here. At every mention of anything of a geographic nature the teacher can say, "That is geography."
2. Get three or four copies of a "Census Portrait of. . . . (the state where you teach)." (These are available for 10¢ each from: Publications Distribution Section, Social and Economic Statistics Administration, Washington, D.C. 20233. Do not send stamps.) There are data based on the 1970 census concerning ethnic groups, racial make-up, income, schooling, workers and jobs, farming, etc. in these four-page folders. A population density map is also included. Look in the *World Almanac* to find a state that has about the same population as yours, and get the same number of copies of that state's "Census Portrait." Have a group of three or four students go through the same process of finding a state about equal in population to theirs. (You will have copies ready for them). Let them study both "Portraits" and make such comparisons as they are able.

GEOGRAPHIC CONCEPTS: location climate natural resources population distribution

GENERALIZATION: Ways of living are influenced by geographic location.

FOR FURTHER READING

Bacon Phillip, ed. *Focus on Geography: Key Concepts and Teaching Strategies.* 40th Yearbook of the National Council for the Social Studies. Arlington, Va.: National Council for the Social Studies, 1970. Chapter 10, "Children's Spatial Visualization," by John Eliot; Chapter 11, "Developing and Using Behavioral Objectives in Geography," by Ambrose A. Clegg, Jr.; Chapter 12, "Building and Using Inquiry Models in Teaching Geography," by James L. Hills; Chapter 15, "Emerging Social Studies Curricula: Implications for Geography," by Lorrin Kennamer, Jr.

Broek, Jan O.M., *Geography: Its Scope and Spirit.* Social Science Seminar Series. Columbus, Ohio: Charles E. Merrill, 1965.

Hanna, Paul R., et al. *Geography in the Teaching of Social Studies.* Boston: Houghton Mifflin, 1966.

James, Linnie B., and La Mont Crape. *Geography for Today's Children.* New York: Appleton-Century-Crofts, 1968.

Manson, Gary, and Merrill K. Ridd, eds. *Geography in Today's Curriculum.* National Council for Geographic Education, 115 North Marion St., Oak Park, Ill. 60301.

Walsh, Huber M., ed. *An Anthology of Readings in Elementary School Social Studies.* Arlington, Va.: National Council for the Social Studies, 1971. "Principles and Practices in the Primary Grades," by Val Arnsdorf, pp. 137-139; "Changing Aspects of Geography and the Elementary Curriculum," by Phillip Bacon, pp. 168-170; "Geography in the Middle Grades," by Lorrin Kennamer, Jr., pp. 155-157; "Curriculum Planning for Geographic Education," by George S. Tomkins, pp. 144-147.

History

> To a ten-year-old, history can be tramping the wilderness with Daniel Boone, raising the flag with the Marines at Iwo Jima, living with seventy-five others 'tween decks on the *Mayflower* in the long voyage across the Atlantic, riding with Paul Revere through the night to Concord town, and floating down the Mississippi with Pere Marquette. It can be an Indian watching the *Santa Maria* and her sister ships drop anchor, climbing the heights of Darien with Balboa, surveying with Washington in virgin territory, imprisonment by Indians with Captain John Smith, and travelling under the North Pole in a nuclear-powered submarine. It can be seeing new homes rise one by one in Jamestown, tasting buffalo meat on the trek by covered wagon across the western plains, smelling exploding gunpowder in many a French and Indian battle, feeling cold water rising to one's armpits in Arnold's march to Quebec, and hearing the great peal of the Liberty Bell on that first Fourth of July.[7]

History is the past. That past may be yesterday, last year, when grandfather was a little boy, two hundred years ago, in the sixteenth century, when Rome ruled the European world, or thousands of other happenings. History is the present, today's events. History is a story. History is a record. Commager says, "There are as many kinds of history as there are historians, and each historian writes his own kind of history."[8] However, down through the centuries certain traditional patterns of organizing material in writing have been developed. Commager delineates these traditional patterns as the chronological, the geographical, the political, the cultural, the institutional, and the biographical.

The chronological pattern has a beginning event or events carried through the succeeding years to the end point determined in the planning. The geographical was more evident when historians of the nineteenth century used to think of history as something that concerned only the European world, that is, Europe, the Mediterranean, and the Americas, although the non-European world occupies two-thirds of the globe. The political pattern seems to be the most convenient to the historian because historical materials are customarily organized along national lines. This approach is popular because it appeals to national pride. "The cultural historian is called upon to know, understand, and explain the ideas of a whole generation, sometimes in many different societies, and to trace their manifestations in the whole fabric of history."[9] Explaining and interpreting the youth culture of the 1960s and 1970s would concern the cultural historian. The biographical pattern is a large part of history. Biography is probably, for the general reader, the most popular form of history.

7. W. Linwood Chase, "American History in the Middle Grades," *Interpreting and Teaching American History*, 31st Yearbook (Washington, D.C.: National Council for the Social Studies, 1961), p. 342.

8. Henry Steele Commager, *The Nature and the Study of History* (Columbus, Ohio: Charles E. Merrill, 1965), p. 15.

9. Ibid., p. 20.

> Man's political systems, his social groupings, his very life style affect the historian and influence his writings. History is not something which exists independently of man; it is something that comes to us filtered through the mind and the imagination of men. . . . History as a record consists of three states or processes, usually so skillfully blended that they appear to be a single one. The first is the collection of what is thought to be relevant facts; but remember, what seems relevant to one person will appear irrelevant to another. The second is the organization of these facts into some coherent pattern; but remember, no two patterns are ever quite alike. The third is the interpretation of the facts and of the pattern; and certainly no interpretations are ever quite alike. Now all of these processes flow into each other. The practiced historian is not ordinarily conscious of these separate steps any more than a skillful baseball player is conscious of the separate steps that go into a decision to strike at a ball. It is impossible to collect the facts in the first place without some theory of relationships among them; after all, what are you looking for? It is impossible to organize them into a pattern without some theory that dictates the pattern. And it is impossible to interpret them except on the basis of the material that has been selected and the pattern that has been drawn.[10]

Some of the many experiences that children may have today reach into the field of history:

1. They compare and contrast ways of living. Grandparents came to settle in this country, or father grew up on a farm.
2. They listen to the tales of the past—stories that great-grandfather may have told to grandfather.
3. They observe or take part in the celebration of national and local holidays. All holidays have historical meanings.
4. They possess relics of a past era—an antique table or chest or something else that has been in the family for generations.
5. They notice place names. How did that building, park, square, street, town, or city get its name?
6. They use maps. Maps tell stories to those who know how to read them and raise questions that history can answer. Compare a map of any continent in an up-to-date atlas or geography with one published thirty-five or forty years ago.
7. They collect coins, stamps, pictures of automobiles down through the years.
8. They read. Interest in historical events may have developed from storybook reading or from some newspaper or newsmagazine reading.
9. They watch television. Curiosity about some things they see may raise questions with a historical basis.

Develop discussion in your classroom. Ask, "What is history?" The experiences listed above will help you in directing discussion.

10. Ibid., p. 5.

One interesting approach to discussion is to ask, "Can you see history, or touch, taste, smell, or hear history?" You could divide the class into groups of four or five students with a secretary writing down the suggestions on which a group agrees. With reports from the groups, a class chart could be made.

Some students might like to write the "History of Craig," or the "History of Janet," about themselves.

HISTORY CONCEPTS: early settlements chronology westward movement the present heirlooms the past change slavery

GENERALIZATION: Growing up one hundred years ago was different in many ways than growing up today.

FOR FURTHER READING

Chase, W. Linwood. "American History in the Middle Grades." In Cartwright, William H., and Richard L. Watson, Jr., eds. *Interpreting and Teaching American History,* 31st Yearbook of the National Council for the Social Studies, chap. 19. Washington, D.C.: National Council for the Social Studies, 1961.

Commager, Henry Steele. *The Nature and Study of History.* Social Science Seminar Series. Columbus, Ohio: Charles E. Merrill, 1965.

Johnson, Henry. *Teaching of History in Elementary and Secondary Schools.* Rev. ed. New York: Crowell-Collier-Macmillan, 1940. This is a classic that should be read by every teacher interested in teaching history.

Kownslar, Allen O., ed. *Teaching American History: The Quest for Relevancy,* 44th Yearbook of the National Council for the Social Studies, Washington, D.C.: National Council for the Social Studies, 1974. Chapter 1, "Is History Relevant?," by Allen O. Kownslar; Chapter 5, "Can We Put Ourselves in Their Place," by Virginia M. Rogers and Ronald K. Atwood; Chapter 9, "Am I Relevant to History?: The Environment," by Allen P. Lawrence. Should be of particular interest to the elementary teacher.

Martin, Edward C., and Martin W. Sandler. "Rejuvenating the Teaching of United States History." *Social Education* 35 (November 1971): 708-739. Suggests many resource materials and where to get them.

Walsh, Huber M., ed. *An Anthology of Readings in Elementary Social Studies.* Arlington, Va.: National Council for the Social Studies, 1971. "In Primary Grades—Today's Discovery is Tomorrow's History," by Joan Alcorn and Ruth Griesel, pp. 148-150; "The Dilemma of History in the Elementary School: Product or Process?" by Ambrose A. Clegg, Jr., and Carl E. Schomburg, pp. 158-161; "The History Component of the Elementary Social Studies Curriculum," by Jean Doherty, pp. 151-154.

Humanities

The areas of humanities such as art, music, and literature are important aspects of all social science disciplines. One might study about an artist who lived during the

Renaissance and was part of a particular school or group of painters. He has historical and sociological dimensions. The artist comes from a certain part of France and his paintings are beautiful and valuable. The individual and his creative product crossed disciplinary lines, but he was a real part of a given setting and was influenced by that setting.

The artist sculpts during a particular era, the musician composes a beautiful aria at a particular point in time, and the writer develops a play over several years. In a very real sense, however, these creative products span time in a most unusual way. Political states and civilizations change, but the works of the artist, the musician, and the writer remain for centuries. The creative individual conquers time in this sense and is able to share his ideas with the generations that follow him.

It is important that people in the social studies recognize and use the creative products of a culture as part of the input about that culture. Not only does such expressive input provide information of a unique kind, it also provides stimulation and encouragement for the children to explore the development of new modes of expression for themselves.

The methods used by artists, musicians, and writers are diverse and not always of immediate use for the classroom. Some of the qualities underlying the actual development of a creative product, however, do have relevance for children. A highly developed skill undergirds every truly creative production. The skill and the difficulty and persistence involved in developing it can be explored with children. The actual production of a work of art requires discipline. Lastly, the creative artist is synthesizing his skill, his thoughts, and his feelings into a convincing whole. He is daring to share his inner self with the world even knowing that misunderstanding and misinterpretation are bound to occur. He is willing to risk himself in order to share a unique idea or sensation. True creativity requires a commitment to the production and sharing of an idea.

The teacher could begin a presentation of social studies lessons with a humanistic base by playing a song that all the students recognize. "America the Beautiful" is one example. Let the students sing along. Go back over the song and look for word images such as "purple mountain majesties." Ask or list the following questions:

1. How could you best illustrate this song?
2. When was the song written and what other events were taking place at this time in U.S. history?
3. Who wrote the song? What experience in the composer's life may have served as a basis for the ideas in the song?
4. Could a history of well-known songs reflect something of the history of the country?
5. Why do people write songs about the country in which they live?
6. Compare the patriotic songs of the United States with those of another country.

Prepare a series of activities for each question, and allow the students to select one question (and accompanying activities) to develop for sharing with the class.

HUMANISTIC CONCEPTS: artistic esthetic expressive

GENERALIZATION: People in different places at different times in history have produced products that are appealing to the senses and are considered creative.

FOR FURTHER READING

Kinney, Jean, and Cle Kinney. *Twenty-one Kinds of American Folk Art and How to Make Each One*. New York: Atheneum, 1972.

Powell, Thomas F., ed. *Humanities and the Social Studies,* Bulletin 44. Arlington, Va.: National Council for the Social Studies, 1969.

Tooze, Ruth, and Beatrice P. Krone. *Literature and Music as Resources for Social Studies.* Englewood Cliffs, N.J.: Prentice-Hall, 1955. In spite of its publication date, a reference that must be available to elementary teachers. For literature and music sources to enrich social studies units it has no equal. The music for many songs is in the text.

SCIENCE

Science is a broad term that refers to systematic knowledge. Science concerns observable facts and the theories and principles related to these facts. The sciences include 1) physical science, 2) biological science, 3) mathematics and logic, and 4) the social sciences which we have just described. Each of the divisions of science concentrates on a facet of organized information. For example, the physical scientist is most concerned with the nature of the universe, and there are many specialties under this broad rubric. Astronomy, physics, geology, chemistry, and meteorology are all special interests of physical scientists. There are even more definitive specializations in each field of science. In physical science under the specialty of physics, one might study and obtain advanced degrees in atomic or nuclear physics, electronics, or aerodynamics.

Biological sciences involve the study of living organisms. Such topics as heredity, bacteria, and the relationship of the organism to its environment are of great interest to the biological scientist. Mathematics and logic are the working tools and skill areas of all scientists. Since scientists are mainly interested in events that can be repeated, they need the tools of mathematics and logic to explain, help describe, and even aid in predicting future events.

The social scientists, of course, are concerned with man and society. This area of science is a difficult one in which to carry out precise experiments because an individual may not act in exactly the same way twice. Social scientists rely on observation, logic, and, frequently, broad sampling to arrive at conclusions.

The scientific method is one of the prime contributions of science to the world of thought. In general terms, the scientific method consists of five steps: 1) stating the problem, 2) forming hypotheses, 3) observing and experimenting, 4) analyzing and interpreting data, and 5) drawing conclusions. There are variations and elaborations on the steps in the process, but using this sequence does help to explain a problem in a logical, orderly way.

The field of science has become a highly specialized one, and yet a clear-cut definition of where one science begins and another ends is most difficult. In a single space launch, for example, almost every scientific specialty is involved. The social scientists are concerned about the persons involved, their feelings and preferences, their comfort and safety. The mathematicians and statisticians are involved in recording volumes of data on the computer so that they can account for and help predict all the events and possibilities. The biological scientist is enthralled with the data such an experiment provides about human reactions to stress, breathing, heart function, and the like. Meanwhile the physical scientist is testing the adequacy of the technological equipment and the reaction of the metals to heat and cold. A scientist in any of these areas cannot work alone, but needs the help of other specialists to provide the most beneficial results.

In many of the topics presented in this book, you will see the overlap of science and technology with the social sciences. It is difficult, almost impossible, to study man without also investigating the inventions and products that he has produced. In the classroom as well, the interdisciplinary approach can be used to examine effectively people, their society, and their universe.

SCIENCE CONCEPTS: proof experiment data

GENERALIZATION: Scientific experimentation and technology have produced rapid changes in people's living environment.

GOALS FOR SOCIAL STUDIES

Social studies is more than content, it is also process. It is the study of the relationships of individuals to their physical and social environment, and the interaction of a person with other people. Young children must learn how to study about people. The process of finding out becomes an important part of the learning that elementary children must pursue. Indeed, social studies for the elementary school child begins to sound more and more complex.

What are the goals and responsibilities of the social studies program?

The ends set up in curriculum guides may appear as objectives, aims, goals, purposes, or even as the social studies philosophy. However these are stated, the social studies program goals should complement and build on the educational goals of the school. The primary goal of the school is to aid in the development of individuals who are knowledgeable, self-directed, and sensitive human beings. The competencies that can be expected of such individuals can be spelled out for the social studies curriculum and will provide direction in program development.

The student who is a knowledgeable, self-directed, sensitive human being can:

1. Demonstrate knowledge and skills related to the social studies content being explored.
2. Work efficiently and productively toward the solution of problems inherent in the content being used and listen to the ideas of other people while producing creative ideas of his own.
3. Investigate and develop a background in the social problems, values, and feelings of people in his own and other cultures.

Knowledgeable person

The social studies must provide the student with a body of knowledge about human beings and society. It can provide information about the past and present that can serve as a base for futuristic projections and extrapolations. Social studies inquiries also produce data that show how human beings have adapted to place or environmental differences and how they have changed these places or adapted them to their own needs.

Since social scientists have ways of recording information that are unique to the social science discipline, children must be given instruction in reading and interpreting these data. For example, recording ideas and information on different kinds of maps is the distinct purview of the social scientist. Therefore, it is the responsibility of the elementary social studies program to provide the students with the needed skills to enable them to glean information from these map sources. What are the specific understandings and skills that are needed to produce students who are knowledgeable in social studies?

Skills. The skills below are instruments for transmitting knowledge and understandings into patterns of behavior. Without these broad information processing skills, the students would hardly be able to use what they know. (In addition, Chapter 9 is devoted to the development of specific map skills, charting, graphing, use of time sense and sequence, and research skills.) What are the skills that a social studies student must have?

Reading
Organizing
Observing
Listening
Defining issues
Making decisions
Expressing ideas clearly
Locating
Weighing evidence

Self-directed problem solver

While knowledge is crucial to any social studies program, the ability to *use* knowledge to solve problems, see relationships, and make decisions is perhaps even more important. It is not enough to produce students who can recite dates of wars and treaties or explorations. The students must know how to relate this information to other events and how to gather data about other topics of interest. In every body of social studies content, there is the potential for using heuristic and hypothetical questions. These involve the mental processes of problem solving and thus involve the student much more directly. The heuristic question, "What if we expanded our national park system to double its current acreage?" will provoke the students' thinking. They will have to consider cost, legislative problems involved, people's feelings for and against the system, new map designs, boundary decisions, and a host of other issues. The social studies program should concern itself with helping students learn to solve problems in a systematic way so that they can become self-directing problem solvers and can continue to grapple with issues when they are no longer in a structured school setting.

Problem-solving skills

1. Problem recognition and definition form an essential first step in the problem-solving process.
2. The collection of data and the judgment involved in deciding on amount and type of data involved are important problem-solving skills.
3. A data summary and analysis phase are a needed part of the process.
4. The formulation of alternative solutions and the selection of the solution that is best for this particular problem are important strategies in the problem-solving process.

5. An evaluation of the practicality of the problem solution is useful and frequently provides suggestions for follow-up and refinement of the problem being examined.

Social person

Every social studies problem should provide the developing students opportunity to explore the role of the self in their own society. Developing the student's self-concept, with an emphasis on the social, political, and economic values needed in a democratic society, is a real part of the social studies responsibility. Learning to respond to the needs of people in one's own and other cultures is also an important part of the social studies education process. Some of the basic values needed to produce a societal person are:

1. The dignity and worth of the individual.
2. A belief in democracy and in the peaceful coexistence of nations.
3. A positive approach to the solution of problems.
4. Respect for people of different races, creeds, appearance, or national origin.
5. A belief in education as a vehicle for self-satisfaction and improvement.
6. Involvement with and concern for the immediate group with which one lives.

The objectives or goals that have been given are broad and inclusive. They are not behavioral, instructional objectives, and would require more specific detail if they are to be translated into instructional form. Examples of behavioral objectives are given with the units in Chapter 2 and the learning packets in Chapter 5.

CURRICULUM PLANNING

The decade of the sixties witnessed curriculum planning to an extent never before known. The seventies have been a time for assessing, refining, and exploring new dimensions based on the results of past labors. The next decade will require a renewed commitment to social studies education—to educating children to live peaceably with one another in a world that reflects economic and social stress.

Curricula now being developed in elementary social studies deal with a rationale involving the social science disciplines of economics, political science, anthropology, sociology, history, and geography, in an interdisciplinary or multidisciplinary organization. Emphases, focus, grade placement, and choice of content will vary. Social studies is concerned with people. People's ways of living cannot really be understood without knowing something of their past (history); their interrelationships with their environment (geography); their groupings and institutions (sociology); their patterns of behavior (anthropology); their production, distribution, and exchange of goods (economics); and their processes of governing (political science).

Certain similarities in content exist at various levels of instruction. The greatest similarities may be found in the early grades, which include such units as Family Life, the School, Our Community, and Communities Around the World. Noticeable differences may be found in grades 4, 6, and 7. Even at these levels one can find similar topics and units, but they are placed in different grades. For example, some schools provide for the study of Western Hemisphere countries in grade 6 and Eastern Hemisphere countries in grade 7; in other schools the reverse may be true.

Overview

The following section presents a grade-by-grade overview that shows the dominant theme or themes for each grade, followed by illustrative topics, units in each grade, and a brief statement of recent trends.[11]

Kindergarten. Local Environment Studies — Short-term experiences and units are provided on home, school, neighborhood, store, service station, how we learn, the airport, trucks, and other aspects of the immediate environment. Current trends are: to provide deeper studies of the home, school, and neighborhood; children and families in other lands; our global earth; and how people change the neighborhood and the community.

Grade 1. Family, School, and Community Life — Illustrative units include: the family; our schools and other schools, the family at work; neighbors at work; community workers; the fire station; the supermarket; families, schools, and neighborhoods around the world; the dairy farm; farm life; and how we learn. Current trends are: to introduce economic, anthropological, and other concepts from the various disciplines, such as division of labor, extended family, and role; to teach map and globe skills in greater depth; to provide comparative studies of families and schools at home and abroad; to compare rural and city life; to consider homes of the future; and begin to develop career awareness.

Grade 2. Community Studies—Units and topics include: community workers; public services; how we get our food, shelter, and clothing; transportation; com-

11. John U. Michaelis, *Social Studies for Children in a Democracy, Recent Trends and Developments*, 6th ed. Copyright © 1976. Reprinted by permission of Prentice-Hall, Inc., Englewood Cliffs, New Jersey.

munication; our community and other communities; living in different communities; and workers around the world. Current trends are: to provide for comparative studies of communities: to extend map and globe concepts; to study and compare changes in communities; to include some historical material on the community; to investigate food, shelter, and clothing in other lands; to emphasize specialization and division of labor within and among communities; to consider future developments: and to develop career awareness.

Grade 3. Metropolitan Communities, City Life, Cities Around the World— Illustrative units and topics include: neighboring communities, different kinds of communities, transportation, communication, urban problems, living in metropolitan communities, communities around the world, pioneer communities, native Americans, development of our community, comparative studies of our community and other communities, and further communities. Among the trends at this level are: increased attention to interdependence among communities; to urban problems, planning, and renewal; to past, present, and future changes in cities and metropolitan areas; to how the community is governed; and to careers in the community.

Grade 4. Our State, Regions around the World, Regions of the United States, Great People in American History—Units and topics that illustrate the diversity at this level are: our state in early times, our state today, living in different world regions, our global world, conservation, area study of India, changing Japan, and how Americans obtain goods and services. Significant trends at this level are: to provide cross-cultural comparative studies; to study historical, geographic, and economic aspects of the home state in greater depth; to give more attention to state government; to study the contributions of individuals from all groups to the development of the state and nation; to explore future prospects and proposals for change; to give attention to environmental problems; and to explore careers and roles of workers at the state level.

Grade 5. Living in Early and Modern America; Regional Studies of the United States, Canada, and Latin America — Illustrative units and topics are: discovery and exploration of America, colonial life, pioneer life, westward movement, contributions of leaders, regions of the United States, relationships with Canada, living in the Americas, and our neighbors to the north and south. Current trends are: to stress relationships among countries in the Americas; to study urbanization in different regions; to explore the impact of scientific and technological developments in the past and present; to give more attention to the contributions and history of minority groups; to include environmental studies; to include law-based instruction on rights and responsibilities; to include new programs such as Man, A Course of Study;* to provide a more balanced treatment of the past, present, and future; and to extend career awareness to the national level.

Grade 6. World Cultures, Western or Eastern Hemisphere — Illustrative units and topics stressing the Western Hemisphere are: early cultures of South America; the ABC Countries, Argentina, Brazil, Chile; living in Mexico; countries of Central America; historical and cultural beginnings in the Western world; and economic and social problems. Units and topics focusing on the Eastern Hemisphere are: backgrounds of American history, Western Europe, Central Europe, Mediterranean lands, Eastern Europe, the USSR, the Middle East, North Africa, Africa south of the Sahara, India, and China. Schools that focus on global geography provide for a selection of units on culture regions and countries around the world. Trends at this level are: to program grades 6 and 7 so that students may study both Eastern and Western culture regions; to highlight interdependence among countries; to explore the problems of developing nations; to consider the work of international agencies; to study the impact of culture on ways of living; to analyze social, economic, and political systems in greater depth; and to explore current problems and possible future developments.

Grade 7. World Cultures, Eastern or Western Hemisphere Studies, Study of Our State, U.S. History — The history and geography of Eastern Hemisphere areas, expecially Europe, are predominant, with emphasis on such units and topics as Old World backgrounds, early man, early civilizations, Greece and Rome, the Middle Ages, and Western European nations. Schools that focus on countries in the western hemisphere tend to stress geography and include units and topics similar to those listed above for grade 6. World geography is offered in some schools, and in several places Our State is studied in grade 7 instead of in grade 4. Much of the work in grade 7 is planned to provide background for units on U. S. history in grade 8. Current trends are: to include studies of the cultures of Asia, Africa, and Latin America; to interrelate state and national history; to include ethnic studies; to explore the problems of new nations; and to study historical, geographic, social, economic, and political aspects of development in greater depth.

Grade 8. U.S. History; The Constitution; Federal, State, and Local Government—Specific topics and units include: exploration and discovery; colonization; the

* Originally developed by The Education Development Center (E.D.C.), these materials are now available from Curriculum Development Associates, 1211 Connecticut Ave., N.W., Suite 414, Washington, D.C., 20036.

thirteen colonies; the winning of independence; the Constitution; building a government; emergence of American patterns of living; the Civil War and Reconstruction; growth of industry and agriculture; enrichment of U.S. life; contributions of leaders; contributions of minority groups; preserving and extending human rights; becoming a world power; relations with other nations; government at the local, state, and national levels; and geography of the United States. The typical practice is to emphasize the study of early U.S. history up to the Reconstruction era with about one-third of the time on later U.S. history; the reverse is generally true in grade 11 in which U.S. history is studied intensively. Current trends are: to provide fewer units and to study them in depth; to provide primary source materials for analysis and interpretation by students; to give more attention to minorities in the history of the United States; to emphasize the interrelationships of federal, state, and local government; to provide case studies on selected aspects of government; to relate historical trends to current problems and future developments; and to clarify the legal rights and responsibilities of all citizens.

Characteristics of quality programs

The total program is a complex of understood purposes, of subject matter content plus generalizations drawn from it, of classroom practice, of learning materials. The Newton program enumerates nine characteristics of a good social studies program.[12]

1. A good program should include a definite statement of scope and sequence, grade by grade. It should be firm in that no teacher should feel free to appropriate content assigned to a later grade. It should be somewhat flexible in that, for enrichment, the scope of successive units should be expandable in depth.
2. In a good program, the content for a grade level should be related to the maturity, experience, and ability (in terms of complexity of ideas) of children of that age. To meet individual differences, teachers still have to vary learning activities to meet each child's talents. Mastery of content and generalizations will be relative to the individual's capacity.
3. Each topic or unit, in a good program, should be relevant to the learner's life. If choices were well made, each unit will contribute to children's perception and understanding of their world and its problems. That this may introduce them to controversial issues at an early age is a merit, not a defect.
4. A good program is relevant to the needs of society. Society may justly demand that those who share its benefits should contribute to its well-being. An industrial society in the twentieth century rests on a base of science and technology for which there is no earlier model. A democratic society cannot afford many non-

12. *Social Studies, Kindergarten through Grade Nine,* Newton, Mass. Public Schools. Reprinted by permission.

participant members. They must take on not only the burdens of conformity, but the burdens of nonconformity, not only the exercise of the right of protest, but the obligations of directing change in constructive ways.

5. A good program will help children grow in their grasp of the concepts basic to the systematic, organized structure of disciplines. This is the process by which information becomes knowledge. Information becomes knowledge as it reveals relationships, as means are derived from it and discovered to be pertinent and relevant to other meanings. With a structure of knowledge available to him, a child has one of the tools he needs to continue to learn. A first step in this direction is the identification of basic concepts. The second step in shaping a program in this direction is building into the teaching process a greater sensitivity for generalizations.
6. A good program gives children an opportunity to study whatever they study in enough depth to acquire a satisfying feeling of mastery. Rather than expose them to summary surveys of broad fields, they should have time and materials to explore more limited topics in detail.

   This position implies several corollaries: (a) Since the time available does not increase, some topics have to be left out. (b) Survey textbooks do not meet our needs for materials. (c) We must identify and supply more extensive study and reading materials but in fewer areas. (d) We have an opportunity to use original source materials rather than secondary summarizing materials. (e) Greater demands will fall on library-type collections of materials and on developing skills in using them. (f) Structuring of teaching plans will call for less emphasis on recall, question-answer responses, more emphasis on thinking and reasoning responses. (g) Where omission of topics leaves blanks that must be filled in to link units, as in history, a careful collateral reading program must be devised to fill them.
7. A good program is based on an interdisciplinary approach.
8. A good program expands pupils' interests. Partly this will occur by study in depth, and partly by emphasizing relevance. In large part, however, it is related to the developing of pupils' concepts of self. In the discovery of relations and of interests, they also discover their own personal uniqueness.
9. A good program requires balanced attention by teachers to its many elements. These elements include:

   a. Acquiring information and knowledge about the cultural heritage we share.
   b. Developing study and learning skills.
   c. Growth in self-concept or self-knowledge for purposeful self-direction.
   d. Building attitudes or tendencies to behavior acceptable in our society.
   e. Learning to appreciate the arts in our culture and the services of others.
   f. Becoming aware of the basic concepts and structure of the social science disciplines.
   g. Developing understanding of the meaning of facts and events.
   h. Formation of permanent interests and sources of enjoyment in the social sciences, history, and the humanities.

i. Developing skill in critical thinking and problem-solving.
j. Discovering habits and skills of good citizenship, including group participation.
k. Developing habits and skills of good citizenship, including group participation.
l. Acquiring an inspiring code of values that might govern personal relationships.

Minnesota Project Social Studies Program

The University of Minnesota Program, developed in a five-year federal project, is being used and adapted now in many states. Resource units may be purchased and duplicated for use in any school system. Curriculum committees vary in adaptation of individual units. Some use them as they have been developed; some make minor changes; others make more detailed changes to fit the community, the teaching corps, or the materials available. Some have introduced individual units into their own curricula.

Dorothy Fraser has described the Minnesota program. The grade-level themes show successive study of family, community, regions, and nation.[13] When the unit titles are examined, however, the content that is used is significantly different from conventional programs. Kindergarteners become acquainted with the globe on which they live and are introduced to concepts of conservation, cultural diversity, and change. First- and second-graders study families, but the families they study are widely distributed in space and time. These families are selected to illustrate cultural variations and similarities and to demonstrate culture change. Most of the content must be considered to be "new."

Third- and fourth-graders study communities, but again the communities are widely distributed in space and time and represent a considerable change in content as compared to conventional programs. Study of political institutions begins specifically in grade 3, and economic concepts and principles are emphasized in grade 4. In the regional studies of grade 5, case studies of limited site locations are combined with brief overviews, replacing the general historical-geographic survey of the Western Hemisphere that has frequently been found in this grade. Some of these are sequent occupance case studies, others are historical-geographic in emphasis.

In grade 6 we find the first cycle of U.S. history planned to articulate with a second cycle placed in grade 10. (Note that this program reduces by one year the time spent on U. S. history as such.) The five chronological units in grade 6 carry the national history to 1876, emphasizing culture contact, culture change, and cultural

13. Dorothy M. Fraser, "Social Studies in the Elementary School: A Case Example of New Content," in Alexander Frazier, ed., *The New Elementary School.* (Washington, D. C.: Association for Supervision and Curriculum Development and the Department of Elementary School Principals, National Education Association, 1968), p. 116. Discusses also curricula in Lexington, Mass., and Madison, Wisconsin.

continuity, as people carry their culture to new places. This treatment is different from the regional studies of the United States in grade 5, where the stress in on changing use of the same environment at specific sites.

CONTENT FRAMEWORK OF UNIVERSITY OF MINNESOTA ELEMENTARY SOCIAL STUDIES PROGRAM[14]

GRADE AND THEME	UNITS
K. Earth as Home of Man	1. Overview: Earth as the Home of Man 2. Our Global Earth 3. A Home of Varied Resources 4. A World of Many Peoples 5. Man Changes the Earth
I. Families Around the World, I	1. Chippewa Family (or Local Tribe) 2. Hopi Family (Change over Time) 3. Quechua Family, Peru 4. Japanese Family
II. Families Around the World, II	1. Boston Family, Early 18th Century 2. Soviet Family, Urban Moscow 3. Hausa Family, Nigeria 4. Kibbutz Family, Israel 5. Culminating Period: Bringing Together what they have learned about Families, their Culture, Social Processes, Social Organization
III. Communities Around the World, I	1. Rural and Urban Communities: A Contrast (Include Own Community) 2. An American Frontier Community: Early California Mining Camp 3. Paris Community 4. The Manus Community (Great Admiralties) in the 1930s and 1950s
IV. Communities Around the World, II	1. Our Own Community 2. A Community in the Soviet Union 3. A Trobriand Islander Community 4. Indian Village South of Himalayas

14. From *Progress Report No. 2.* (Minneapolis: University of Minnesota Project Social Studies Curriculum Center, November 1965).

GRADE AND THEME	UNITS
V. Regional Studies	1. The United States a. Overview: Development of System of Regions b. Sequent Occupance Case Studies (Local Area and Six Others) 2. Canada a. Overview: Development of System of Regions b. Historical-Geographic Case Studies of Six Regions 3. Latin America a. Overview: Various Ways of Regionalizing b. Historical-Geographic Case Studies Emphasizing Three Periods in Four Regions 4. Case Study of One Small Region of Africa
VI. The Formation of American Society	Emphasis on Culture, Culture Contact, Culture Change, and Cultural Continuity 1. Indian America 2. Colonization of North America 3. American Revolution 4. Westward Expansion 5. Civil War and Reconstruction

The outline below indicates a major focus of a social science discipline in each grade and the other disciplines from which content is drawn.

THE SOCIAL SCIENCE DISCIPLINES IN THE MINNESOTA CURRICULUM[15]

GRADE AND THEME	MAJOR FOCUS	OTHER DISCIPLINES
K. Earth as Home of Man	Geography*	Anthropology
I. Families Around the World, I	Anthropology*	History, Sociology, Economics
II. Families Around the World, II	Anthropology*	History, Sociology, Economics
III. Communities Around the World, I	Anthropology*	History, Sociology, Economics, Political Science

15. From *Progress Report No. 2.* (Minneapolis: University of Minnesota Project Social Studies Curriculum Center, November 1965).

GRADE AND THEME	MAJOR FOCUS	OTHER DISCIPLINES
IV. Communities Around the World, II	Economics*	Geography, Anthropology
V. Regional Studies: U.S., Canada, Latin America	Geography*	History, Anthropology, Sociology, Economics
VI. The Formation of American Society	History*	Geography, Economics, Anthropology, Sociology, Political Science

Write to Selective Educational Equipment, Inc., 3 Bridge Street, Newton, Mass. 02195 for the catalog on "The Family of Man." This social studies program is based on the work of the University of Minnesota Project Social Studies Curriculum Center. The catalog details the materials in each unit kit, including authentic artifacts, graphic materials, and other media and lists the contents of the resource guide for the teacher.

Adaptation and substitution

There are any number of programs in social studies in the elementary school that have been developed in the 1960s and 1970s through funded projects, with government or foundation aid, or by textbook publishers. Many school systems have adopted a program lock, stock, and barrel; others have made adaptations.

The Chelmsford, Massachusetts Elementary School District is one of the systems that has used the Minnesota program for years, making adjustments and adaptations or instituting some alternative content as committees, individual teachers, and the social studies coordinator have constantly evaluated the results. The program for the first four grades in 1965 has been outlined above. It remains very much the same today. In grades five and six there is considerable change, however, which is sketched below.

GRADE V. PEOPLE, ENVIRONMENT, AND TECHNOLOGY

A. People and People

1. Your Rights and Responsibilities as an American citizen (based on work of the Civic Education Committee at UCLA). Liberty under law; freedom of expression; freedom of religion; equal protection of the law; due process of law
2. Values in Action (based on work of Fannie Shaftel, Jack Fraenkel, and Lawrence Kohlberg). Value clarification; analysis of values; moral dilemmas

* Course focuses primarily upon one discipline and deals with it fairly systematically, but draws on other disciplines.

B. People and Environment
   1. Geographic Features
   2. Individual Skills Program

C. People and Technology (based on work of Education Development Center, Cambridge, Mass.)
   1. Tooling Up: An Introduction to People and Technology
   2. Case Study on Whaling. How the system worked; implications of the system
   3. Community Field Study

D. People, Environment, and Technology
   1. Technology and the United States. Impact of technology on way of life; industries and technological systems in the United States; analysis of technological systems; technological systems and the environment; make your own world; 2000 A. D.
   2. Optional Specialty Projects; Technology and Canada; Technology and Latin America

GRADE VI. AREA STUDIES: APPLICATION OF MAJOR SOCIAL SCIENCE CONCEPTS FROM GRADES K THROUGH V

A. Europe
   1. Overview. Geographic features; people and technology; interdependence and intradependence; family life; government; Europe through the ages
   2. Specialty Reports Applying above to Selected Countries

B. The Middle East
   1. Three Major Religious Beliefs
   2. Effect of above on Jerusalem
   3. Geographic Features
   4. People and Technology
   5. Middle East Turmoil
   6. Culture. Specialties: bazaar

C. China
   1. Inquiring About China
   2. Geographic Features
   3. China and Its People. Village life versus city life; social organization; government; people and technology; education; role of China in the world

D. Africa
   1. Overview Using Africa Inquiry Maps (based on work from Project Africa)
   2. Acquiring Energy—Ghana Case Study (based on work of the Education Development Center). Ghana and Ghanaians; energy resources; building a dam—what happens to the environment; traditional and modern aspects of Ghanaian life; impact of dam on six Ghanaians; Ghana and technology; a question of values
   3. Optional: Application of generalizations from #2 to other African nations

ASSESSMENT OF A SOCIAL STUDIES PROGRAM

In the climate of reform and revision that has developed during the last decade in relation to the social studies curriculum there have been necessary and desirable attempts to provide a rationale and an assessment of an elementary program. One of the most noteworthy and useful practically is found in *Guidelines for Elementary Social Studies.*

We report here the twelve guidelines with mention of some of the ideas discussed under each. Although these guidelines were made to analyze and assess any program already built, or to be built, thoughtful perusal of their development in the pamphlet will provide a teacher with many helpful ideas that could influence the curriculum in the individual classroom under any program.[16]

1. *Are the major purposes of the program clearly stated in terms of pupil behaviors realistically attainable, and are they consistent with the philosophy of a democratic society?* What is it we want pupils to learn? What should pupils know or be able to do when they leave the program?
2. *Is the program psychologically sound?* Do the practices and procedures required by the program enhance or inhibit the self-fulfillment of individual pupils? Psychological soundness may be detected in the types of pupil activities suggested and must be questioned in the kinds of materials used.
3. *Does the program show evidence of providing for balance in its attention to cognitive, affective, and skills objectives?* Ideas, facts, concepts are important, as are the various specific skills, but so too are the affective components—values, attitudes, ideals, and feelings. Balance among the three should be reflected in the total program.
4. *Does the program provide for sequential and systematic development of concepts and skills that are believed to be important?* There are times and places where sequence is essential to effective teaching and learning. The grade in which a child is situated has almost nothing to do with what he knows. Instruction must be planned in accordance with the learning status of indivdual pupils.
5. *Are the criteria for the selection of substantive content clearly specified in the program?* There must be a clear rationale for the inclusion of some topics and subjects and the exclusion of others. With the increasing of skills associated with thinking as a major outcome of social studies instruction, greater attention will need to be given to the selection of subject matter to achieve such goals.
6. *Is the program of instruction relevant to the lives of the pupils?* Do the learning activities, the resources, the subject matter, and the skills make sense to the pupils, and do they regard them as vital? Relevance and meaningfulness are powerful forces in motivating a learner.

16. John Jarolimek, *Guidelines for Elementary Social Studies* (Washington, D.C.: Association for Supervision and Curriculum Development, 1967), pp. 11-27. Reprinted with permission of the Association for Supervision and Curriculum Development and John Jarolimek.

7. *Is the scope of the program realistic in terms of the contemporary world and the backgrounds of today's pupils?* The modern social studies program needs to be cosmopolitan in character and global in scope. Most pupils will live a major portion of their lives in urban environments in the twenty-first century.
8. *Are the learning activities and instructional resources consistent with the stated purposes of the program?* Purposes and objectives of social studies programs can be achieved only through the learning activities and instructional resources used by the pupil. One does not develop thinking abilities of pupils by having them learn only the conclusions that have been made by others and summarized in textbooks.
9. *Does the program provide adequately for differentiated instruction?* No program in social studies can be rated strong unless it comes to grips with the variety of individual differences among pupils. Variations can be made in objectives, in content, or in methodology. Differentiated instruction is essential at all levels of ability.
10. *Is the program one that teachers will understand and be able to implement and support?* Curriculum guides that do not clearly assist the teachers in their work are of little value. The planning and implementation of curriculums in social studies must include attention to teacher involvement and in-service activities.
11. *Are the curriculum documents sufficiently structured to provide teachers with direction, yet flexible enough to allow individual teacher initiative and creativity?* Curriculum documents should be highly *structured* in terms of purposes, objectives, concepts, and skills to be included; methods of selecting content; and similar matters dealing with the definition of the intent and character of the program. They should be *flexible* in matters dealing with actual teaching and working with pupils.
12. *Is it possible to evaluate the program in order to establish with some degree of confidence the extent to which major purposes have been achieved?* Without some type of evaluation—formal, informal, systematic, or catch-as-catch-can—it is not possible to improve programs. The more systematic, objective, and broad-gauged the evaluation is, the more likely that it will yield reliable and valid feedback for program improvement.

The assessment of a total program is comprehensive and requires the exploration of overall patterns and ideas as well as attention to detail and specifics. Educators of the 1980s will find many challenges and rewards in planning and implementing programs that meet student needs. High-quality programs are needed to produce lifetime learners.

THE TEACHER AND THE SOCIAL STUDIES PROGRAM

Teacher support of a program is crucial. When a teacher presents a topic or a program with great enthusiasm, the students are frequently carried along by the sheer weight of the teacher's interest until their investigation takes on a fascination of its own. Children may even learn irrelevant bits and pieces of information because of teacher influence. This is not recommended as the most beneficial or lasting motivation, but it is one motivation and dozens of examples can be cited to give evidence of it. The teacher can make or break the worst or the best program ever devised; this is of great importance because of the initial thrust and the continued support the teacher can lend to a program.

However, the teacher has more to bring to any program than enthusiasm. The teacher also brings a knowledge of the resources (community, library, media) available in a particular setting and knows the level of cognitive functioning of the specific group of students who will be exposed to the program. Both of these elements will require adjustment and adaptation of a standard program simply because in the area of resources and level of cognitive functioning variation is inherent. The teacher must be responsible for the adaptation that will be needed to make a program viable for a particular class, be it the second grade or the sixth.

Some new programs are based on subject matter (e. g., anthropology) in which the teacher may have had little or no formal training. This places yet a further demand on the most versatile person. It is necessary to become knowledgeable in these subjects, and the teacher must either read extensively in this content area, or take formal courses, or both in order to understand the background of the program well enough to serve as a resource person for the students when they investigate the content of the specified program.

Published programs change slowly and new texts and other materials are not often purchased yearly by a school system. Therefore, the teacher is also given the task of refining, updating, and providing supplemental materials that will help children recognize the tentative nature of knowledge. This is a large order because the elementary teacher must carry on an informal updating in all subject areas. Is it any wonder that teachers become known as great borrowers and collectors of resources and information?

The elementary teacher has an important part in shaping young students for tomorrow's world. The social studies program has a share of this responsibility. The two, teacher and program, must work together to provide the finest possible learning conditions and materials for developing young minds.

NEW DIRECTIONS

Variables that are gaining momentum for the late seventies and eighties should be considered in updating or refining an existing program. The major emerging trends are that:

1. The thrust of the behavioral sciences has been broadened to include the humanities. An emphasis that is more comprehensive and inclusive in gaining a realistic picture of today's society and its problems is emerging. A more integrated collection of subject matter is used to describe man and his world.
2. The topics that are studied more frequently allow direct student involvement in finding out about the subject. Interviews, surveys, questionnaires, and opinionnaires, as well as graphing and charting the results of the information, are the tools of primary grade children as well as more advanced students.
3. There is considerable evidence that more material and time is being spent on subcultural and/or ethnic minorities. Topics such as sexism, racism, and brotherhood are part of many school curricula. In short, an effort is being made to emphasize more current national and individual concerns.
4. A comprehensive intercultural view is becoming important. Social studies teachers are still concerned with a world view or a global frame of reference, but there is an inclination toward humanizing the particular culture or concept being studied. For example, in examining a topic such as "third world problems," teachers tend to select a year in the life of a boy in India to point out the problem more concretely.
5. There is a developing emphasis on more variety in student products. In the past, students have developed reports or drawn pictures to share the results of their investigations. Now, many classroom teachers are encouraging the development of poems, songs, strategic games, and designed experiments to demonstrate knowledge.
6. Open-class structures are promoting the development of individualized instruction packets. These packets most often provide choices of activities, and they also provide for partner, small group, and teacher-directed options. There is an increased emphasis on the use of media and the use of activity cards to achieve more student choice. Contracts and self-evaluation are often part of these learning packets. Learning centers include the learning packet activity suggestions as well as the media needed to carry out the activities. Such centers are an important part of the educational future.
7. There is a strong emphasis on attitudes and values, which will no doubt continue. There may perhaps be an increased stress on personal integrity and responsibility. This would seem to be a natural outgrowth of the seventies' federal government problems. Methods that permit student involvement in real-life problems will be used increasingly. Simulation techniques such as role playing, the use of games both commercial and teacher made, and dramatic play will be a part of this emphasis.
8. The emphasis on career education has come to the elementary classroom where simple skills can be developed that will aid the student in getting jobs in the immediate community. Student attitudes toward employment are also being explored.
9. A number of schools are now teaching units on consumer education or advertising or propaganda because this general area is so important to the life of the child. There can be no question that skills and careful decisions are needed for

spending income from childhood throughout adult life. The elementary school will assume an increasing amount of responsibility for such practical education.

10. The needs for skills development in all subject areas is receiving a renewed emphasis in both the United States and Canada. Social studies skills such as map reading and interpretation, graphing, information processing, and data-sharing skills are a part of this larger skills emphasis and can be seen in classrooms from kindergarten through twelfth grade.

FOR FURTHER READING

Banks, James A., ed. *Teaching Ethnic Studies,* 43rd Yearbook of the National Council for the Social Studies. Arlington, Va.: National Council for the Social Studies, 1973.

Beyer, Barry K., and Anthony N. Penna, eds. *Concepts in the Social Studies,* Bulletin No. 45. Arlington, Va.: National Council for the Social Studies, 1971.

Haas, Glen, ed. *Curriculum Planning: A New Approach.* Boston: Allyn and Bacon, 1977.

"In-Depth Evaluations of Social Studies Curricular Projects, Programs, and Materials." *Social Education* (Special Issue, November 1972).

Jarolimek, John, and Huber M. Walsh, eds. *Readings for Social Studies in Elementary Schools.* 3rd ed. New York: Macmillan, 1974.

Joyce, Bruce R. *New Strategies for Social Education.* Chicago: Science Research Associates, 1972.

Michaelis, John U.; Grossman, Ruth H.; and Lloyd Scott. *New Designs for Elementary Curriculum and Instruction.* New York: McGraw-Hill, 1975.

Social Studies Curriculum Guidelines. Arlington, Va.: National Council for the Social Studies, 1971.

IMPROVING INSTRUCTION THROUGH THE UNIT PROCEDURE

Chapter two

It would be difficult indeed to justify educationally the assign-study-recite-test plan of conducting social studies. See what happens when you ask a question calling for a single fact. Hands go up; you call on one child for an answer; the other children in the class do nothing. Second question, second child, second answer; again the rest of the children do nothing. And so it goes. But pupil participation and involvement in the learning process are essential.

One method of organized pupil participation is the unit plan. The unit plan describes the learning experiences in which the teacher will involve the student. It is a curricula design that is teacher oriented, but one that has an underlying philosophy of student participation and involvement. Teaching social studies by the unit plan is more widely advocated than any other procedure. There is, however, no magic in it. It still requires a quality teacher to do a quality job.

The unit has been described in many ways, but a simple operational definition may be helpful. A unit is an organized body of information, learning experiences, and instructional materials that is designed to produce significant learnings for students.

The resource unit is a considerable amount of preplanned material for the teacher, produced without reference to any particular group of children. But there still remains much important planning to be done by the teacher throughout the unit.

In long-range planning, the teacher chooses from the resource unit as well as he can at this stage what to include in a teaching unit, what to leave out, and what to modify according to his experience and inclinations and the needs of his particular class. He will note the instructional materials recommended, which include the bibliography, and find out what is and is not available from the school, the central office, public library, and other sources.

As the unit proceeds, the teacher needs to do short-range planning: review progress and problems encountered by students and make adjustments in plans conditioned by pupil-teacher planning; check availability of materials, interests, and needs of pupils, determine the pace of progress. These adjustments should be reviewed and replanning done for a week ahead.

The necessity of careful daily plans cannot be stressed too emphatically. No social studies period should begin without the teacher knowing generally what he and every pupil in the class will be doing throughout the period.

Cooperative planning between the teacher and the student for more specific objectives contributes much to the success of the unit. This provides for a cooperative evaluation of the unit and the objectives developed in relation to it.

In this chapter we will explore the elements in a resource unit and examine a daily lesson plan that might represent the plans for implementing a single learning experience in a unit. No direct attempt will be made to point out all the similarities and differences between a learning packet and a unit, but the reader will see the similarities immediately. One comparison will be developed deliberately. The learning experiences portion of the unit and the developmental activities of the learning packet will be examined, and transfers from unit to packet and vice versa will be demonstrated. The teacher can then readily redevelop his own materials along the lines that are needed.

PLANNING THE RESOURCE UNIT

If you are fortunate enough to teach in a community where a curriculum guide has been developed, you will have resource units for your grade. You may find resource units in other courses of study and other source materials that are helpful. Many teachers find great satisfaction in developing a resource unit or cooperating with fellow teachers in its production. Indeed, many methods students have tried their hand at writing their own units. One class did this and reported this to be the "best social studies class we ever had." If you want to really understand the thinking that goes into a unit, build one. A single experience such as this will clarify myriad questions. The following outline will help you get started on building a unit.

I. **Analysis of Content**

A. *Overview:* A descriptive statement indicating the phases of the topic to be emphasized and why it is important to the learners for whom it is planned.

B. *Content Outline:* Shows the subject matter scope of the unit.

II. **Objectives**

A. *Knowledge*
B. *Problem Solving Skills*
C. *Attitudes and Values*

III. **Learning Experiences**

A. *Approach, Opener, or Starter Activities:* Several suggested ideas that the teacher may develop and use as a means of arousing interest and setting the stage to introduce the unit.

B. *Developmental Activities:* The crux and body of the whole unit in operation. Carrying on the developmental activities constitutes the assimilation or working period of the unit. The activities should be specific in type and provide for the various levels of maturity, interest, and ability of the class members. This section of the unit includes learning experiences that provide for the *intake* of information and the development of content thinking skills and social skills, as well as for the reinforcement of these skills.

C. *Culminating Activities:* Usually a final group activity which results from drawing together all of the values gained in the unit. It should, if possible, create a sense of completion of one problem and, at the same time, arouse an interest in the next problem.

IV. **Evaluation**

Samples of the instruments or techniques that illustrate how the teacher intends to gather evidence that the objectives of the unit have been developed and achieved. In actual operation they are an integral part of instruction. Should include both measurement and appraisal items.

V. **Bibliography**

A. *Children's Books:* An annotated list, in complete, approved form, of any books useful to children in carrying out the activities of the unit.

B. *Teacher's References:* A list of professional, content, and reference books, magazine articles, and other printed materials useful to the teacher in preparing for, planning, and guiding the unit.

VI. **Instructional Materials**

A list, in complete organized form, of the films, slides, exhibits, records, realia, etc., available for use by the teacher.

Over the years, several different classifications of units have been offered. Probably the most useful are simply resource units and teaching units. The resource unit is a collection of instructional materials and activities organized to develop major understandings of a sizeable topic, such as "The Farm," "New Frontiers in a New Nation," and "Latin America." Its activities, subject matter content, and even major understandings are much more than any one class will or should do. Its material is organized without any specific classroom in mind. No matter where the teacher may find it, it can serve the purpose of preplanning. It can always be in a growing state, for in truth it is never finished. Now to turn to the phases of developing the outline above of the resource unit which you may be writing—your preplanning.

Getting Started

When beginning to develop a unit, it is helpful to sketch out a list of the questions or curiosities that one has about the topic. Getting the ideas flowing is an important first step in unit development. Let us take an example. Select a topic that is of interest and jot down the abbreviated questions just as they occur to you.

Topic: The Automobile

Who invented it?
How have production processes changed?
What is the average cost of a car?
How much gas is used by cars in the United States yearly?
Do certain age levels choose certain types of cars?
What are related inventions?
What businesses depend on the car industry?
How has the car affected our way of life?
What problems has the car created?
What kinds of solutions are proposed to the problems?
How many people are employed in the auto industry?

This is only a partial list, but it will convey the idea of spontaneity and the lack of order or precision that is to be expected in an initial listing. Now begin to collect questions that have some similarity. This group of questions has a common element:

How has the car affected our way of life?
What problems has the car created?
What kinds of solutions are proposed to the problems?

Look for other groupings or categories and jot them down. Grouping the questions together will help structure a content outline.

Once the grouping is done, and before the outline is formalized, write one clear sentence that summarizes the whole. One way to think about this is to try to write down the ideas that students who studied this content might remember five years from now. For example, "The automobile is a complex machine that has provided new opportunities for people, but it has also created problems that must be solved." One would not assume that the student would remember or state the idea in exactly this way, but the sense of it might remain. This sense will also help the teacher-designer to place emphasis on the elements in the units that have the most potential for contributing to this overall idea.

Now the designer is ready to expose these beginning ideas to a friend or colleague or an instructor. Discuss the ideas and ask for reactions so that some check on the unit is provided early. In addition, look up the topic in several books and find the ideas these resources convey. Correlate these with the categories and beginning ideas that have been jotted down.

The result of this effort should be a content outline. The content outline for a unit is a deliberate effort to order and organize the content that began as a random assortment of questions and ideas. The teacher-designer is now ready to formalize both an overview of the whole and the content outline that will serve as the basis for the unit.

Analysis of Content

In the *Overview,* you write a descriptive statement indicating the highlights and emphasis. For a fifth grade unit on "New Homes in a New World," the following was written:

> By 1625, Spanish, English, French, and Dutch settlements had been established in North America. A company of English merchants had provided funds to make possible the first English settlement at Jamestown. The Pilgrims, seeking a place for freedom of worship, founded Plymouth. Within the next ten years thousands of Englishmen settled in nearby parts of Massachusetts. Dutch merchants established trading posts along the Hudson River which shortly developed into towns. The English, Dutch, and French had come to stay in the New World. The years ahead were to show remarkable growth in population.[1]

The *Content Outline* is most frequently written in the customary outline form, sometimes in great detail as a "telling" outline, sometimes in briefer topical form.

Objectives

In the outline for a unit three broad areas for the delineation of objectives are listed: knowledge, problem-solving skills, and attitudes and values. Unit objectives are most often stated in behavioral terms and are derived from the interaction of the social studies content and the broad educational goals. Figure 2.1 gives an example of the

1. Teacher's Guide for *Makers of the Americas* (Lexington, Mass.: D.C. Heath and Co., 1963).

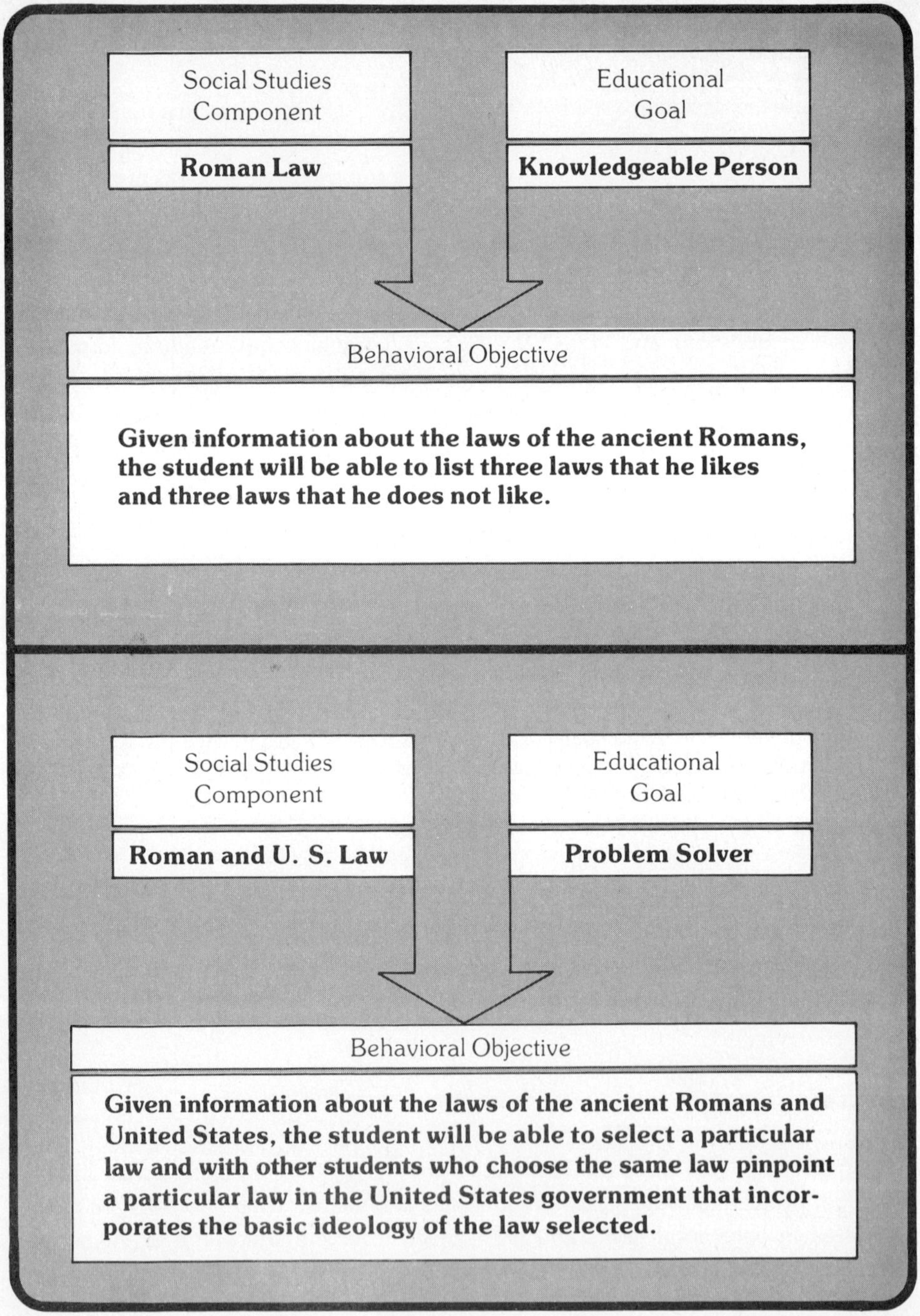

Social Studies Component

Roman Law

Educational Goal

Knowledgeable Person

Behavioral Objective

Given information about the laws of the ancient Romans, the student will be able to list three laws that he likes and three laws that he does not like.

Social Studies Component

Roman and U. S. Law

Educational Goal

Problem Solver

Behavioral Objective

Given information about the laws of the ancient Romans and United States, the student will be able to select a particular law and with other students who choose the same law pinpoint a particular law in the United States government that incorporates the basic ideology of the law selected.

content being considered and the educational goal desired. The resulting behavioral objective is spelled out for two different goals.

A behavioral objective is composed of three parts: (1) the entering condition; (2) expected student behavior (sometimes called terminal behavior); and (3) the criterion or level of performance that is acceptable. Below is an example of a behavioral objective, the learning experiences that should produce this behavior, and a suggested evaluation of the experience.

I. **Behavioral Objective** After (a) viewing a film dealing with the process of clothes manufacturing, (b) the student will write (c) an accurate* description of the role people play in this manufacturing process.

Comments:

a. "Viewing a film dealing with the process of clothes manufacturing" is the *condition under which a specified behavior will occur.*
b. "The student will write" is the *expected student behavior* that is to occur as a result of planned instruction.
c. "Accurate description" is the *performance level* that will be accepted.

II. **Learning Experiences** (steps taken in sequence to reach the desired terminal behavior)

1. Show film: Wool (*From Sheep to Clothing*) (EBF 385)
2. Ask students to write a paragraph telling about the contributions people make in producing cotton clothing.
3. List steps, with the students, in the production of wool.
4. Have students draw sketches of the human activities that go into making a coat.
5. Discuss the children's drawings, and organize the pictures in a sequence. "What happens first, second, etc."

III. **Evaluation** (Evaluative technique) Have each student write a paragraph describing the people's role in the manufacturing process. Trace the manufacturing process from beginning to end.

*Accurate shall be defined as: (1) number of roles described; (2) logical in terms of sequence of behaviors shown in film.

FIGURE 2.1. Example of a Statement of Behavioral Objective, Learning Experiences to Achieve That Objective, and How Objective Will Be Evaluated.

In writing a behavioral objective the part that frequently creates problems for the writer is the section referred to as *student behavior* or *expected student behavior*. Care must be taken here so that the student behavior is stated in terms that are measurable. Some means of assessing the behavior is required, and this means that the behavior prescribed must be in some way observable. It is possible to read a paragraph that a student has written and assess it. It is much more difficult to assess the student's appreciation of music unless this is represented in some observable manner. If a teacher is satisfied that attendance at a concert represents appreciation, then the observable behavior, the attendance, may well be stated as the objective. If something more than attendance is required, what is it, and how will the teacher know that it has been accomplished? Many behaviors can be assessed and products that are complex and contain multiple behavioral outputs can be examined in small components for purposes of improvement and assessment. Below are examples of some terms that are observable behaviors and some terms that are not observable and are thus difficult to measure.

OBSERVABLE BEHAVIORS	DIFFICULT TO MEASURE
Reciting	Understanding
Writing a paragraph	Gaining insight
Listing	Perceiving
Describing	Feeling
Naming	Enjoying
Drawing	Acquiring
Sketching	Appreciating
Delineating	Comprehending

Some sample objectives used in a Grade 6 unit on "The Middle East" should provide a concrete example dealing with a specific topic. As the unit develops the student should achieve the following objectives:

1. Given general information on the Middle East through the use of film, visuals, and artifacts, the student sets up hypotheses on the area relating to religion, environment, technology, and lifestyle.
2. Given three of the major religious beliefs in the world the student is able to compare and contrast the following characteristics:
   a. Each religion teaches belief in a supreme being.
   b. All have certain laws that govern their belief.
   c. From religion man has developed certain customs, values, and lifestyles.
3. Given the fact that Jerusalem is an international city for the three major religions

of the world, the student is able to compare and contrast the effect these religions have on life in the city.

4. Given a map of the Middle East and North Africa, the student is able to identify the countries, major topographical areas, climate, bodies of water, and principal cities.

Examples of behavioral objectives for a second grade are presented in Chapter 5 in "The Zoo Community" learning packet.

Knowledge. In considering the understandings and main ideas students get in social studies, one must consider the different social sciences and their relationships to the units developed. An interdisciplinary approach is recommended for the elementary school, but it is recognized that any one particular unit may emphasize one social science more than another. Some units have been developed with the intent of emphasizing one social science (Senesh Economics Units) and developing other social sciences as they relate to this. For a broader discussion of the contribution of each social science see Chapter One.

The development and organization of content for the teacher proceeds from broad concepts, to main ideas, to specific factual examples. However, the learning sequence for the child is reversed: the student starts with specific instances and develops a main idea dealing with a broad concept.

The acquisition of specific content-related skills is sometimes required for developing an *understanding* or *main idea*. It is very easy to list twenty or more skills in connection with any unit; it is not very helpful to do so. Surely, many skills are used in some degree, but list only those that could have considerable attention because of the activities suggested. Sometimes a unit lends itself especially well to the introduction or further use of a particular skill.

When materials are selected from a resource unit for a teaching unit, the teacher must be sure that the skills collected coordinate with the activities collected. No single skill is likely to be developed in one unit, but each skill listed should be specific. To say "Develop map and globe skills" is scarcely helpful. "To determine distance on a map or globe by using a scale" is more directive in the activities to be developed. (See page 327 for map and globe skills.)

Problem-solving skills. In a social studies unit it is not enough for the student to memorize content. Students should be involved in developing ideas and synthesizing information. One of the most important functions of the school and the social studies class should be to produce continuing learners; that is, to produce students who value learning and the learning process. Persons who have developed ideas with materials and research findings that support these ideas have the potential for becoming continuing learners, because they have been involved in the problem-solving process and the process they have used is available for use again and again with other and different content. Problem-solving processes are an important part of a unit if one wishes to produce students who can deal with research materials and can continue to deal with real social issues throughout their lives. Whenever the problem-solving approach is used content that is not exclusively social science may be needed to solve the problem at hand. For example, science and mathematics may be needed to deal with the problem of population control. This provides for a natural integration of content areas and is an effective way to learn.

The use of the problem-solving process is an important teaching strategy. In far too many classrooms children memorize, drill, and recite, and are too seldom engaged in asking their own questions, hypothesizing about answers and ideas, and searching for verification of these hypotheses. Problem solving provides for student choice and selection of problems and student involvement in the cognitive process used to solve these problems.

A number of different techniques for actively involving students in the problem-solving process have been developed in the past decade. Materials have been produced to implement these techniques in the classroom, and a variety of labels have been used to describe them. One of the broader terms used to describe student involvement in research and problem-solving is inquiry.

Attitudes and values. Attitudes and values are difficult not only to teach or develop but also to write about in connection with a specific unit. We are concerned with attitudes toward other people (even when these people are present only in books and films), with appreciation of contributions of people past and present, and with respect for the individual wherever and whatever he is.

We will examine some of the areas that concern the student and on which units of work might be focused. The current issues in our society, government as it relates to the individual in a democracy, and understanding other cultures (international understanding) are some of the areas one might examine with students. Each of these is a highly sensitive area and cannot be explored without considering the values held by the person doing the investigation. Chapter 7 deals with this topic in detail.

Learning Experiences

Approach or starter activities. Starter activities are used to initiate a unit. One or more of these may be used as motivation to enlist interest, raise questions, and provide discussion as a basis for pupil-teacher planning requiring further exploration through a variety of learning materials. A resource unit might be quite specific in the suggested approach activities. The approach or starter activities should provoke the students' curiosity and generate an element of excitement about the new topic. The "need to know" about an event or person or a group of people can provide a powerful stimulus for children as well as adults. Such curiosity can survive the inevitable encounters with information sources that may be dull, irrelevant, or too difficult to understand and will drive the students on to sources that do apply to their projects. Among the starter activities teachers have used are:

1. Pictures and slides to show comparisons.
2. Map and globe study.
3. A story and music to introduce folklore of a culture group.
4. A museum visit to see certain collections, or a field trip.
5. Newspaper or magazine articles concerned with current affairs in a region.
6. An exhibit in the classroom—travel posters, realia, etc.
7. A letter from a visitor to a country or from a resource person.
8. Bulletin board display (pictures, charts, advertisements of products, etc.).
9. Continuation of a time line that has been constructed in an earlier unit.
10. Selection from a contemporary book read to children (of the historical period under study).
11. An extemporaneous dramatization.
12. A film or filmstrip, TV program, newscast.
13. A common assignment in reading—perhaps a biographical sketch.
14. An excerpt read from a diary or other document.
15. Planning of an automobile trip or a long plane trip.
16. Collections of stamps and coins.
17. Exploration of children's or teacher's previous experiences with the topic.

Developmental activities. It is through developmental activities that progress is made toward achieving the objectives of the unit: the knowledge, the problem-solving skills, the attitudes and values. The list below illustrates the types of learning activities that have a place in units at one time or another. A teacher can use this list to build activities for a unit by asking the question about each of the activities below, "Can this activity be used as a means of learning at this grade level in this particular unit?" For example, apply this question to the activity "note-taking" under Research. "Can note taking be used as a means of learning by a third grader in a unit on food?" It certainly can, so the teacher can write an activity: "Have one pupil, or a small committee, make a list of the fresh vegetables and fruits available in the supermarket." And so on, raising a question about each activity as a possibility. Remember that the intake of information provides opportunity for some form of expressive activity, and several means of taking in information should be provided.

Do not ask students to begin a unit, for example, by discussing what they know about Ancient Rome. Provide a stimulating input of information that all students can enjoy before asking for an output of ideas. Some input of information and some suggested output such as brick and mortar provide the most effective teaching/learning procedure. Development of a variety of ways to express the processed ideas should also be encouraged. Some examples of different activity possibilities are:

LEARNING ACTIVITIES FOR SOCIAL STUDIES

Research	Reading, writing, interviewing, note-taking, collecting, using references, map work, reporting
Presentation	Telling, announcing, describing, giving directions, reporting, demonstrating, dramatizing, pantomiming, exhibiting, relating events, illustrating
Creative Expression or Experience	Writing, drawing, sketching, modeling, illustrating, painting, sewing, constructing, manipulating, dramatizing, comparing, singing, imagining, role playing
Appreciation	Listening, describing, viewing, reading
Observation or Listening	Observing, visiting places of interest, viewing pictures or films, listening to recordings
Group Cooperation	Discussing, conversing, sharing, asking questions, helping one another, committee work
Experimentation	Measuring, collecting, demonstrating, conducting experiments
Organization	Planning, discussing, outlining, summarizing, holding meetings
Evaluation	Summarizing, interviewing, asking questions, criticizing[2]

Discussion activities. Discussion is and should be an essential part of many of the activities of the unit. Class discussion serves two main purposes. It contributes to getting and giving information, offers opportunities for children to evaluate together what has been done and decide what needs to be done, and explores various possibilities before actual decision making. Secondly, it provides the teacher with a favorable time for evaluating the group process as well as the individual pupils. There should be much discussion in planning an exhibit, a time line, a large map; collecting pictures; preparing to write diaries, letters, poems; and in developing many other activities.

One must not confuse the term "discussion" with "recitation." Discussion is not just another name for recitation. A recitation is "reciting a prepared lesson by pu-

2. John Jarolimek, *Social Studies in Elementary Education*, 4th ed. (New York: The Macmillan Company, 1976), p. 127. Reprinted by permission.

pils before a teacher." A discussion is "give-and-take talk; a going over of reasons for and against." Discussion in a class may arise in many ways:

1. "Talking Together" in the pupil activities at the ends of units in textbooks suggests questions for discussion. In most cases the answers are not in the story and they call for active thinking and reasoning by the pupils.
2. Comparisons and contrasts.
3. Questions asked by a pupil about ideas for which he cannot find the answers.
4. Separating major and minor ideas when learning to outline.
5. Discrepancies in the accounts of an event in different textbooks.
6. Differences arising from matters of opinion.
7. Planning an activity.
8. The need for further investigation of a topic.
9. Talking over the implications or meaning of a story.
10. Clearing up misunderstandings and clarifying thinking.
11. The report made by a pupil or a committee.
12. The formulation of the generalizations or understanding of a unit.

The daily recitation period in which the teacher tries only through routine questions to find out how well the children have memorized textbook material provides practically no discussion and probably little else of real value. The discussion period that seeks through thought-provoking questions to raise problems growing out of the unit provides the conditions for fruitful discussion, when wisely guided. This discussion emerges from class situations. The teacher should see that the threads of a discussion are drawn together so that all students understand the conclusions reached and decisions made.

Culminating activities. Concluding activities as the unit draws toward its close, culminating activities that pull together all of the strands on which individuals, small groups, and the class have been at work, and summarizing activities that raise questions are all pretty much the same piece of cloth. The questions:

Where did we start?	Focuses attention on the original pupil-teacher planning.
Where have we been?	Focuses attention on the major undertakings and synthesis of information.
Where are we now?	Focuses attention on what has been learned and the formulation of generalizations.
What is next?	Focuses on what has been left undone or unfinished and directs discussion toward the next unit.

As a culminating activity, the day of the show for parents and guests or the Mexican luncheon for the principal, supervisor, and custodian, or like performances, are things of the past unless they can be educationally justified as learning experiences for boys and girls. Students should be aware that variety in ways of presenting ideas is attention getting. Students can use overhead projector outlines, bulletin board summaries, poetry and songs they have written, or even role-playing of the interactions that they hypothesize might take place in a given situation. Creative expressions provide for an unusual synthesis of feelings and information and add greatly to the understanding of the entire class. The culminating activity for a unit may vary from a single summary statement to a full-blown production. The magnitude in terms of time and expressive output should be determined by the students in the light of the ideas they wish to convey.

Evaluation. Evaluation is concerned with determining any modification of the behavior of the learners in terms of significant understandings, attitudes, and skills. Is the child a different person now because he has spent several weeks on this unit? Questions like these must be answered:

1. Do the children understand that . . . ? (Here one takes the *understandings* that were stated in declarative sentence form under the *objectives* for the unit and turns each sentence into a question.)
2. Have the children grown in ability to . . . ? (Here one lists the problem-solving skills that received particular attention during the unit.)
3. Have the children developed . . . ? (Here one is concerned with the attitudes and values designated in connection with unit.)
4. Have the children shown achievement in tests constructed on the instructional materials used in the unit? (Tests can show command of important facts and understandings, problem-solving skills, special skills, etc.)

These are the questions to ask, but the means of determining the answers are not indicated. The section of Chapter 10 on Evaluation provides some suggestions.

DAILY LESSON PLANS

Planning for each lesson period is a requisite for good teaching. Unit planning provides the broad base for an extended sequence of activities, but individual daily lessons require additional preparation. The extent and detail of the daily lesson plans will vary considerably. If the class has been divided into small groups to begin a research activity the previous day, the plan may be to continue the activity. On the other hand, the lesson may introduce a new idea in a unit of work, and the teacher's planning and follow-up will be fairly extensive. Let us examine a typical lesson plan outline in which the main parts are clearly identified, and then look at a sample lesson plan that follows this outline.

Outline for Lesson Plan

A. Purpose of lesson: State in broad terms the idea you hope the students will retain.

B. Behavioral Objective: Be specific and state in measurable terms.

C. Opener (Motivator): Get the students involved—relate to real life if possible.

D. Learning Activities:

1. Some choice should be available to students.
2. Some variation in procedure from total group to individual response or team interaction should be included.
3. Some variety in input and output mode should be planned. That is, the students can read about a topic, see a filmstrip, or go on a field trip to gather information. Different ways of expressing what is learned should be designed. Reports, musical compositions, poetry, and art work can all be used effectively to express ideas.
4. Some input and some output should be planned. Do not give huge amounts of information without the opportunity for expressive output. Questions: If you plan to discuss some particular topic with the class, list the questions you will use.

E. Summary and Futuristic Thrust: Pull together the ideas that have been dealt with in the lesson. If possible, finish with something like, "And tomorrow we are going to learn something exciting that the scientist discovered," or, "Think about this question: 'What is the most important service the policeman gives you?' We will discuss your answers tomorrow."

F. Evaluation: If a formal evaluation is planned, delineate it here. Show quiz example, questions for written response, etc.

G. Materials: List books, films and all media.

Lesson: I Am an American

A. Purpose: To present a broad view of the cultural heritage of an American in preparation for studying the "United States: Two Centuries of Growth."

B. Objectives:

1. Given a filmstrip and record, "I Am America," the students will sing the songs that are part of the American heritage, such as "My Country 'Tis of Thee."

2. Given an opportunity to share in teams, the students will describe a place in the United States that they have visited and the partners will try to guess the location of the place.
3. Given materials, the students will each make a flag for use in the Day Care Centers.

C. Opener:

1. Prepare the students for the filmstrip. Tell them that they will be trying to identify certain places in the United States and special symbols that they see that represent the concept of our country.
2. Use the filmstrip and record "I Am America."

D. Learning Activities:

1. Instruct the students to sing along with the songs that are familiar to them.
2. Discuss filmstrip in a general way. Then, divide the class into teams. Have each student describe either a symbol or a place depicted in the filmstrip. Have the partner guess what his teammate is describing.
3. Prepare the students for making flags for use at the Day Care Centers. Raise questions about number of stars, number of stripes, order of stripes, etc.
4. Provide strips of red paper. Use white background. Provide stars and a cut-out blue patch.
5. Have students make flags in teams.

E. Summary and Futuristic Thrust:

1. Raise questions about the flag as a symbol. Provide students with an opportunity to select some specific details about this symbol for a one-paragraph report to the class next time.
2. List a few beginning suggestions: "Color Me Red, White, and Blue," "Take Good Care of Me," "Where Was It I Saw You Last," "You Do Get Around."

F. Evaluation:

1. Check the product (flags) the teams have produced. Look for accuracy and beauty.
2. Check each child in terms of the following continuum:

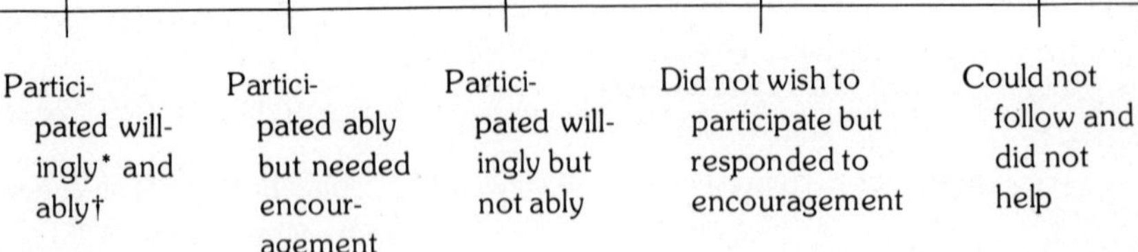

*Willingly—general positive attitude toward project

†Ably—could follow theme

G. Materials: Filmstrip and record "I Am America"; Flag strips and tape, stars, background.

STRATEGIES FOR SUCCESSFULLY IMPLEMENTING A UNIT

Designing and implementing a unit of content in which the students are both involved in some planning and provided with a range of choices in the learning process is a complex task. There are several strategies the teacher can use to meet the challenge this presents more effectively. Implementing the inquiry process, effective grouping and regrouping of students, asking thought-provoking questions, and careful daily planning of lesson procedures are all skills that will contribute to a successful unit. Let us examine each of these skill areas in detail.

The Inquiry Process

The purpose of the inquiry process is to engage the students in the active process of learning to develop their ability to "find out for themselves." It involves them in raising questions, making some educated guesses (hypotheses) about possible answers, testing those answers through search for data, and coming to a decision or conclusion.

Many teachers will recognize that they have used the inquiry process in varying degrees in parts of a unit. Our treatment here of inquiry does not imply that it is unknown to practicing teachers. We hope this presentation will be helpful in initiating it where it has been little used, and that it will provide an example of a problem-solving process.

In any classroom procedure, it is wise to examine the sequence of behaviors that make up the total process, as well as the role of the students and the teacher in the process being used.

The basic model. The basic model or strategy of engaging in social inquiry can be helpful to the teacher in understanding and directing the problem-solving process. Social inquiry depends on imagination and orderly consideration of evidence. This basic model may be conceived in terms of tasks. It is, in fact, a group of behavioral objectives in problem solving.

1. Identify the problem
   a. Raise questions
   b. List relevant items
2. Categorize the subtopics underlying the problem

3. Select one component or subtopic and hypothesize possible outcomes
4. Plan the data development stage
   a. Plan data collection
   b. Collect data
   c. Organize data
5. Analyze data
   a. Look for alternative solutions
   b. Examine accuracy and dependability of data base used
6. Share results
7. Evaluate
   a. Effectiveness of process
   b. Adequacy of product
   c. Raise new hypotheses
   d. Plan the next phase of inquiry

Students' role in inquiry process. Children should be active agents in their own learning process. We talk about children formulating their own hypotheses for investigation. Perhaps they do, but they may not think of the learning process in such sophisticated terms. It would seem that children first of all engage in the inquiry process because they are curious about something or because they need to know something for a particular reason. They may find a number of different topics interesting and choose one to pursue. Having chosen a facet of a subject, the students then delve into several sources, see contradictions and different viewpoints, and collect the ideas and data that seem relevant in satisfying their own curiosity or needs. Some final exploration and sharing of their views and conclusions seems to be the natural response to the compelling curiosity that began the inquiry.

One might see the student's role as follows:

1. Is curious or feels a need to know about something.
2. Ranges over a variety of sources and chooses a field of concentration from among competing stimuli.
3. Narrows the search to more specific questions.
4. Recognizing that the input of information is customarily followed by some output of relevant data, the student collects data and engages in critical thinking (i.e., chooses among contradictory and differing opinions).
5. Shares the data with others and raises more questions to explore later.

Student guide for inquiry. The students may use the following outline of primary questions as an aid in carrying out the research (inquiry) process.

Researchers are people who ask questions and carefully search for information to answer the questions. They examine the information, organize it, reach conclusions on the basis of the information, and share their findings with others. The following outline tells you how to do research. You will want to refer to this outline often.

I. How do you begin research?*

A. You choose a topic and decide what you want to know about it.
B. You think about the topic and ask yourself questions about it.
C. You list the questions you want to answer.
D. You make an outline of the topic and important subtopics.
E. You find out where information about your topic is available.

II. How do you collect information about your topic?

A. You learn how to get information from different sources.
B. You take notes and classify the information you collect in the library.
C. You write letters and collect information by mail.
D. You learn how to read maps, charts, and graphs.
E. You learn how to interview people, make surveys.

III. How do you organize the information you collect?

A. You organize the information by listing main ideas.
B. You can organize the information by time sequence.
C. You can organize the information by comparison.
D. You prepare graphs, charts, maps, and visual aids.
E. You keep a research diary.

IV. How do you prepare a report to share the information you have?

A. You outline the report and write a rough draft.
B. You prepare the visual aids that will appear in the report or will be used when you present the report to the class.
C. If the report is to be oral, you prepare 3 x 5 cards for each subtopic and write out the first and last sentences.
D. If it is a group project, you coordinate your report with the other students.

V. How do you evaluate your research?

A. You review the sources you used to see if you had several resources of different kinds.
B. You check to see if your resources give fact or opinion and whether there are biases in your resources or your conclusions.
C. You see if your research gave you or other people new ideas.
D. You discuss your report with your teacher.

*Primary question example

Children's choice. We saw the inquiry process demonstrated in a first grade classroom. This structure was developed by the teacher to provide motivation for the children to pique their curiosity, and to make them aware of research procedures such as those listed above. The media specialist and the librarian gathered together all the materials, book and nonbook, on Hawaii. Children were given an opportunity to look at a limited sample of the materials which dealt with a range of topics. Each day some time was devoted to providing the individual youngsters with information about different topics. For example:

Monday	Susan examines booklet on pineapples
Tuesday	Susan looks at filmstrip on *Homes of Hawaii*
Wednesday	Susan listens to record of Hawaiian music
and so on . . .	

Following this exposure, the students were given an opportunity to choose a topic about which they would like to become the "experts." The remaining materials for the topics were then provided for the individual or group that chose a certain topic. On most topics a booklet, a filmstrip, a record or tape, and in some cases a film were provided. The idea was to provide reading stimulus, picture stimulus, auditory stimulus, and a combination of these so as to make research profitable for as wide a range of students as possible. The students could manage most media by themselves but needed help with the tape recorder and the 16mm film projector.

It was suggested that the students prepare a picture, that they write a sentence or two about their topic, and that they think about the things they would read and see and be prepared to tell the other children a little about them.

Before the final sharing session the teacher had the children discuss the things they would need to think about when they were presenting their research to the class. These first grade children suggested the following:

1. Speak loudly enough for everyone to hear.
2. Have pictures large enough to see from the front or pass them around.
3. Don't say "ah-h."
4. Be brief.

Finally the children proudly shared their findings with the class.

In this program a strong emphasis was placed on arousing curiosity in children. Curiosity is a strong motivating force for learning and stimulates the child naturally and more effectively than other external pressures will. Curiosity creates a questioning stance.

Questions: The basis for inquiry. Pursuing questions that come from an individual, a class, or a small group discussion can be stimulating intellectual work. The inquiry process can be carried on by an individual, a group, or a class working through small groups. The question may be a big question, or a small question which leads to a big question, or a small question which remains small but whose inquiry potential should be realized. Here is a sample of questions with different potentials:

1. Is Canada or Mexico more like the United States? Why?
2. How would you describe your town (or the United States) to a foreign child?
3. What do maps and globes tell you about Great Britain?
4. What do maps and globes not tell you about Great Britain?
5. (An artifact is shown.) What is it? Who used it? How was it used? Etc.
6. If we plan a trip to Finland what would we expect to see?
7. Many questions can arise from raw data such as statistical tables.
    a. Overseas travelers by year, by sea, by air
    b. South American countries with population, area in square miles, density per square mile
    c. Number and percentage of voters voting in the last state election
    d. Number and acreage of farms in the states of the United States and value per acre
8. How do we know that the cave man existed?
9. Begin a series of questions dealing with your research topic, "What would happen if . . . ?"
10. Is a big city in a foreign country (Cairo, Tokyo) like a big city in the United States?
11. Look at a map of any large area of the world and try to explain why a large city (such as London) is located where it is. What would it take to prove the hypotheses true or false?

Some techniques for stimulating small group discussion and for creating a basis for inquiry about a topic are to:

1. Use a film without the sound turned on.
2. Use a film loop with a small group.
3. Use a filmstrip from the Critical Thinking Aids series.[3]
4. Project a slide or show a picture of a place that will not be studied in detail during the year and have pupils (probably in small groups) list the things they think might

3. Modern Learning Aids, P.O. Box 302, Rochester, N.Y. 14603. One hundred filmstrips on events in U.S. history (e.g., "Gold Rush," "Slavery in America"). The first fifteen frames tell a story up to a point. The class divides into groups to discuss what happens now, what decision they think was made, etc. Groups report and there is discussion. Class returns to the filmstrip which in several more frames raises questions for further discussion. The last frame reveals the historical outcome.

be true about the place. Tell them where it is and let them read to check on their guesses.

5. Ask a group of children what they think about a certain topic. Tape record their comments. After study in this unit topic, have the students listen to what they originally said and discuss what was revealed.

Teacher's role in the inquiry process. The inquiry-oriented teacher realizes that there is more to learning social studies than *intake* (collecting information), storage (memorization of facts), and retrieval (producing information for a test or answering a teacher's questions). Student speculation in building an hypothesis for research also is necessary. Such speculation may lead up blind alleys, but blind alleys, dead-end streets, and alternate routes are all a very real part of research and experiencing some of these increases learning. Therefore, the teacher allows time and guidance and support for students in the research operation.

The teacher also provides materials and resource suggestions. He serves as a diagnostician when called upon to do so, but he also encourages the students to diagnose their own needs.

The teacher in the inquiry process may provide the focus questions for the investigation as well as connecting questions along the way. A focus question should delineate: (1) the general type of response, and (2) the area of concern. For example: Can you list (type of response) the machines (area of concern) that you saw in the General Motors factory? Other kinds of questions include supportive questions (Can you add something, Jane?), summary or generalizing questions (Can you put all these ideas into one sentence?), and explaining questions (Why do you think this happened?).

In the inquiry process the teacher generally asks questions rather than provides answers. The ability to ask good questions is imperative.

The teacher can also provide the stimulus for gathering data by direct means by suggesting the use of interviews, surveys, questionnaires, and direct observation schedules. Frequently students do not think of these possibilities because they are not used in all classrooms. Nearly any concept or topic can be enlarged upon and enhanced by using such techniques. For example, if the student is studying the broad topic of Transportation and the subtopic "Cars," it would be interesting for him to identify as many of the makes of cars as possible and then check a local street after school to see how many cars of each type pass that spot in half an hour. He may wish to find out why people purchase a certain make or model. How much money is spent on cars in the automotive industry generally? How many jobs does it provide for people? What problems have automobiles created? What related industries are affected by changes in the auto industry? An endless number of questions can begin with a simple direct observation and provide an exciting self-generating inquiry base for the student.

Conditions for inquiry. Suchman says three conditions seem to be essential for the process of inquiry.[4] The teacher can aid in the inquiry process by providing these conditions.

1. *Focus.* To say "Think about it" does not provide focus. "Look at this and watch what happens." "How can you account for such a thing?" "What evidence is there for this?" "Is there a better way to live?" Confronted with such questions the students have no answers but can be aided to develop some.
2. *Freedom.* To lead a child step by step in his social learning is a limitation of freedom. Children must have the opportunity to make choices as to what *data* they get, get next, and next, and what ideas they pull out of storage (their own and other sources) to try out on the data they take in. The teacher can grant freedom to do this in the students' learning environment but it is a freedom, developed over a period of time, that the students have to accept and use.
3. *A responsive environment.* They cannot inquire except through gathering data. If they do not have an environment from which they can obtain the data they want when they want it, and in the sequence in which they want it, there can be no inquiry.

The three conditions listed here are the result of certain teacher behavior that produces a good learning environment. This kind of teacher behavior simply sets the stage for inquiry.

It is assumed in much of the literature dealing with inquiry that the student is the inquirer. It does not seem logical to expect a student to be alive, curious, and fascinated with learning unless there is some evidence of this in the teacher. Curiosity need not die with an A.B.or B.S. degree, and the attainment of adult years. A teacher who enjoys learning about new ideas and investigates them in a scholarly way may provide a beneficial model of learning for the young student.

In many cultures all over the world the chief way of learning is by imitation. Perhaps it is unwise for us to ignore this potential in our society. The "teacher-proof" materials that have been packaged and provided for children would seem to ignore "teacher-model" potential. Because we feel that the teacher himself must be an inquiring, active, involved individual if he is to understand and help develop the process of inquiry in others, it would seem that some training along these lines might be in order. If the teacher himself is an inquirer, he will recognize the value of questions and tentative, partial answers. He will also see clearly the needs for alternatives and for a broad range of experiences that intensify the individual's interests. His role as a teacher of inquirers will be to encourage exploration, help build connections, and help make relationships more explicit. He will be a person who is keenly aware of other persons

4. J. Richard Suchman, *Inquiry: Implications for Televised Instruction* (Washington, D.C.: National Education Association, 1966), pp. 27-29.

and their needs and will endeavor to maintain and guide the individual student in the learning process.

Grouping procedures

Organizing children in groups or pairs is an effective way to carry out many assignments. There are many advantages to group activities, and the use of groups in a unit provides the students with a number of skills.

1. Group work requires each child to participate actively:
   a. Listening and reacting to the opinions of other children
   b. Formulating and presenting an opinion
   c. Recording and summarizing group opinions or findings
2. Many children are able to participate at a given time.
3. Children are encouraged to work and think independently of teacher direction and reaction.
4. For many children the small group is a proving ground. Shy or reluctant children are more likely to interact with a few children than with the total class.

Successful group work does not just happen. It requires patience and some planning with the children.

1. For the first experiences make the assignments short. Have children consider only one question or examine only one picture. The assignments can be increased later.
2. Vary the tasks.
3. Set up the groups as far apart as space allows—there will be more noise and physical activity than when children work alone.
4. Experiment with groups of from two to five (never more). For younger children use fewer children per group.
5. Be sure the assignment is clearly related to work going on in the class.
6. Be sure each child understands the assignment. Give it in writing.
7. Before group meetings discuss assignment with group leaders. When desirable, write the assignment out for each group leader. Discuss their responsibilities.
   a. Try to get each child to participate in planning the process to be used
   b. Try to keep discussion relevant
   c. Try to get children to talk quietly one at a time
   d. Try to help children see that all members of the group are happier and can participate more effectively if the decisions are reached by consensus rather than by "voting down" the minority

Provide leaders with questions requiring more than one-word answers and with supplementary questions to consider different possibilities. The leader must be able to keep discussion alive.

8. Sit for a few minutes with each group. Listen to comments and observations. Make suggestions to help discussion and possible ways to report back to class.
9. Provide time for evaluation. Each group should try to judge its effort and success.

   a. What were we supposed to do?
   b. Did we do it?
   c. Did we finish our job? Why not?

10. Sometimes tape a group discussion. Play the tape to the class. The class will like evaluating the taped discussion.

Informal or impromptu grouping is the easiest and most frequently used. There are several ways of arranging such groups. One can literally "draw a number out of a hat," or group quickly by numbering off or using tables of students. In grouping of this type, the task assigned is usually of short duration, since neither topic or associates were chosen by the student.

Sociometric grouping is usually employed when the duration of the project is fairly extensive. If one works for a great length of time on a project, he may be more productive if he works with congenial colleagues. Developing a sociogram for a group does require some time and effort on the part of the teacher. Grouping and choices change over time and task. One might use the following general guidelines for developing sociometric grouping.

SOCIAL DISTANCE SCALE

This scale is used to assist you in organizing groups for work purposes in your classroom. Distribute dittoed forms like the one below or simply have each student write his name on a slip of paper followed by a 1—2—3 listing.

Student ____________________

Question: Who would you prefer to work with you?

1. ____________________
2. ____________________
3. ____________________

DIRECTIONS

1. Conduct the choice-making task casually.
2. Keep the responses confidential.
3. Suggest that you are available to help clarify any question the student has.
4. *Do not*
   a. assist the student in making choices
   b. allow the students to discuss their choices.

Base the *work* groups on the following (read aloud):

There are some people you like to work with better than others. We will be working in groups to produce research reports for the class. Such reports require a number of different contributions such as art work, creative ideas, speaking skill, etc. Please indicate on a slip of paper the person you would most like to work with in such a group. Now list two other choices. When you finish, your paper should be numbered 1, 2, 3, with a name following each number.

If you wish to use the groups for purposes other than *work* groups your statement of purpose must change. Children's choices for different task assignments may not be the same. Once the student's choices have been made the data might be first recorded as shown below. The first column names the students making the choice followed by three columns for their choices in order.

	1ST	2ND	3RD
Ann—	Emma	Opal	Jane
Beth—	Jane	Mary	Vera
Charlie—	Dan	Walter	George
Dan—	Charlie	Larry	Walter
Emma—	Jane	Vera	Ann
Frank—	Charlie	Walter	Dan
George—	Robert	Charlie	Frank
Henry—	Charlie	George	Sam
Jane—	Ann	Vera	Emma
Kate—	Vera	Mary	Jane
Larry—	Beth		
Mary—	Vera	Ann	Emma
Nancy—	Vera	Ann	Mary
Opal—	Walter	Jane	Vera
Robert—	Beth	Sam	Emma
Sam—	Henry	Walter	Beth
Vera—	Jane	Dan	Ann
Walter—	Charlie	Beth	Henry

FIGURE 2.2 Recording Sheet

	Ann	Beth	Charlie	Dan	Emma	Frank	George	Henry	Jane	Kate	Larry	Mary	Nancy	Opal	Robert	Sam	Vera	Walter
Ann					3				1					2				
Beth									3									
Charlie																		
Dan																		
Emma									3									
Frank																		

In listing choices for the actual grouping task, it is useful to think of these choices in a reverse number system to the recorded list above. That is, Ann chose Emma first, Opal second, and Jane third. If one wishes to give most weight to first choice, since this is the most preferred person, a numbering of 3 for Emma, 2 for Opal, and 1 for Jane on the recording sheet will give the proper idea of leadership and isolation. (*See* Figure 2.2.)

In following through Ann's three choices one can see the relative popularity of these particular girls. One might also observe, upon completing the chart, the sex polarization. This is a fifth-sixth-grade group and fairly typical of this age range.

In using the charts, one develops groups beginning with the isolates or near isolates and gives them one of their choices if possible. The sociogram alone cannot be the sole determiner of the group. Certain task variables (could these children do this particular chore?) and psychological factors (not placing three or four aggressive, non-cooperative types in the same group, for instance) must also be considered.

Group work evaluation. It is a good idea for students to assess their own success or failure as a group. A checklist like the following may help them to do this effectively. (Duplicate this checklist.)

You may have done your research with a friend, or as one member of a group. If you did, the work sessions should be evaluated. You can use the following checklist to find out how well you worked with others. How well did you perform as part of a team?

	ALL OF THE TIME	MOST OF THE TIME	SOME-TIMES	NEVER
Cooperated in planning research presentation				
Participated in choosing a leader				
Listened to other people's ideas				
Abided by group decisions				
Took a share of responsibility for getting the research report done				
Completed tasks				
Respected the feelings of others				
Suggested new ideas for benefit of the research report				
Contributed in the reporting session				

How well did you come out on the Group Work Evaluation scale? Were most of your check marks in the "All of the time" column? If most of yours were in the "Never" column, you will need to work harder at this skill next time. Jot down your ideas for improving the "Never" or "Sometimes" checks on your list.

Use of study guides

In carrying out a unit of instruction it will be necessary for the students to complete some information gathering on their own. A study guide is a set of questions based on a particular reading or a specific media input. It is a listing of the problems to be solved, tasks to be done, objectives to be achieved, and materials to be used suited to the abilities in a class. Guides should be used only as a part of the total program; exclusive or heavy use is not profitable.

It is important to provide a buildup of information in the organization of study guide questions and other curricular materials because responding to these provides for the expressive output in which the child will be involved. Study guides frequently take the form of questions. If one is to provide for a logical buildup of information and an opportunity for the child to express this in a reasonable way, then care must be taken in the questions provided. A question sequence should be formulated in the order of the psychological steps that are required to answer the questions. Listing kinds of questions use the most simplistic kind of logic. These should be used in the early stages of content intake. Questions beginning with "what" or "when" seek to ferret out important details. More complex questions dealing with more important ideas that require some inferential reasoning powers should be used later. Questions that ask "how" or "why" require more processing of information and should come toward the end of the study sequence.

Two samples of study questions will serve to illustrate the difference between the simple intake of information which might produce a person who knows many facts and the intake of information combined with a problem-solving approach to the information and/or situation being investigated.

Sample A. The following study questions are suggested as a guide for the *factual intake of information* from books, films, and pictures. Duplicate for each child or print on a large chart. You may want to divide the list into smaller parts for small groups of children or state references within a small range of pages if there are severe reading problems in your class.

INFORMATION GATHERING SEQUENCE

1. What did these people eat?
2. When did they get their food?
3. What kind of tools did they have?
4. Where did they get their tools?
5. Who used the different tools?
6. What did these people teach their children?
7. How were the children taught?
8. Who taught the children?

Sample B. The following sample of questions involves a factual base and some use of problem-solving processes. This sequence goes from what and when to why, from a simple response to a more difficult one.

REASONING SEQUENCE

1. What group raided the ships at the Boston Tea Party?
2. When did this happen?
3. How was the group able to carry out this act?
4. Why did they decide to do this?
5. What was the reaction to this in Boston?
6. How do you think you would have reacted as an English merchant? Why?

Team use of study guides. When study guides are used by pairs or teams of three, recall is reinforced by oral response and by confirmation of answers by partners. Answer sheets enable the teams to find mistakes immediately; thus a self-directing, self-correcting learning situation is available for improving the intake of ideas.

1. The teacher prepares a set of questions covering specific material in the order in which the answers are to be found in the book or other media source, with pages or paragraphs or frames sometimes indicated. Answers are provided on the back, or on the bottom or side which is folded over to conceal them; some teachers prefer separate answer sheets.
2. Children work in pairs or teams of three. They read the paragraph, view the media, read the questions in the study guide, consult on answers, write the answers on a separate sheet, and check their answers against the answer sheet.
3. When all pupils have completed the work on their study guides, class or team discussion may follow. Since the guides have assured the coverage of facts, the team discussions should require elaborative or critical thinking.
4. Study guides may be provided for pupils who have difficulty in learning, or different guides with different purposes may be designed for varying needs of groups within the class.
5. If in social studies chapters the ideas are covered in too superficial a manner for bright pupils, study guides may be prepared for teams to answer. They will move rapidly. When the answers have been completed or checked, pupils progress to library references on the same topic.
6. Guides can provide developmental instruction to recall, in outlining, or other specific skills.
7. Guides may be prepared that require oral summaries, with the partner checking against a list of ideas in the selection. Written summaries may be checked in the same manner.
8. Steps in outlining may be taught through study guides, beginning with the task of selecting best topics for paragraphs, then progressing through writing topics, writing minor ideas under major headings, filling incomplete outlines, and, finally, the complete task of outlining.
9. Since workbooks are learning aids rather than texts, children profit by consulting each other before answering workbook questions. Each pupil may write the answers, or a single workbook may be used to record the team answer.
10. Inattentive pupils may be helped by team use of study guides in listening, following lists of questions to be answered during listening. The speaker pauses at intervals to allow teams to answer the questions. The same method may be used in connection with motion pictures.

Suggestions for preparing study guides. Since a study guide is built to go with a particular media source, no illustration is given of a specific guide or worksheet. Rather we present suggestions which can be developed with your chosen materials.

1. Locate the following on the map.
2. Answer the following by marking *true* or *false*, after reading pages____________.
3. Do the exercise on page ____________ in your book.
4. Would you like to live in this region? Give your reasons.
5. Questions answered by direct quote, using words from the book. What is? What did? What things? What animals? What happened? How long ago? Where? Which?
6. Look at the map on page ____________ and answer these questions.
7. Look at the maps (rainfall, natural resources, population) and answer these questions.
8. Complete the following sentences.
9. Complete the following outline (fill in the blanks).
10. Some of the eight sentences below tell why the ________________ . Place a check mark before the five correct statements.
11. For vocabulary: Match the words in Column 1 with the correct meanings in Column 2.
12. Choose the best ending. (Multiple-choice-type questions.)
13. Categorizing: Here are two headings; put the following items under the proper heading.
14. Name the three countries that ________________.
15. List ____________.
16. Draw ____________.
17. Study guide suggestions for bright students:

    a. As review or for quickly organizing facts, they can use the guides that emphasize facts.
    b. "How" and "why" discussion questions.
    c. Encyclopedia and reference reports, oral and written.
    d. Project assignments in map making, charts, etc.
    e. Outlining.
    f. Written summary report.
    g. Questions involving critical and elaborative thinking.

Questioning techniques

Good questions provoke good answers. Most people, at one time or another, have been enthralled by a give-and-take question-and-answer session. One person may have heard a celebrity being interviewed on a talk show; another person may have observed as a clever courtroom lawyer built a case for his client by asking probing questions; and yet another individual may have listened as a teacher responded to a pupil's thinking and helped the student develop his ideas more fully by using a skillful questioning strategy. In each case, the viewer may have been almost astounded at the amount of information and ideas the careful questioner was able to draw forth. The individual being questioned may have been almost as surprised as the onlooker to find that he knew so much about the topic. The individual who listens to another analytically and follows this careful listening with thoughtful questions can be helpful in any group discussion. The classroom teacher needs both of these skills. There are some general ideas that a teacher can consider in becoming a more effective questioner.

1. Take what children say seriously. It is always possible to shrug off a remark a child makes as irrelevant or poorly thought out. It is wiser to assume that children intend to be a part of the thinking that is taking place in the classroom. A chance remark may shed new light on a topic. If each remark cannot be dealt with in detail as a discussion proceeds, ask the child to jot down the idea and talk to you later about it.
2. Listen for what the student is trying to say. Ask questions about the intended message as it applies to the topic at hand. Allow time for rephrasing an answer or comment.
3. Do not be distracted by minor grammatical or spelling errors in an initial exploration of an idea. Correct them later. One student writing a list on the board wrote "wisdon" instead of "wisdom." Before allowing the ideas to continue, the teacher said caustically, "You mispelled wisdom," and the student had to correct the word before the group could proceed. Surely this did not demonstrate the use of wisdom on the part of the teacher. The entire list might easily have been put in order later.
4. Try to think about the topic to be discussed from several different angles. When a student responds to a question in a somewhat unique way, think honestly. "Could this be interpreted this way? Is this another possible way of looking at the ideas presented here?" Such an approach will help you to question more intelligently and more thoroughly.

Sometimes a whole series of questions must be used to provide the information necessary to finally conclude a topic. Some sequences of questions have been shown to be more productive and more useful in summarizing information than others. Let us examine those that research has shown to be most effective.

Questioning sequences. In research done by Taba, Levine, and Elzey, the thinking skills have been divided logically into three cognitive tasks to facilitate their implementation in the elementary social studies classroom.[5] In connection with these tasks, question sequences have been developed that lead children to mobilize their thinking.

5. Taba, Levine, and Elzey, *Thinking in Elementary School Children* (San Francisco State College, Cooperative Research Project No. 1574, 1964.)

The first of three tasks deals with concept formation. The students are asked to list, group, and categorize a body of information.

Task two deals with the interpretation of data and the development of generalizations. In this task students are encouraged to look for similarities and differences in items of data and to develop general statements based on their observations.

The third task is the application of principles. Questions dealing with this task ask children to hypothesize about the data and to explain and support the prediction they have made.

These tasks organize the steps toward abstract thinking in an hierarchical order (not unlike Bloom's *Taxonomy*) and, by skillfully using inductive question sequences, help the student arrive at a high level of thinking. The cognitive tasks are based on an inquiry-oriented, research rationale. That is, children are expected to choose some facet of the broad content emphasis, collect data, organize it, and present the data in a summarized form to others.

In research reported by Taba, short sequences of teacher-pupil interaction were identified in tapescripts dealing with the culmination of the children's research effort.[6] Recurrences of certain broad question sequences were found, as well as a high-level general statement or a high-level inference associated with these sequences. It is not possible to give the exact question sequence because the number of responses and number of questions depends upon the topic and the teacher's sense of timing.

The modules (short sequences of teacher-pupil interaction) that were found to recur were the following:

A. *Additive Module*—The teacher asks "What else? What more can you add?" etc. Having solicited a number of contributions, the teacher repeats briefly the various contributions and seeks once more for additional information.

Teacher: (Repetition)—"We've talked about architecture, the calendar, the government, and the musical instruments. (Additive question)—What else did the Romans contribute?"

Child: "They had a lot of basic designs for today's transportation. Their ships were improved and were the best up to the 1700s."

Teacher	+ (the additive question)
Student	statement
Teacher	+
Student	statement
Teacher	+
Student	statement
Teacher	repetition, +
Student	high level general statement.

6. Hilda Taba, *Teaching Strategies and Cognitive Functioning in Elementary School Children* (Washington, D.C.: U.S. Office of Education, Cooperative Research Project No. 2404, 1966.)

B. *Reflective Module*—The teacher simply reflects students' questions by tossing the ball back to them—"Someone want to answer that?" "What do you mean by that term?"—finally, repeating the gist of the comments and asking for clarification.

Child: "Well, Florida is pretty close to the Tropic of Cancer."

Teacher: "All right, Florida is close to the Tropic of Cancer, so what is that going to mean, John?"

Child: "Well, it's going to be warmer than some other parts of the country."

Teacher	reflect (tossing question back)
Student	statement
Teacher	reflect
Student	statement, or possible question
Teacher	repetition and reflect contribution or question.
Student	high level general statement

C. *Explaining Module*—Simple use of "Why?" "Can you explain?" etc. by the teacher. The teacher uses some form of an explanatory question several times and then repeats the contributions and asks for a final summation.

Teacher	why?
Student	explains
Teacher	why?
Student	explains
Teacher	repetition of the several explanations, why?
Student	high level inference

D. *Backward Chain*—Child begins with broad general statement (e.g., All developing nations need help from richer nations). The teacher asks him to give specifics to back up the statement (What do you mean they need help?). This clarifies the statement for the student, the rest of the class, and the teacher.

The modules provide some general ideas regarding questioning that might be useful for classroom teachers. It is interesting to note that in all cases a sequence of the same general kind of questions is suggested, not just a single question. This allows for a collection of responses rather than a single "right" response.

The modules also suggest that repetition by the teacher is productive if followed by a final response from the children. When one listens to his own response, it somehow clarifies the communication and the effect the communication has had on others. It may also provide an opportunity to organize a more succinct summarial statement. Teachers frequently use repetition to complete a lesson.

A more productive use of repetition allows the students to make the final statement of summary following the teacher's brief repetition, thus producing generalizations in a very natural way. For example,

Teacher: "All right. There's another point. You've brought out the military strategy. You've mentioned the well-trained soldiers. You said they had great leaders, good roads, and a good location on water. What else can you say about this? What can you say about the Roman victories?"

Child: "Rome was powerful and won many battles because of several reasons. Mainly they had a good location and very strong, smart citizens."

This allows the child rather than the teacher to summarize, and it provides an opportunity for encouraging the children to finalize the research ideas.

Levels of questions. Questions can be phrased in several ways, requiring different amounts of cognitive work in shaping a response. Following roughly the levels of cognitive processes provided in Bloom's *Taxonomy* a hierarchy of questions can be developed.

1. Knowledge Questions. Several simple questions that evoke factual or informational responses are provided under the section on *Study Guide Questions*, Other examples include:
   a. What is the title of the book?
   b. When did the Civil War officially begin?
   c. What is meant by the "extended family"?
2. Descriptive Questions. Questions of this type require elaboration, discussion, and usually more detailed description than the knowledge questions.
   a. Single-Focus Descriptive:
      (1) Tell about the difficulties encountered by Lewis and Clark on their famous expedition.
      (2) Describe the route taken by the Cherokee Indians that is called the "Trail of Tears."
   b. Double-Focus Descriptive:
      (1) Compare the living conditions of the Northeast Woodlands Indians with those of the Plains Indians.
      (2) Contrast the unwritten food and eating taboos of the Bulu tribe with those of the middle-class American.
3. Application Questions. Practical applications require not only that the individual know the data, but also that he apply it or the ideas generated by it to a new situation. This, then involves an additional mental operation.
   a. How would you begin a unit on culture using the ideas on concept formation developed by Taba?
   b. Here is a map of your community drawn on a one inch graph. Can you draw this using a quarter-inch graph scale?

4. Analysis Questions. When one analyzes, he separates or breaks down or distinguishes the component parts of something. Analytical questions require individuals to carry out this general process mentally in order to produce a response.

   a. Which of the processes pictured below would be most apt to provide a careful evaluation of the product developed?
   b. Which type of propaganda technique is shown in the statement, "Statistics show that . . . ?"

5. Heuristic Questions. Heuristic questions are valuable because they promote research into unproved areas and frequently encourage thinking about that which cannot be proven. They serve to guide research or reveal alternative aspects of a topic. Responses to heuristic questions typically require both analysis and application in a predictive manner.

   a. What would Native American/New American relationships have been like if all settlement west of the Mississippi had been stopped by the U.S. government?
   b. What might happen if the World Trade Organization were not supported by the major powers?

6. Evaluative Questions. Questions in this category require information, the ability to describe, the application and analysis of data, the consideration of alternatives, and the respondant's own thoughts and feelings about the topic.

   a. Consider the migrant workers in the Sacramento valley. What do you think is their most immediate need, and what legislation would you recommend to care for this need if you were a state legislator?
   b. How would the people around beltway 495 respond if the decision to double the lanes for traffic were announced? How would you respond if you were one of the homeowners whose property bordered the affected expansion area?

It should be abundantly clear to the reader that there are many ways in which questions can be used to promote learning. There are also a number of different types of questions that require a different mode of cognitive attack. The use of questions in different settings, as well as the use of many of the higher-level questions, are stimulating for both student and teacher.

FOR FURTHER READING

General

Hanna, Lavone A.; Potter, Gladys L.; and Robert W. Reynolds. *Dynamic Elementary Social Studies—Unit Teaching.* 3rd ed. New York: Holt, Rinehart & Winston, 1973.

Jarolimek, John. *Social Studies in Elementary Education.* 5th ed. New York: Macmillan, 1977. Chapter 2, "Planning for Teaching the Social Studies."

Michaelis, John U. *Social Studies for Children in a Democracy.* 6th ed. Englewood Cliffs, N.J.: Prentice-Hall, 1976. Chapter 3, "Planning Units of Instruction."

Preston, Ralph C., and Wayne L. Herman, Jr. *Teaching Social Studies in the Elementary School.* 4th ed. New York: Holt, Rinehart & Winston, 1974. Chapter 4, "The Unit."

Sanders, Norris M. *Classroom Questions: What Kind?* New York: Harper & Row, 1966.

Smith, James A. *Creative Teaching of the Social Studies in the Elementary School.* 2nd ed. Boston: Allyn and Bacon, 1975. Chapter 6, "Unit Teaching."

Selected Bibliography on Inquiry

Allen, Rodney F.; Fleckenstein, John V.; and Peter M. Lyons, eds. *Inquiry in the Social Studies.* Arlington, Va.: National Council for the Social Studies, 1968.

Banks, James A., and Ambrose A. Clegg, Jr. *Teaching Strategies for the Social Studies.* 2nd ed. Reading, Mass.: Addison-Wesley, 1977.

Beyer, Harry K. *Inquiry in the Social Studies Classroom: A Strategy for Teaching.* Columbus, Ohio: Charles E. Merrill, 1971.

Estvan, Frank J. *Social Studies in a Changing World.* New York: Harcourt, Brace & World, 1968. Chapter 13.

Hunkins, Francis P. *Questioning Strategies and Techniques.* Boston: Allyn and Bacon, 1972.

"Inquiry-Oriented Teaching." In *An Anthology of Readings in Elementary School Social Studies,* edited by Huber M. Walsh, pp. 23-53. Arlington, Va.: National Council for the Social Studies, 1971. A series of brief expressive articles.

Jarolimek, John, "Focus in Inquiry," *Social Education* 33 (May 1969): 533-550. Five articles on inquiry.

Ryan, Frank L.; Joyce, Bruce; and Marsha Weil. *Exemplars: Models of Teaching.* Englewood Cliffs, N.J.: Prentice-Hall, 1972. Chapter 8.

Ryan, Frank L., and Arthur K. Ellis. *Instructional Implications of Inquiry.* Englewood Cliffs, N.J.: Prentice-Hall, 1974.

THREE EXEMPLAR UNITS

Chapter three

The first illustrative unit in this chapter is one on "The Telephone." It can be developed in an early primary grade, or even the kindergarten. The subject is an important one. Teachers will find adaptation to their particular groups fairly easy.

"Colonial Life in America" shows what one fifth grade teacher actually planned in teaching such a unit. She did not have a resource unit in which someone had done the preplanning for her. Using her past experience and some notes, Miss Wiggin built a teaching unit. Her long-range plan for this unit is reproduced from her plan book without any editing. The material printed in italics has been added in order to call attention to certain important points.

The third unit is one that emphasizes attitudes. The "Black American" deals with a current issue in our country and an implementation of democratic values. It touches on a sensitive area in our culture and attempts to provide emotional involvement in the issue, as well as informational input.

A PRIMARY UNIT ON THE TELEPHONE

I. Analysis of Content

A. *Overview.* The telephone is an important part of everyday life in many parts of the world. Business is conducted, friendships are cemented, and many services are arranged over the telephone. Emergencies can be reported and lives saved as a result of the rapidity of telephone services. As a widely used effective means of communication, the telephone has no equal. For the reasons mentioned, it is important that children learn to use the telephone themselves and take messages on it for other people.

B. *Content Outline*

1. How we use the telephone
   a. Know your own number
   b. Know how to place a call
      (1) directory, use of it
      (2) get correct number
      (3) dialing procedure
      (4) sounds, what they stand for
      (5) personal list of numbers for easy referral
   c. Know how to receive a call
      (1) identify person and/or residence
2. Telephone courtesy
   a. Answer promptly
   b. Take a message
   c. Speak clearly
3. Emergency use of the telephone
   a. Dialing procedure
   b. Data needed to report an emergency
      (1) full name
      (2) address where help is needed
      (3) reason help is needed
4. How the telephone works
   a. Invention of Alexander Graham Bell
   b. Sound
      (1) vibration—sound waves
      (2) hearing sounds—eardrums, brain

II. Objectives

A. *Understandings.* After the students have completed the activities in this unit, each child will:

1. Say and write his home telephone number
2. Identify at least one courteous behavior
3. Write full name and address, also be able to give it verbally upon cue
4. Give the name of the inventor of the telephone
5. Label a sketch of the ear

B. *Problem-solving Skills*

1. Use a classroom directory and place one phone call correctly
2. Accept one call and give proper identification
3. Take a message in which a return call is requested, and correctly give the message and number to the party requested
4. Place an emergency call in a role-playing situation in the classroom
5. Make sound by vibrating a rubber band

C. *Attitude Development*

1. Decide what people would be most needed on his personal list of numbers
2. Report an emergency clearly and carefully in a role-playing situation

III. Learning Activities

OBJECTIVE	MOTIVATOR ACTIVITIES	MATERIALS
To involve students and interest them in the use of the telephone.	1. a. Show film *Telezonia*. b. Discuss the four children in the film. c. Have each child draw a picture of something in the film that he particularly liked. e.g., the magic land, Mr. Tell, or Ms. Question Mark.	Film—*Telezonia*, from C & P Telephone Film Library—Baltimore. In other states call the public relations department of the telephone company. No charge for films used in schools; movie projector; drawing paper; crayons
2. To help every child learn his telephone number.	2. a. Give each child a slip of paper on which to bring his phone number from home. b. When the numbers come from home, provide each child with a piece of construction paper. (Let the children choose a sheet that is the color of their house.) c. Have the children draw the outline of their houses on the paper. d. Cut out the houses.	Construction paper (various colors), crayons, scissors

OBJECTIVE	MOTIVATOR ACTIVITIES	MATERIALS
	e. Write the telephone number in large black letters on the roof of each house.	
3. To reinforce the phone number of each child.	3. a. Use the materials from activity #2 for a bulletin board in which the houses line streets in the local school community.	Bulletin board, border materials, lettering, children's telephone houses, felt-tip pens
	3. b. Have the children help to locate each house. Each child can review the telephone number and address of his house.	
4. To acquaint the children with the idea behind a telephone directory.	4. a. Make a list of the children's names on the board. Introduce the idea of last name first.	Chalkboard, chalk, visible alphabet
	4. b. Have the students place these names in a new list in alphabetical order.	
	4. c. Give the students a ditto sheet with four or five names and accompanying phone numbers to order alphabetically (e.g., Briggs, Janet R. 359-6826; Milligan, Ruth 987-8394; Tyler, Robert 597-8934; Hall, Ellen F. 263-9001; Doty, Paul 783-4602. *Note*: The numbers should not change, but should accompany the same name in the new alphabetized list.	Ditto sheet
5. To teach the children dialing procedure.	5. a. Make some cardboard telephone shapes. Give each child one phone shape and let him color his own phone.	Cardboard telephone shapes
	5. b. Hand out the dial circle with ten holes in it. Have the students fasten these to their phone shapes.	Dial circle

OBJECTIVE	MOTIVATOR ACTIVITIES	MATERIALS
	5. c. Label the numbers. Teacher may help with numbers and letters.	
	5. d. Have a student call out his phone number while all other students using their individual phones dial the number.	
	5. e. Repeat this procedure a number of times using different callers and numbers.	
6. To acquaint the children with the sounds they may hear from or on the phone.	6. a. Play the tape for the children. Discuss it with them.	Tape of busy signal, phone ringing, phone ringing after you have dialed recording answer.
	6. b. Prepare a ditto that will allow each child to identify the sounds on your tape.	Ditto, ear phones, and tape recorder
	6. c. Let the children play the tape and complete the accompanying worksheet on their own.	
7. To allow students to practice receiving and sending calls.	7. a. Have two children sit across the room from each other with working practice phones. Have one dial the other and identify himself.	Two play phones, or teletrainer borrowed from the local telephone company. (A teletrainer consists of two activated telephones and a speaker control unit. It will give a dial tone, busy signal, and a ringing signal.)
	7. b. Have a message left for someone to return a call. Teacher should check out each child using a check list:	
	7. c. Have each team member carry out both roles.	
	7. d. Have a number of teams do this. Eventually have every student in the class do this chore although it need not be done all at one time, nor in front of entire class. Teacher should have a	

CALLING CHECKLIST	DIALED CALL PROPERLY	IDENTIFIED CALLER	GAVE MESSAGE CLEARLY
Anne Brown			
John Crane			
Bob Davis			

RECEIVING CHECKLIST	RECEIVED CALL PROPERLY, IDENTI-FYING RECEIVER	GAVE INFORMA-TION IN A MANNERLY WAY	RECORDED ALL DETAILS NEEDED FOR RETURN CALL
Anne Brown			
John Crane			
Bob Davis			

FIGURE 3.1. Telephone checklists

OBJECTIVE	MOTIVATOR ACTIVITIES	MATERIALS
	complete checklist for all class members when the procedure is finished.	
8. To help children consider carefully the problem of bad manners or poor training on the caller. Using the telephone is a way of communicating with each other. We create an impression even in answering a phone.	8. a. Have a child call you. Mumble with one, hesitate with another, take a message inaccurately, hang up before the person has finished talking, chew gum into the phone, don't identify receiver. 8. b. Follow through on the inconvenience this creates and the feelings the caller had about this behavior. List these ideas on the board.	Children cued to behavior in advance; play phones, chalkboard, chalk

OBJECTIVE	MOTIVATOR ACTIVITIES	MATERIALS
9. To have students identify an abbreviated personal phone list.	9. a. Ask the children to make a list of names of the people they might call most often in a week.	Paper, pencil, construction paper
	9. b. Help each child make his own alphabetically ordered, practical, everyday directory.	
	9. c. Make a cover for the directory out of construction paper.	
10. To reinforce the idea that in telephoning we are communicating with each other.	10. a. Show the film *Experiments*.	Film—*Experiments*, C & P Telephone; movie projector, paper cups, string
	10. b. Discuss the ideas on communication developed here.	
	10. c. Allow teams of students to replicate the paper-cup telephone.	
11. To practice the emergency procedures needed	11. a. "Because this is very important we will do this together. Each of you will give your own name. We will call from this home address and report an accident." Place address and family name on the board. Now dial and have the students report an accident and request the emergency unit. Go over this until the students are able to give the information slowly and carefully. Give: (1) name calling—"who"; (2) home address—"where"; (3) kind of problem, help requested—"why."	Cardboard, phones, chalkboard
	11. b. Discuss the option of reporting any accident to the nearest adult and the need	

OBJECTIVE	MOTIVATOR ACTIVITIES	MATERIALS
	for specificity in making such a report. The same information questions as in 11. a. can be used.	
12. To learn to use the telephone in an emergency.	12. a. Have several role-playing teams set up. Have them rush in, dial the operator, and report an accident or fire, leaving out one detail.	Chalkboard, chalk
	12. b. Have this happen during reading class or following recess—at several times throughout the day.	
	12. c. Pull the ideas together and analyze the problem the negligence of the caller created for the emergency squad. Accent again the three W's of emergency calling.	
	12. d. See the "Learning Center Blueprint" dealing with emergency calling in *Instructor* (August/September 1976), pp. 64-66.	*Instructor* (August/September 1976)
	12. e. Check with the phone company and get emergency numbers stickers for each child to take home and stick on the home phone.	
13. To acquaint the students with the inventor of the telephone.	13. a. Show the film *Here is Tomorrow*.	Film—*Here Is Tomorrow*, C & P Telephone Co.; movie projector
	13. b. Ask the children to each think of something important in the film. They should plan to state this for the class in one brief sentence. (Film deals with Alexander Graham Bell as a creative inventor.)	
14. To experiment with sound and see how the telephone is based on scientific principles.	14. a. Explore how sound is generated with the children.	Rubber bands of different thicknesses

OBJECTIVE	MOTIVATOR ACTIVITIES	MATERIALS
	Group the students in twos. Give each team a rubber band.	
	14. b. Have one student stretch the rubber band between his thumb and forefinger. His partner plucks the strand. Note the vibration of the band.	
	14. c. Have the class listen to the sounds from rubber bands stretched to different lengths.	
	14. d. Examine the science book, and set up a simple circuit for the children to see the effect of a closed circuit. Allow them to close the circuit and ring the bell that it connects. Show that the same principle works when a light is substituted.	Devito, Alfred, and Gerald H. Krockover, *Creative Sciencing Ideas and Activities for Teachers and Children* (Boston: Little, Brown, 1976), pp. 226-229.
15. To experiment with the way sound travels.	15. Fill a pan with water, and after the surface is quiet, drop a small stone in the middle. Have students observe circular waves that are produced. Compare this verbally with how sound waves travel.	
16. To explore the human ear as the receiver of sound waves.	16. a. Show the film *A Sense of Hearing*.	Film—*A Sense of Hearing*, C & P Telephone Co.; movie projector, a ditto
	16. b. Discuss the film briefly.	
	16. c. Have the students label the ditto showing the ear and its connection to the brain.	
17. To help students to review and generalize on what has been covered in the unit.	17. a. *A Culminating Activity*. Plan a trip to the local telephone office.	Permission slips, transportation
	Plan and carry out a mural showing some of the things the students saw.	Butcher paper, crayons or paint

OBJECTIVE	MOTIVATOR ACTIVITIES	MATERIALS
	17. b. *Alternate Activities.* Provide each student with a list of names and some detail to be transmitted about a class party (e.g., Bring five sticks of gum for the party.): Barbara Ellis 345-9683; Anna Jackson 345-3214; Reginald Otis 345-8637; Ralph Parish 345-9381; Arthur Nolan 345-1367. Hand this list to one student who must properly convey the message by phone to all the people on the list. (Other details might include games, equipment, drinks, food, time of party, date, schedule, etc. *Note:* Any detail omitted or called in error will seriously affect the success of the party.) This will serve as a mini-evaluation tool.	Slips of paper with names
	17. c. View *Telezonia* again. Discuss.	

IV. Evaluation. Evaluation will be based on the quality of work completed as well as several checklists and a post-test.

Post-test

1. Write your full name and telephone number.
2. List one courteous telephone behavior.
3. Give your home address.
4. Name the man who invented the telephone.
5. What are the three W's of emergency calling?

Let the students complete the following self-administering, self-scoring, fill-in-the-blanks on their own. (Can be taped for younger children.)

Inventor

My name is_____(1)_____. I invented the telephone in (2) . Mr. __(3)__ was my assistant. One day I called him from another room. He heard me on the__(4)__. I said____(5)____.

(1) Alexander Graham Bell
(2) 1875
(3) Watson
(4) receiver
(5) Watson, come here

Provide the answers above in mixed order. Let the students select the correct ones to fill in the blanks.

Telephone Manners

1. Always speak___(1)___.
2. Don't__(2)__with the telephone.
3. When the phone rings answer___________(3)_________.
4. Lions roar, but we must___(4)___with a normal tone of voice on the telephone.

(1) clearly
(2) play
(3) promptly or right away
(4) speak

Provide answers in mixed order as in previous exercise.
Check the following products for accuracy.

1. Sketch of the ear.
2. Alphabetized ditto.
3. Ditto of phone sounds.
4. Lists from Activity #7.
5. Order of personal telephone directory.

V. Bibliography for Teacher and Student

The Telephone Book. Racine, Wisc.: Golden Press, Western Publishing Company, 1974.

Foster, Ronald M., Jr., ed. *Satellite Communication Physics*. Bell Telephone Laboratories, 1963.

The following are all published by the Bell Telephone System and should be obtainable through your local telephone office: *The Birth and Babyhood of the Telephone; How the Telephone Works; Alexander Graham Bell; The Magic of Your Telephone; Machine Talk; Voices around the World*.

Puzzles

Have each pupil choose a puzzle, *easy* or *hard* or both. The teacher gives oral directions.

Easy

Across

1. When in trouble call the ________ .
2. Short name for telephone.
3. Last name of inventor.
4. Busy signal.
5. When you wish to speak on the phone you ________ your party.
6. Before you dial, listen for a dial ________ .

FIGURE 3.2 a, b. Examples of Easy and Difficult Crossword Puzzles

Difficult

1 B	E	L	L			2 D	I	A	L
3 4	1	1		4 P	O	L	I	C	E
	5 D	I	R	E	C	T	O	R	Y
6 P	H	O	N	E		7 B	U	Z	Z
8 A	B	C		9 P	O	L	I	T	E
	10 N	U	M	B	E	R	S		
	11 O	P	E	R	A	T	O	R	
12 A	R	E	A	C	O	D	E		

Across

1. Inventor of the telephone.
2. You __________ the number of the person you wish to speak to.
3. Number for local information.
4. When you need help call the __________ .
5. The telephone book is called a __________ .
6. Short word for telephone __________ .
7. Busy signal.
8. Alphabetical order is sometimes called __________ order.
9. When you talk on the phone you should be __________ .
10. In the directory you will find names and telephone __________ .
11. When you don't know whom to call, dial the __________ .
12. When you dial long distance numbers you must dial the __________ __________ first.

FIGURE 3.3. Individual evaluation checklist

Name____

ANSWERING THE TELEPHONE

Observe the following questions:	YES	NO
1. Was the telephone answered promptly?		
2. Was the greeting pleasant?		
3. When taking a message was the caller's name and telephone number asked for courteously?		
4. Was the message taken down or repeated?		
5. Was the pupil polite when telling the person who called that he had reached a wrong number?		

USING THE TELEPHONE

Observe the following questions:	YES	NO
1. Did the pupil listen for the dial tone?		
2. Was the number dialed correctly?		
3. Was the dial finger wheel brought all the way to the finger stop each time?		
4. Did the pupil remove his finger and allow the wheel to return by itself after each letter or numeral dialed?		
5. Was the telephone held correctly?		
6. Did the pupil replace the receiver properly after completing the call?		

VI. Instructional Materials

Zim, Herbert S. and Shelly, James R., *Telephone Systems.* New York: William Morrow and Company, 1971.

Darwin, Len, *What Makes a Telephone Work?* Boston: Little, Brown and Company, 1970.

We Learn About the Telephone, American Telephone and Telegraph Company, 1964.

The Telephone and How We Use It, Bell Telephone System Litho in U.S.A. 8-57.

Films: "*Telezonia*," *Experiments, Here Is Tomorrow, A Sense of Hearing* From C & P Telephone Film Library, in Baltimore, Md. No rental charge for schools.

(In other states contact the public relations department of the phone company.)

Tapes: Two tapes will be needed to complete the activities; the teacher makes these for Activity #6.

Equipment: 2 play telephones, paper cups, butcher paper, drawing paper, crayons, paint, movie projector, tape recorder, scissors, felt-tip pens, dittos, rubber bands, chalk, and chalkboard.

Let us see what one fifth-grade teacher actually did in teaching a unit on "Colonial Life In America." She did not have a resource unit for which someone had done the preplanning for her. Using her past experience and some notes, Miss Wiggin built a teaching unit. Her long-range plan for this unit is reproduced from her plan book without any editing. The material in italics has been added in order to call attention to important points.

UNIT ON COLONIAL LIFE IN AMERICA (New England, Middle Atlantic, and Southern States)[7]

Purpose: to help youngsters recognize the differences which existed during the early life of America due to various factors, among them land and environment, and to recognize how these differences influenced our lives and created certain basic problems in them.

Understandings:

1. Among the thirteen original colonies people and purpose differed because of
   a. cultural heritage,
   b. land and climate.
2. Because of these differences certain problems arose.
3. However, certain problems were shared by all
   a. trading;
   b. relationship with England, government;
   c. differences in religion.

Organization:

1. Children have, as a total class, examined certain characteristics of the early colonies, have observed through maps and filmstrips that differences did exist, and have set up certain questions for which they want an answer as part of their study.

7. Judith Wiggin, Harrington School, Lexington, Mass. Reprinted by permission.

This is where the teacher used her starter or initiatory activities—discussion, looking at books, seeing filmstrips, etc. This class used three days doing these things. On the third day the class considered a long list of questions on the chalkboard. Miss Wiggin had been writing these questions as they were raised since the first day.

2. Organize class into research groups with a "leader" appointed in each, except for small group directed by the teacher. Groupings are indicated on attached card.

Miss Wiggin often made notes of various kinds on 3 × 5 cards and attached them with paper clips to pages in her plan book.

There were twenty-six children in the class. Nine were assigned to the New England colonies, nine to the Middle colonies, and eight to the Southern colonies. There were three groups of three each in the New England grouping, and the same for the Middle colonies. (Sometimes a study group might have four, but it is best not to have more.) Miss Wiggin appointed a leader for each of the small groups, six in all, and met with them separately before the first meeting of the groups to discuss with them their responsibilities and how to get started. Responsibilities of group leaders are to:

a. *Make the initial selection of books with the teacher.*
b. *Discuss questions on the guide sheet with group, and add any others.*
c. *Assign, or obtain mutual agreement upon, the specific question or questions on which each individual will work alone.*
d. *Conduct sharing time at the close of each work period, leading the group to make suggestions to the individual.*
e. *Know what difficulties his colleagues are in so he can get help if necessary.*
f. *Know status of accomplishment of his group at all times.*

The research guide on p. 99 was given to the leaders at their meeting and distributed to the members of the groups at the beginning of the first work period. The questions in this guide were assembled and edited by the teacher from those written on the chalkboard in the initiatory period and two or three others were added which she thought desirable.

3. Provide children in New England and Middle Atlantic groupings with materials to guide in locating information, their purpose being to find as much as possible about their particular area through use of:

   a. multi-text references
   b. encyclopedias: *World Book, Compton's, Wonderful World, Britannica, Jr.*

c. individual filmstrip viewers *(Note the use by one individual only for information. Many of the filmstrips would not be seen by others in the group or class.)*
d. pictures—Colonial America series
e. atlases
f. fictional reading materials (library)
g. poetry
h. current literature—magazines

4. Each group of children will be responsible for finding out in detail about specific area or topic concerning Colonial Life (see research guide).
5. Smaller group of eight children who will study about Southern life will use a basic text: *Colonial America* to work with the teacher in guided reading gaining skill in:

   a. locating specific information about a topic
   b. interpreting pictures to gain knowledge
   c. relating map information to what is read
   d. organizing information into a final sharing activity

Taped lessons: History of Young America

These eight children have reading problems. They are given prestige in their class because they will be the only group to present any information to the class on the Southern colonies. The teacher spends some time every day with this group. The tasks they undertake when the teacher is not with them are nearly always in teams (two or three each) instead of individual work. They support each other in mutual aid, which is desirable. Such children need considerable help, which is often supplied as needed by detailed work sheets and very specific directions for using the various instructional aids.

Taped lessons have all kinds of possibilities, limited only by the ingenuity of the teacher. For one lesson Miss Wiggin built an outline over some material in History of Young America, filling in the main headings. She recorded on tape all of the directions for putting in the details, waiting long enough after each for the children to write. The children, sitting around a table, plugged in earphones, listened, and performed.

6. Along with general research, the following activities will be included to provide for various levels and interests:

   a. Examining a region through relief, rainfall, growing season maps to be able to describe and picture what one's surroundings would be like, availability of rivers and bays, quality of soil, weather, and to locate another similar region.

b. to examine maps on the colonial settlements noting possibilities for trading—European, South American, and North American
c. to compare growth in population maps, to list reasons why people originally settled where they did; why they either moved inland or remained along the coast.
d. judging from pictures the relationships of colonists to Indians; kinds of punishments imposed; problems with making a living; difficulties in climate; uses of natural resources
e. retelling from an individually viewed filmstrip the most important information
f. compiling a list of terms peculiar to a particular colonial region—illustrating and using vocabulary
g. comparing pictures of a colonial city and its modern counterpart to note changes and offer explanations for these
h. reading a recent news item and discussing its relationship to the colonial period
i. noting areas of knowledge which colonists excelled in—giving reasons why (e.g., fishing)
j. making a large chart comparing the three areas. *This was never used during the unit but became the concluding or culminating activity through a whole class discussion under the direction of the teacher.*
k. learning more about special colonial figures to discuss importance at that time:

Ben Franklin	William Penn
John Adams	George Washington
Sam Adams	Thomas Jefferson

l. finding out about modern whaling methods and comparing with those used in colonial days
m. constructing examples of buildings, tools, household equipment, transportation; finding out about specific jobs, lumbering, blacksmith, candle and soap makers
n. discussing through panels problems of the regions then and now
o. discussing what qualities were needed for settlers to make a success of a new colony; giving reasons for opinions from examples
p. comparing colonial education with modern—listing differences and similarities; also examining samples of early school equipment—primer
q. making a museum collection of dolls representing clothing worn in various parts of the colonies
r. listening to samples of folk songs and folk tales from these areas
s. role playing:
   (1) a day in the life of . . .
   (2) a meeting of Puritans to decide on cases against the law and giving out punishments
t. telling original stories about the colonists (How I felt when . . .)

u. showing the progress of a particular industry through a series of pictures (self-drawn)
v. writing letters or diaries giving accounts of your life as a colonist
w. dramatizing important events in life of colonies
x. writing puzzles entitled "Who were they?" about certain groups of colonists
y. newscasting about the recreational activities of the day
z. reading literature actually published at that time: *Poor Richard's Almanac*
aa. preparing an exhibit of colonial homes
bb. outlining history of a particular colony
cc. Believe It or Not!

Whole group lessons:

1. Using index to encyclopedias
2. Making comparisons and contrasts about the ways of life in the three areas
3. Sharing fictional reading

Additional activities:

1. Using *Enchantment of America* series to examine more thoroughly the features of the region being studied
2. Specialty reports

Where did Miss Wiggin get her suggestions for all these activities? From teaching a similar unit in the past, or from a card file of activities she indexes under her unit titles, or under units she might build some time. Activities for the file are found in textbooks, magazine articles, curriculum guides of other schools, publications of the National Council for the Social Studies, current events publications, and publications of many organizations, including commercial ones. Finally, activities came from her own ingenuity.

Not all activities in the unit on Colonial Life were used. Others were added as the unit proceeded. Suggestions from the list were made by the teacher as she worked with each of the small groups. During the course of the unit, activities proposed by some of the children were also carried out.

Social studies in Miss Wiggin's class is scheduled at least one hour a day. Since language lessons have no subject matter content of their own, activities in the language period may often be concerned with social studies material too. Some art periods are used on art activities useful in a current social studies unit.

The daily social studies period may be thought of as having three parts:

1. *Conference*—at the beginning for a quick check to see that all groups and individuals know exactly how they are going to use the work period; for bringing to the attention of the whole class pertinent information; or sometimes to present briefly needed practice or review.
2. *Work Period*—the major portion of the period when individuals and groups are busy on activities. The teacher is constantly on the move among the groups, directing, guiding, stimulating, and prodding, and also working with a special group, such as, the slow learners.
3. *Check-off and Planning*—Every day toward the close of the period, chairmen should report the status of their group's work and plans as they see them for the next day. Sometimes the teacher will note things to have ready for tomorrow.

Only through experience and the particular demands of the day will the teacher be able to determine just how much time needs to be allotted to each of these three parts. Actually, it makes no difference whether the divisions show plainly or not, as long as the three elements are present in the social studies class.

In the unit on Colonial Life there came the time when the groups on the New England, Middle and Southern colonies wanted to share their information and their production with the rest of the class. This may be done periodically during the unit or done all at once in bringing the unit to a conclusion. Try each way in different units, or some of both in the same unit.

Miss Wiggin says that unit teaching requires careful planning, as does any good teaching. She did her long-range planning in producing the unit above. She did her short-range planning before each new week by reviewing and evaluating the work of the week before. She made decisions about what lines of inquiry should be abandoned, what should be cultivated, what should be stressed and what minimized; determined what materials were needed; recalled what problems were being faced by what individuals; and then plotted the week ahead (in writing). At the end of each day she did her daily planning for the next in light of what she had learned as she had circulated from group to group and had heard at check-off time. She used colored 3×5 cards attached to a page in her plan book on which she made notations about new activities to be started by different individuals or groups, materials needed, suggestions she wished to make, an interview to be arranged, a question for the music teacher, and similar ideas to forward the learning experiences of the children.

The unit procedure is a form of organization that calls upon all of the good methods in handling materials and activities ever used by quality teachers. To a degree, unit teaching might be described as a "type of behavior and attitude of mind" of the classroom teacher.

QUESTION GUIDE FOR READING

As you are reading, you will be learning about each of the following topics:

1. People
2. Homes
3. Occupations
4. Clothing
5. Education
6. Recreation
7. Problems

Try to find as much as you can: These questions will give you some ideas.

1. What interest did the people in your region have in the New World?
2. Was religion important to these people? If so, how was it an influence in their way of life?
3. What jobs did the man of the family have? How did the women and children work?
4. What kinds of tools and equipment did they use in their jobs?
5. How did their choice of crops to grow make their living conditions different?
6. What were their homes like? How were they furnished? Where was the cooking done? What kinds of utensils did they use in their cooking?
7. Who were the wealthy colonists? How did they live?
8. What was the typical town like? Describe its plan or arrangement.
9. How did the people dress? Of what materials were their clothes made? How were their clothes made?
10. How did the people enjoy themselves? Did they have much leisure time?
11. In what ways did the colonists provide for the education of their children? How did the education of boys differ from that of girls?
12. What were their means of travel and communication? Did they have mail service?
13. How were the sick and diseased cared for? Did they have doctors and different kinds of medicine?
14. What problems did they face in their daily lives? (food, heat, for example)

Suggested Reference List

The Growth of America, pp. 77-91
Our Country's Story, pp. 105-114
America's Frontier, pp. 95-111
Makers of the Americas, pp. 125-158
History of Young America, pp. 71-83, 96-105
New Ways in the New World, pp. 145-165

Some Books to Find at the Library

Barksdale, Lena. *The First Thanksgiving*
Clifford, Harold B. *America, My Home, Then and Now*
Comfort, M.H. *Children of the Colonies*
Daugherty, James. *The Landing of the Pilgrims*
De Angeli, M. *Elin's America* and *Thee, Hannah*
Duffe, Marcelle L. *New Amsterdam Colonial Days, New England Colonial Days,* and *Southern Colonial Days*
Hall-Quest, Olga. *How the Pilgrims Came to Plymouth*
Lenski, Lois. *Puritan Adventure*
Maloy, L. *Wooden Shoes in America*
Mason, Miriam. *William Penn*
Prescott, D.R. *A Day in a Colonial Home*
Saunders, Lucy, and Carrie Willis. *Those Who Dared*

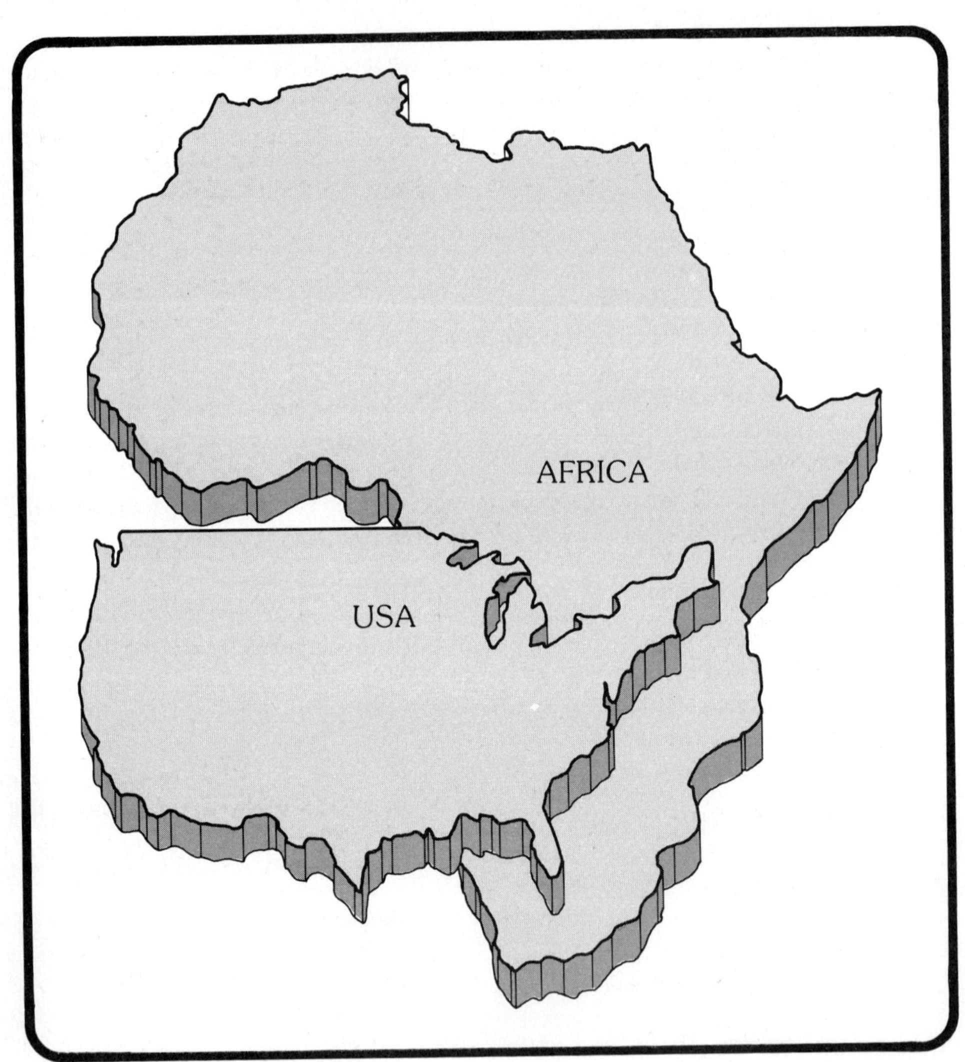
AFRICA
USA

THE BLACK AMERICAN: AN ILLUSTRATIVE UNIT

Subject and Grade: 6th-8th grade social studies. Approximate time: 9-10 weeks*

I. Analysis of Content

A. *Overview*. One of the most pressing challenges facing the teacher in American classrooms today is to respond to the need for a realistic approach to the Afro-American, his unique situation in American society, and his contributions to that society. This unit on Black Studies is intended to give students a strong background of factual information regarding the Afro-American, to give them an understanding of the situation the black man finds himself in today, and to help them develop positive attitudes toward black Americans. It is designed for students who have little or no personal knowledge of the black American.

During the introductory lessons, the class will be asked to list on the board specific situations that the black faces today. Students will then be asked to group these listed items into categories (e.g., housing, violence, etc.). Students will select a category on which to work for a group presentation to be given at the end of the unit. Students may also do independent research on any area of Black Studies they wish during the unit, and will be given library time to develop this. An effort to collect the products of the independent research would be profitable for class sharing.

B. *Content Outline*. An historical approach shows the development of and reasons for some of the present-day problems. Involvement in current issues and possible action modes for students should be emphasized.

African Culture
Slave Trade
Slavery
Civil War, Emancipation
Supreme Court Decisions
Segregation
Racism
Black Achievement
Civil Rights Movement

II. Objectives.

The objectives listed under headings are repeated in the Learning Activities section of the unit opposite the activities that will help achieve the objective. The order of objectives is different in the Learning Activities section because one does not develop all Knowledge Objectives followed by Problem-Solving Objectives, but rather provides for rotation of input and output of information.

**Adapted from a unit for Grades 6-8 by Bonny Schmidt-Burleson*

A. *Understandings (Basic Knowledge).* Given information and an opportunity to assimilate the information about each of the following topics, the students will demonstrate knowledge of them.

1. The African continent
2. Early African culture
3. The slave trade
4. The historical background of slavery in America
    a. The Civil War
    b. The emancipation of the slaves
    c. The Supreme Court decisions; especially *Separate but Equal*
    d. The legal and illegal attempts to limit the number of possibilities open to the freed slaves.
    e. Black achievements
5. The Civil Rights movement

B. *Problem-Solving or Cognitive Objectives.* Given a problem situation, the students will demonstrate their ability to use logical thought processes in finding solutions to the problems. Specific topics follow:

1. The effects of change of residence
    a. personal-temporary
    b. personal-permanent
    c. other person(s)-temporary
    d. other person(s)-permanent
2. The influences of sections of the country and socioeconomic status on people's opinions about the Civil War.
3. The achievements of black Americans—researched by students, shared with class.
4. Preparation of a bulletin board on important events in the Civil Rights movement.
5. Presentation and class evaluation of group research efforts.
6. Analysis of solutions to open-ended stories dealing with prejudice.

C. *Attitudinal (Appreciation) Objectives.* Given situations that are emotionally charged, students will be able to decenter and assume the roles of persons in situations described in role-playing sessions. Situations should:

1. Develop feeling for the discomfort of crowded conditions and the feelings that accompany giving and/or receiving commands.
2. Develop feelings about cultural uprooting, loss of cultural ties.
3. Provide the student with an opportunity for emotional involvement with the predicament of a slave.

4. Defend beliefs regarding war based on research of a section of country or socioeconomic group.
5. Provide for emotional involvement with victims of segregation and racism.
6. Provide involvement in situations involving prejudice.
7. Provide for specific action possibilities for high level valuing: the action component.

Additional activities provide for further problem-solving situations and for additional examination of values and attitudes. No specific objectives are listed for these because they are optional and are suggested to provide some alternatives for individualizing the unit emphasis.

Basic books: Goldstone, Robert, *The Negro Revolution,* (New American Library, New York, 1956), $ .95; Neufeld, John, *Edgar Allan,* (New American Library, New York, 1968), $ .60.

Beginning with these books the author would suggest the use of as many of the references from the bibliography (see pg. 114) as possible.

III. Learning Activities

OBJECTIVES	LEARNING ACTIVITIES	MATERIALS
To introduce Africa, the continent	1. Teacher stimulates interest in Africa by showing film of African continent.	Film projector; film—*African Continent: An Introduction,* University of Maine, 16 minutes, $4.00.
To develop knowledge of early African culture	2. Teacher marks on large map the areas the students will study and the students mark these on their own maps.	Large map of Africa, individual maps of Africa
	3. Teacher motivates students with media presentation of African culture using folk tales, slides, records, and realia.	K. Arnott, *African Myths and Legends;* Record: *African Music,* Folkways Records and Service Corp.; "Africa" (Classroom Pictures), Informative Classroom Pictures Publ. Goldstone, *The Negro Revolution.*
	4. Students are asked to read the prologue in the text about early African culture and answer study questions for class discussion. *Study Questions:* a. Meroë, capital of the ancient kingdom of Kush, was once a great city. What can	

OBJECTIVE	LEARNING ACTIVITIES	MATERIALS
	we tell about life in the city from the ruins we find today?	
	b. The ancient kingdom of Ghana was very wealthy. How did the Ghanians gain this wealth?	
	c. People of Timbuktu were famous for skill in one area. What was this area?	
	d. One great early East African civilization still exists today. Which is it? How long has it been independent?	
	e. What caused the decay and downfall of these great African civilizations?	
	5. Teacher reads chapters 6 and 12 of *Things Fall Apart* (the wrestling match and the wedding) on tape and the students listen at listening stations to learn about Ibo culture before the white man came.	Chinua Achebe, *Things Fall Apart;* tape recorder, ear phones.
	Additional activities for student involvement. (Do at least one)	
	a. Students prepare bulletin board on African art.	Bulletin board, art materials.
	b. Students design African masks of cardboard.	Cardboard, string, and paint.
	c. Students write own folk stories in the African tradition and design enactments around these.	
	Additional activities for individual students.	
	a. Read Achebe's novel, *Things Fall Apart*, or *No Longer At Ease,* and write report.	
	b. Explore folk myths and stories further.	K. Arnott, *African Myths and Legends*

OBJECTIVE	LEARNING ACTIVITIES	MATERIALS
	c. Explore African influence on art and on today's fashion trends.	
	d. Study African poetry.	Hughes, *Poems from Black Africa*
To present factual information about slave trade so that students are aware of misery endured by slaves	6. Teacher shows diagram of interior of slave ship and discusses the trade with students, showing the trade routes on world map. Be brief.	Overhead projector, diagram of slave ship, world map.
To develop a feeling for the discomfort of close conditions and the feelings that accompany giving and/or receiving commands	7. In a role-playing situation, students are lined up as slaves in rows of fours with four "slave dealers" to be picked by students. "Slaves" are given some chore to do and the "dealers" are to see that they do this while remaining crowded together. See pages 38-39 in text for suggested chore and description of condition. Roles will then be exchanged in order that dealers may role-play slaves.	Goldstone, *The Negro Revolution*
	8. Describe Africa at the time of slave trade for the students. Show pictures of art and dwellings if these are available.	
	9. Review United States (primarily Southern colonies) at the time of slave trade.	
To develop specific knowledge of personal change into a generalization about permanent moves for large numbers of people	10. Teacher guides students through the following cognitive processes leading to emotional involvement.	
	a. Teacher asks students to name things in their community with which they are familiar and make them feel at home, such as school, church, movies, the way people talk, the hot dog stand; these are listed on	

OBJECTIVE	LEARNING ACTIVITIES	MATERIALS
	board. *(Listing—involving concept formation, categorizing.)*	
	b. Teacher asks which students have travelled, moved from town to town, or gone camping. *(Intellectual involvement.)*	
	c. List on board what things were missed when students left own home town. (*List—involving categorizing.*)	
	d. Teacher asks students if any of them have ever travelled alone. (*Intellectual involvement.)*	
	e. Teacher asks them to imagine that they are not just travelling alone but are moving away for ever and ever. (*Hypothetical deductive thinking.*)	
	f. Students are asked to write composition on how they would feel in such a situation. (Teacher may wish to remind students of Rip Van Winkle.) (*Emotional involvement.*)	
	g. Students in small groups discuss how different America was from Africa and how the slaves must have felt. (*Generalizing, summarizing.*)	
To give students historical background of slavery in America	11. Students to read Chapter 3 on slavery in text and answer study questions. *Study Questions:* a. What influence did the cotton gin have on slavery? b. Why was cotton especially suited to slave labor?	Goldstone, *The Negro Revolution*

OBJECTIVE	LEARNING ACTIVITIES	MATERIALS
	c. Where did the slaves work? Who decided where they would work?	
	d. What were slave codes?	
	e. What fraction of southern people owned slaves?	
	f. How did the poor whites feel about slavery?	
	12. Review study questions as total group.	
To provide the student with emotional involvement in predicament of a slave	13. Case history: Dred Scott Case. Teacher reads paragraphs on Dred Scott (page 37 in *Black Americans*) and asks students to recall what they read in chapter three in text about Dred Scott.	Lincoln, *The Black Americans*
	a. Students to reenact courtroom scene, playing parts of Roger Taney, Dred Scott, Dr. Chaffee, and Mrs. Chaffee, as well as of the other judges.	
	b. Underground Railroad. Teacher reads to students pages 80-82 in text about underground railroad and daring escapes. Does the class know of anywhere where daring escapes are being made today for the sake of freedom (Berlin)?	Goldstone, *The Negro Revolution*
	c. Artistic expression of what it felt like to be a slave. (Songs, poems, stories, drawings.)	Art supplies.
	d. Study Negro spiritual by playing records and singing songs as a class.	Record player, record of spirituals, sheet music of American folk music.
To give students historical background of Civil War and Emancipation, and to provide an opportunity to gather information,	14. Students read Chapter 6 in text. Class divided into five groups: Northern freedmen, Northern whites, slaves,	Goldstone, *The Negro Revolution*

OBJECTIVE	LEARNING ACTIVITIES	MATERIALS
logically organize it, and defend it—dealing with sections of the country and socioeconomic levels as they influenced opinions about the war.	Southern aristocracy, and poor white Southerners. Groups to defend their role regarding the Civil War. Class discussion to center around value of these roles and the emotions involved. *Additional activities for individual students:* a. Show in color slave states, free states, border states.	Outline maps of United States
	b. Student reports on Frederick Douglass, Nat Turner, Harriet Tubman.	
To give students factual background of Supreme Court decisions (especially *Separate but Equal*). To develop student knowledge of white attempts (legal and illegal) to limit the job possibilities open to the freed black.	15. Students to read Chapters 7 and 8 in text and answer study questions. *Study Questions:* a. After the war, were the "slave codes" replaced by other codes? What were they? b. What were the Fourteenth and Fifteenth Amendments? How did later Supreme Court decisions influence them? c. Who gave final legal sanction to segregation? What influence do you think this had on the black? d. What improvements did the Reconstruction governments initiate? e. How was the stereotypical image of the black built up? f. What type of work did the freedman do after the War? g. Who formed the Ku Klux Klan and why?	Goldstone, *The Negro Revolution*
	16. Class discussion on study questions with special emphasis on how the black was legally stripped of his rights.	

OBJECTIVE	LEARNING ACTIVITIES	MATERIALS
To give students emotional involvement with victims of segregation and racism.	17. Teacher reads *Black Misery* to class, using opaque projector to share illustrations with class.	Hughes, *Black Misery;* opaque projector
	18. Students are divided into two groups and told that one group will be "white" and the other "black." They must sit at separate sides of the room; "blacks" are to carry "whites' " books, wash blackboards, be last at the drinking fountain, etc. Class is not told that in a few days the roles will be exchanged. (Whites make the rules for blacks in each case.)	Depending on the local situation, some teachers may wish to carry out activities 18, 19, 20, 21.
	19. Students look for signs of discrimination in own community.	
	20. Class reads Neufeld, *Edgar Allan*. Small-group discussion on why the family made their decision as they did.	Neufeld, *Edgar Allan*
	21. Students are asked to recall their feelings and experiences during the segregated situation initiated in activity #18. They are to write their own "Misery is. . ." definitions patterned on *Black Misery* and illustrate them.	
	Additional activities for student involvement:	
	a. Black American to talk to students about his experiences growing up in America.	Resource Person
	b. Teacher reads "No Day of Triumph," "Go Up for Glory," "The Long Shadow of Little Rock" from *Growing Up Black* on tape and students listen at listening stations.	David, J., *Growing Up Black* (This book is not recommended for general student use, but for teacher selection and readings.); tape recorder and ear phones
	c. Students are given a list of books about well-known	

OBJECTIVE	LEARNING ACTIVITIES	MATERIALS
	black Americans. Students who select a book will be given an opportunity to share.	
To provide informational background on black achievements. To have students develop research reports for sharing.	22. Class divides into small groups and picks one of the following topics to explore black achievement in that field: art, music, science, politics, show business, sports, literature. Students may wish to present their findings to a fourth-grade class.	
	23. Assign small groups separate chapters in these books. 24. Following the above experiences, the students should discuss black accomplishments, and the odds against which they were won.	Goldstone, *The Negro Revolution;* Florence Jackson, *The Black Man in America, 1932-1954*
To develop knowledge of civil rights movements.	25. Class reads Chapter 11 and Epilogue in text.	Goldstone, *The Negro Revolution*
To provide students with information as well as an opportunity to collect and organize data dealing with civil rights.	26. Class makes bulletin board of significant events which happened recently or are happening now in the field of civil rights. *Additional activities for student involvement:* a. Local civil rights worker talks to students about his work. b. Research into founding and purposes of NAACP, CORE, SCLC.	Magazines, newspapers, art supplies (Display could be made for hall bulletin board.)
To provide for research sharing.	27. Provide a class session for book reports about black Americans. 28. Presentations by groups formed at the beginning of the course.	
To provide involvement in situations dealing with prejudice. To	29. Role-playing with open-ended stories regarding prejudice	Shaftel and Shaftel, *Role-Playing for Social Values*

OBJECTIVE	LEARNING ACTIVITIES	MATERIALS
provide an analysis of solutions suggested in role-playing stories dealing with prejudice.	("Second Prize," "Josefina," Shaftel and Shaftel). Analyze solutions and feelings.	
To provide specific action possibilities for high level valuing (action component).	30. Class decides where we should go from here and what we (as sixth- and eighth-graders) can do. Some class time could be spent on discussing this topic. ing this topic.	
	Additional activities for student involvement:	
	a. Exchange program with inner-city school.	
	b. Article for school newspaper on course work.	
	c. During access or free time, some students may wish to play "Blacks and Whites," a game similar to "Monopoly" but with special hardships and challenges to the players who elect to be black.	"Blacks and Whites," Psychology Today Games, P.O. Box 4762, Clinton, Iowa, $5.95 (Teacher should review game and may wish to modify the directions.)

IV. Evaluation

A. *Content Evaluation*

1. Final examination
2. Quick quizzes given after content area study during the unit.
3. Information used in role-playing sessions.

   Designate three students to judge reality of solution in keeping with described persons and/or background information. Question "Could this really happen?" may be used.

B. *Problem-Solving Evaluation*

1. The teacher will carry out careful analyses of general statements produced as a research effort. Generalizations can be judged on the basis of several criteria:

   a. Accuracy
   b. Relevance
   c. Inclusiveness
   d. Tentativeness ("most of the time")
   e. Use of comparison

f. Cause/effect

g. Good sentence structure

h. Dynamism ("the one that makes us curious")

It is assumed that a student will meet some, not all, of these criteria in a given summary statement. The teacher may check written statements at any time to see the kinds of criteria that are represented. No letter grade is necessary.

2. Student evaluations of individual or group research presentations are valuable. The students may use a checklist. The following is a brief sample:

Name of Pupil Giving Report

Title of Report	EXCELLENT	GOOD	FAIR
1. Was knowledgeable about the subject	E	G	F
2. Presented report in an organized way	E	G	F
3. Emphasized important points	E	G	F
4. Answered questions asked	E	G	F

Additional criteria may be suggested by the class.

Completed checklists should be given the reporter to provide him an additional learning tool.

3. A joint teacher-pupil evaluation of the success of group participation can be carried out. Again a checklist may be used, or the teacher may conduct a general discussion with each separate group using standard questions such as:

   a. Did all group members participate in planning the report?

   b. Did all persons contribute to the final report?

   c. Did group members work together in solving the research problem?

4. It is possible to analyze the solutions in *role-playing*.

   a. Count the number of solutions proposed.

   b. Count the number of antecedent/consequent statements made (Example: *if . . . then*)

C. *Attitude Evaluation*

1. Pre- and post-measures are suggested here. The items following will give the teacher an indication of the individual child's feelings about blacks. To instruct the pupils in marking before the pretest, use an illustration on the board.

   Discuss the sample, then proceed to pretest. The child marks in the space near the word he thinks describes the black. This test is given *before* and *after* the unit to see if there has been any change in the students' perceptions of blacks.

POLICEMEN							
Like +	=	=	=	=	=	Dislike –
Pleasant	=	=	=	=	=	Unpleasant

BLACKS						
Good	=	=	=	=	=	Bad
Pleasant	=	=	=	=	=	Unpleasant
Busy	=	=	=	=	=	Lazy
Ugly	=	=	=	=	=	Beautiful
Weak	=	=	=	=	=	Strong
Fast	=	=	=	=	=	Slow

2. Read the story to the class. Have each child write his response in as much detail as he wishes. Collect the responses and role-play two or three solutions. Both written responses and enactments may be judged on the criteria listed below. The pre- and post-written responses may be analyzed for individual change. They may also be totaled to provide information about change in the whole class.

   *Pretest story** Imagine that this is Halloween night and you are with your friends. You come to a street corner and see five black children across the street. Someone in your group of friends yells to the children, "Hey, why are you wearing dark masks?" The other kids in your group start to laugh. You would . . .

   *Posttest story** Imagine that you are visiting a friend of yours out of town. You decide to go swimming at the public swimming pool. Getting into line to pay your admission, you notice a young black boy in line just in front of you. As he gets up to the booth to get his ticket, the lady says there is no ticket for him but then offers to sell you and your friend two tickets. You would . . .

   Criteria for judging responses
   - non-involvement
   - inquiry
   - verbal debate
   - say or do nothing

*Adapted from N. Kogan and M. Downey, "Attitude Scale Toward Blacks" in Shaw, Marvin E. and Wright, Jack M. *Scales for the Measurement of Attitudes*. New York: McGraw-Hill Book Co., Inc. 1967.

asking why
argues in disagreement
physical and verbal involvement
physical contact or saying what he is going to do about it.

3. Interaction with other students in discussion groups regarding issues may be taped, transcribed, and coded for levels of sensitivity, number of proposed solutions, and pro- or anti-black statements.

FOR FURTHER READING

Fiction for Children

Achebe, Chinua. *No Longer at Ease*. Fawcett Publications, 1960.

______. *Things Fall Apart*. Fawcett Publications, 1959.

Arnott, Kathleen. *African Myths and Legends*. Walck, 1963.

Hughes, Langston. *Not without Laughter*. Collier-Macmillan, 1969, (lst printing, 1930.)

Lipsyte, Robert. *The Contender*. Bantam, 1967.

Neufeld, John. *Edgar Allan*. New American Library, 1968.

Nonfiction for Children

Adams, R. L. *Great Negroes Past and Present*. Chicago, Ill.: Afro-American Publishing, 1963. Illustrated.

Burt, Olive. *Black Women of Valor*. New York: Julian Messner, 1974.

Courlander, Harold. *Negro Folk Music U.S.A.* New York: Columbia Univ. Press, 1963.

Goldstone, Robert. *The Negro Revolution*. New York: New American Library, 1956.

Greenfield, Eloise. *Paul Robeson*. New York: Thomas Y. Crowell, 1975.

Hamilton, Virginia. W. E. B. DuBois. New York: Thomas Y. Crowell, 1975.

Haskins, James. *Fighting Shirley Chisholm*. New York: Dial Press, 1975.

______. *The Picture Life of Malcolm X*. New York: Franklin Watts, Inc., 1975.

Hughes, Langston. *Black Misery*. New York: Paul S. Eriksson, 1975.

______, ed. *Poems from Black Africa*. Bloomington: Indiana Univ. Press, 1963.

______, and Milton Meltzer. *A Pictorial History of the Negro in America*. 3rd rev. ed. New York: Crown Publishers, 1968.

Jackson, Florence. *The Black Man in America, 1932-1954*. New York: Franklin Watts, 1975.

Lincoln, Eric. *The Black Americans*. New York: Bantam Books, 1969.

Tobias, Tobi. *Arthur Mitchell*. New York: Thomas Y. Crowell, 1975.

Towne, Peter. *George Washington Carver*. New York: Thomas Y. Crowell, 1975.

Teacher References

Aran, Kenneth, et al. *The History of Black Americans*. United Federation of Teachers. Teaching suggestions are varied, stimulating, and realistic. Each unit is followed by a bibliography and other resources.

Banks, James A. *Teaching the Black Experience: Methods and Materials*. Belmont, Calif.: Fearon Publishers, 1970.

Bohannan, Paul. *Africa and Africans*. Natural History Press, 1964. (See Doubleday)

Bontemps, Arna. *American Negro Poetry*. New York: Hill and Wang, 1963.

Brink, William, and Louis Harris. *Black and White*. New York: Simon and Schuster, 1965.

David, J., ed. *Growing Up Black*. New York: Simon and Schuster, 1969.

Drimmer, Melvin, ed. *Black History*. New York: Doubleday, 1968.

Lomax, Louis E. *The Negro Revolt*. New York: Harper & Row, 1962.

Patrick, John J. *The Progress of the Afro-American*. Westchester, Ill.: Benefic Press, 1970.

Shaftel, Fannie R., and George Shaftel. *Role Playing for Social Values*. Englewood Cliffs: Prentice-Hall, 1967.

Wright, Rose. *Fun and Festival from Africa*. New York: Friendship Press.

Wyne, Marvin D.; White, Kinnard P.; and Richard H. Coop. *The Black Self*. Englewood Cliffs: Prentice-Hall, 1974.

ADVANTAGES OF THE UNIT PROCEDURE

1. The variety of materials and activities provides for individual differences in interest, ability, and achievement.
2. An increasing measure of responsibility is placed upon the pupil.
3. There is emphasis upon the development of understandings rather than upon the accumulation and memorization of isolated information.
4. The teacher, too, is forced to acquire extensive and significantly focused information for himself.
5. Many unit topics require the introduction of material more up-to-date than any provided in a textbook.
6. The unit emphasizes multiple sources of information (the multi-media approach). The pupil is moving in and out of "reading" as the only source of information.
7. The unit encourages critical thought and independent thinking.
8. The unit provides opportunity for functional use of skills in useful activities.
9. There are real opportunities to work on real jobs with other people.

CAUTIONS

One must not fall into the trap of believing that a highly recommended procedure in itself can prevent pitfalls for the unwary teacher. There are cautions to be observed.

1. One should not expect all good social studies experiences in a school year to be incorporated into units.
2. A unit does not go on for a specified length of time. It might be twelve weeks long or only one day long. Attainment of the objectives set up determines its length.

3. It is most unlikely that any teaching unit should be repeated in the entirety of its details in any succeeding year; the individual children are different, some materials should be added and some dropped, some content may need to be expanded or contracted, and even the teacher should be different because of his previous teaching of the unit or because of experiences he has had since then.
4. Mere gathering of information does not guarantee its use in a meaningful way.
5. Since a source unit contains more suggestions for activities than should be used in any teaching unit, the teacher must maintain a proper balance in activities, e.g., between intake activities and output activities, and between types of learning activities (reading, writing, discussion, dramatization, etc.). In primary grades, particularly, the amount of visual materials seems to have a positive correlation with the success of the activity.
6. Be sure that the individual is steered into various types of activities, so that one student isn't always reading, another only drawing, or another only doing map activities. Keep a simple checklist.
7. Variety and quantity of activities do not guarantee quality learning experiences or provision for individual differences in a significant way.
8. Avoid the danger of directing planning and activities through *telling* rather than *guiding*.
9. As the unit progresses, always hold in mind the objectives set up for the unit. They serve as beacons to keep you on course.

IMPROVING SERVICES TO THE INDIVIDUAL CHILD

Chapter four

In a democracy one of the primary beliefs is that each person is valuable and should be given an opportunity to develop his potential to its fullest. While this belief has not been implemented adequately for all minority groups (e.g., Native American, Black American, Spanish-American, and others) it is still a goal and an ideal worth striving for.

If a teacher gives more than lip service to this democratic value, then the classroom will surely reflect his concern for each pupil. The teacher's ability to deal adequately with the individual and his needs can strongly affect the student's attitude toward school, and perhaps toward education in general. Such an emphasis—or lack of it—might make study seem interesting or dull, stimulate or deaden intellectual curiosity, widen or restrict horizons, and create or destroy an appreciation of differences within the classroom. There can be little argument that attention to individual differences is important and necessary.

No administrative plan or curricular pattern can provide for all the alternatives that individual differences necessitate. Ability grouping, grouping within the classroom, and/or curricular plans for high, average, or low achievers may lessen the range of differences in a given setting, but will not resolve the issue totally. The problem of dealing with individual differences rests squarely with the teacher as an instructional problem and must be dealt with as such.

The first step would logically be a careful analysis of the differences in the classroom. There is, however, no diagnostic instrument that will analyze for the teacher all the facets of a child's behavior, indicating specifically how to develop satisfactory social studies experiences for each child. Since this is the case, perhaps at least some broad areas in which differences occur should be examined to help provide rough evaluation tools as a prerequisite to dealing with differences effectively.

In the past, educators have made efforts to provide for children with learning difficulties. Considerable reliance has been placed on IQ testing, and rough categories of children's abilities have been devised to describe students' learning potentials. The "slow learner," the "gifted child," the "low achiever," and the "superior student" have been used to describe certain test ranges of students. The problem with these descriptive labels is that they "label" the child, and children are categorized and pigeon-holed by merit of a score on a test. Sometimes the individual child becomes of secondary concern and the differences between children the primary consideration. The reverse is preferred. More recently we have become aware of a range of differences and needs and some attempt is being made to deal with these needs. Specifically, then, what are some of the differences one might find in a typical classroom?

DEVELOPMENTAL DIFFERENCES

In the elementary school there is a great range in physical and emotional maturity. Some general knowledge of these variations may help the teacher in providing for the children at a given grade level. Below is a thumbnail characterization of each age level in the normal elementary school. These characteristics tend to be typical of the group but are not necessarily true of each individual in it.

Five-year-olds are curious and eager to learn, are usually serious and businesslike, are cooperative, need adult support emotionally, like to observe others, are interested in the immediate environment, have only vague concepts of remote time or places, want to be helpful, like to work and play with small groups, need frequent short rest periods, and are beginning to learn to control small muscles but are not yet capable of fine finger work.

Six-year-olds are inclined to be noisy; resent direction but also overconforming; may be easily hurt by correction or disapproval; may react by showing temper or hitting; are self-assertive and aggressive; want consistent and orderly routine; enjoy dramatic play; want to be "first"; are not interested in highly organized games; want approval from the teacher; need suggestions to make decisions; avoid things they cannot do; ignore sex, race, and social status in choosing friends; are eager and highly active but easily fatigued; and are in a period of great physical change.

Seven-year-olds have wide interests, are eager to please but may set goals too high for themselves, complain easily, worry somewhat about place in family and school group, enjoy talking, tend to be highly competitive, work with absorption for periods, increase their mastery of skills, still seek approval of teacher in preference to peers, often exaggerate, have better eye-hand coordination and better use of small muscles, are increasingly sensitive to feelings and attitudes of other people, and are reaching for independence but not sure of themsleves.

Eight-year-olds are impatient—especially with themselves, are critical of people and may be demanding of adults, begin to want prestige in the group and may seek it through boasting, are eager to be considered grown-up, dramatize anything, have a high sense of humor, imitate friends, like active games, show more enthusiasm than good judgment, are full of energy, like to argue, and are not as dependent on the teacher but are still sensitive to criticism.

Nine-year-olds can manage independence, are growing more independent and more cooperative, like competition, make strong response to loyalty and patriotic appeals, have self-motivation as their most important characteristic, have awakened sensitivity to social approval of group, have individual positive likes and dislikes, desire to work independently, are challenged by a task, have ideas and interests of their own, are capable or carrying through planned projects with a minimum of adult urging, need recognition and deserved praise, and need adults to treat them as individuals.

Ten-year-olds use language to express the rights and feelings of others, are very responsive to praise, feel they must be as much like their peers as possible, demand less time and attention and begin to prefer respect for increased maturity, resent being told and want to participate in decisions, are interested in how things are made and in books that are realistic, are critical of self, and have more defined individuality with indications of the types of adults they are going to be.

Eleven-year-olds and *twelve-year-olds* find it important to escape too much adult domination, present many problems as preadolescents, identify with peer group rather than authority, are interested in other people's ideas, develop the capacity for thought and reasoning on problems of their own, respect good sportsmanship, want prestige in own age group, are cooperative and industrious, have a keen sense of competition, may be demonstrative, are eager to please, and strive for independence.

DIFFERENCES IN LEVELS OF ABILITY, RATE OF LEARNING, PERFORMANCE

Within a given classroom there are differences in the quality of work produced. Part of this variation in achievement stems from a range in ability. All children are not equally able in all areas of emphasis in schools. Therefore, it is necessary to adapt instruction to various levels of ability. In the regular class situation teachers must be willing to adjust instructional materials and learning activities to the demonstrated level of the pupil. Maximum learning efficiency depends on the right materials and the right activities for the right child at the right time. A second reason for differences in achievement in a group of students is the rate of learning. The speed at which one learns affects performance as critically as the ability to understand the task at hand. The rate of performance may also be critical in the accomplishment of the task at hand.

A third grade child described the effect of some of these differences rather well. He said, "My friend and I are tied for the best in math in the class. I can do problems that are harder, but if it's just figuring, he's faster than me." This eight-year-old has a reasonably good concept of level of ability and rate of performance in dealing with mathematics. He sees the value of understanding, but, also, the value of speed in operation.

All children do not learn the same information nor develop skills within the same time limit. The regular classroom plans should be flexible enough to allow some pupils to learn faster than others, to allow others to proceed at a pace that will result in success at different levels, and to encourage zeal for learning. Because of the range of ability and rate of learning and/or performance, it is wise to develop one's classroom materials with an eye to a minimum performance level. A number of more complex, alternative suggestions for the same basic learning experience can provide challenge for the range of students in a given class situation. Examples of this follow.

Learning experience minimums and alternatives

The following illustrations for different grade levels show how possibilities for the individual child may be drawn from typical class activities for all children.

SOME MINIMUM ACTIVITIES	BEYOND MINIMUM ACTIVITIES
GRADE 1	
On the board the teacher lists different workers in the neighborhood as the students name them.	Classify the various kinds of workers: (a) those who make things, (b) those who do things for us. Then further classify (b) group into: those who distribute goods those who protect us those who perform services for us those who teach us What other workers do you know who were not named under (a) or (b)? Why not?
Where does the supermarket get the goods it sells?	Which of the three meals at home costs the most? Why? Make a chart to show the differences.

SOME MINIMUM ACTIVITIES	BEYOND MINIMUM ACTIVITIES
GRADE 2	
Ask children to gather information about the countries from which their parents and grandparents came.	Find out in what ways homes in some of these countries of national origin are similar or different from homes in our city. Present your findings to the class.
In what ways does electricity help us?	Make three posters, each with pictures of electrical appliances that: (a) provide light, (b) provide heat, and (c) provide power to do work.
GRADE 3	
Study various means of transportation in the community.	(a) How do you decide which mode of transportation to use? Can you find any information on which mode is used most in this country? What does it cost to go to a large city three hundred miles or so from your home by different modes of transportation? (b) Propose a plan for cutting down the high accident rate of automobiles. Present the plan to your class for discussion.
Study rubber trees and where they grow.	How is synthetic rubber made? Do a survey in places where rubber goods are sold to find out about uses of synthetic and natural rubber. Find out what things used to be made of rubber—natural or synthetic—and are now made of something else. Why?
GRADE 4	
Sing some American folksongs.	Compose the words of a folksong.
Make a bulletin board display of the Four F's of Norway (farm, fish, forests, fiords).	Do a pupil specialty on Oslo, Norway, properly supported with visual materials.
GRADE 5	
Make a chart on the New England states listing the principal products with the principal place of growing or manufacturing.	Make a series of charts: (a) List the New England states with their populations in order. (b) List the states with their areas in order. (c) List the fifteen largest cities (name their states) with their populations in order. Compare the three charts and devise a new chart of information about the six New England states that comes from thinking about the comparisons.
Choose the ten places in the United States you would recommend that a foreign tourist see and give the reasons why. Use various	Have two or three children take an outline map of the United States and put on it the locations of all cities of more than 100,000

SOME MINIMUM ACTIVITIES	BEYOND MINIMUM ACTIVITIES
means of transportation (jet, train, automobile, bus) to get to the ten places, telling why you decided on each means at different times.	population without putting in the names. They then study the map and see what statements they can make as they look at the distribution of these cities.
GRADE 6	
Have groups of three write down lists of places they would like to visit in Spain, Portugal, and France, giving reasons. Each group could report, compare, and make a composite list.	Prepare a travel brochure on "Advice to American Tourists Preparing To Visit France, Spain, and Portugal." Tell of preparations for travel and of major places people should visit to gain an understanding of the culture, living activities, and historical interests of these countries.
Organize committee reports on the five natural regions of the Soviet Union. Make a bulletin board display to show where these areas are located and the value of each.	Have individual reports with suitable visual materials on (a) our relations with the Soviet Union, (b) United Nations activities involving the Soviet Union, (c) the Soviet Union and her neighbors, and (d) news inside the Soviet Union, which will give information and help bring understanding to the rest of the class.

DIFFERENCES IN SOCIOECONOMIC BACKGROUND

Until recent years particular experiential difference has received little attention in our schools. Though it was given little attention, it was in existence, nonetheless, and many children lacking some of the advantages of the typical middle-class child were unhappy, disoriented, and sometimes ashamed and embarrassed because of the differences they felt between their home and the school. Many children in ghetto and in rural areas left school as soon as the law permitted in an effort to escape this conflict. While physical escape may partially solve the problem, psychological escape from the effects of long-term abasement may not be as readily accomplished. Even the student who refused to quit because he knew within himself that he was able to compete began to question his own ability. If he clung to belief in himself, he was an exception indeed—but he could not erase the scars such prolonged struggle created.

At the present time there is more emphasis on and more investigation of the backgrounds and interests of various socioeconomic groups. It might be useful for teachers to be aware of the particular differences that could affect classroom performance.

Reading difficulty

Numerous studies have dealt with the reading levels of culturally different students. There are factors other than socioeconomic ones that contribute to reading difficulties. However, since reading problems are of major concern for people who work with minority groups and with individuals from low income groups, we will develop the topic in this context. It has been fairly clearly established that the reading levels as determined by standardized achievement tests are lower for such youngsters. Children from these socioeconomic groups often respond to pictures or direct involvement more readily than they do to reading or auditory stimuli for extended periods of time.

Some of the reading-related differences teachers need to be aware of are that:

1. Reading just has not become a part of the lifestyle of the child.
2. The child finds difficulty in expressing thoughts orally and in writing (i.e., in expressing middle-class thoughts in middle-class language).
3. Listening vocabulary is much larger than reading vocabulary.
4. Speaking vocabulary is less diversified; there may be differences from the meanings usually associated with words.
5. The child may show a preference for concrete, specific ideas over abstract, general ones.

Because reading skill is so important in our culture, it would seem that some general suggestions for dealing with the problem are in order. The suggestions do not attempt to deal with the intricacies of phonics instruction nor the progression of reading skills. Rather, they are "helpful hints" that can be used at any stage of reading development.

Suggestions for improving reading

1. Provide suitable reading material (e.g., materials that deal with the realities of their lives). There is scarcely an area studied in middle grades that doesn't have library books on the subject written at lower reading levels. In the references (p. 000) look at books by Eakin, Huus, Spache, and Tolman, and the March 1972 and 1973 and December 1974 issues of *Social Education* for recent lists of quality social studies trade books.
2. Read a short section for a single purpose, not several purposes.
3. Give a résumé of a section before the slow learners do silent reading.
4. Use books in which illustrations reveal content meaning.

5. Type a sentence or two, or a question, and clip to pictures from magazines or newspapers or to postcards.
6. Have teacher-written reading material on the unit topic.
7. Have a good reader read the material to a group of slow learners, interpreting, commenting, and asking and answering questions.
8. Have pupils read a short selection, then select one of four statements as the best one for a summary of the selection.
9. In many reading activities have pupils work in pairs, supporting each other in a common answer or action.
10. If you have a tape recorder, record the material from the textbook on tape, making necessary explanations as you go. Be chatty, even humorous. Later, using earphones, low achievers can follow along in the text, without the direction of the teacher.
11. Give special attention to vocabulary growth through specific planning.
12. Use visual appeal widely. Much knowledge can come from pictures, and labels and captions provide some reading practice.
13. Adjust the curriculum to emphasize fewer concepts with as much variety and detail as possible given to each concept.
14. Keep both reading and writing assignments short.
15. Widely space the teaching of skills to provide more time for practicing and learning the skills.

The results of failure

Most of us look back to past successes to pull us through periods of failure, but for some children failure is too often merely the expected outcome. This buildup of failure may lower the child's level of aspiration and he may show a tendency to give up easily or to want to try something else. Because of this he may enjoy tasks that have reasonable "time-to-completion" factors. The following suggestions might help the teacher to deal with this accumulation-of-failure problem.

1. Concentrate on activities that can be completed fairly quickly yet fit within the framework of the class unit.
2. Make sure students know the purpose of the activity.
3. Provide checklists or charts to record progress toward goals and check off each item as completed. This provides frequent reinforcement.
4. Find different ways of providing repetition and drill.
5. Don't feel obliged to "cover" units. Develop central ideas and major topics rather than too much detail.

6. Make allowances for "off" days—some days things just don't click, so don't force issues and further alienate the student.
7. Provide frequent doses of positive reinforcement and de-emphasize comparative evaluation (comparing one child with another). Substitute individual progress assessment whenever possible. Do not use "put-down" techniques with children in the class in an effort to get a higher level of achievement. Comments that can be interpreted as negative references to the child's ability must be avoided.

DIFFERENT INTERESTS

Children, like adults, have a range of interests. The opportunity to choose among alternatives and pursue one's fascination can be motivating. Enrichment is taking place when a child's understanding of a topic or idea, or his interest in it, is broadened or deepened. Enrichment activities should encourage initiative, develop and broaden interests, increase levels of skill, and challenge the full use of abilities.

To allow for a range of interests and provide for enrichment activities in learning are therefore important. Some of the broad suggestions for doing this in a typical classroom are:

1. Present a number of ideas in a variety of ways.
2. Provide opportunities for expressing ideas in different ways and at different levels of complexity.
3. Provide alternatives or electives for selecting topics to be developed by each child.
4. Include materials from different levels of difficulty and complexity for children to use.
5. Provide help and suggestions in the child's development of ideas for presentation to the class.

GENERAL SUGGESTIONS FOR DEALING WITH DIFFERENCES

It is important to give special help at points of weakness in learning development. Since children are different, they need help in different areas or aspects of social studies at different times. All pupils do not need extra help in map reading, in historical relationships, or in outlining, for example. The regular classroom should be characterized by direct teaching to the point of error or weakness only to those children who need the assistance. However, certain guidelines might provide help in the improvement of classroom operations in general.

When the teacher is introducing the lesson it is wise to:

> Review yesterday's work and examine the connection between it and today's work;
> Make sure the students understand and share the purpose of the day's activity;
> Exercise great care in giving directions—be specific.

As the class session proceeds:

> Provide book and non-book materials (e.g., pictures, realia, films, audio-tapes, etc.) to stimulate interest;
> Reduce the amount of verbal and abstract presentation and encourage wide participation in the development of ideas;
> Use variation in procedure within a class period. Use demonstrations whenever possible. Direct experience on the part of the child should also be planned and carried out;
> Be sure that students are aware of criteria used when they are going to be evaluated on a particular project.

The differences among children are many. It is not possible that all persons have an extremely high ability, nor desirable that all students perform at a rapid rate. It would not be expected that all students have a uniform experiential background. In fact, life would be less interesting if these conditions did exist. Because individual differences are a reality, let us deal with them by providing the best possible opportunity for each individual to succeed in his own way, at his own rate.

Because children in a given classroom are at different developmental levels, come from a variety of socio-economic backgrounds, and have a wide range of interests, it is incumbent upon the school in general and the teacher in particular to provide instruction that allows each student to participate actively in the learning process. Individualized instruction systems strive to do this very thing. "In an individualized teaching program, it is recognized that there is no standard student. Each student is a unique individual who learns in his own way and in his own time."[1] The student's uniqueness and individuality can be nurtured by allowing him to work on a completely independent basis where he explores a special interest or develops a particular skill. Volumes have been written about individualizing instruction, programmed instruction, and computer-assisted instruction, all of which are designed to provide input and output opportunities appropriate to the special needs of the individual student. Why, then, do social studies teachers concern themselves with this problem?

In social studies, providing for the individual is important, but, by definition, the social aspect of the student's learning is also the concern of the social studies pro-

1. William M. Bechtol, *Individualizing Instruction and Keeping Your Sanity* (Chicago: Follett, 1973), p. 3.

gram. "It must be pointed out that some students do not learn well using only the independent mode. This mode can be a very 'lonely' way for a student to achieve his learning objecttives and it should not be overused."[2] In a small group the "individual student's interests and learning style can survive; yet it is large enough so that other students can provide spark and stimulation."[3] Students thrive on the social interaction and mild competition provided by a small group.

Besides being a "lonely" way to learn, completely independent instruction does not provide the child with the opportunity to develop the social skills that are needed all through life. One of the goals of the social studies program is to aid the child in acquiring skill in working with others. Skill is listening, getting agreement, incorporating sub-ideas, and building partial ideas into a practical whole are all skills that are developed by *doing*. Students need opportunities to try out these social skills on a regular basis.

Group size variables

Here are some activity suggestions that can be applied to individual, partner or small group, and teacher-directed learning situations. The activities are planned to provide practice with working in different group situations. Examine these general suggestions and then combine the ideas with the three modes of dealing with differences that are developed in detail on pp. 141-173. *Bonus Box Ideas, Learning Packets,* and *The Pupil Specialty*.

Individual Activities. Any pupil needs more opportunities to check his information and knowledge than any question-and-answer recitation provides. Teachers need to use their time to better advantage than calling upon individual children to answer factual questions, but some factual information is needed in every learning packet.

Self-directing learning exercises prepared in advance can be used more than once. Children working alone can carry on without supervision, and, furnished the answers—as they should be—can do their own checking. You will think of many kinds of exercises to go with your own curriculum. Some ideas are suggested here with an illustration or two under each. They can be extended into longer exercises.

1. Write the name of the country you would be in if you were
    a. climbing Mt. McKinley
    b. boating on the Thames River
    c. looking at the Taj Mahal

2. Ibid., p. 58.
3. Ibid.

2. Use a globe.
   a. What country is between 40° Lat. N. and 120° Long. W. and 10° Lat. S. and 60° Long. W.?
3. Put in an envelope slips of cardboard with a geographic term written on each: e.g., delta, plateau, valley, tributary, etc. Have some pictures in the envelope. Match term and picture.
4. Make silhouettes of the separate continents. Mount each. Be able to recognize each continent by its shape no matter how it is turned.
5. Look at a map of the United States. Using your home state as a reference point, ask a series of questions like:
   a. If you traveled due west, what state would you go into?
6. With either your home town or home state as a base, use a globe or world map in your geography book.
   a. Which is further away? Berlin or Athens? Lima or Paris?
   b. What direction is Mexico City?
7. Make sets of cards with the correct answers on the back:
   a. Map symbols
   b. Pictures of types of work. Identify the work.
   c. Pictures typical of a country. Identify the country.
8. Look at a World Rainfall Map in your textbook. (Typical of other exercises that could be prepared on pattern maps, or of exercises that may be in your text.)
   a. What is the title of this map?
   b. What does the darkest color stand for? the lightest?
   c. How much rainfall does the southeastern part of the United States receive? Central Australia? East Coast of Australia?
9. Here are other suggestions you can develop.
   a. A group of pictures. Answer for each: what season is it?
   b. A group of pictures of scenes in three or four countries that have been studied. Which pictures are about country X, about country Y, about country Z?
   c. Pictures with well-known landmarks (Christ of the Andes, canals of Venice, Leaning Tower of Pisa, etc.). Write name of each.
   d. Individual pictures with multiple-choice item identification. Choose the right answer.
   e. Small piece of a map—three multiple-choice items, one of which is correct.
   f. Series of descriptive sentences about a place. Do you recognize the place?
   g. Prepare a series of questions to be answered from interpretation of a graph.
   h. Using the scale to measure distances on a map, how far is it by air from Paris to Berlin? New York to Mexico City?
   i. Arrange pictures in chronological order.
   j. Match pictures and captions.

k. Match cities and descriptions.
l. In what bodies of water do the following lines of latitude and longitude cross?
m. In what countries do the following lines of latitude and longitude cross?

Partner or small-group activities. The teacher needs to examine critically how much actual participation there is in a discussion of a total class group. Even a lively give-and-take discussion usually involves only eight or ten out of a class of twenty-five. An alternative is a small-group discussion (four or five), all on the same question, reporting back to the class through secretaries (which will occasion further discussion).

Sometimes the stage is set for discussion with the whole class, then the students adjourn to small groups, and then reconvene for group reports. The occasion could be the development of a chart on regulations for a field trip or a checklist on pupil behavior as a good citizen, appraisal of a film, or a summary of what has been learned in a unit. Sometimes group discussions are taped, and the teacher can analyze them later. Hearing its own recording may well spark further appraisal by the group. After the first taping or two, children will virtually ignore the presence of the recorder.

Three basic kinds of small-group discussion can be considered. One would be a discussion that deals with an exchange of information by a few students following a research period. Another would be a rather free discussion in which new ideas are being generated and explored (sometimes referred to as "brainstorming"). A third would be a discussion in which feelings are explored. It is assumed that in each setting the teacher provides a focus for the group and then uses a sequence of questions. Different sequences would be used as deemed appropriate by the teacher.

Small-group discussion provides the opportunity for using knowledge acquired by other methods. After information has been presented through textbooks, motion pictures, lectures, demonstrations, television, field trips, or any form of mass presentation or individual learning, small-group discussion is an excellent means for student planning, organizing, integrating, and using the knowledge.

Purposes of the group

1. To adjust to differences in level of achievement.
2. To adjust to rates of progress.
3. To provide enrichment through extending the depth and breadth of learning.
4. To increase the understanding of concepts.
5. To increase the retention of knowledge.
6. To develop thinking abilities—elaborative, organizational, and critical.
7. To aid the development of initiative in learning.

8. To aid the pursuit of independent investigation—allowing for different interests.
9. To aid in self-directed learning when suitable materials are available.
10. To contribute to social personal learning through practice in working with others, sharing knowledge, giving and receiving criticism, and mutual aid in learning—providing for positive use of differences in background.
11. To provide an opportunity for shy students to speak out and share ideas.
12. To allow students to clarify ideas by exploring vague ones with a few peers before submitting them to the entire class.

How to organize and work with a group

Groups should be made up of from three to five students; a larger number seldom works well. Members may be pupils of differing abilities or backgrounds in almost any congenial combination. Pupils usually seem willing to have the teacher designate the teams. Teams should be temporary and changed frequently.

1. The group is presented with questions, and the students are given suggestions for recording their answers.
2. In a group a chairman, as well as a secretary, may be selected. The chairman will serve as the organizer and the group leader. The secretary should be able to record rapidly. Both chairman and secretary may be chosen by the group or by the teacher. For younger children the teacher will need to work more actively on note taking. A tape recorder and cassette could be used if the teacher is needed by two groups simultaneously.
3. During discussions, the teacher should be active, moving among the groups, giving assistance when necessary, settling problems that arise. As the groups mature in their work, the teacher may provide less supervision.
4. Each secretary reports the group product to the class. Other groups check their answers as each secretary reports and report only additions and corrections.
5. Small-group discussion, followed by some class discussion of the composite report, generally replaces class recitation. More responses and better attention result if chalkboard lists, ditto stencils, or overhead transparencies are used to make these sharing sessions more enjoyable.

Note. If, during the process, members are unable to work together, or if one creates a disturbance, have the offending pupil(s) work alone at the same tasks. Such action is usually adequate to ensure future cooperative effort. Sometimes it may be necessary for the teacher to sit with the group or with the pupil that is causing problems and work out a solution to the problem. Working in a group is a learning experience. It requires social skill and will require practice and teacher assistance from time to time to help the operation run smoothly.

High-level questions for the group. The effectiveness of group discussion depends upon the quality and type of questions asked or the problem set. If thinking is to be developed in the classroom, a major opportunity is provided by designing questions that require various types of thinking.

1. For recall, the teacher prepares a test or list of factual questions—the *who, what, when, where,* and *how many* type.
2. For greater intellectual effort, questions are asked requiring multiple answers and relationships, such as order or sequence of events; major ideas under different heads; products, causes, and results.
3. For inference, questions are asked that go beyond the materials presented—why the action took place, what is likely to happen next, what would be the result of a different action, etc.
4. For integration, questions that call for relationships of new knowledge to old are asked—in what way is this like previous situations? how does it compare with other areas, periods, or techniques?
5. For elaborative thinking, which is also required by inference and integration questions, problems are posed calling for things to be done and inquiries to be made, unanswered questions are presented, and other tasks calling for relationships and applications are set.
6. For critical thinking, questions ask for evaluation, better ways of accomplishing the task, most significant points, evidence of bias or prejudice, suitability for use in particular situations.

Planning is essentially elaborative thinking, calling for any suggestions, ideas, activities, or possibilities. The group product is likely to be better than the sum of the individual products without stimulation by discussion.

Teacher-directed activities

Teachers can direct the total class in activities in such a way that every pupil is involved all the time, but this requires planning and organization. There is nothing more tedious than the class in which one student goes to the chalkboard and twenty-nine others wait for a response to be recorded. If the laboriously written response can even be seen by all the children, it will be a minor miracle. If there are no errors in the response, a second mini-miracle will have occurred.

Teacher-directed activities can provide for maximum pupil participation and a minimum of the problem noted above. We call these *Every Pupil Response Techniques.* In the usual question-answer recitation where the teacher is checking knowledge or understanding of facts, only one child can be called upon. Others who are ready to respond are denied the opportunity. There is a better technique that can be used for a rapid survey of facts, as a quick low-level review, or to help determine the need for additional instruction. The technique consists of providing each pupil with response cards.

The teacher asks a question, makes a statement, or gives a word. Pupils hold up the appropriate response card for the teacher to see. To illustrate:

1. Each pupil has three cards, marked *T, F,* and *O,* standing for *True, False,* and *Opinion*. The teacher has a whole series of statements, such as:
   a. Texas is larger than Indiana (use your home state in place of one of these).
   b. New Orleans is at the mouth of the Mississippi River.
   c. Boston would be more interesting to visit than San Francisco.
2. Using just two cards, *T* and *F,* or *Yes* and *No,* pupils can respond to a series of true and false statements.
3. The teacher writes on the chalkboard three names with the response card number for each. Pupils use three response cards with the numbers, *1, 2,* and *3.*

1	*2*	*3*
Oregon Country	Texas	Louisiana Territory

   Then the teacher gives phrases like these:
   Purchased from France
   Became a republic
   "Fifty-four forty or fight"
   Lewis and Clark
   Sam Houston
4. It is not difficult to think of a number of categories. For example,
   Three Scandinavian countries
   Three or four continents
   Three persons
   Clothing materials: animal, plant, man-made
   Part of the plant we eat: leaves, seeds, root
   Countries: island, seacoast, inland
   Eastern Hemisphere, Western Hemisphere, both hemispheres
   City, state, country
   Colonies: New England, Middle, Southern
   Spanish, French, English
   North of the equator, at the equator, south of the equator

A variation of the card technique is that of printing an answer at the top of a sheet of paper, holding it up for the teacher to see, and folding it back after use, ready for the next question or statement.

What is to be done with wrong responses? Remember that the purpose is a quick survey of a large number of facts: explanations delay this.

1. Avoid temptation to explain and reteach; it invites inattention on the part of those who have the correct response and it wastes their time.
2. Wrong answers may arise from the ambiguity of the questions or from interpretations that permit other answers. This calls for analysis when bright pupils give different answers.
3. Sometimes the wrong card is picked up unintentionally; stress alertness.
4. When the class divides evenly on answers, explanation is required; even the correct answers may result more from guessing than from knowledge.
5. Many wrong answers from the same pupils require a later separate review for them, with some possible reteaching.

In many activities there are advantages in the whole class working together with teacher direction and planning. Some teacher-directed total class activities are:

1. Introduction of a unit; brief activities at periods during the unit; and its concluding activities.
2. Demonstrations—machines, processes, "how-to-do-its".
3. Field trips—planning, organizing, executing, evaluating.
4. Exhibits and displays—classroom, school, and community.
5. Films and filmstrips—for common background and discussion; differentiated tasks assigned.
6. Listening to reading—poetry, stories, vivid descriptions, and personal accounts.
7. Plays and dramatizations—enjoyment and understanding.
8. Discussions—building group standards, checklists, behavior rating scales, reactions to reports, current affairs.
9. Choral reading—patriotic, American, cultural themes.
10. Appreciation—basic American beliefs, folksongs, commemoration holidays.
11. Recordings—music, voices of the famous, foreign languages.
12. Radio or television programs—special events.
13. Class planning—assemblies, other activities.
14. Listening to explanations and directions.
15. Hearing specialty reports from individuals, committee reports, and discussion.
16. Team discussions phase in and out of whole-class participation activities as secretaries of the team groups report back the results to the class, where further discussion may take place. Team discussions in whole-class activities provide a constant change of pupil role, from audience to participant.
17. Possibly the introduction of a new skill, but this is generally inappropriate since learning rates and needs for subskills instruction differ so greatly among individuals.

Specific program suggestions

How can a program be provided in which a student can select activities, but still learn to work in harmony with other individuals? Three separate ways of dealing with differences will be spelled out in this chapter and specific exemplars will be provided in Chapter 5. You may wish to select one approach for your classroom, or you may incorporate or recombine the ideas into a new holistic approach that will be workable for the special needs of your students.

Bonus box ideas. One way of dealing with individual differences is to provide a bonus box containing a wide variety of suggestions for students' use in dealing with any topic of their choosing. Such ideas might be used in addition to the standard curriculum; they may even be used by the teacher to stimulate thinking when building new materials for use with the students. (Activities follow in Chapter 5.)

Learning packets. A second and more extensive technique for dealing with individual differences is the use of the learning packet. A learning packet consists of a collection of activities and resources that provide instruction on specified objectives. It includes a built-in management system (frequently in the form of contracts) and evaluation strategies. The packet is designed for student use and is therefore located in an easily accessible area in the classroom. Sometimes realia, pictures, and media are placed with the actual instructional cards or sheets in a particular spot, on a designated table, or in a specified corner, and the whole collection is referred to as a learning center. Packets provide for a range of learning experiences, and the student can select the activity that is most meaningful for him.

ADVANTAGES OF THE LEARNING PACKET

1. Permits substantial amount of direction by the pupils in cooperation with the teacher.
2. Provides for better use of time by pupils and teacher.
3. Provides motivation of learning by eliminating frustration or boredom caused by too difficult or too easy level or rate.
4. Allows the teacher to study the children in varied social situations.
5. Provides greater enjoyment of learning as children like to choose the specific activity they will carry out.
6. Fosters desirable interaction among children.
7. Allows for more accurate evaluation of each child's progress by both the child himself and his teacher.
8. Encourages multiple approach to learning.
9. Makes provision for enrichment of learning for all pupils.

10. Provides for varying amount of practice in skills areas according to individual student's needs.
11. Allows children to work at a pace that is comfortable for them.
12. Helps to inspire creativity and an atmosphere conducive to learning.

LIMITATIONS OF THE LEARNING PACKET

1. Requires organizational ability on the part of the teacher.
2. Requires consistent and systematic supervision by the teacher.
3. Demands teacher-made materials.
4. Disturbs those who like relatively quiet rooms.

The pupil specialty. An additional strategy for individualizing instruction is the pupil specialty. There is content developed at nearly all grade levels where the individual student can select subtopics or special interests and develop a research report on them. The report might be referred to on an activity card in a learning packet, or it might be suggested as a special extra credit in a particular unit. In any case, it allows the individual an opportunity to develop his own unique interests and style and to use his best judgment about his own scholarly effort. A great deal of guidance may be needed by some students in order for them to produce a quality report.

A pupil specialty is an activity in which a child uses research tools to find out as much as possible about a topic, area, or project. It helps him pursue his particular interests and develop proficiency in research, organization, and presentation skills. As the pupil specialty program develops within a classroom the quality of reporting improves significantly. The specialty report is presented orally, but has several marked distinctions from the usual oral report. As compared with the ordinary oral report, the specialty report:

1. Is really an oral-visual report because it requires displayed material.
2. Is far more comprehensive in depth and breadth.
3. Uses a wide variety of sources.
4. Wants contributions and aid from parents.
5. Has a distinctive follow-up.
6. Has a considerably higher motivation value.
7. Promotes prestige of the individual.

Definite educational purposes are served by the pupil specialty. It:

1. Provides for differences in learning rates and levels of ability.
2. Encourages self-expression.
3. Teaches the children to budget their time wisely.

4. Is self-directing. (Self-directing assignments are preferred by children.)
5. Results in the use of many and varied references and sources.
6. Often offers the opportunity to do a construction activity with purpose.
7. Makes schoolwork challenging to the bright pupil by raising the level of instruction to his ability.
8. Provides a program for differentiating and enriching instruction.
9. Makes effective use of pupil time after the completion of daily tasks.
10. Provides an opportunity for developing self-discipline through independent study.
11. Provides an opportunity to broaden children's interests.
12. Develops skills such as locating information, selecting and evaluating pertinent material, organizing, participating in research activities, taking notes, compiling bibliographies, writing letters, using expression, reporting, developing display and artistic arrangement, labeling, using higher mental processes, and applying critical analysis.

TEACHER'S RESPONSIBILITY IN MEETING INDIVIDUAL DIFFERENCES

Providing instruction that is most meaningful for each student is a difficult task. The teacher must play a large part in providing the necessary instruction because he is closest to the primary participant—the child. "Teachers are potentially the most sensitive, flexible, and divergently responsible components of any instructional system."[4] At least two separate roles can be described.

First, the teacher has an immediate function in relation to the total unit or packet of material dealing with a specified content. Bruner says that the teacher serves to activate, maintain, and guide the learner in this self-directed learning process. This role requires considerable knowledge of both children and resources. Besides the general responsibility of motivating and guiding, there are several specific competencies that are required of the teacher at given points in the unit. The teacher must serve as:

1. Research director with small groups,
2. Discussion leader using good questioning strategies,
3. Role-playing specialist to direct small-group interaction, and
4. Aide to students with media and resource materials.

4. Stuart R. Johnson and Rita B. Johnson, *Developing Individualized Instructional Material* (Palo Alto, Calif.: Westinghouse Learning Press, 1970), p. 4.

The teacher can serve a second function in a program where providing for individual differences is the primary focus—as the responsible person to contact the librarian or media specialist. The responsibilities in a program where students are engaged in a number of different activities are many, and they can be handled best by dividing them among the individuals involved in the program. The media specialist and/or librarian can profitably serve along the following lines:

1. Assist small groups in the location and use of media and book materials.
2. Provide a pleasant atmosphere in which to collect and organize research findings
3. Confer with teachers regarding content that will be covered and materials that will be needed
4. Advise teachers about recent materials and make suggestions about the possible uses of these new materials
5. Consult and counsel students and teachers about variety in presenting or sharing data with others

There is no doubt that the teacher who considers it his obligation to provide for the individual differences in the classroom has assumed a large responsibility. Preparing materials for a bonus box, a learning packet, or a specialty report consumes time and requires tremendous organization skills. Keeping resources circulating and groups working successfully requires another skill and more time. Individualized instruction is a demanding master, which requires the best talent and highest commitment. It is a challenge, and one teachers can meet with careful preparation and a real concern for each child in the learning situation.

ASSESSING LEVELS OF INDIVIDUALIZED INSTRUCTION

In an article entitled "Instrumentation for Teaching and Instructional Management," Glaser and Cooley delineate the components of an individualized instruction program. They list the following components:[5]

1. The outcomes of learning are specified in terms of competency to be attained and the conditions under which they will be attained. The outcomes of instruction are described in terms of measurable performances and assessable student projects. Subgoals will be specified and ways to reach the objectives suggested.
2. Diagnosis of the initial state of the learner upon entering the instructional system is important.

5. Robert m. W. Travers, ed., *Second Handbook of Research in Teaching,* AERA publication (Chicago: Rand McNally, 1973).

3. Alternative instructional procedures are made available through multi-materials or automated devices.
4. Performance is observed and repeatedly assessed. In the early learning of skills the assessment is almost continuous. This assessment is used as the basis for the next instructional unit.
5. Instruction proceeds as a function of the relationship of assessment to performance in a "cybernetic" fashion.
6. The system collects data in order to improve itself.

It is obvious that some of these components are more observable than others. For example, items two, three, and four seem to be visible in the classroom. The checklist in Table 4.1 spells out these components in more detail. Use the checklist to determine the degree of individualization that could be observed in your classroom.

TABLE 4.1 INDIVIDUALIZED INSTRUCTION OBSERVATION SHEET

	STRONG EVIDENCE	SOME EVIDENCE	LITTLE EVIDENCE	NO EVIDENCE
Students using pre-tests	____	____	____	____
Students using media	____	____	____	____
Students using book references	____	____	____	____
Students demonstrating self-direction	____	____	____	____
Using time well	____	____	____	____
Requesting help when needed	____	____	____	____
Students using contractual agreements	____	____	____	____
Students working independently or in small groups	____	____	____	____
Students using self-scoring posttests	____	____	____	____
Students selecting topics or materials	____	____	____	____

The second part of an individualized instruction evaluation program depends more directly on the student. It is necessary to determine whether or not the student sets the goals and whether or not he decides on the direction his project will take in the future. To do this, the simplest and most direct method would seem to be to use a questionnaire administered informally and verbally.

STUDENT QUESTIONNAIRE

1. Did you choose this topic yourself?
2. Do you like to study this way?
3. Did you complete a contract?
4. Are you using more than one book for your report?
5. Are there any good films or pictures that you can use?
6. Can you go as fast as you wish in this subject?
7. What will you do next?

An assessment can be made for each separate packet on each body of content, but the foregoing strategies are good general ones to keep in mind. The categories and questions suggested will help the teacher assess the success of individualized instruction in his particular classroom.

FOR FURTHER READING

Banks, James A., and W. W. Joyce, eds. *Teaching Social Studies to Culturally Different Children.* Reading, Mass.: Addison-Wesley, 1973.

Bechtol, William M. *Individualizing Instruction and Keeping Your Sanity.* Chicago: Follett, 1973.

Brunk, Jason W. *Child and Adolescent Development.* New York: Wiley, 1975.

Frost, Joe L., and Glenn R. Hawkes, eds. *The Disadvantaged Child.* Boston: Houghton Mifflin, 1970.

Hoffman, Alan J., and Thomas F. Ryan. *Social Studies and the Child's Expanding Self.* New York: Intext, 1973.

Johnson, Stuart R., and Rita B. Johnson. *Developing Individualized Instructional Material.* Palo Alto, Calif.: Westinghouse Learning Press, 1970.

Lapp, Diane; et al. *Teaching and Learning Philosophical, Psychological and Curricular Applications.* New York: Macmillan, 1975. Chapter 4, "Education: Personalized."

Michaelis, John U., and Everett Keach. *Readings on Strategies in Elementary Social Studies.* Itasca, Ill.: Peacock, 1972.

Rogers, Vincent R., and Thomas P. Weinland, eds. *Teaching Social Studies in the Urban Classroom.* Reading, Mass.: Addison-Wesley, 1972.

Sperry, Len. *Learning Performance and Individual Differences.* Glenview, Ill.: Scott, Foresman, 1972.

Walton, David A., and John T. Mallon. *Children and Their World: Teaching Elementary Social Studies.* Chicago: Rand McNally College Publishing, 1976.

INDIVIDUALIZING INSTRUCTION EXEMPLARS

Chapter five

Three separate ways of dealing with differences were presented in Chapter 4. Specific exemplars of these different ways are developed in this chapter.

BONUS BOX IDEAS

Children enjoy selecting an activity for additional credit or for fun. Following are a number of ideas you can use and add to for your classroom. Place each of these suggestions on a 3″ by 5″ card and arrange either alphabetically by major idea or in categories (e.g., artwork, media suggestions, social activities, etc.)

1. Be a continuing "expert" throughout the year on national affairs, or some phase of world affairs, or some geographic area such as Africa or South America.
2. Make posters, paintings, murals, etc., on topics of particular interest.
3. Exchange letters with children in foreign countries.
4. Illustrate and/or annotate a booklet on a specific subject.
5. Help classmates with their work.
6. Give talks to other classes, supplemented by audiovisual materials.
7. Make specialized pattern maps showing topography, natural resources, population distribution, farm products, and the like.
8. Prepare readings for days of special historical interest.
9. Assume responsibility for a project or problem more involved or more difficult than those being worked on by classmates.

10. Consult advanced reading materials and interpret as a contribution to the class (e.g., a second-grade youngster with fifth-grade reading ability).
11. Make charts that require analyses and comparisons to produce.
12. Make a chart showing the designs of early coins and contrast them with present-day coins.
13. Make independent visits to historic spots for background material.
14. Plan an assembly program on a special topic.
15. Prepare a bibliography for the class or for another grade.
16. Be a research person for the class unit. Assemble material that will provide additional information. Read and present that material not used by other members of the class.
17. Preview, evaluate for appropriateness, and present films and filmstrips.
18. Suggest independent or group activities in art, creative writing, music, and drama pertinent to a unit (such as Transportation or Canada) and carry out some of them.
19. Keep in touch with the best in children's books. (Perhaps some arrangement can be made with the school or public librarian to skim new books before they are put into circulation.)
20. Do organizational thinking: recall exercises requiring listing or categorizing.
21. Do critical thinking: evaluation in relation to criteria, questions of how and why, comparing and contrasting.
22. Do elaborative thinking: uses, inferences, relationships of new knowledge to that already possessed, determining sources of information.
23. Probe *behind* events of the day and the acts that led up to them.
24. Build a dictionary of technical terms used in social studies materials.
25. Work on a community project in such a way that an actual contribution is made.
26. Write a play or a television or radio script.
27. Prepare a demonstration of folk games or dances.
28. Make a time line showing how the life spans of inventors overlapped; also place on it important historical events.
29. Construct an electric map.
30. Demonstrate the operation of irrigation.
31. Do a specialty report on an assigned topic in connection with a unit.
32. Make an after-school or weekend excursion, not possible for the class, in connection with the unit being studied.
33. Compose biographical riddles on inventors, statesmen, explorers, etc.
34. Conduct a neighborhood survey—danger spots for young children, inspection of bicycles, homes providing a place for flag display, etc.
35. Plan a "Hall of Fame" for a country other than the United States. Display it on the bulletin board.
36. Be responsible for an original "Cartoon of the Week."

37. Make a list of the ten countries in the world having the largest population. Are there any similarities among them? What, if any, are major differences?
38. A working pair of pupils look at an unlabeled picture of tall buildings in a city. What city is it? What further kind of evidence is needed to make a decision?
39. Present a pair of pupils with unlabeled pictures of a number of cities in foreign countries, in each of which, if observed closely, one might find something to identify the city (one individual in distinctive dress, one small sign, a distinctive bridge, a well-known landmark for a traveler, etc.).
40. Listen to a story read, then do your own interpretation of the story (in writing, art, pantomine, etc.). If put on tape the story can be repeated more than once, and the student can listen to it whenever he chooses.
41. A weekend field trip to compare "our town" with a nearby city. On the trip check items in a notebook about "our town" or "my part of the city" against the same items about "the city."
42. Develop ideas of the traffic problem into and out of the city. Use a large blank sheet of paper—one dot for "our town" and one dot for "the city." Have children take home questionnaires to be filled out by parents who travel to and from the city. Mark the different routes on the map with yarn. Indicate each family's travel route with a small auto cut from construction paper. Use road maps to determine what other towns add to the traffic.

LEARNING PACKETS

The organized activity cards and materials that make up a learning packet provide a strong stimulus for learning in the classroom. They require a high degree of organization to build, but are extremely flexible and self-directed once they are complete.

Packet development

Learning packets have been developed in which the variables of individual study, team learning, small-group interaction, and teacher-directed activities, as well as variation in time investment and level of accomplishment, are all taken into account. The packets can be used in learning centers and added to or changed with relative ease once the overall packet organization has been developed.

The theme of a packet can be drawn directly from a specific scope and sequence requirement in a given school system or developed from a teacher and/or student choice of topic. The packet may be based on a concept like "Revolution" or a topic like "The Zoo" or "National Parks." Frequently the choice is partially dependent upon the amount, type, and level of back-up materials that are available to expand the subideas that are a part of the content selected. In other words, the teacher does not usually say, "We will explore the topic 'Tribalism in Africa' for our next social studies packet," unless he has checked out the library and media center to determine whether or not materials are available on this topic for the required grade level. If the learning packet idea is successfully implemented, it will use multiple approaches to learning and will undoubtedly require supplementary reading materials as well as media resources.

Since the cards present only a brief sequence of instructions, some coordinating system with reference to accompanying dittos, special resource materials, and/or booklets will need to be worked out. One teacher was developing a learning packet on automobiles. Each activity card was shaped like a small car, since young children would enjoy choosing a car to have at their desks as they worked on an activity. Some system was needed to coordinate the activity described on the card with the raw materials (games, dittos, etc.) needed to carry out the activity. The teacher placed a numbered hubcap on the rear wheel of each automobile in the packet. This hubcap number corresponded with a numbered envelope or folder of materials that would be picked up by the student at the same time he selected the activity card. This organization system was a good one and saved both students and teacher much time in looking for needed resources.

Activity card guidelines

Activity cards are the major part of the learning packet structure. The following suggestions will be useful in developing cards for student use:

1. The cards are for children to read and use—vocabulary and sentence structure should be kept simple and direct.
2. Numbering the sequence of "things to do" will help children proceed more efficiently.
3. The number of separate instructions on a card should be limited to three or four items. DO NOT CROWD THE CARD! (Children will avoid crowded, confused cards.)
4. Some cards should be designated for the individual child, some for teams or partners, some for small groups and some may be teacher directed or "have to" cards for everyone.
5. If a sketch or graph or organizing schema is required, provide an example on a corner or on the back of the card.
6. Some reference to materials or corresponding work sheet will be needed to help students move along easily without unnecessary questions.

Figures 5.1 and 5.2 show two examples of activity cards.

FEAR

Individual
or
Partner

Materials: Resource Box
Magazines

One of the ways to get people to buy a product is to instill fear of pain, health risks, dangers to children, etc. that may occur without this product.

Directions:

1. Use the resource box to locate advertisements that use this technique.
2. Check the label on the back (fear). See if you can list the danger or fear the advertisement is presenting.
3. Find several examples of your own. Label them and add them to your folder.

FIGURE 5.1

RULES AT THE ZOO

Teacher directed
"Have to"

Materials: List of suggestions
from the local zoo

Directions:

1. Discuss some rules that would be helpful at the zoo (staying with partners, etc.).
2. List rules on the board.
3. Have children copy rules for their scrapbooks.

FIGURE 5.2

Eye appeal is an important consideration in designing a learning packet. People at all age levels are attracted to colorful pictures and clearly readable materials. Teachers have designed zoo wagons, doghouses, and camping trailers out of construction paper and contact paper. These activity-card containers are designed to accent the topic as well as provide interest. For example, a zoo wagon may carry cards shaped like elephants that provide activities on the "Zoo Community." The doghouse accents a unit on "Pets," and the camping trailer a "Recreation" emphasis. Other teachers have used shoeboxes or plastic lunch box containers and have covered them with contact paper or pictures. Primary students especially are initially fascinated with such innovative materials and continue to enjoy the activities in a well-planned, creative learning packet. Both packet containers and activity cards can add appeal to the entire unit.

Cards may vary in size from 5″ x 8 ″ to full page size for younger children. They may be typed or printed on plain cards, or dressed up in the shape of bright flags, balloons, dogs, or fish depending on the topic and the grade level. In any case the cards should be clear and carefully proofread before sharing them with children.

What is included in a packet?

The following list delineates the topics that are usually found in a learning packet. Tabs or bright colored dividers between sections will help the students locate the section they wish to work on more readily. (Alternative titles are given in parentheses because teachers sometimes use different headings to designate certain topics.)

- Overview of Topic
- Content Outline
- Behavioral Objectives (Competencies) *
- General Procedure and/or Information Cards
- Motivator(s) (Opener, Initiatory Activities)
- Developmental Activities (Learning Experiences)
  - Individual Activities
  - Partner or Small Group
  - Teacher Directed

  (major portion of the packet)
- Culminating Activities
- Assessment (Pretest/Posttest, Evaluation)
- Children's Books
- Teacher's Books
- Media

An illustration of a primary Zoo Community Packet will serve to define each of these components.[1] Materials for the teacher as well as for the students are placed on cards.

*Since many activities and choices are provided for students, the cards that specifically develop the objectives should be labeled "Have to" or "Required." This will guarantee minimum coverage of skills and objectives.

1. Zoo Community Learning Packet prepared by Phyllis Strake Chansler for use with young children. Reprinted by permission.

Overview. An overview is a brief statement that can be written for either teacher review or for student edification. It gives the overall emphasis of the packet and may include some of the broad purposes one might consider in using the material. For her second grade packet Chansler wrote this overview about Zoo Community for her own use.

> Since the earliest times man has been interested in animals. Man has kept animals caged for his own enjoyment and entertainment. The zoo is a special community of some of these animals. Man may study these more closely in the zoo than in their natural habitat. According to Robert Johnson, Director of Education at the Baltimore Druid Park Zoo, most zoos have four main objectives. These objectives are:
>
> 1. *Recreation.* People come to the zoo to relax and enjoy themselves.
> 2. *Education.* People come to the zoo to learn about the animals. Our goal is not just to teach facts about the animals, but also to provide the visitor with new attitudes, especially a respect for animals.
> 3. *Conservation.* Zoos have a major responsibility to help preserve animal life, especially those species that are rare and endangered. The long-range plan is to have a pool of animals that can be returned to the wild, if and when this is appropriate.
> 4. *Research.* The zoo attempts to develop improved techniques of animal husbandry and veterinary care.
>
> The children will learn about all of the objectives but will concentrate mainly on the second one, education. They will learn about this objective through field trips, research projects, reading and writing, films, and art projects. Man's fascination with animal life begins at a very early age so the zoo community should prove to be an interesting and exciting project for any group of children. This packet was prepared for use at the second grade level. It will last around six weeks, being lengthened if the children remain interested and shortened if their interest wanes.

Content outline. A content outline includes the salient ideas to be considered and provides both student and teacher an advanced organizer so that they can check on the general information and ideas that will be developed fully in the packet.

1. How to identify animals
   a. color and size
   b. shape
   c. movement
   d. habitat—country
   e. food

2. How does the zoo obtain its animals?
   a. trade with another zoo—most common now
   b. bought from dealers
   c. located on safari
   d. donated by nations and people
   e. born or hatched at the zoo
3. How do animals adapt
   a. their natural habitat
   b. zoo surroundings
   c. people help zoo animals
4. Jobs for people at the zoo
   a. zoo keeper
   b. veterinarian
   c. vendors
   d. ticket takers
   e. clean-up people
   f. guides
5. Rules for the visitors at the zoo
6. Finding your way at the zoo
   a. maps
   b. symbols and signs

Behavioral objectives. Behavioral objectives are objectives that state clearly the entering condition, the expected student behavior, and the level of acceptable performance (see pp. 45–49).

1. After completing the unit on the zoo community, the child will name at least fifteen zoo animals.
2. After completing the classification portion of the Zoo Packet, the child will place his fifteen zoo animals in separate classifications by color, size, habitat, and original country.
3. After completing the unit, the child will express orally at least two ways animals adapt to their natural habitats and two ways that people help the animals adapt to their new environment at the zoo.
4. After viewing the film *Zoo* (from Friends of the Zoo, Washington, D.C., 1974), the child will state three different jobs people have at the zoo.
5. After studying about the signs and maps at the zoo, the child will cite at least three different symbols used at the zoo and be able to follow and make his own map.
6. Before the actual zoo field trip, the child will orally report the basic safety rules for children at the zoo.

General procedure and/or information cards. If all students are to fill out a contract, it can be provided under General Procedure. The contract will be dittoed. Figure 5.3 provides an example from the Zoo Community Learning Packet.

Several other types of cards might be provided here. An example of a business letter and an envelope may be needed for some packets. Field trip instructions or checklists may also be provided under the "Procedure" or "Information" tab at the beginning of the packet.

Motivator(s), opener, initiatory activities. A motivator or opener is an activity that will spark interest in the topic being developed. Two or three alternatives should be provided so that one can certainly be carried out. Sometimes films do not arrive when ordered or field trips do not work out. Provide an alternative initially and the problem is resolved. Figures 5.4 and 5.5 provide examples of such alternatives.

Developmental activities. The largest number of cards and materials in a learning packet will be contained in this section in which the ideas that have been sketched in the content outline are developed through a variety of activities for students. Different kinds of activities and several levels of difficulty from which students can select the one most appropriate to them should be presented in the packet. All cards should present a *short* sequence of procedural tasks. Nearly all of us select tasks that look easiest; so keep all cards roughly the same length. Activities should be provided for all topics and subtopics in the content outline.

CONTRACT Your name________________

Use a different animal for each activity so you will have twenty different animals. There are twelve "have to" cards in the activity box. You may choose any eight other activities and sign your contract below.

Card Number	Date Started	Date Finished	Your Name	Teacher's Name

Signature ________________

FIGURE 5.3. A contract form

BE A FRIEND

Teacher Directed
"Have to"

Material: Film from Friends of the Zoo, Washington, D.C.

Directions:

1. Watch film
2. Be on the lookout for:
   a. jobs at the zoo
   b. different animals
   c. food of animals
   d. special signs in the zoo
3. Discuss the film
4. If time permits go over film again.

FIGURE 5.4

BORN FREE

Teacher Directed
"Have to"

Material: *Elsa*, by Joy Adamson (New York: Pantheon Books, 1961)

Directions:

1. Read aloud day by day the story about Elsa, the lion cub that was born free.
2. This may motivate children into learning more about lions and other animals.

FIGURE 5.5

It is important that the students know the number of people needed for a given activity. There are obviously a number of clever ways to designate the number of persons for whom the activity is designed to operate most effectively. One teacher marked the cards that were an activity for one student with a stripe across the top of the card. A partner, team, or two-person card had stripes on both ends of the card. A small-group card was bordered on the top and both ends, while a total-class card was banded on all four edges.

Let us consider each of these grouping variations separately and take into consideration some of the specific reasons for the grouping as well as activities that can be carried out successfully with each special group.

There are the *Individual Activities*. Frequently the student can work effectively by himself. What kind of activity cards are best for the individual cards? There are reports and creative expressive outputs that can be carried out on an independent basis with maximum use of time, skills and talents. Figure 5.6 is an example of a self-directing, self-correcting *Individual Activity* card.

ANIMAL IDENTIFICATION

Individual *Materials:* Teacher-made tape of zoo animals recorded at a local zoo. (Use any number of animals, in any order that is convenient)

Directions:

1. Listen to the tape all the way through.
2. Go back and stop the tape after each of the ten animal sounds. Write down the name of the animal that made that sound.
3. Check your answers with the answer card at the back of the card file.

ANSWER CARD FOR ZOO SOUNDS TEACHER TAPE

Check your answers:

1. lion's roar
2. seal's bark
3. myna bird talking
4. elephant trumpeting
5. monkey chattering
6. parrot squawking
7. hippopotamus's roar
8. bear's growl
9. eagle scream
10. people talking

FIGURE 5.6

Figure 5.7 demonstrates an *Individual Activity* card that does not include a self-correcting card, but does include an illustration that will help clarify instructions for students.

SCALE—DRAWINGS

Have to Individual

Materials: Ditto sheet with animal on large graph and matching blank smaller graph sheet.

Directions:

1. Make a scale drawing on the smaller graph to match the large drawing.
2. Be careful to try to make it exact.

Example:

Copy The Picture

FIGURE 5.7

Some of the activities in a learning packet will be designed for *Team* or *Partner Activities*. Team activities are based on the assumption that children can learn from one another. The emphasis is on *learning*, not on evaluation or marking. The children work together on learning tasks, not on tests. Working in pairs makes learning more secure and more sociable, and it provides for more individual practice than the usual recitation and so-called discussion.

Students, especially those in intermediate grades, like working in pairs. The success of paired practice depends in part upon the congeniality of the pair and the particular emphasis they are exploring. For example, they might be paired for reading level, enterprise, interests, or certain personal qualities. Figure 5.8 is an example of a Partner Activity.

ANIMAL IDENTIFICATION

Have to Partners

Materials: Chalkboard list of animals

Directions:

1. Divide children into pairs. Have them classify the animals listed on the chalkboard. Let them work for about ten minutes.
2. Have pairs join other pairs to form teams of four. Have the pairs compare lists and come up with a major classification.
3. Let children name categories, using a name that would tell something about why the animals are grouped together.

FIGURE 5.8

For *Small-Group Activities* the cards can indicate a small group discussion or role-play and an impromptu group can be formed to carry out this task. Figure 5.9 is an example of a small-group activity. This approach to the grouping task is the easiest and most frequently used. There are several ways of doing this. One can group quickly by rows, or have students number off, and have all 5's meet in a certain place, all 4's together, etc. In grouping of this type, the task assigned is usually of short duration since neither topics nor associates were chosen.

Some activity cards will indicate *Teacher-Directed Activities*. (See Figure 5.10.) The teacher may wish to have the whole class begin a unit of content together and may provide an exciting or challenging first experience for the students. There are other activities throughout the unit and perhaps a final assessment that can best be done under teacher direction. In the usual question-answer recitation where the teacher is checking knowledge or understanding of facts, only one child can be called upon. It is hoped that the typical teacher/student total class discussion may be used with care and that other alternatives involving more students at a given time will be considered.

ANIMALS IN OUR SCHOOLROOM ZOO

Have to Group

Materials: Long roll of butcher paper, pencils, paint or crayons

Directions:

1. We are going to make a mural of our zoo.
2. The class will be divided into five groups. Each group will decide what group of animals it wants to draw.
3. After the mural is finished we will make a map of our zoo.
4. Each group will design some symbols for the map legend that their section is preparing.

FIGURE 5.9

ANIMAL IDENTIFICATION

(Teacher help needed to make molding material.)

Teacher directed

Materials: Sawdust, white glue, water, bowl, and paint

Directions:

1. Mix sawdust with thinned glue to form molding material.
2. Shape animal that we find at the zoo. (Look at example in display case at the doorway.)
3. Let animal dry over night.
4. Paint your animal the right color and add any designs the animal may have.
5. Save your animal by putting it in the display case until we make our animal exhibit.

FIGURE 5.10

Students need to learn to work in large groups, to express ideas clearly, and to share the results of their research efforts, so we have *Total Class Activities*. The teacher may direct these activities or the students may plan the total class involvement. In many of these activities there may be nonparticipants in varying degrees, but there are advantages in the whole-class group process of working and being together. Figure 5.11 provides an example of a total class activity.

RULES AT THE ZOO

Teacher directed
Total class

Directions:

1. Discuss some rules that would be helpful at the zoo.
2. List rules on the board. (Staying with partner, etc.)
3. Have children copy rules for their scrapbook.

FIGURE 5.11

Culminating activity. The final activity should pull together a number of concepts and ideas that have been developed throughout the developmental activities section. The activities should provide the student with the opportunity to generalize about the content learned, as well as perhaps demonstrating a practical application of the content. Figures 5.12 and 5.13 are culminating activity cards.

CULMINATING ACTIVITY

Have to

This animal zoo will be presented to the Kindergarten and First Grade classes.

Directions:

1. The class will be divided into groups of three.
2. Each group will decide what zoo animal they want to be.
3. Each group will make signs telling what zoo animal they represent, what country they are from, what they eat.
4. Two people will make masks out of paper plates that look like the animal. The other person will be the zookeeper for the animals.
5. The group will help look up the answers for any questions they may think of that the younger children might ask about their animal.
6. The zookeeper will answer the questions when the children come to the zoo.
7. There will be a ticket taker, who will also make the tickets.
8. There will be a map made of our zoo.
9. Some children may be asked to be guides.

FIGURE 5.12

CULMINATING ACTIVITY

Have to

Directions:

1. Plan a field trip to the zoo. (National Zoo or Baltimore Druid Park Zoo, depending on time and money)
2. Discuss safety rules with children before zoo trip.
3. Have permission slips signed and returned.
4. Get parent help as aides.
5. Have checklist for children to do while riding bus. What did you see on the way to the zoo?
6. At the zoo, have zoo-hunt dittos for the children.

Example of ditto:

1. My name means river horse. Who am I?
2. I am sometimes called a bear but I really belong to the raccoon family. Who am I?
3. I sometimes grow to eighteen feet tall and my baby is six feet tall. Who am I?

FIGURE 5.13

It is recommended that this field trip serve as a general finalizing stimulus that can then be developed by the teacher to look again at the ideas stressed in the outline. It should serve as a basis for much verbalization, a necessary component of the development of the young child. (*See* pp. 194–197 for field trips.)

Bibliography. Also on cards as part of the learning packet should be a bibliography of children's books for the students and one of useful adult books for the teacher.

Media. This category should include films, filmstrips, study prints, records, tape cassettes. As useful references in some learning packets there might be included the names of resource people and possible field trips that parents might carry out with their children.

Evaluation. Deals with level of achievement of a student on a particular packet in terms of the objectives specified.

1. Did children remain interested in the animals?
2. Were the activities diversified enough to hold their interest?

3. Do the children seem to respect animal life more and are they less apt to tease animals (and people)?
4. Do the children realize all animals depend on one another for many things in life?
5. Do the children understand the reason for rules and regulations?
6. Do the children accept differences in animals and people as a good thing?
7. Do the children seem concerned about a healthy environment? Perhaps interest in pollution and environmental clean-up could follow this unit.
8. Most of the evaluation of this unit will come from direct observation of the students by the teacher.

Figure 5.14 presents a card with both pre- and posttest items, but there are a number of other evaluative strategies that have been used throughout the learning packet. Such things as student participation in role playing, art work, responding to questions about a filmstrip are all products that can be examined.

The pretest is given before the student commences the packet. The information gained from the cursory preexamination will help the teacher to guide the child in filling out the contract of activities. If the child misses all the "names of jobs people do at the zoo," the teacher should make certain that this particular child contracts to do some activities that will meet this need. The contract can be checked along with the pretest to see whether or not more activities are needed to strengthen a weak area. These may be chosen by the teacher and student in conference.

PRETEST AND POSTTEST

Have to

I will use basically the same test for both areas:

1. Can you name fifteen zoo animals?
2. Can you name the country each of the above animals come from? Name them in order.
3. How do homes in the zoo differ from the natural homes of the animals?
4. Name three jobs people have at the zoo.
5. Name or tell about three different signs or symbols at the zoo.
6. What are two safety rules for the children to follow when they are at the zoo?
7. Where does the zoo get its animals?
8. Why do you like to go to the zoo?
9. What animal in the National Zoo did the United States get as a gift from China?

FIGURE 5.14

Self-Evaluation checklist for your learning packet

When you have developed a learning packet, using a checklist is a handy way to determine whether or not all elements in a process have been covered. Any items in the "NO" column should be carefully examined. Could they be improved?

I. CONTAINS APPROPRIATE COMPONENTS	YES	NO
Overview	___	___
Content Outline	___	___
Behavioral Objectives	___	___
Motivator	___	___
Activities	___	___
Individual	___	___
Partner/Small Group	___	___
Teacher Directed	___	___
Culminating Activity	___	___
Evaluation	___	___
Materials		
Books	___	___
Media	___	___

II. APPROPRIATE CURRICULUM DESIGN	YES	NO
Topic appropriate for grade level	___	___
Instructions clearly and briefly given	___	___
Instructions given in second person or as a command	___	___
Contract in evidence	___	___
Accompanying handouts/worksheets	___	___
Cards using sequencing (e.g., numbers or letters)	___	___
Behavioral objectives are measurable	___	___
Motivator can certainly be carried out and/or alternatives are provided	___	___
Evaluation clearly assesses objectives	___	___

III. PHYSICAL APPEARANCE	YES	NO
Creative packaging	___	___
Color coding and/or clear delineation of type of card (e.g., individual or partner)	___	___
Tabs or demarcation of sections of packet	___	___
Cards attractively presented	___	___
Proofreading evident	___	___

Teacher's follow-up evaluation

	WAS A DEFINITE PROBLEM	NEEDS SOME MORE ATTENTION	WAS VERY SATIS-FACTORY
Did this learning packet provide for maximum learning for all students in the class?			
1. Allows for changes of physical position—moving about, standing, sitting, or working on the floor	___	___	___
2. Provides a balance between individual and group work	___	___	___
3. Permits self-checking by the child or easy checking by the teacher	___	___	___
4. Includes three-dimensional, manipulative materials as well as paper and pencil tasks	___	___	___
5. Provides opportunities for children to develop a sustained interest in an activity, extending over several days	___	___	___
6. Provides some activities that are open-ended and have no right answer	___	___	___
7. Includes a variety that allow for different learning styles—uses media for visual, auditory stimulation	___	___	___
Was this learning packet structurally efficient?			
1. Materials are out where the students can get them easily when they need them	___	___	___
2. Ways of keeping track of who has participated in this packet are clear	___	___	___
3. Media are readily available for student use	___	___	___
4. Coordinated system between cards and accompanying dittos moves smoothly	___	___	___

UNIT/PACKET TRANSFER STRATEGIES

Any learning packet or unit stands on its own, usable just as it is. A trainee or teacher may have developed one or more topics using one particular structure. A number of hours of preparation time in locating materials, as well as considerable thought in organizing activities and content, will have been invested in the development of the chosen structure. For any one of several reasons, the teacher may now wish to use another structural design. For example, it is possible that the teacher's choice of material organization has gradually changed, and the teacher now wishes to use an alternate curriculum design. There is always the possibility that a teacher may move to another school system where one particular design is in vogue, or where the principal strongly recommends that a given structure be used. It is also possible that the methods class professor has a certain preference for one type of curriculum design, and now the cooperating teacher under whom one is student teaching is more at ease with another structure. For any or all of these reasons, a teacher needs to be prepared to restructure a body of curricula materials that have been carefully prepared. The skill needed for this task can be readily learned; it will provide the teacher with the best possible opportunity to use materials and ideas in other ways.

It is possible for the learning packet to be used in a more traditional class setting where the teacher directs more of the activities. The activities can be numbered in sequence and the individual cards are in a sense rewritten. *See* page 145 for a sample Activity Card.

OBJECTIVE	LEARNING ACTIVITY	MATERIALS
To introduce scale so that students can use this in many ways in content areas	5. a. Hand out scale drawing of the lion on a matrix. b. Give children smaller matrix for reducing the lion in size. c. Tell the children a story about a mighty lion and a mouse and a magician who could make the lion smaller so that the mouse could be his friend. Elaborate.	Ditto sheet with animal on large graph, smaller graph paper.

It is, of course, possible to effect the same kind of change from unit to packet and card file. Let us take an example from "The Black American" unit.

OBJECTIVES	LEARNING ACTIVITIES	MATERIALS
To give students historical background of Civil War and Emancipation, and to provide an opportunity to gather information, logically organize it, and defend it—dealing with sections of the country and socioeconomic levels as they influenced opinions about the war.	14. Students read Chapter 6 in text. Class divided into five groups: Northern freedmen, Northern whites, slaves, Southern aristocracy, and poor white Southerners. Groups to defend their role regarding the Civil War. Class discussion to center around value of these roles and the emotions involved.	Goldstone, *The Negro Revolution*
	Additional activities for individual students:	Outline maps of United States
	a. Show in color slave states, free states, border states.	
	b. Student reports on Frederick Douglass, Nat Turner, Harriet Tubman.	

This unit activity could be rewritten into several activity cards, shown in Figures 5.15, 5.16, and 5.17.

HOW GROUPS FELT ABOUT THE CIVIL WAR

Have to
Small Group

Materials: Goldstone, *The Negro Revolution*

Directions:

1. With several other students choose a topic from the following list: Northern freedmen, Northern whites, slaves, Southern aristocracy, or poor white Southerners.
2. Find out about the role of the group you chose before and during the Civil War.
3. Discuss it as a group. Talk about the values the people in the group shared.
4. Present your ideas to the class.

FIGURE 5.15

POLITICAL DIVISION DURING THE CIVIL WAR

Individual *Materials:* Maps of the United States

Directions:

1. Get a map of the United States.
2. Mark the slave states, the free states and the border states. Use a design that is easy to understand.
3. Make a legend that identifies your markings for others.
4. Make a list of the states in each category to go with your map.

FIGURE 5.16

MEET MY FRIEND

Individual *Materials:* Books and resources on Frederick Douglass, Nat Turner, Harriet Tubman.

Directions:

1. Select an individual from the resource file of materials.
2. Read about this person, looking for fine points of interest that the ordinary reader might miss.
3. Prepare a report for the class. Make your person "come alive."
4. Give your report.
5. Ask for a show of hands from those who would like to read more about this person.*

*This is a good way to determine how interesting you really made the report.

FIGURE 5.17

What are the rules to remember in making these transfers?

LEARNING ACTIVITIES FOR LEARNING PACKETS

1. Include more specifics in the directions.
2. Provide for only brief activity and follow-up. For additional activities rely on additional cards.
3. Write in the imperative or the second person.
4. Include a list of the materials a student will need.

LEARNING ACTIVITIES FOR UNITS

1. Give objective along with the activity.
2. Be brief and only suggest an idea. (The teacher must elaborate on it independently.)
3. Provide for students to work on several similar activities at the same time.

THE PUPIL SPECIALTY

The pupil specialty is an individual research process in which suggestions and specific materials are provided for the student. The teacher is given special permission by the publisher to duplicate the materials that follow in this chapter. All the specialty material that follows is intended for student use. Its source should be given.[2] When the sheets are clipped together they can be made into neat little booklets, one for each pupil who is doing a pupil specialty.

2. Charles L. Mitsakos, Social Studies Coordinator, Chelmsford, Mass. School System, has, with a number of teachers over the years formulated a very useful pattern of checklists from a earlier unpublished presentation of the Pupil Specialty Guidebook developed by George H. Moore of the Wellesley, Mass. Public Schools. Reprinted by permission.

INTRODUCTION

The topic that you have chosen for this project is a very important one. You are probably the only person in the class who will be working on this subject. Your friends are depending on you to do a fine job.

You will have to use many different types of materials, such as books, magazines, encyclopedias, filmstrips, and films in order to find interesting information about your subject. Seek out valuable information.

The steps that will help you to prepare your project are:

1. Taking notes based upon the various materials that you use.
2. Organizing a display that will explain your project to the viewer.
3. Presenting a report of your findings to the class.

Remember that your teacher and the library staff will be very glad to help you. GOOD LUCK!

Understanding my subject

Subject title:

Reason for choosing this topic:

WHERE TO LOOK FOR MATERIALS

Directions:

Some items have been checked by the teacher in the following list, showing some of the materials in which you will find information on your subject. After you have used the materials checked in the second column, put a check mark next to that item in the first column.

1	2		1	2	
____	____	Adventure Stories	____	____	Newspaper Files
____	____	Almanacs	____	____	Other Sources of Material
____	____	Bibliographies	____	____	Play Indexes
____	____	Biographies	____	____	Textbooks
____	____	Dictionaries	____	____	Atlases
____	____	Encyclopedias	____	____	Charts
____	____	Graphs	____	____	Films
____	____	Historical Stories	____	____	Filmstrips
____	____	Indexes to Free Materials	____	____	Hero Stories
____	____	Library Card Catalogue	____	____	Maps
____	____	Magazine Indexes	____	____	Pictures
____	____	*National Geographic* Magazines	____	____	Recordings

WHERE TO GO FOR MATERIALS

Directions:

Some places have been checked on the following list, showing some of the places you may go to collect information. After you have gone to the places checked in the second column, put a check mark in the first column. You may go to many other places for information on your subject. If you do this, write the names of those places on the blank line and check the first column.

1	2	
____	____	Libraries
____	____	Town Hall
____	____	Historical Societies
____	____	Museums
____	____	Historical Sites
____	____	________________________
____	____	________________________
____	____	________________________
____	____	________________________

PEOPLE TO SEE AND WRITE TO FOR INFORMATION

Directions:

Follow the same directions as you did on "Where to Go for Materials."

1	2		1	2	
____	____	Resource People	____	____	Factories
____	____	Town Officials	____	____	Manufacturing Companies
____	____	Teachers	____	____	Travel Agencies
____	____	Librarians	____	____	Chamber of Commerce
____	____	State Guide Books	____	____	State and Government Agencies
____	____	Churches	____	____	Other

People and places I have contacted:

Name ____________________

Address ____________________

Name ____________________

Address ____________________

Name ____________________

Address ____________________

Name ____________________

Address ____________________

HOW TO ORGANIZE YOUR RESEARCH MATERIALS

After you have taken notes from all possible materials, people, and places, you are ready to put all your information together and to prepare to report your findings.

Follow this procedure for organizing your report.

1. From your research notes, put all the information and material for one item together.
2. Read all notes under each topic.
3. Write a sentence or two giving the most important ideas that your notes tell you. (Be sure that your sentences are well written.)
4. Make a sequence card—a single card listing topics in correct order for reporting.
5. Add the names of all materials used in your bibliography.

THINGS TO CHECK FOR IN YOUR WRITTEN REPORT

After you have finished the first draft, ask yourself the following questions. If the answer is yes, put a check mark in front of the item. If the answer is no, be sure you get it done before you begin your final report.

______Have I organized my report into topic paragraphs?

______Is what I have written interesting, accurate, and thorough?

______Have I checked my report to make sure that I have not included things that I don't quite understand or words that I don't quite know the meaning of?

______Have I checked my report to make sure that there is no copying directly from resources except for brief supportive quotes?

______Is my report well written, following the rules of good English?

Indenting all paragraphs.

Remembering to capitalize all words that should be capitalized.

Spelling all words correctly.

Placing all punctuation marks in their proper places.

______Have I had a fellow classmate or friend read over my first copy?

IDEAS FOR PRESENTING MATERIALS

You will be limited to ten minutes for giving your report. Yet you probably will have materials which you could talk about for much longer. If you can't talk about everything you want to, perhaps you could show and display material which the other boys and girls could see after your report. Making your report interesting is very important. Everyone wants to hear you talk, but they also want to see what you have done. There are many, many ways to do this. Check the items that you think will make your report one of the most effective. You can use any or all the space in the room you want.

______Books	______Maps
______Chalk Boards	______Models
______Charts	______Models of People, Places, Things
______Clippings	______Murals
______Dioramas	______Opaque Projector
______Film Slides	______Overhead Projector
______Filmstrips	______Pictures
______Films	______Posters
______Foods	______Records
______Magazines	______Tape Recorder

THINGS TO CHECK FOR IN YOUR ORAL REPORT

After you have chosen the things you want for your report, ask yourself the following questions. If the answer is yes, put a check mark in front of the item. If the answer is no, be sure to get it done before you report.

______Is my information accurate?
______Is the material important to my subject?
______Did I exhaust all sources of information?
______Do I know my subject well?
______Have I put it in good order for reporting?
______Do I have new and interesting words for my report?
______Are my facts and events in the order in which they happened?
______Is the beginning of my report going to make the class interested?
______Have I prepared my report so that I know the order in which I will be presenting my material?

THINGS TO CHECK FOR IN YOUR DISPLAY

When you have gathered your display materials and are ready to put them up around the classroom, ask yourself the following questions. If the answer is yes, put a check mark before the item. If the answer is no, be sure you get it done before you display your material.

______Do all of my materials have labels?
______Do the labels explain the materials?
______Is the bulletin board arrangement neat and attractive?
______Do my materials stick to my subject?
______Is it easy to understand what I have written?
______Did I choose interesting and different ways of presenting my materials?
______Have I picked someone to help me put up and show my materials?
______Do I have a good surprise poster for the advance publicity?
______Do I have all of the necessary equipment to give my report?

THINGS TO REMEMBER WHEN REPORTING

There are many things to remember when giving a talk before a group. Here are some of the important ones. Try to remember them when you are speaking before the group. Underline the ones that are most important to you. Write below any other rules that you feel you need as a reminder.

1. Speak with a strong voice so that everyone can hear.
2. Look at your audience when you speak to them.
3. Pronounce your words clearly.
4. Speak in complete sentences.
5. Explain new terms to the class.
6. Stand aside when you are pointing out pictures or maps or places.
7. ______________________________
8. ______________________________

CHECK UP AFTER YOUR REPORT

Make up five good questions to ask the class after you have completed your report. Perhaps some members of the class will want to ask questions of you.

EVALUATION

Following your report your teacher may ask the class to discuss your report in groups of five pupils. After a short discussion the secretary of each group will be able to give you one or two comments on the things which were most effective, and also one or two suggestions for improving your next report. The group will have copies of the pupil checklist.

PUPIL CHECKLIST FOR JUDGING A SPECIALTY REPORT

Here are some things to think about when deciding what the reporter did best and what he should try to do better.

1. Showed he was well acquainted with his subject
2. Spoke in a clear voice
3. Presented his report in an organized way
4. Brought out important points
5. Looked at his audience while speaking
6. Made sense in the things he said
7. Used visual material to clarify his report
8. Visual material was easily seen
9. Visual material was used to illustrate important points
10. Visual material was not just used to start or finish report but used throughout report.
11. Visual material was well labeled
12. Visual material was held so all could see
13. Spoke from notes
14. Summarized important points
15. Answered correctly most of the questions asked
16. Held the interest of his audience

IMPROVING LEARNING THROUGH DIRECT EXPERIENCE

Chapter six

Every student is part of a community—a community that can provide valuable, direct-experience learning for children who have a variety of interests and come from different backgrounds. It is possible to use direct-experience learning in planned situations outside the classroom in the community proper, and to bring in resources for sharing information within the school. The goal of direct-experience learning is to provide a more relevant, obvious tie-in between the workaday world and the student's classroom learning environment. In order to stimulate the child and involve him more fully in the world around him, new systems of education are being considered and more active learning strategies have been developed.

"Educators and parents throughout the country are trying alternative forms of education which are less restrictive and more beneficial to the growth of children's minds and spirits. Their main concern is that classrooms become more humane and involving places for children."[1] New ways of organizing the school are needed if the community and the direct experiences provided by the environment are used to the best advantage.

OPEN EDUCATION

One new approach to learning and to the organization of the school is currently being explored in many parts of the country. The "open education" emphasis is an attempt to reorganize several components of the school program so that students can be

1. Barbara Blitz, *The Open Classroom: Making It Work* (Boston: Allyn and Bacon, 1973), p. 3.

more directly involved in learning about the world in which they live. The development of an open classroom is an attempt to meet the unique needs of each child and directly involve him in the school and community in which he lives. This new approach to education, referred to as "open education" or "open classroom," is a loosely structured collection of ideas and means different things to different people.

Open structure

Schools-without-walls. The idea of open space is an integral part of the open education concept—open space within the classroom arrangement and outside the formal classroom learning setting. Philadelphia's Parkway Program is probably one of the most well-known projects in which students are encouraged to learn both in the school and in the community. "Students there have classes throughout the city, often taught by non-professional educators. . . . Schools-Without-Walls students invariably work in TV stations, hospitals, newspapers and local court rooms."[2]

Within the class the feeling of openness can also be provided for the students, and this is important. "The spatial arrangements, the materials and the organization of time and routines will all communicate your feelings and intentions to the students."[3] In fact, many new buildings are being built to convey the feeling of openness. These come in a variety of shapes from rectangles to hexagons and octagons, and can be seen from San Francisco to Boston. These new shapes frequently contain facilities such as teacher preparation alcoves, built-in media centers, and study areas that further accent the basic openness, direct-involvement notion. "Spaces of varying size and shape accommodate 75 to 100 children and permit one-to-one, small-group, class-size, and total unit activity. . . . Space utilization encourages maximum flexibility and an environment conducive to many types of learning activity."[4] Figure 6.1 shows one use of a large, open space. The structure of the room and the use of large spaces allows more flexibility in teaching arrangements. Frequently a lead teacher or team leader is designated for an open space, and several other certified teachers and interns or teacher aides are all assigned to a pod, planet, unit, or space. These arrangements encourage team teaching and the use of special teacher talent. The decisions about instruction are typically made in planning sessions. ". . . differentiations are made cooperatively by the unit staff on the basis of preparation, experi-

2. Robert D. Barr, "Diversifying the Social Studies: The Trend toward Optional Public Schools," *Social Education* 38 (March 1974): 239.

3. Blitz, *Open Classroom, p.84.*

4. Herbert J. Klausmeier and Richard E. Ripple, *Learning and Human Abilities Educational Psychology*, 3rd ed. (New York: Harper & Row, 1971), p. 235.

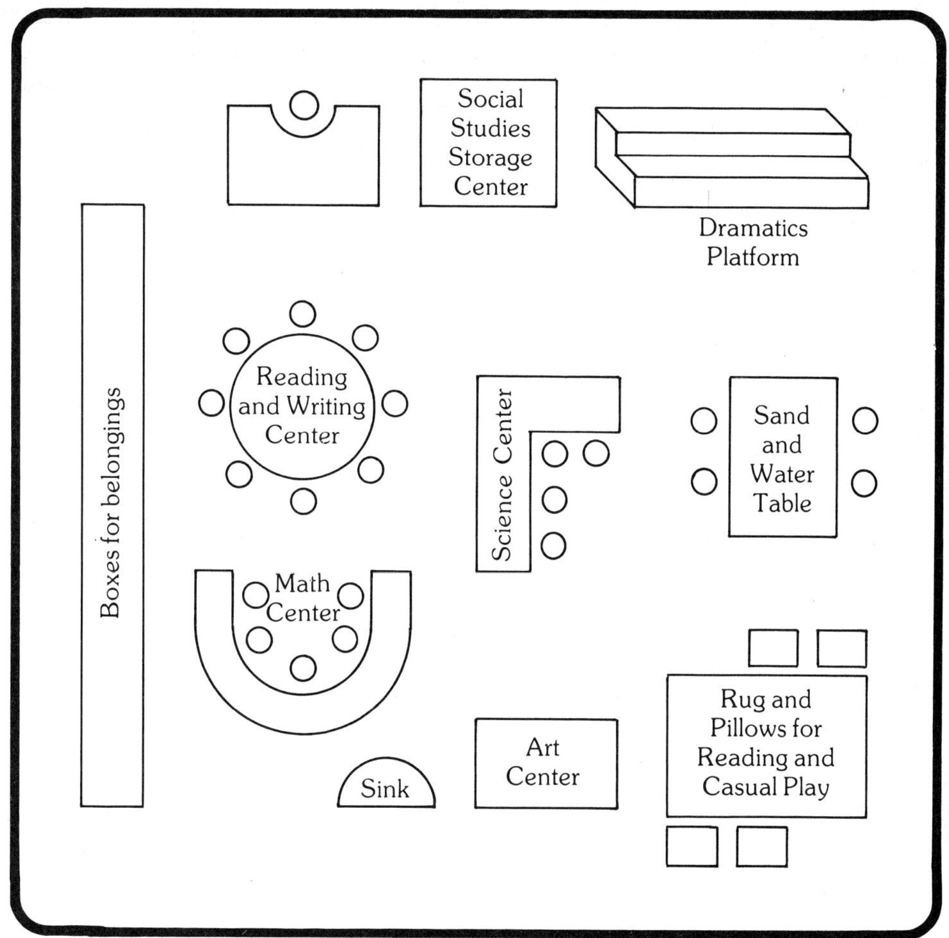

FIGURE 6.1 From Barbara Blitz, *The Open Classroom: Making It Work* (Boston: Allyn & Bacon, 1973), p. 106. Reprinted by permission.

ence, leadership, and interests of each staff member.[5] For example, one teacher may plan and carry out the primary responsibility for a learning center or a unit on National Parks because this is a particular interest of that teacher. Other teachers will work with this teacher in carrying out some of the activities involved, such as a field trip to a park. The plans for the cooperative activities are made during the special planning session.

5. Klausmeier and Ripple, *Learning*, p. 232.

In order to have team teaching proceed effectively regular team planning sessions are needed. In an assessment of the open space schools in greater Boston in 1973 a teacher survey showed that all teachers felt that more planning time was needed. Team teaching demands close coordination of efforts and careful scheduling of time and materials.

Open self-contained classroom. It is possible to gain some of the advantages of open space in the traditional self-contained classroom. Learning centers can be designed so that the students are able to move about freely in such a classroom. Figures 6.2 and 6.3 show two sample room arrangements.

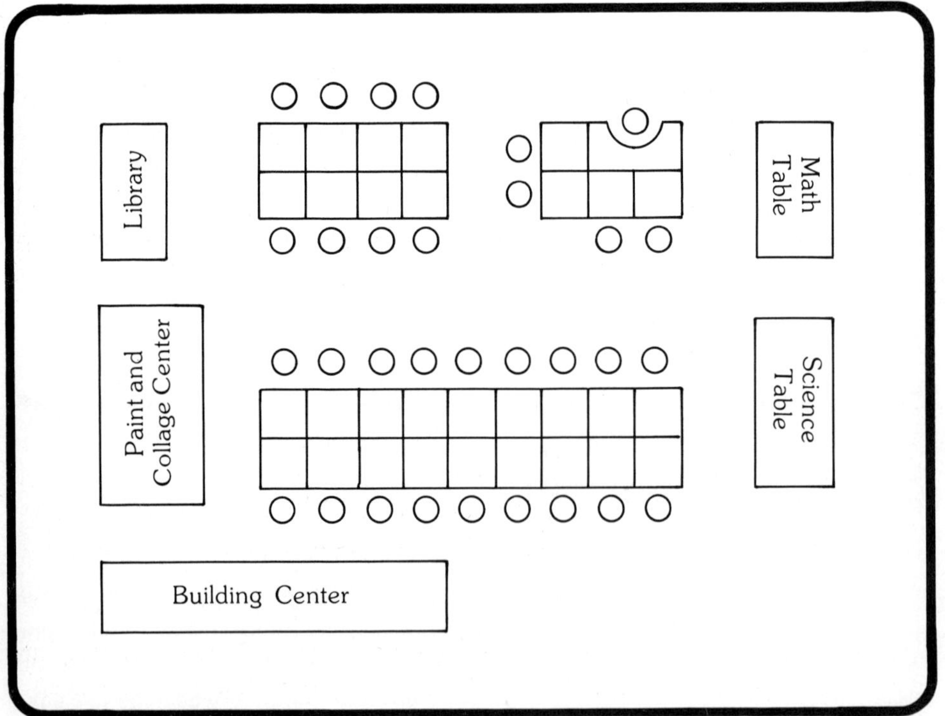

FIGURE 6.2. From Blitz, *Open Classroom*, p. 103. Reprinted by permission.

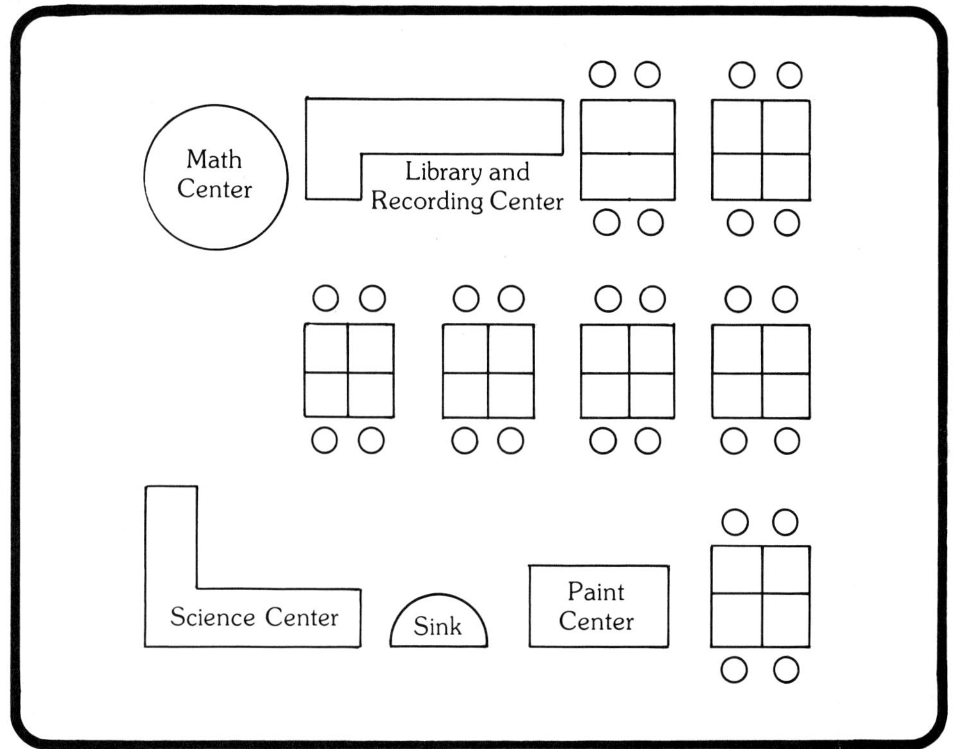

FIGURE 6.3. From Blitz, *Open Classroom*, p. 104.
Reprinted by permission.

Open content

When people talk about open classrooms they are sometimes referring to the content the students are covering in the class and the method of selecting that content. There is an underlying assumption that there will be a degree of choice for students in an open classroom.

Choosing freely. In some schools the students actually choose any topic that appeals to them. "The student is free to choose among options or to choose none of them."[6] He can select some ideas presented in materials in the class or can select any

6. Mario D. Fantini, "Alternative Schools and Humanistic Education," *Social Education* 38 (March 1974): 245.

other topic he wishes. For example, a student may decide that he is particularly interested in flowers. The range of topics related to the original interest in flowers is quite broad. The teacher serves as a resource person and provides books, media, and actual experiences that will extend and further refine the student's initial bits of information, without pushing or overdirecting the student. Textbooks are used as references, not as books to be read from cover to cover. All content may be based on an interest of this kind with no attempt being made to separate out the various disciplines. The student may wish to know what kinds of tulips there are, where they come from, how expensive various bulbs are, how to order and what shipping rates are, how you produce a new strain of tulip, what is the best soil for tulips, and how to arrange the blooms so that they are pleasing to the eye. Social studies, language arts, arithmetic, science, reading, and art will all be involved in satisfying the student's curiosity about flowers. The development of this interest about flowers may be only a beginning. The student may choose to develop other subtopics or may delve into a tangential topic which captures his attention, such as shipping regulations or international tariffs.

When this approach to learning is used the student is taught the skills as the need arises. For example, he learns to write a business letter because he wishes to order some tulips.

Choosing from alternatives. There are many classrooms in which students are provided with three or four alternatives from which to make their choices. One class was provided with this choice:

> Here are four topics dealing with the early settlers of New England: The First Mayflower Journey, The Winter of 1620, The Native American Inhabitants, The New Land. Select one of these topics and prepare a research report, a collection of poems, a play, or a diary report about your topic to share with the class.

In the example, a choice of topic is given, and a choice of processing and sharing is also given. On occasion the sharing phase is left completely open and no suggestions are made to the student as to how he is to process and share information. He is simply given the topic choice, and must himself decide on the strategy that would best represent the information and ideas gathered about that topic.

When a number of alternatives are provided, the teacher has the opportunity to collect resources for students' use in advance. This allows the teacher to be free of the "resource person" role during the actual work sessions and to use the time more effectively—for example, helping students work in groups or instructing individual students who need special work in skills areas.

Open methodology

The way in which the content is developed by the teacher and the student is part of the central concept of "open education." Method refers to the way in which the ideas are developed and expanded. Any system that deals with learning and the use of ideas must concern itself with both the input and the output processes, that is, how the student obtains information, and how he represents it or shares it with others.

Open input procedures. It is possible for students to gain information in many different ways. Direct experience procedures such as surveys, interviews, and field trips provide a base for collecting data, and in the open classroom students are given a number of ways to gather the information they need. While the teacher may make suggestions about input mode (books, musical compositions, slides, interviews), the final choice for gathering the necessary data should be the student's right and responsibility.

The use of direct experiences as an input process is not a new idea. Pestalozzi, an eighteenth-century Swiss educator, used direct sense experiences in learning. "The use of realia in lessons, the teaching of geography via field trips, the learning of arithmetic by solving actual problems that concerned the pupils, the procedure in instructing from known to unknown, and from concrete to abstract"[7] were all a part of Pestalozzi's method of instruction. Many kinds of input are available today that were not a part of Pestalozzi's world. The use of all sorts of technology—films, tapes, TV and other media—has expanded the student's options for input of information and ideas.

Open expressive output. In the open classroom the student is expected to produce, but the emphasis is on the honest, cognitive involvement that the student demonstrates rather than on the product itself. "Each child must be respected, listened to, cared for and consulted. His unique qualities must form the basis for his continuous progress within the educational environment provided for him."[8] The output that each student provides is important—even crucial—to determining next steps and more advanced challenges.

All children do not produce reports with equal skill and/or enthusiasm. A number of alternatives should be provided that each child can demonstrate most effectively the things he has learned. "Pages from books or magazines can be made into

7. Richard E. Gross, ed., *Heritage of American Education* (Boston: Allyn and Bacon, 1962), p. 259.

8. Michael J.Malinowski, "Open Concept at the Secondary Level" (Paper reproduced for Greater Boston Council for the Social Studies, 1973), p. 1.

transparencies with the proper duplicating equipment."[9] Children can use overhead projectors for shadow pictures, and students have invented some truly interesting role-playing situations using fingers as characters or black silhouettes on the machine which are projected to life size on the screen. Some students may wish to demonstrate actively a particular skill they have learned. They may wish to dance a Highland fling or the tarantella or sing a song. Still other students may wish to write a poem or draw a picture of one element in their search that affected them deeply.

In one program each student was encouraged to be creative. ". . . the individual is exposed to a curricular cycle which is entitled, *Me, the Creator and Craftsperson*. It is interesting to note the focus on the 'me' and exposure to such techniques as film-making, theater improvisations, anatomical drawing, and culinary arts as tools for increasing the creative potential of the individual."[10] The fact that one can communicate ideas in many ways is frequently overlooked by adults as well as children. The reemphasis of this fact can be a part of the learning process.

Teacher guide role. In the more traditional classroom the teacher has a major role in the instruction that is carried out. Careful planning, variety in presentations, new ideas, and enthusiasm are all a part of the traditional teacher's stock in trade; so are they a necessity for the teacher in the open classroom. The teacher does not become a nonentity that serves as part of the classroom furnishings. Quite the contrary, the expert open classroom teacher has all the qualities mentioned and more. He must be open to student concerns and find new and clever ways of getting children to express themselves. One individual in writing about open classroom teachers says that they are supportive and are schooled in "attending"—a very apt expression. Teachers give hand and eye contact as well as other kinds of attention to the students, and this helps promote effective communication.

The atmosphere the teacher creates is informal, but emphasizes the importance of each individual. The teachers make an effort to help the student feel positive about learning, and they emphasize the importance of each individual's feelings. Magic Circle is a discussion, group interaction idea used at the Gridley Bryant School in Quincy, Mass. The lead teacher, Pat Drew, works very effectively with this technique. Students sit in a circle, usually on the floor, and discuss some personal feeling. Everyone is asked but not required to contribute to the idea being considered. One particular strategy is to select an individual in the group and contribute some *positive* comment about the person. The comment should be something that is rather unique, that everyone may not know. This tends to provide many small incidents, frequently

9. Evelyn Berger and Bonnie A. Winters, *Social Studies in the Open Classroom* (New York: Teachers College Press, 1973), p. 22.

10. Fantini, "Alternative Schools," p. 245.

personal interactions, that add up to a certain rather impressive whole. Even a student who has been having problems will begin to see himself in a different light. The Magic Circle technique is an example of one that can be used in an open space school to reinforce the informal feeling, while at the same time providing a stimulus for positive behavior.

The teacher serves as a resource person, as a researcher, and as an interested party in the projects being developed by the students. But, good teaching is good teaching in the traditional classroom or in the open classroom. Planning and assessment strategies; an able, flexible mind; and human kindness are requisites for any good teacher in any time and place.

Open time use

The fourth and final variable that we will discuss in connection with the open classroom is the way in which the time is used. Time is one of the student's most valuable resources.

Using school learning time. Open classrooms tend to provide a more flexible approach to the use of time for learning. There are times when students work in certain areas for designated time spans. On occasion, however, the content or problem being considered may require more time, so the schedule is readily reorganized to fit a particualr need. Indeed, in some open space schools no schedule is developed, as such. The use of time in the open classroom varies from complete lack of scheduling or organizing to setting up blocks of time for certain subject areas.

Using time for learning. The real objective of the open classroom is to involve the student more directly in the learning process—to foster a strong "need to know." If this is accomplished, the student will learn and pursue an interest not only during school hours, but also after school and even during holidays and vacations. Students begin to use their surroundings as a resource; counting out forty-five minute class periods becomes a thing of the past. Students volunteer to help in computer centers, in pet stores, in extended care facilities for the aged, and in other parts of the business world. Jennings writes, "We're discovering how potent community based learning is —internships, jobs, travel, exchanges, volunteering, community study. . . . We're learning how potent active participation is —responsibility for a real task, serving on interviewing committees, tutoring younger students, planning together, building a playground, investigating local firms for pollution, working in a bakery or conducting a poll."[11] All these activities sound exciting and are loaded with learning potential. They

11. Wayne Jennings, "Social Education in an Open School," *Social Education* 38 (March 1974): 253-254.

span time confinements and demand that (perhaps compel is a better word) the learner continue to investigate after the traditional school day has ended. They will require extra teacher time—extra commitment—on occasion. An old-fashioned idea (commitment) for the new-fangled concept of open education.

FOR FURTHER READING

Blitz, Barbara. *The Open Classroom: Making It Work.* Boston: Allyn and Bacon, 1973.

Hertzberg, Alvin, and Edward F. Stone. *Schools Are for Children.* New York: Schocken Books, 1971. Paperback.

Kohl, Herbert R. *The Open Classroom.* New York: Random House, 1969.

Larkin, James M., and Jane J. White. "The Learning Center in the Social Studies Classroom." *Social Education* 38:(November 1974): 698-710.

Morlan, John E., *Classroom Learning Centers.* Palo Alto, Calif.: Fearon, 1974.

Nyquist, Ewald B., and Gene R. Hawes, eds. *Open Classroom: A Source Book for Parents and Teachers.* New York: Bantam Books, 1972. Paperback.

Silberman, Charles E., ed. *The Open Classroom Reader.* New York: Vintage, 1973. Paperback.

Taylor, Joy. *Organizing the Open Classroom.* New York: Schocken, 1972.

DIRECT EXPERIENCE IN THE COMMUNITY

The idea of using community resources to enhance and extend the student's learning opportunities has been mentioned briefly. Let us explore the community as an information source in more depth.

Why study the community?

There are several reasons for studying the local area:

1. It allows you to see democracy in action.
2. It shows the importance of the individual in action.
3. It provides an opportunity to work with ledgers, local laws, tax rates, etc.—the raw materials of social science.
4. It gives you a chance to see how your area relates to the nation, and helps you gain insight into the way people work together.
5. It gives you an opportunity to identify an area where you might be of service to other people.
6. It helps you locate possible employment opportunities for youth and adults.

Research topics about your community

If you decide to begin your career as a social scientist by studying your local community, a wide range of topics are available on which you may begin your research:

People, settlement, conditions of living	Growth of the town
Business and industry	Education
Trade and communications	Labor and labor unions
Professions and occupations	Arts and crafts
Government	Recreation
Religion	Transportation

Places to look for information

There is a number of places you can go to get information directly:

Museums	Graveyards
Historic sites or monuments	Post office
Farms	Bakeries
Bus transportation centers	Shoe repair shops
Air and railway terminals	Drycleaning establishment
Stores and restaurants	Files of local newpapers
Power plants	Printed local history
Mines, mills, factories	Histories written but not printed
Resort areas	Physical remains
Town hall (government center)	Account book of a family or business
Courts	Diaries
Town parks and forests	Old pictures
Persons who know local history	Oral sources—participants in events

How to begin research on the community

The following boxed sections may be copied on ditto stencils and reproduced for use by your students.

EXPLORING YOUR COMMUNITY

Perhaps one of the best ways to find out about your community is to ask questions. Whether you live in a small town like Eastham, Mass., with a population of 2,300; or in a large town or small city like Thomasville, N.C., with 15,000 population; or a large city of 110,000 such as Cedar Rapids, Iowa; or a city of more than half a million like Seattle, Washington, you can ask these questions about your home, or about your town or city.

1. Why did the first settlers choose this place to live?
2. Do we get food from farms near here?
3. How many schools of different kinds are there?
4. Did Native Americans ever live in this area?
5. How are goods and people transported?
6. Who makes the rules or laws for our community?
7. When was our community settled?
8. Have people from other countries settled here?
9. Do we manufacture any products here?
10. How many different ways do people earn their living?
11. When people are not working, how do they spend their leisure time?
12. Are the schools the same as they were fifty years ago?
13. Is a newspaper published in our town? If not, why not?
14. Is the population increasing or decreasing?
15. Why is our town the size it is?
16. How does a man get to be the tax collector?
17. Is all of the leisure time used just for having fun?
18. Is there anyone living here who knew our town long, long ago when it looked different?
19. Why do dogs have to be licensed?
20. Does the state highway go right through the town? Why or why not?

Now go over the twenty questions and put those that belong together in groups (e.g. #1 and #4). Having the questions placed in groups helps you find labels for the information you are curious about. Then you can look it up in resource books, and talk with resource people.

After the questions are sorted into groups, give a title or label to each category (division or group). To get started we will give you the titles of the categories for the questions. Some questions may fit in more than one category. You may go over the questions alone or in small groups and decide under which category each question belongs, and then write opposite the category title the number of the question.

OUR COMMUNITY	
1. People	________
2. Growth	________
3. Business and Industry	________
4. Transportation and Communication	________
5. Occupations	________
6. Education	________
7. Government	________
8. Leisure, or use of free time	________

Now let's go further in organizing for research. Work with a friend or two and discuss the topics developed. Choose one of the eight topics above. One of you should serve as the secretary. Copy down the questions under the topic. Now add more questions that the group can think of concerning the category. Probably your group can raise eight or ten questions or more.

Be sure to keep a complete copy of the questions developed to share with the class in the final report.

Now that you have raised questions about a topic, you want some answers. Where can you find the answers to questions about a community?

Getting information. There are a number of ways of finding out about an event, a person, or a place. (To the teacher: When you make ditto stencils for the following items, allow space for answers or provide a separate answer sheet.)

1. We have seen it. This is *direct observation*.	What are some of the things I know about my community because I can see them myself? List.
2. We have been told about it. This is *word-of-mouth*.	What are some of the things I know about my community because I was told about them? List.
3. We have read about it. We call this *written information*.	What can I read about my community? In what? List.
4. We have seen pictures or a map. This is *graphic information*.	What can I learn about my community from pictures and from a map? List

DIRECT OBSERVATION

Try direct observation yourself. Stand on a corner with a friend for five minutes. Each of you record everything you see. Do not talk to each other.

Now compare your reports. Write down things you both mention.

Things only I mention.

Things only my friend mentions.

ANOTHER DIRECT OBSERVATION EXERCISE

When you observed on the corner you may have seen so many different things that your list and your friend's list are quite different. The lists may also be a mess! An observer can be *trained* to look for certain kinds of information. Stand on the same corner again for five minutes and record what you see, using this observation checklist. Again compare with your friend. (You may want to adapt this list to your situation.)

OBSERVATION CHECKLIST

1. Number of cars

   ____

2. Number of trucks

   ____

3. People who cross the street

   ____

4. Dogs on leashes

   ____

5. Dogs that are loose

   ____

6. People eating food

   ____

7. Number of times light changes

   ____

8. Number of people

   ____

9. People talking together

   ____

Was your information more like your friend's this time?____________________

Were your notes easier to read?____________________

Did you see something you could not record on your checklist?____________________

What are the advantages of the checklist?____________________

What are the disadvantages of the checklist?____________________

WORD-OF-MOUTH

Information from another person may come to you by word-of-mouth. Someone may give you information about your community, or you may ask a question about it. When you want several kinds of information, it is wise to have your questions written down for the interview. Sometimes when you have not done any planning, the conversation rambles and takes so many turns that the information you need may not be in your notes at all. Here are sample questions for an "Old Timer Interview." You may wish to add some questions of your own. Choose an older person that you know who has lived a long time in your community and ask him these questions.

1. Name?
2. Why did you choose to live in this area?
3. How long have you lived here?
4. How many people lived here when you came to this area?
5. What major changes have taken place here?
6. How did these changes affect you?
7. What problems did these changes create?
8. What problems did the changes solve?
9. What do you see as a possible future for this area?

If it is possible, tape the interview so that you can play it over several times. One can gather more information this way. Of course, you will need the person's consent to tape the interview.

WRITTEN INFORMATION

You may need to use the library or send letters to gather written information about your community. Knowing how to write a good letter and to use the library are even more important when you are studying about a topic that is not close at hand.

You can find out a great deal about your community by reading old newspapers, looking at old account books, and by reading the letters or documents that were written long ago by people in the town or city. The local historical society frequently has collected much information from written sources that it will share with you.

GRAPHIC INFORMATION

You can learn a good deal about your community from pictures and maps whether you live in a small village or a large city.

Your teacher, school librarian, or public library may have picture files that you can use. Families and friends may have pictures of the community that show old buildings, fashions in clothes, and different kinds of transportation. It will pay to examine pictures carefully.

Perhaps you will find an old picture of a street that shows buildings that are no longer there. What has taken their place? What else do you find in the old picture that wouldn't be in a picture taken today? It will probably be more fun working with a partner than working alone to discover how many things in a picture taken one hundred years ago, or sixty years ago, or even twenty-five years ago, are no longer there.

Maps of communities (especially small towns) are probably more difficult to find than pictures. You can inquire about them through merchants, real estate firms, chambers of commerce, librarians. If none are available you could make a map of the streets in your neighborhood, or the downtown area, or roads going out into the country. (To the teacher: See item 4 on page 342 for the source of a topographic map of your area. Every classroom should have one. You will find it rich in information.)

It is clear that there is much potential in a community for learning. Not only can students gather information about a specific area, but they can also learn the processes used in getting information. For elementary school children, "how to do is as important as what to know." The process used can be repeated.

Let us examine in more detail another direct experience strategy for gathering information in a community—a field trip.

Field trips

There are a number of places in a community and within driving distance that provide information and enhance the learning situation for students. Some of these are listed on p. 185 under "Places to Look for Information." As a teacher you will need to plan with care, because while the field trip provides many opportunities for learning, it also carries with it an assortment of possible problems. Bus schedules, parent accompaniment, permission slips, money involved, illnesses, lunch facilities, and myriad other details can make for chaos. The teacher can make a field trip—a direct experience in learning about an area—a valuable one. No field trip should be taken that doesn't have the possibility of turning out first-rate. It is to that end that we make our suggestions.

Stage one. Before any arrangements are made for a specific trip, define the purpose of purposes that will be served by it. Will it provide a learning experience not possible in the classroom, lead to further learning activities, or increase the accuracy of specific concepts? There are some other questions to be considered before a final decision is made on a field trip:

1. Is this the most efficient and effective way for the children to get the needed information and experience?
2. Will the whole class benefit from this trip?
3. Is the expenditure of effort, time, and money justifiable?
4. Would it be better for a committee to go and report back?
5. Could the same results be obtained if parents took their own children?

Stage two. When making plans for a specific trip, use the checklists below, for teacher and student. Check off or mark "NA" (not applicable) every item on the check line before you start the trip.

TEACHER PREPARATION

____ 1. Do you know now in what way what is to be learned on the trip will be useful in the social studies?

____ 2. Has the principal, or proper school official, given permission for the trip?

____ 3. Have arrangements been made and confirmed with someone at the trip's destination? Have you been through the trip beforehand to evaluate the suggested sequence of the activities?

____ 4. Is there a guide (either the teacher or a guide at the destination)? Do you know the area well enough to serve as an efficient guide if one is not provided?

____ 5. Are all transportation arrangements in order?

____ 6. Do you haved signed permissions from all parents?

____ 7. Have you a time schedule to which you will be able to adhere?

____ 8. Did you check to see if one day rather than another would provide more learning experiences for the children?

____ 9. Do you have additional adults to go on the trip? (Plan a ratio of one adult to ten children or less.)

____ 10. Will you be back at the school long enough after the trip before school dismissal to have pupils list three or four of the big ideas learned, so when asked at home what they learned today they will have an answer?

____ 11. Do you plan to use a variety of activities? Of the many that could be involved in the total process, for example, are reading, interviewing, note taking, drawing, observing, asking questions, summarizing, evaluating, and speaking. Will the class get considerable learning mileage out of this demanding, time consuming activity?

PUPIL PREPARATION

____ 1. Did you carefully develop a need in the pupils for the trip?

____ 2. Do the children understand the specific purpose or purposes of the trip?

____ 3. Are questions listed whose answers should come out of the trip?

____ 4. Are any individual or committee responsibilities planned for?

____ 5. Are other instructional tools to be used in preparation, such as reference reading, films and filmstrips, records, pictures?

____ 6. Do the students have any kind of checklist on which items can be checked off as accomplished on the trip?

____ 7. Is some particular pupil to express the group's thanks to individuals who have helped or guided them?

____ 8. Was there cooperative discussion of what constitutes proper and courteous conduct of pupils?

____ 9. Are rules for safety worked out, such as:

A buddy system requiring two children to be with each other during the trip

Stop at the corner and wait for the teacher or an adult

On the bus, talk quietly, stay in your seat, do not change places, and do not disturb the driver.

Stage three. This stage is the trip itself. If plans have been carefully made and executed to this point, only a few further suggestions remain.

1. At the destination, organize quickly and get started.
2. It is usually best for the teacher to head the group with the conductor, but a traffic rear guard should be maintained (an adult and two responsible children). Neglect of this precaution has caused more delay and trouble than any other single factor of management.
3. Questions by pupils should be encouraged, because information given on the spot makes a permanent impression.
4. The teacher should be alert in offering suggestions to note takers at crucial times during the visit. One teacher prepared sealed envelopes to be opened at certain places during an industrial visit. The plan was a success.
5. Spending money for candy or food should be discouraged unless the trip involves a picnic lunch or meal.
6. If transportation conditions allow, there should be some kind of profitable activity on the return trip.
7. Check item 10 in Stage Two, *Teacher Preparation*.

Stage four. The follow-up is the crux of the whole field trip experience. Further activities are carried on and outcomes are evaluated. Allow variety in the follow-up activities and do not leave yourself open to the criticism made by one little girl: "I don't like field trips because I'm always thinking about the composition we'll have to write when we get back to school."

Possibilities for activities include:

1. Group discussion based on answering questions formulated before the trip and raising questions to be considered for further study.
2. Individual or group reports based on preplanning.
3. Creative projects, exhibits, dramatization, writing, bulletin board display, scrapbooks, art work.
4. Map work.
5. Visual aids to amplify, clarify, and organize impressions on the trip.
6. Provisions for a written record, group or individual, of the experiences, impressions, and learnings gained.

7. Thank-you notes.
8. Items for the school paper or local press.
9. Chart of new vocabulary words.
10. Make a list/photo story to share with parents of some of the interesting things seen and done.

Evaluation by the boys and girls should include:

1. How well did our plans succeed?
2. Were our questions answered?
3. Any new interests discovered?
4. If we were to plan it all again, how could we improve?
5. Would we recommend this trip to next year's class? Why?

Evaluation by the teacher should cover:

1. Effectiveness of the trip in relation to the purposes. (See Stage One, p. 194)
2. Improvements in planning for another time. What should have been done to make it a better learning experience?
3. Evidences of growth in self-reliance and self-control, courtesy, ability to observe, critical thinking, appreciations, skills (note taking, interviewing, reporting, etc.), new interests engendered.

The principal's office should have a file on field trips in connection with units of work showing the information indicated below and kept up to date by each teacher after a field trip.

Name
Address
Whom to contact for arrangements
Expense (if any)
Time required
General comments
Major learnings

Resource persons

It is wise to have a central file (in the main office) of people who can provide special resources. This card file should give name and address, phone number, and specialty, as well as the age level for which this person has served as a resource.

Many parents, business people, and professionals are willing to assist in making children's learning experiences more challenging. People may have collections of artifacts, travel experiences and slides, hobbies, or special talents or be willing to serve in a helping role on field trips, parties, and the like. Some individuals may be willing to be interviewed at home or in their offices, studios, or other places of work. This can add a dimension of reality to the information that a simple classroom talk may lack.

When a person is called upon to help, he should be given some preparatory information. It is important for the visitor to know the age level of the children involved, any special room accommodations that exist, the general preparation the students have had on the topic, and the amount of time that is planned for the session.

If the students are to interview the resource person, have some questions prepared in advance. It is usually wise to start with prepared questions and then allow students to ask spontaneous questions once the session is moving. Tape-record the session so that the students can review the information later.

The assessment of the effectiveness of the resource persons available to the school is important. Although many people have talents and training in specific areas, not all of them can communicate effectively with large groups of children. The checklist in Figure 6.4 might be filled out on the back of each card in the file of resource persons. For particular speakers other items may be important. As resource persons are used you may find that additional categories need to be added to the above list.

FOR FURTHER READING

Brehm, Shirley A. *A Teacher's Handbook for Study Outside the Classroom*. Columbus, Ohio: Merrill, 1969.

Brown, James W.; Lewis, Richard B.; and Fred F. Harcleroad. *A-V Instruction: Materials and Methods*. 4th ed. New York: McGraw-Hill, 1973. Pp. 330-336.

Dwyer, Robert L. "School Camping Programs: Ecology in the Outdoor Classroom." *Social Education* 35 (January 1971): 74-77.

Howland, Adelene E. *How to Conduct a Field Trip*. How-to-Do-It Series. Arlington, Va.: National Council for the Social Studies, 1962.

Hug, John W., and Phyllis J. Wilson. *Curriculum Enrichment Outdoors*. New York: Harper & Row, 1965.

CAREER EDUCATION

In primitive societies and even in colonial times in our country children were shown the employment opportunities that were available to them by their parents or relatives. The range of possibilities for any one individual was not unlimited and the most com-

DATE: TEACHER: GRADE: SPEAKER'S TOPIC:	OUT-STANDING	GOOD	FAIR	POOR
Appears to be an expert in the field				
Spoke clearly and used appropriate vocabulary				
Used pictures, slides, realia				
Involved the students in the learning process				
Responded well to students' questions				
Provided suggestions for follow-up research (bibliography, materials)				
Comments:				

FIGURE 6.4

mon method of instruction was a direct-experience apprenticeship. This was as true in the kitchen as it was in the hunting forest. The individual might actually try his hand at several kinds of work and then choose the one for which he had most talent. Today it is impossible for students to try out the range of jobs available to them. It is even difficult to obtain information on all the employment opportunities that exist. There are more than twenty thousand different occupations in the United States alone. How can a student prepare for such a world of work? The answer seems simple enough: the school should prepare the student for an adult world in which myriad alternatives exist, both in the world of work and in basic life choices. Surely this should be a part of social studies education. It is, however, a responsibility that requires considerable energy and creativity.

What is career education?

According to one expert, "Career education consists of all the activities and experiences through which individuals prepare themselves for work."[12] Yet another says, " . . . it somewhat defies a very precise, discrete definition."[13] Marland, considered by

12. Kenneth Hoyt, "Straight Answers on Career Education," *Today's Education* 64 (1975): 60.
13. Keith Goldhammer, "Career Education and Social Studies," *Social Education* 37 (1973): 484.

many the father of the current career education emphasis says, "Career education, then, in the broadest, most philosophical sense, is really a change of mind and a change of heart."[14] A change of mind and a change of heart from what to what? This is not absolutely clear. Is this due to accident or confusion or by design?

Career education is a broad idea that is perhaps more a message than a specific entity that can be defined by narrow parameters. It does not come to you packaged with canned objectives and checklist evalualtion sheets. Career education may differ from community to community and from region to region. "If there is a central message in our conception of career education, it is to cry out against this absurd partitioning of the house of education, this separation of subject from subject, of class from class, this false and destructive distinction between the liberal academic tradition on the one hand and the utilitarian-vocational tradition on the other."[15] Perhaps this spells out more clearly the change of mind and heart that is needed—a change from the artificial, self-seeking layering of education and learning to a more genuine and realistic program for the learner. "The idea behind career education is this, that there is basically neither an academic nor a vocational track in the curriculum. Our job as educators is to help every human being become capacitated to the fullest extent of his potential."[16]

The preceding discussion is rather idealistic and is really motivational fuel for the teacher. Before the teacher can actually deal with the concept in the classroom, however, some more solid suggestions are needed. What are the qualities that one can expect to find in a career education program? Such a program:

1. Is for all students at all levels.
2. Reflects what is known about how careers develop.
3. Provides for collaboration between the educational system and other phases of business and community.
4. Is learner centered in goals, methods, and evaluation.
5. Provides for specific skills acquisition.
6. Helps students examine their attitudes toward career opportunities.

Introducing students to careers

If these are the characteristics of a career education program, what shape will these characteristics assume in your classroom? First, an introduction to the "World of

14. Sidney P. Marland, Jr., "Career Education, Not Job Training," *Social Education* 37 (1973): 501.
15. Ibid., p. 504.
16. Goldhammer, "Career Education," p. 486.

Work" or to the careers one might choose can be presented systematically at each grade level. If the faculty work closely together and coordinate efforts from grade level to grade level, a sizeable number of career options could be explored by the time a student completed elementary school. It is a good idea to call on local townspeople to serve as resource people in this introductory phase. The now defunct Rocky Mountain Educational Laboratory used this strategy in an effort to acquaint the teachers attending their workshops with the career possibilities in an area. The persons invited to the sessions were electricians, auto body repairmen, builders, and plumbers. They were individuals who had been involved in their careers for a fair amount of time, and had hired or supervised others in the same career. Teachers were given an opportunity to question these people about the qualities they wanted most in a young person entering their trade. The teachers also inquired about the specific skills needed, salary ranges, and particular problems in a given career area. The dignity and ability of the resource people involved in this training program was impressive. Their answers were direct and to the point. They were no-nonsense men and women who worked in a demanding, competitive world. Individuals like these contribute tremendously to a training program for teachers. They also contribute very positively to children's concepts of the world of work which they must enter. You might request something similar for an in-service training sequence.

Academic skills

Career experts tell us that high-level technical skills and vocational entry skills must be taught, as well as an introduction and a general education on careers. "It seems, then, that schools should expose students to a broad range of career possibilities, help them narrow down their area of choice, and provide the actual skills that will be needed in several specific job areas."[17] What kind of skills are needed? Academic skills are needed in every job. Let us examine two common employment areas: food preparation and service, and motor vehicle operation and service. There are reading, language, mathematics, and social skills for each of the work areas mentioned. The following lists show a sizeable number of academic skills for the two work areas mentioned. Other similar lists may be developed for any number of job categories.

17. Martha Tyler John, "The World of Work," *Instructor* (December 1974), p. 39.

ACADEMIC SKILLS NEEDED FOR FOOD PREPARATION AND SERVICE[18]

Reading

- Name on time card
- Days of the week
- Streets and addresses
- Can labels
- Directions for equipment use
- Items on menu
- Recipes
- Waiter's order slips
- Inventory sheets
- Schedules
- Orders from chef

Writing

- Sign name
- Mark containers to go out
- Mark sandwiches to go out
- Order from menu

Oral Language

- Understand directions
- Speak politely to customers
- Suggest items on menu

Mathematics

- How to stack
- Tell time
- Full and empty
- Count to fifty
- Size
- Read thermometer
- Concepts of one to ten
- Add up sales check
- Judgment of small numbers
- Pay small bills
- Car sizes
- Make change
- Hours worked
- Fractions to eighths
- Weights and measures
- Punch amount on ticket
- Compute price from weight

Spelling

- Own name
- Kinds of sandwiches
- Kinds of coffee
- Other items of food

18. These skills lists were produced by Gerald Benjamin as a result of a survey of the job areas presented. The results of the survey were provided in a mimeographed paper entitled "Academic Skills Required in Each Job Area," Boston University, 1970.

ACADEMIC SKILLS NEEDED FOR MOTOR VEHICLE OPERATION AND SERVICE

Reading
- Oil gauge
- Labels on cans
- Car names
- Telephone names
- Driver's test
- Simple directions

Reading
- Job order blank
- Manufacturer's directions
- Names of tools and parts
- Street names
- Names of customers

Mathematics
- Read meters
- Make change
- Compute bill
- Figure sales tax

Writing
- Items of sales
- Items on job order

Oral language
- Speak clearly and politely
- Give clear direction or map information

Mathematics
- License plate numbers
- Telephone numbers
- Count number on items
- Pressure gauge
- Time schedules
- Gasoline pump

Spelling
- Items on sales slips
- Items on job orders

Teacher application. There are several possible uses of the lists that have been provided. An incorporation of the skills into the standard curriculum and an overt recognition of related job areas is one direct and fairly easy use of the academic skills lists. It is clear that many of the academic skills demanded are taught in the elementary school.

We recommend as the skill is taught that the teacher show directly how it is used in several careers. For example, if the children are learning to count to one hundred, the teacher could then explore with the children the way in which a person employed in a grocery store might use this skill. "Do you think a grocery store worker would ever need to know how to count to one hundred? In what ways might he use this skill?" Such a practical application would provide motivation for acquiring the skill and would at the same time give students a more clearly defined concept of the work category being considered. This application can be readily used with primary grade students.

It is also possible for the teacher to assign an occupation to a small group or several groups for discussion. The group could talk about and list examples of specific instances in the assigned category where they think the suggested skills would be used. They may wish to observe a particular worker on their own after school to check out their hypotheses. The group could also be asked to prepare a list of demonstration possibilities to give evidence of the skills listed. If more than one group has dealt with a job category, a "sharing and comparing" session can be arranged by the teacher. For carrying out their demonstrations of the skills, the students will need materials and media to aid in the sharing process.

The third possibility that could be used is an individual approach to applying academic skills to specific job areas. If this approach is used, the teacher can provide reading materials as well as other materials at a learning center. The lists of academic skills needed are provided on cards. The student selects or chooses one job area in which he wishes to demonstrate competency. He then develops a contract (see Figure 6.5), and collects evidence to fulfill his contract. With the teacher's help the student plans a small group sharing demonstration.

The following materials would be useful for demonstrating the academic skills mentioned on the lists. Other materials might be needed, especially if other academic skills lists of work categories are developed by the teacher.

Order blanks
Blank checks
Bill of sale
Time cards
Thermometers
Recipes
Insurance policy (or information)
Measure (dry or wet)
Play telephones
Simple maps
Menus
Old telephone directories for street addresses and phone number references
Sized cans (6 oz., 8 oz., 13 oz.) with cost of the items—for unit pricing skill
Media for Student Use:

1. Tape recorder (cassette)
2. Overhead projector with clear transparencies and felt tip pens or grease pencils
3. Butcher paper for charts
4. Folders
5. Dittos

INDIVIDUAL CAREER CONTRACT

Grade ____________________ Student ____________________

Date ____________________ Teacher ____________________

Career Choice: ____________________

I. Skills I will use:

A. ____________________

B. ____________________

C. ____________________

D. ____________________

II. Materials or evidence I will prepare to demonstrate the skills:

A. ____________________

B. ____________________

C. ____________________

D. ____________________

III. Date to be finished: ____________________

IV. Resources to be used:

____

FIGURE 6.5

Attitudes toward careers

Provision of skills is important, but the exploration of attitudes and feelings associated with careers is perhaps equally important. It is beneficial for students to think about the "others" their career choices will affect. One very real dimension of career satisfaction is the pleasure the career gives to the worker because he serves others. For some people the altruistic need is a strong one, and some degree of service rendered in a career will make the job more tolerable, indeed more desirable. Attitudes toward people and toward helping others might be examined in everyday classroom situations. Role-playing vignettes such as those proposed by Shaftel and Shaftel will help students consider their own feelings about others.

The satisfaction gained from financial reward is, of course, another dimension of careers. Part of the mathematics lessons might include comparative salaries, rates per hour, possible living area for the required job, and so forth.

The classroom can provide the forum in which students can examine their own feelings and the attitude of their peers about different careers. One very direct, practical way to evoke responses and provide a forum for the students to examine their own attitudes is to provide an open-ended, real-life situation for discussion or role playing.

The following is an example of such a situation and the actual solutions provided for the problem when it was presented to children at first, third/fourth, and seventh/eighth levels. The children were given the following vignette:[19]

Mother: You are the mother of three children and you are a lawyer and work from 9-5 every day. You are working on a very exciting case right now. Your husband has just come in the door from work. His boss has arranged a three-week business trip over Christmas for him. The children want the whole family to go. Act out what you will do now.

Father: Your boss has just arranged a great business trip for you. The children would be on school vacation. Your wife is a practicing attorney. You have just come in to tell her about your big chance.
Act out what will happen now.

Students were asked to discuss their ideas of what would happen.

19. John F. Cuber, Martha Tyler John, and Kendrick S. Thompson, "Should Traditional Sex Modes and Values Be Changed?" *Controversial Issues in the Social Studies: A Contemporary Perspective*, 45th Yearbook (Arlington, Va.: National Council for the Social Studies, 1975), p. 110.

GRADE 1 RESPONSES

Anne:	We go without her and when she's done with the case—then she can go.	Join us later
Barbara:	. . . get everyone to help her so she'll get finished faster.	Get help
Billy:	Make the trip when the case is over, postpone vacation.	Postpone trip
Irene:	Cancel it, and then go in the summer.	Cancel and go later

GRADES 3-4 RESPONSES

Kevin:	I would ask the people who had the problem to get another lawyer.	Another lawyer
Phil:	I would like to tell my boss that I would like to take the trip at another time.	Postpone trip
David:	I would tell my boss to wait till my wife got a vacation and then we could go on the fantastic trip.	Cancel and go later
Anne:	I would try to solve it at home and then when I was finished I'll call my husband and then I say I'm gonna come.	Join us later
Kevin:	Instead of going on an airplane or going some place far away I'd go in a camper and we would drive, let's say around Massachusetts and we could go to Cape Cod and over the weekend and drive around and then when she said she had to go the office all we had to do is drive the office and they're still on their trip and they go exploring all around in the woods.	Lost focus
Jim:	I would tell the wife to drop the case and wait until after vacation cause she needs the vacation cause she works every day.	Drop the case

GRADES 7-8 RESPONSES

Bob:	She shouldn't go. . . . she shouldn't go because she got herself into that, it's her responsibility—that's her job to defend somebody.	Stay home and defend

Jane:	But if she was a good enough lawyer she could do it quick enough so that she might even make the trip but if she can't go she can go another time . . . she's making plenty of money!	Go on her own another time
All at one time:	Discuss it in the family. Get the feelings of everyone in the family.	
Charlie:	Suppose they wouldn't mind not being without a mother on that trip and they would want her to defend this guy. Suppose he was innocent—they wanted her to defend him so they could go on the trip and she could stay and, maybe for a week and if the trial is in the beginning of the week she can take a plane down and join them.	Join them later
Bob:	Maybe take the other week another time if they could afford to give him an all-expense trip couldn't they give it to him another time.	Cancel and go another time
Jane:	If they would have had two weeks, they forfeit the first three or four days for the trial and then all go for the other ten.	Forfeit a few days and all go later
Teacher:	*What could the mother do?*	
All at one time:	Have another lawyer take her place.	Another lawyer.
Jack:	A judge has to be a lawyer, right, well, if she was a woman judge, maybe she had to pass up a trip—so she could understand how this woman feels and let her go . . .	Another time for the trial

Teaching about career options, the acquisition of academic skills, and the practice of psychomotor skills as well as exploring students' attitudes toward careers are important parts of any social studies curriculum. We recommend that teachers spend some time on each of these skills. For example, if the students are studying about the family, then a subtopic dealing with the careers that are represented in the class might be explored with the children. At each grade level there are opportunities for career emphasis and the specific suggestions provided in the foregoing section can be used in total or in part at any grade level.

Students need to learn to think about the future—to project. It is beneficial for them to experiment with the consequences of change before the changes take place. The following hypothetical situation encourages them to be futuristic problem solvers:

There are indications that the work week will be shorter in years to come. Let us assume that you only have to work twenty hours a week for your full-time job and that you can bargain with your employer for the organization of the time you put in for him. You must present a logical case. Prepare for your appointment with your boss so that you can respond to questions such as these: (1) "Will this schedule be most beneficial for the company?" (2) "How will this proposed schedule keep you in constant touch with our aims and policies?" For your own benefit, think about the following questions. How will you spend the other time you have? Will you take up a new hobby? Learn a new skill? Discuss your plans with a friend.

FOR FURTHER READING

Croft, Doreen J., and Robert D. Hess. *An Activities Handbook for Teachers of Young Children*. 2d ed. Boston: Houghton Mifflin, 1975.

Gannit, Walter V. "Occupational Preparation in the Elementary School." *Educational Leadership* 28 (January 1971): 359-63.

Hoyt, Kenneth B., et al. *Career Education and the Elementary School Teacher.* Salt Lake City, Utah: Olympus. Available in paperback.

Linder, Bertram L., and Edwin Selzer. *Your Work and Your Career.* New York: W. H. Sadlier, 1975.

Lorton, Mary Baratta. *Activity-Centered Learning for Early Childhood Education*. Menlo Park, Calif.: Addison-Wesley, 1972.

Ryan, Charles W. *Career Education Program (Grades K-6)*. Boston: Houghton Mifflin.

Shaftel, Fannie R., and George Shaftel. *Role-Playing for Social Values.* Englewood Cliffs, N.J.: Prentice-Hall, 1967.

ECOLOGY

This topic requires an integration of subject content in order to solve a problem. Students can become directly involved in the complexities of a real-life problem that encompasses the questions of energy shortage, pollution, food shortage, pesticides, conservation of resources and wildlife, and land and water use. "Ecology is an integrative science which uses, as its tools, the findings from isolated or factionated scientific disciplines and weaves its analyses into unique, comprehensive explanations."[20]

One can view the overall ecological system as extremely complex and therefore unapproachable, or as a more understandable living system whose component facets can be examined.

20. Martha C. Sager, "Ecological Balance of Planet Earth," *Social Education* 35 (1971): 47.

Ecosphere curriculum design

> One way of viewing the earth is in terms of its great envelopes: the lithosphere, pertaining to the nonliving solid earth; the atmosphere, describing the nonliving gaseous envelope; the hydrosphere, designating the nonliving aquatic aspect; and the biosphere, including all the living organisms taken as a whole, exclusive of the nonliving environment. The envelope of the mind, or 'neosphere' to encompass the collective human mind of the earth, or the 'thinking layer,' is now being accepted as another of the earth's spheres.[21]

If one studies ecology from the broad ecosphere perspective, a curriculum can be developed that presents the topic in a systematic fashion and provides an opportunity for the student to examine one facet of the topic. The unit design that follows is especially useful when one is considering a topic that, like ecology, has many facets. It gives the teacher a structured organization of resource materials and a defined sequence at the same time as it provides the student with a range of topics and guides him in locating and using relevant sources and materials. It also systematically provides for social interaction and student/teacher evaluation.

Figure 6.6 presents the basic flow chart for the ecology curriculum design. It shows the general sequence of steps in a complete cycle for the initial introduction of ecology to the final student presentation of information and findings on his chosen subtopic.

The specific examples of the development of the multi-media network expand the flow chart into Figure 6.7.

General introductory stimulus

A film or field trip can be used effectively from which the entire group may develop certain research categories. (The Taba technique of list, group, and categorize is useful here.[22] For the unit on ecospheres, resources for the following anticipated categories should be collected: hydrosphere, biosphere, atmosphere, lithosphere, and Neosphere. Children occasionally suggest other categories of interest to them and a collection of resources dealing with a new topic is manageable and is readily accomplished. In this connection a media specialist and/or librarian are extremely helpful.

21. Helmut K. Buechner, "An Ecosystem Approach to a Livable Environment for Man" (Paper presented to the National Council for the Social Studies in New York, 1970).

22. A series of tasks were developed by Hilda Taba in research dealing with children's thinking processes. Task 1 deals with concept formation, and in order to aid children in the formation of social studies concepts the following process was delineated: (1) listing what was seen, (2) grouping together items that are similar, and (3) categorizing the collection or group. For more detail see Hilda Taba, *Teacher's Handbook for Elementary Social Studies* (Reading, Mass.: Addison-Wesley, 1972).

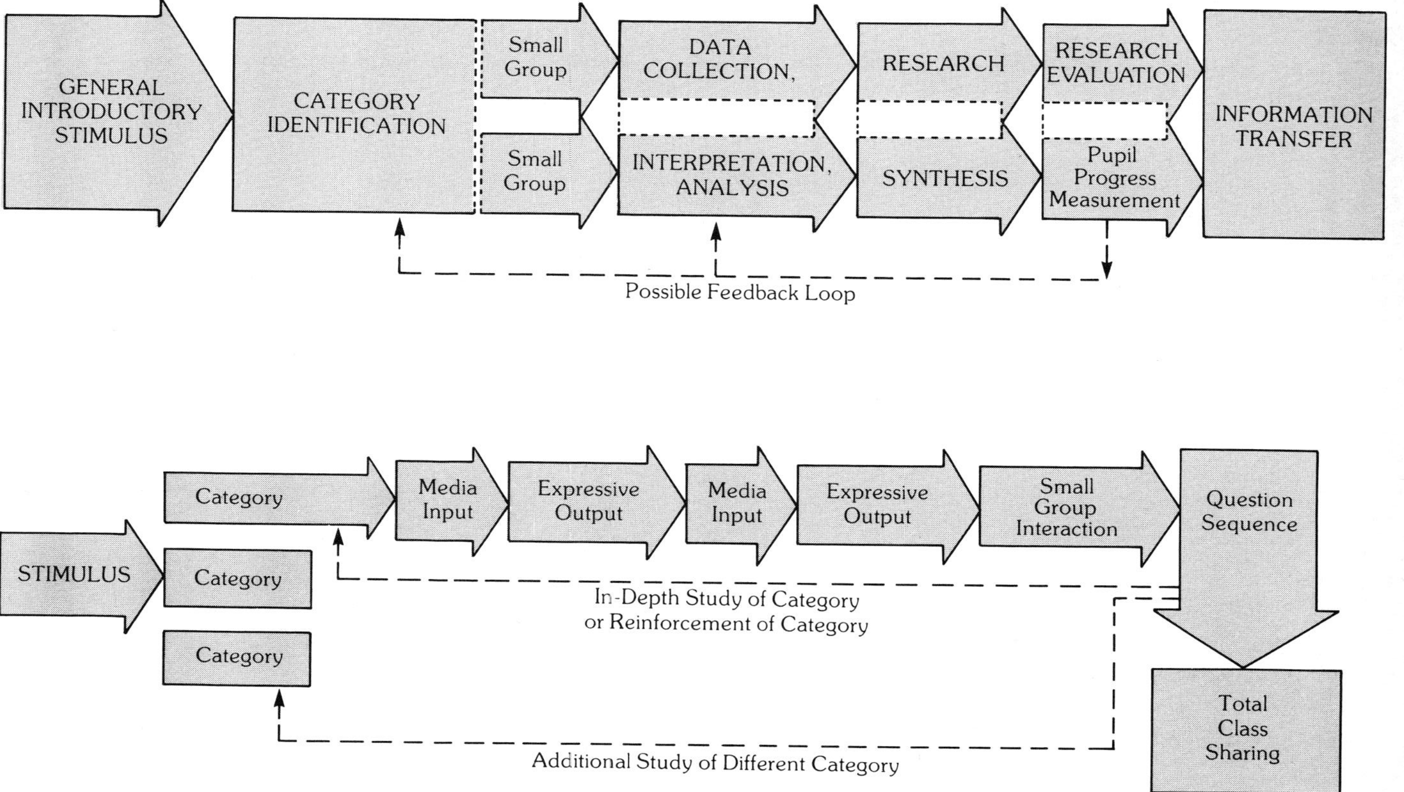

FIGURE 6.6 A Systematic Approach to Curriculum Design

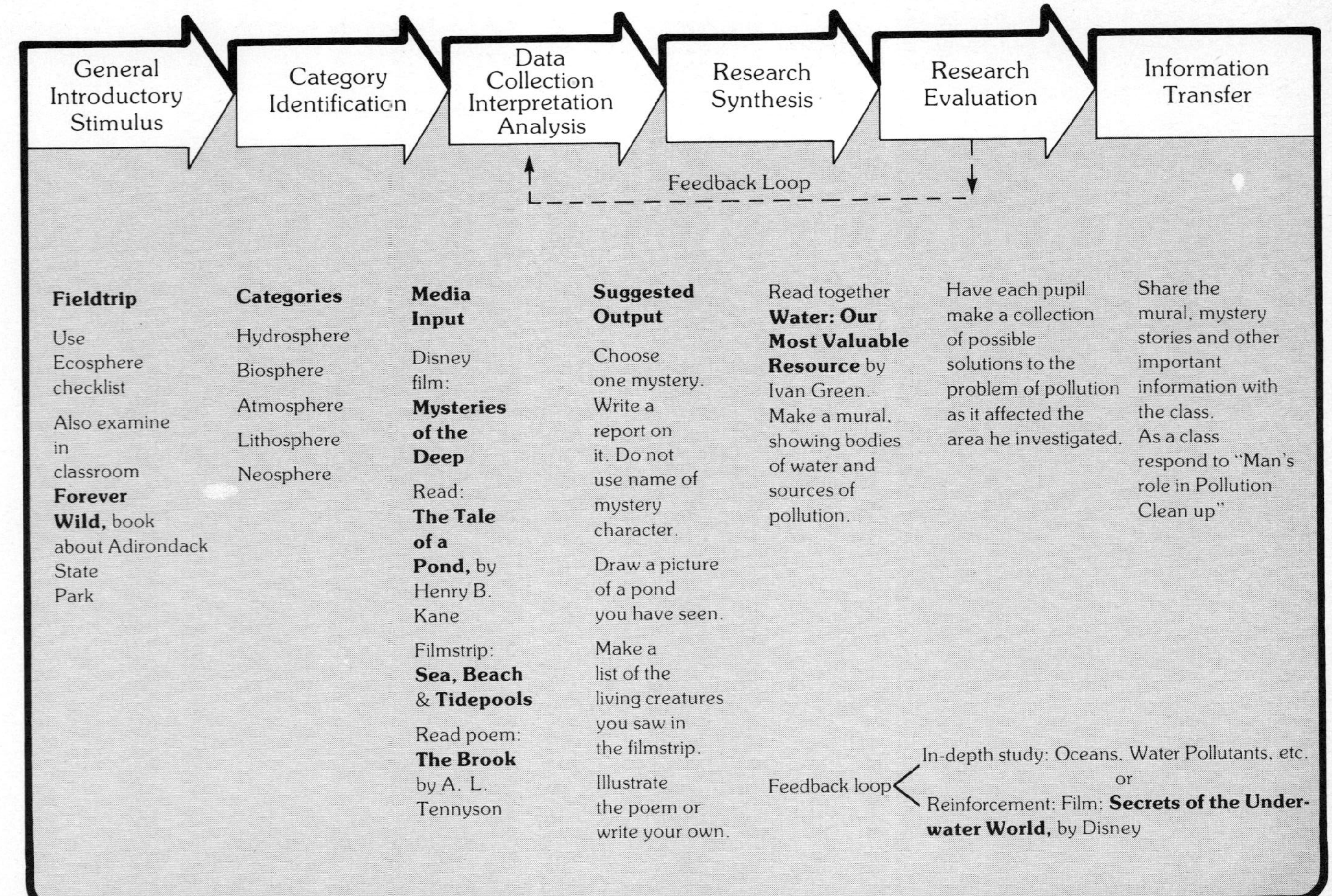

FIGURE 6.7. A Specific Systematic Approach to Curricular Design

An ecosphere field trip checklist is provided for use as a follow-up to a field trip in the vicinity of the school. When you return from the field trip you will be ready to use this checklist. It can be completed as a total class project or reproduced and filled in by each child separately. If the checklist shows that existing conditions are detrimental to the environment, the teacher may wish to help the students gather additional data and plan a course of action for improving the area.

Data collection, interpretation, and analysis

There are two stages of data collection for each category (e.g., hydrosphere, etc.). First, the concrete data pertaining to the concept are collected by the members of the groups; then, after the small group interaction and pupil progress evaluation stage, some of the students may wish to collect more or different data about their topic.

During each stage of the data collection, a child goes through a sequence of similar steps using different media. The sequence is somewhat arbitrary and depends on the teacher's preference. Some teachers allow the children to use the media when and where they wish, rather than in a specified sequence. Others follow a strict sequence of media utilization. The approach may depend partly on the class members and their ability to carry out independent research.

After a child uses the audiovisual media (film, book, opaque projector, etc.), expressive output is suggested. Here again there is a wide range of freedom in the extent to which the teacher may specify the desired output. Some teachers allow the students to design their own expressive activities and to follow them through. Others suggest a few specific activities and require the children to follow them.

Research synthesis and evaluation

After each child in a group has completed the sequence of activities in the data collection phase, the group meets to coordinate the material it has collected. The teacher serves as a small group specialist when directing the group's activity.

When the group has completed the collection and synthesis of materials pertaining to the category being studied, an evaluation is carried out. This may be in the form of

1. a sequence of questions dealing with a content emphasis. For example:
   Describe the different kinds of water pollutants you saw.
   What are some of the water resources of the United States?
   What is the effect of too much raw sewage being poured into a river?

ECOSPHERE FIELD TRIP CHECKLIST

Biosphere

What living things did you see?

1. What types of plants and trees grow here?

Plants:

Grasses ☐ Small bushes and shrubs ☐
Flowers ☐ Hay or grains ☐

Trees:

Birches	☐	Cedars	☐	Pines and firs	☐
Maples	☐	Oaks	☐	Elms	☐

2. What type of vertebrae live here?

Birds:

Pigeons	☐	Swallows	☐	Crows	☐
Sparrows	☐	Robins	☐	Chickens	☐
Bluejays	☐	Pheasants	☐	Other	☐

Reptiles:

Snakes ☐

Amphibians:

Frogs	☐	Salamanders	☐	Toads	☐

Mammals:

Squirrels	☐	Mice, rats	☐	Deer	☐
Chipmunks	☐	Rabbits	☐	Skunks	☐

Man ☐ (number in your range of vision) Porcupines ☐

Over 200 ☐ 50-200 ☐ Under 50 ☐

Fish: (list kind if you saw any living fish)

3. What types of living things did you see?

Mosquitoes	☐	Spiders	☐	Ticks	☐
Flies	☐	Fleas	☐	Bees and hornets	☐

Hydrosphere

What water did you see?

☐ Ocean ☐ Lake ☐ Pond ☐ River ☐ Stream

Water movement:

☐ Rapid ☐ Sluggish ☐ Trickle ☐ Stagnant

Appearance:

☐ Clean ☐ Brown ☐ Murky ☐ Green with algae ☐ Black and thick

Refuse:

☐ None ☐ Little ☐ Some around edges ☐ Floating away from shore ☐ Clogged with refuse

What methods are used to keep water pure?

Screens	☐	Chlorination	☐	Aeration	☐
Debris raked	☐	Pipes	☐	Forced air	☐
Grid chamber	☐	Bed of stones	☐	Other	☐
Raw sludge removal	☐				

Atmosphere

What did you see when you looked at the sky?

Blue, clear sky ☐ Cloudy ☐ Hazy ☐ Smoke from smokestacks ☐

Lithosphere (pertaining to nonliving solid earth)

What types of soil did you see?

Dark and rich ☐ Sandy ☐ Clay ☐ Hardpack and bare ☐

Covered with vegetation ☐ Scarcely covered ☐ Bare ☐

What types of rocks did you see?

Sandstone ☐ Igneous ☐ Granite ☐ Shale ☐ Other ☐

Neosphere (the "thinking layer" of the earth)

What man-made things did you see?

Means of transportation:

Cars	☐	Streetcars	☐	Bicycles, motorbikes	☐
Buses	☐	Planes	☐	Other	☐
Trains	☐	Horses	☐		

Factories for production of goods:

Clothing	☐	Steel mills	☐	Canning	☐
Shoes	☐	Oil refineries	☐	Car	☐
Pulp mills	☐	Chemical plants	☐	Other	☐

Dwellings:

Homes	☐	Duplex	☐
Farms	☐	Apartments (many stories)	☐

Stores:

Clothing	☐	Drug stores	☐	Furniture	☐
Food	☐	Hardware	☐	Restaurant	☐
Sports	☐	Music	☐	Other	☐

2. a problem situation that demands a solution. For example:

   The country of Egypt has little water. Several dams have been built to save the spring rains for later use; still, much of the water rushes down from the upper Nile and is wasted before the dry season begins. The dams also keep back much of the valuable top soil, which washed down over the fields in the Nile valley and served as a natural fertilizer. What solutions can you suggest to this new problem?

3. a social problem situation requiring personal identification and involvement. For example:

   The people in a certain state wish to dispose of their garbage. They do not wish to pollute the lake that separates them from the adjoining states. Therefore, under careful regulations, they burn their garbage. The prevailing winds carry the stench of the burning garbage for miles at night and is now interfering with tourism in the neighboring state as well as bothering the natives. What action may be taken by the offender? the offended?

The performance of each child is cooperatively assessed by the teacher and student and a decision is reached about the need for reinforcement or the possibility of an in-depth study of a related topic chosen by the student.

Reemphasis or in-depth study—feedback loop

Following the decision regarding the child's performance, he again goes through the data collection, interpretation, and analysis step. During the second stage of data collection, he either reinforces or extends his previous study. In the former case he uses new media that reinforce the category he has previously studied. In the latter he either makes an in-depth study of the same concept or he chooses a new category for study.

Group information exchange

Different ways of exchanging information have been devised by teachers. Some have each child present a brief report to the class and others encourage the children to devise their own method of presenting information to the class. These techniques include the presentation of plays, puppet shows, songs, or reports using visuals the children have made. Some individuals develop a pupil specialty. Some teachers collect information by conducting class discussions in which they emphasize the major ideas presented for each concept.

Alternative ecology curricular proposals

The program or unit is comprehensive and deals with the entire ecology topic. There are other ways to introduce the topic and provide a somewhat more direct experience oriented emphasis for children. In some cases only a few specific activities are suggested; they should serve as examples to stimulate the thinking of the reader.

Developing one topic as an example. It is possible to select one facet from a related collection of issues, such as:

Endangered species
Energy shortage
Pollution
Natural resources: use and misuse
Pesticides
Population explosion
Food needs

Once the topic is singled out, the teachers and students must then seek creative ways to explore the various aspects of the topic. Let us select an example and explore it here.

Topic: Pollution
Subtopics
- Air pollution
- Water pollution
- Earth pollution
- Noise pollution
- Pollution of living things

Select one subtopic
- Air pollution

The schema presented in Table 6.1 will give an introduction to the sources of air pollution, its source as well as proposed solutions. Much more development is needed in each cell of the matrix, and the expansion of the data in the matrix becomes the basis for research. Polluted air in turn pollutes water, land, and living things.

Add to the matrix suggestions for some *direct-experience* activities to develop further the air pollution subtopic. One experiment would be:

TABLE 6.1 MATRIX

POLLUTERS	MEANS OF POLLUTION	POSSIBLE SOLUTIONS
People	Cars Oil burners Burning waste	1. Instigate concern 2. Walk, use bikes, join car pools 3. Do not burn waste 4. Use electric heat
Community and city	Industry Mass transportation Burning waste	1. Create anti-pollution laws 2. Create mass transit system to eliminate pollution (e.g., electric cars) 3. Create better methods to dispose of waste
National and international	Industry Destruction of national forests Use of poisonous gases in wartime International transport	1. Give money for research to develop pollution controls 2. Create more national parks, reforest large areas 3. Change priorities from war to universal survival 4. Get international anti-pollution laws

Smear several glass slides with Vaseline. Place them in several different areas in and around the school. Leave them for a few days. Collect and place on a piece of clean, white paper under a bright light, or use a microscope and study them. Compare the slides. Make a sketch of the school and number the places where the various slides were placed. In which area was the air the dirtiest?

Additional activities include:

1. The automobile is a major source of air pollution. Observe a downtown area during rush hour. Could you see evidence of slow-moving traffic contributing to air pollution? What evidence was there? Draw a picture of what you saw.
2. Go to a local manufacturing plant and ask the plant manager to explain the method used by the plant to control smoke emission. Take notes and make a report to the class. (This, of course, must be carefully cleared with plant and school administrative authorities by the teacher.)
3. Visit a garage and talk to the mechanic there. Ask him to explain pollution control devices for automobiles. Draw a side view of one and an outside view of the same device.
4. Write a research paper about smokestack screening devices. How do such devices help protect people? What problems are involved in their use?

Supporting a general statement. Now let us use an example of a different facet of ecology to illustrate how a more deductive approach could also be used effectively. The teacher may present the student with a series of generalizations, and the students working either singly or in small groups can gather evidence that will elaborate on and refute or support the statement. The students may present lists, pictures, skits, or real-life examples to expand the idea and clarify the statement they select. Some examples on the topic of *Natural Resources* would be:

1. People use natural resources to satisfy their needs and wants.
2. Some natural resources are not replaceable.
3. There are some natural resources that can be replaced with careful planning.
4. Some natural resources are abundant.
5. The amount and kind of natural resources available in a society influence the way of life of the people in that society.
6. Over a period of time the demand for specific natural resources changes.
7. Conservation is the wise management of resources and is necessary for the general public.

Carrying out ecology activities. It is also possible to build a series of activity cards that students can carry out on a largely independent basis. A few examples to focus their attention on the ecology topic include:

1. Build an ecology library of books, materials, pamphlets, film sources, etc., for the whole school to use. Plan to write for materials, and organize and catalog the materials. Set up a special display table, and give volunteer lectures to other classes explaining the materials that are available.
2. Develop with the students an ecology vocabulary. Have each student develop a booklet in which he records the words that are new to him. Plan a weekly sharing session for ecology vocabulary growth.
3. Recycling project: Organize efforts to collect glass or newspapers or tin cans, find a recycling plant, and make the necessary arrangements to organize the "drive" and to get materials transported to the plant.
4. Visit a park on a nice day. Observe carefully the people within viewing range. Make one list of the things they do that show care for the ecosphere and another of things they do that harm the ecosphere.
5. Explore a "chain of change" in the ecosphere. Select an object to study carefully—for example, a new apartment building being built near you, or a new automobile that your parents have just bought. Make a list of resources required to produce this object. Make another list showing the people and other systems that will be affected by the object now that it is produced.

Participating in outdoor education projects. Still another way to acquaint the students with the ecological problems around us is to involve them in an outdoor living experience. This requires planning similar to that for a field trip, but more extensive. There are several reasons for developing an outdoor education program.

1. Resources are abundant. Many different ecology systems are available for direct investigation.
2. The investigations that take place are based on observation, reading, research, and comparisons. Such inquiry-oriented learning has a lasting impact.
3. There are many opportunities to interact with other students and adults. The setting is informal and the atmosphere allows many special talents and new friendships to emerge.
4. Positive attitudes about the environment and about learning as well are an outgrowth of a successful outdoor education program.

Because of the outdoor living experience, ecology discussions take on more meaning, and action suggestions can be more carefully and realistically explored. Activities can be planned to take place before, during, and after the experience to give maximum mileage to the effort.

FOR FURTHER READING

Books

Miles, Betty. *Save the Earth: An Ecology Handbook for Kids*. New York: Alfred A. Knopf, 1974. An excellent source of simple, practical projects and information for ages 7 to 11.

Peters, Richard O. *How to Teach About Human Beings and their Environment.* How-to-Do Series. Arlington, Va.: National Council for the Social Studies, 1976. A number of practical classroom activities are provided here, along with an extensive, useful bibliography.

Sale, Larry L., and Ernest W. Lee. *Environmental Education in the Elementary School.* New York: Holt, Rinehart & Winston, 1972. This 200-page paperback provides extensive material for use in the classroom and highly useful factual information for the teacher.

Walsh, Huber M., ed. "The Environment." *Social Education* 35 (January 1971): 57–83. Four articles on ecology with many valuable references to government and private organization sources of materials.

Other Materials

Eco-News. Environmental Action Coalition Inc., 235 East 49th St., New York, N.Y. 10017. An eight-page monthly subscription newsletter oriented to today's urban children, grades 4 to 6. Each issue explores a different environmental problem children will recognize.

Ecology: Nature and Needs (grade 4); *Habits and Habitats* (grade 5); *Problems and Progress* (grade 6). Xerox Education Publications, Education Center, Columbus, Ohio 43216. Each booklet is forty-eight pages. Check cost.

Litter-Prevention, a First Step to Improve the Environment. Keep America Beautiful, Inc., 99 Park Avenue, New York, N.Y. 10016. This is a guide of suggested litter-prevention activities for elementary schools. It presents ideas for the classroom, for schoolwide projects, and for community action. Free.

To Save the Earth. Educational Services, National Wildlife Federation, 1412 16th St., N.W., Washington, D.C., 20036. This is an action guide for improving our environment; describes how one class and teacher can make an environment quality survey of their own area. Free.

Air Pollution. National Wildlife Federation (see address above). Written in story form especially for young children, explaining some of the major causes of air pollution. Offers suggestions for the kind of things they could do to become involved. Free.

Outline for Teaching Conservation in Elementary Schools. U.S. Department of Agriculture, Soil Conservation Service, Information Division, Washington, D.C. 20250. A concise, practical guide that teachers can readily adapt to urban, suburban, or rural schools. Objectives are suggested for each grade level. Free.

IMPROVING PUPIL INVOLVEMENT BY EXPLORING ATTITUDES AND VALUES

Chapter seven

"Attitudes are learned, emotionally toned predispositions to react in a consistent way, favorable or unfavorable, towards persons, objects, situations or ideas."[1] Attitudes and values are based on both the information the individual has assimilated and the emotional response specific stimuli evoke. Klausmeier and Ripple differentiate between tastes, attitudes, and values in this way: tastes are specific and temporary; attitudes are more complex and somewhat more lasting; and values are general and relatively permanent. It is almost as if these components were placed on a "change specific/generic" continuum from specific and easiest to change to most general or complex and most difficult to change. For example, one might presently have a taste for reading about the Napoleonic Wars, have a positive attitude toward learning French History, and value history generally. Over a period of time the individual's taste may change and he may prefer Ancient Chinese History, have a positive attitude toward Oriental History and history generally, and still value history and reading historical accounts.

In this chapter, we are especially concerned with the more general and more lasting attitudes and values that students possess and with helping to develop positive attitudes in children. If one is to do this, a number of factors must be considered. First, it is necessary to determine what positive attitudes or attitude clusters need to be developed. Second, it is necessary to decide on the strategy for developing or changing the attitude clusters defined. To make this second decision, the following subideas

1. Herbert J. Klausmeier, and Richard E. Ripple *Learning and Human Abilities* (New York: Harper and Row, 1975), p. 518.

must be considered: (1) the amount and kind of information and emotional persuasion that is provided; (2) the kind of group setting in which the information is given; (3) the extent of acquaintance of members of the group; (4) whether the attitude involved is being reinforced, or whether the individual is being given information that is inconsistent with his present thinking; and (5) the amount of time that is allowed for developing, exploring, and deciding about the topic under consideration. If a rapid barrage of information is provided in an emotional one-sided manner for a large group where none of the members know each other, and the information is contrary to the strongly held opinions of some of the members, these members may become more certain that their point of view is the reasonable one and that the other party point of view is erroneous. Time to assimilate, a comfortable group setting, and some opportunity to interact and explore ideas has more potential for producing change than the opposite conditions.

With these general ideas in mind, let us examine some value areas and develop both definition and practical classroom implementation suggestions for personal, democratic, economic, and moral and ethical values.

PERSONAL VALUES

In the personal value category one would explore the individual's feelings about himself, his self-concept, and his notions about his place in society as he relates to others. "As one grows he identifies himself according to sex, race, physical appearance, achievement and the like. He also evaluates himself. His self-description and evaluation comprise his self-concept."[2]

Listening to this first grader: "See what I can do. I can run and jump. I look good. I feel good. There is nothing wrong with me," one would assume that the child has a positive self-concept. The self-concept is the impression one has of his physical, mental, emotional, and social selves. Jersild says, "The self includes, among other things, a system of ideas, attitudes, values, and commitments. The self is a person's total subjective environment; it is the distinctive center of experience and significance. The self constitutes a person's inner world as distinguished from the outer world consisting of all other people and things."[3]

The inner self is strongly affected by the society in which one lives. Self-concept, then, is developed as the individual compares himself to others and to inferred cultural expectations. Failure to measure up to cultural expectations produces low self-esteem. A high-school dropout says, "I really haven't done anything, but I

2. Klausmeier and Ripple, *Learning*, p. 219.

3. Arthur T. Jersild, *In Search of Self: An Exploration of the School in Promoting Self-Understanding* (New York: Columbia Univ. Press, 1952), p. 8.

would be somebody anyway if I had finished high school." Another one says, "I am seventeen and in the tenth grade, and I still don't read good. And when you can't read, you soon get discouraged."

There is nothing inherently wrong with not finishing high school; thousands of people have not finished high school, and could not, or cannot, read. But this boy feels personally inadequate because of his failure ("I haven't done anything") In the cultural setting in which he lives, this demonstration of skill is deemed important. Because he cannot provide this demonstration of knowledge and skill, the student feels less than adequate as a person. He has a poor self-concept.

Unfortunately, the example cited is not an isolated one. Many people feel inadequate because of academic failure and many others feel inadequate socially or in terms of physical appearance or accomplishment.

> The base for inadequacy is the comparison between the cultural standard that surrounds the individual and his own estimate of how well he measures up. It is clear that either the cultural standard or the individual's estimate could be changed to bring about a more positive self-concept.[4]

The individual estimate is probably easier to change on a short-range basis, since the cultural standard of a large group would shift more slowly.

How can the school help the student to clarify his personal value category? The school deals with children and young people who are just beginning to identify themselves as unique human beings. If they are going to come to terms with plurality and change in society, students will need a strong, positive image of themselves as individuals. The school can provide information and opportunities for the students to examine their feelings about self; in so doing it may help these individuals build positive self-concepts. The teacher who deals with sensitive areas such as self-concept should use care and consideration with each student involved. Embarrassing situations and naïve exposure of student problems should be avoided.

Self-concept

The brief unit that follows is designed to aid the classroom teacher in a beginning self-concept emphasis.[5] It is clear that a positive picture of self does not develop on command at the conclusion of a sequence of activity. Long-term examination of self and a continuous building of self-confidence will be needed for the student to develop a positive self-concept.

4. Diane Lapp et al., *Teaching and Learning* (New York: Macmillan, 1975).

5. Adapted from John F. Cuber, Martha Tyler John, and Kendrick S. Thompson, "Should Traditional Sex Modes and Values Be Changed?" *Controversial Issues in the Social Studies: A Contemporary Perspective*, 45th Yearbook (Arlington, Va.: National Council for the Social Studies, 1975), Chap. 3.

Who am I?

INSTRUCTIONAL TASKS

I. Identify unit objectives. (Initial activity should motivate and provide definition.) An activity may take one or more class sessions depending on the amount of information covered and the age level of the children involved in the exercise.

INSTRUCTIONAL ACTIVITIES

I. Complete all of these activities:

A. Use the record "Free to Be You and Me" and the filmstrip *The Joy of Being You*. Discuss these. (See student bibliography, p. 228.)

B. Have three or four "This Is Your Life" presentations of well-known individuals by students who have had an opportunity to prepare carefully the data in advance. (Presentations might vary, including overhead sequence, skit, radio, tape. Should include persons from different ethnic backgrounds.)

C. Provide a number of books about people who are well-known in different fields of endeavor. Samples should include representations from several ethnic backgrounds, and people who have overcome physical handicaps. These books can be read independently by students as follow-up of the filmstrip/record presentation. (See p. 229 for some suggestions.)

INSTRUCTIONAL TASKS

II. Provide information input and an opportunity for concept formation and a base for data collection and organization. (This one activity may be spread over several days.)

INSTRUCTIONAL ACTIVITIES

II. A. Review the materials used previously. Have a heading on the board or chart, "PEOPLE." Point out that *people* refers to all ages, sizes, races, nationalities. Encourage the students to contribute a variety of ideas to each list as the class builds it. Now place subheadings on the board and collect ideas from the students to fill them in. Here are some suggestions that you may add to or change to fit your objectives. (These become How People Look, etc.)

1. Look
2. Feel
3. Communicate
4. Learn
5. Work
6. Play
7. Plan for the Future

B. When the board or chart is completed, have each student on a sheet of paper change the word PEOPLE in the heading to I. (So these become How I Look, etc.) Then have each student describe each category in some detail privately with you. This will not be shared with the class.

INSTRUCTIONAL TASKS	INSTRUCTIONAL ACTIVITIES
III. Provide for an exploration of problem areas and the negative feelings that accompany the problems.	III. A. Have the class review the subcategories that have been explored before. Read excerpts from stories that deal with handicapped individuals, children who are fat, tall for their group. Use the Shaftel and Shaftel (1967) role-playing stories on being rejected or left out, on being different from the group.
	B. Now explore each category. Jot down problems that bother people about "Looks," for example. Use the original list of specific items, but do not feel limited to it, nor bound to a one-to-one match of problem to item. Some may be skipped, some added.
	C. Refer back to activity II. B. Have each student examine his list of "I"s. Instruct each student to identify problem areas individually as was done above in III. B. with the group.
IV. Use group interaction to define and explore possible improvements.	IV. A. Divide the class into small groups. Have each group take the responsibility for suggesting solutions to the problems in one category. Allow time for discussion of feelings about the problems, but ask for specific solutions in a list from each group at the conclusion of their discussion.
	B. Complete the chart or collect on the board the group suggestions for dealing with PEOPLE problem areas.
V. Arrange for specific action component. (Providing practice helps stabilize the attitude.)	V. A. On single sheets of paper have each student thoughtfully select one self-concept component in which he is most interested. Have each student specify his present level of achievement and the goal for the future self. (Keep the projections within the realm of reality.)
	B. Instruct the students in drawing flow charts, and then have each one draw a sequence of steps that will lead to the final goal he has just described. Have each student select a first step that is a small increment in which he will surely succeed. Positive reinforcement is important. For example:

Toward a More Physically Attractive Me

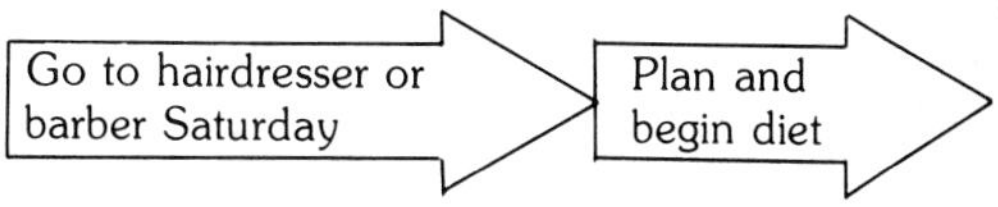

Go to hairdresser or barber Saturday → Plan and begin diet

INSTRUCTIONAL TASKS	INSTRUCTIONAL ACTIVITIES
	C. Allow each student to select a partner to help him carry out his initial steps and to serve in a "Buddy" check system later, or have each student keep a "New Me" diary in which he records progress in dealing with a problem area.
VI. Develop positive feelings about self while working on the improvement plan.	VI. A. Have the students form an informal circle. Have them select a person on whom to focus their attention.
	B. Suggest that each student make a positive comment about that one person. Perhaps tell something about the person that you think others would not know. (Some teachers call this the "Magic Circle" technique.)
	C. Be sure to keep the "positive" statement rule operating, and then summarize the ideas submitted.
	D. Carry this out with each member of the class. (Probably several days or brief sessions for several weeks will be required.) The self-improvement plan will have enough time to begin to show results.
VII. Suggest other areas in which the participants may apply the strategy on an individual basis. (The individual may be able to utilize the process in modifying other attitudes that he wishes to change.)	VII. A. Have students write about, draw, or otherwise express the most important thing they learned in the unit.
	B. Ask each student to think about the next problem area he wishes to deal with.

STUDENT BIBLIOGRAPHY

Dimensions of Personality. Elementary Grade Series. Dayton, Ohio: Pflaum, 1972.

Thomas, Marlo. *Free to Be You and Me*. New York: McGraw Hill, 1974.

The Triple I Series. Grades 1–6 (Self-Identity). New York: American Book, 1970. Includes emphasis on minority groups.

Family

One's own family is usually thought of as part of a personal value system. For a long time we studied the family from a limited perspective. Materials have now been developed that help the child to explore the family from a more realistic point of view. One-parent families, families with adopted children, as well as the extended family and the variety of nuclear families, are all part of the emphasis that new materials provide. The sample of recent books listed below are high-interest low-vocabulary books that will hold even the poor readers' interest. For further information write Raintree Editions, a Division of Advanced Learning Concepts, Inc., 205 West Highland Avenue, Milwaukee, Wis. 53203.

Feelings Between Brothers and Sisters, Conta and Reardon
Big Sister, Little Brother, Berger
A New Baby, Berger
Are We Still Best Friends?, Barkin and James
Feelings Between Friends, Conta and Reardon
A Friend Can Help, Berger
I'd Rather Stay Home, Barkin and James
Sometimes I Hate School, Barkin and James
Being Alone, Being Together, Berger

DEMOCRATIC VALUES

The second values cluster that influences our thinking can be described as our democratic beliefs. We are concerned with learning, living, and practicing the ways of democracy. Democracy is a way of doing things with other people. Living in a democracy implies action that evidences the acceptance of responsibility. The good citizen has certain positive attitudes:

Is aware of the importance of meeting basic human needs and is concerned with the extension of the essentials of life to more individuals.
Gives allegiance to the ideals of democracy.
Practices the kinds of human relationships that are consistent with a democratic society.
Recognizes social problems and endeavors to help solve them.
Possesses and uses knowledges, skills, and abilities to facilitate the process of democratic living.[6]

Donald W. Robinson, director of the Civic Education Project of the National Council for the Social Studies, says "no citizen in any age can be complete if his citizenship training does not include these four factors:

gaining information or knowledge
learning how to use that knowledge analytically—to think
having appropriate feelings or affective reactions
taking some kind of action as a citizen.

6. Stanley E. Dimond, *Schools and the Development of Good Citizens* (Detroit: Wayne Univ. Press, 1953), p. 37.

Civic competence is based on information that comes to students from a wide variety of sources and in many different ways, but receiving information is only the first step in civic education. Considerable disagreement may exist on *how* needed citizenship skills, understandings, and attitudes can and should be developed. Democracy can only be learned by being experienced.

Among the ways to get at the meaning of democracy are:

1. *Study of the beginnings and growth of democracy,* especially in our own national history. Children should understand that it is more than a heritage, for it "must be won anew by each generation." It is not likely that democracy will be studied as a separate unit: the historical elements in it will be material used in other units, problems, or topics. The specific use and grade placement of activities will depend upon the maturation level of the children and the curricular content they have had or are having. Point out any facts of democracy as they arise in social studies and in daily living.
2. *Development of patriotic feelings and appreciations.* The pledge of allegiance, the national anthem and patriotic songs, dramatization, television programs, appreciation of the contributions of those who have come before us, realization that common folk as well as famous men and women were important in our history, the love of our land, and concern for the disadvantaged are all constituent parts of patriotism and ways of getting at some meanings of democracy.
3. *Direct approach to an analysis of the characteristic elements of democracy.* What should democracy mean to boys and girls in the elementary school? Just what elements compose the democratic idea and ideal? An attempt has been made to state the fundamental principles of democracy in words that can be understood by middle-grade pupils. The illustrative examples are merely suggestive, many on the level of childhood experiences. They should be greatly expanded in discussion with children, and further applications should be made to wider areas of American living.

The democratic ideal

MEANINGS	ILLUSTRATIVE EXAMPLES
Democracy means respect for the individual.	
We are always willing that others should have the same rights and privileges that we claim for ourselves.	Do not ask for special privileges; no special "rules" for others that do not apply to ourselves.
We want every individual to feel free to take part with his group in deciding what to do.	Give proper consideration to each person's suggestions; allow each one to take part.
Each person should have the opportunity to develop himself to the best of his ability.	In school, share duties and opportunities with all; provide opportunities for all kinds of talent and ability.

MEANINGS	ILLUSTRATIVE EXAMPLES
We cultivate the habits and manners of ladies and gentlemen for they show our consideration of others.	Speak politely; do not call "names"; listen while others speak; do not make comments about appearance or looks; do not make fun of others who lack skills we may possess.
Those in authority will treat others under them fairly.	Teachers and pupil leaders do not play favorites; each one feels he is treated fairly.
Democracy means cooperation with others.	
Most of the work of the world is done through cooperation. People and nations are interdependent.	Many people make the things you want and buy. You depend upon others for food, safety, etc.
We work together to make life good for each person in the group—school, community, state, nation, world.	Older children look out for younger ones on the playground; share apparatus on public playground.
We believe that the good of all must be considered above personal interests.	Do not play radio and TV too loudly; obey rules about riding bicycles on sidewalk; behave properly in public places.
Successful social living depends upon getting along with others.	Be a good neighbor; take turns; be courteous even to those you do not like.
To be idle is to be unfair to others.	Take responsibility; do not slow up the work of the group by being idle.
We are willing to work for the common good.	Contribute ideas and talents on group projects; don't be selfish; be a team worker, not just an individual star.
We know that not all persons have equal abilities and we are willing to recognize the abilities of others.	Give up your chance to someone who will do a better job; give praise to the other person.
Democracy means productive thinking—thinking problems through in a way that results in helpful action for the good of all.	
It is important for people in a democracy to do group thinking.	Plan together for the success of school activities; think through ways of solving our problems together.
We should make decisions on the basis of all the known facts.	Distinguish between fact and opinion; gossips do not.
Discuss disputes or issues intelligently on the basis of facts, not feelings.	Discuss qualities of candidates for election, treatment of minority groups; discuss issues involved before voting on school activities.
Democracy means that free men have duties as well as rights; obligations as well as privileges.	
We must obey the laws of the land.	Obey city bicycle laws; pay taxes.

MEANINGS	ILLUSTRATIVE EXAMPLES
We must show good sportsmanship in yielding to the decision of the majority.	No hard feelings and willingness to do what the majority wants.
Each has a duty to participate in the work of a democracy.	Do not let the other fellow do the work just because he is willing; no shirking.
Each should be willing to work with his greatest skill on whatever work his fellows assign him for the good of all.	Do willingly the assignment made by a committee chairman.
Democracy means freedoms for people under its government that cannot be found in the government of a dictator.	
Freedom of worship.	Go to the church of your choice.
Freedom from want.	Charitable organizations.
Freedom of assembly.	Meetings of any group not forbidden.
Freedom of speech.	Criticism of unwise actions of public officials.
Freedom of the press.	Editors, not the government, decide what will be printed.
The right to trial by jury.	No trials by a secret police.
Freedom from search and seizure.	Police must have a warrant to make a search.
Rule by the majority.	Our laws are made by majority vote.
Rights of the minority.	Rights of criticism and freedom.
Universal education.	Public schools for all children.

Skills and techniques required for democratic action

The teacher might use the list below as a checklist. Read through the skills and techniques, decide which are suitable to the maturity level of your pupils, and then write opposite each one the opportunities your children have, or could have, for learning and practicing them. They are not to be considered as so many additional separate things to teach. If interpreted correctly they serve to indicate to the good teacher that certain emphases he is already making are contributing to learning skills and techniques needed for democratic living, and to reveal oversights and lack of emphasis in other directions. By the end of the sixth grade, a child should have a certain degree of ability in skills and techniques required as a member of a group, such as:

1. Sharing in discussion intelligently; participating in group thinking.
2. Maintaining an open-minded attitude in discussion.
3. Cooperating with others in work and play.
4. Cultivating attitudes of good will and service.

5. Choosing leaders wisely.
6. Participating in the government of the school.
7. Recognizing rights and property of others.
8. Appreciating the contribution of others to personal and group living.

Skills and techniques required in self-control and self-direction, such as:

1. Discovering certain tasks to be done.
2. Having respect for oneself and others.
3. Assuming personal responsibility.
4. Exercising initiative and making plans.
5. Carrying plans through to realization.
6. Having respect for authority.
7. Putting oneself in the other person's place.
8. Accepting civic duties.

Citizenship organizations in the school

If students come to value democratic ideals, they will need to have direct experience with these ideals. School should be a place where democratic techniques can be practiced—a small democracy in which children live. Abundant opportunities for pupil responsibility, initiative, and action exist in all of our schools and communities.

When a school is ready for it, some type of student council or other citizenship organization can be an effective agency. Every elementary school should have some kind of all-school council, league, or club.

Suggestions. In organizing a student council for the first time teachers need to set the stage by having children consider some worthy endeavors that should be undertaken for the good of the school or the community. Discussion as to the means to be used to accomplish these things will probably lead to suggestions of some type of pupil organization. The discussion phase of what to do and how to do it should be unhurried and thoroughly explored. Well-formed purposes must precede the initiation of the organization itself.

Active membership may be confined to the upper grades, but there should be representative membership of all grades. In line with the all-school student council, effective classroom organizations with their officers, even down through the first grade, are frequently formed.

The number and kind of officials, the constitution and by-laws, the committees, the frequency of meetings, and other features of the new organization are best determined by the nature of the local situation. It is better to start with as simple an organization as possible and add to its activities and officials as need arises than to start with a towering superstructure that may fall under its own weight.

To imitate in organization form a town or city government plan is usually not so effective as something more simple. Desirable activities for children do not coincide well with the activities of town and city departments and officials.

Pupil organizations should provide for the participation of as many children as possible in its affairs through the course of a year.

Reports from many schools all over the country show pupil citizenship clubs and student councils assuming responsibilities for:

1. Beautification of building and grounds.
2. Safety patrol.
3. Lost-and-found department.
4. Cooperatively planned assembly programs.
5. School newspaper.
6. Junior Red Cross.
7. Milk distribution and collection of money.
8. Committees for bicycles, lavatories, lunch room, fire drill, flag, care and repair of physical education supplies, school signs, publicity, ushering at assemblies.
9. Pupil assistants in school library.
10. Development of special clubs: photography, model airplanes, etc.
11. Raising funds for particular school purposes.
12. Active cooperation in various community enterprises.
13. Monitors and helpers for many purposes: bell, orchestra, bulletin boards, flower arrangements, attendance, ditto duplicating, operators and helpers in audio-visual aids.

Living democratically

Teachers have found the questions below helpful in their analyses of democratic living opportunities in their own schools. Teachers found where they stood in reference to *Complacency* (where not much is happening), to *Adaptation* (something valuable is beginning to happen), and to *Productive Action* (where positive answers show considerable democracy in action).

LEVEL OF COMPLACENCY

1. Is all building and classroom administration in the control of teachers and principal?
2. Are patriotic exercises in classroom and assembly a substitute for real action?

3. Is the learning of assigned lessons the only job for which the pupils feel responsible?
4. Is student government regarded as a useful tool for securing conformity to school rules and regulations established by teachers and administrators?
5. Do you believe that the teacher must do all the planning in order for the class to achieve satisfactory goals for the year?
6. Is there a tendency to practice for citizenship in years to come rather than to be active citizens now?

LEVEL OF ADAPTATION

1. Are children allowed to make group decisions only on those things you know will make little difference in your planning?
2. Are citizenship activities ever chosen on the basis of display or publicity value?
3. Do you appoint leaders and committees?
4. Do you have a student council or other pupil organizations because other schools do?
5. Did you form a pupil organization first and then cast around to find things for it to do?
6. Do you think it a good practice to pattern a student government plan after the form of the local community government?
7. Is there unquestioned acceptance by the other children of most suggestions made by the more aggressive members of the group?

LEVEL OF PRODUCTIVE ACTION

1. Do your pupils develop concern for the common welfare and then do something about it?
2. Do pupils learn the meaning of, and regularly practice, the delegation of authority, the division of labor, and cooperative undertaking by groups?
3. Have they formed any kind or kinds of citizenship organizations to accomplish certain purposes? Were the purposes thought through before any kind of organization was attempted?
4. Do your pupils apply the pronoun "we," not "they," to experiences in school?
5. Are pupils gaining experience in committee work and becoming accustomed to serving as leaders and to following leaders?
6. Are your student organizations allowed to make and carry out decisions about significant concerns to children?
7. Are student committees, conferences, elections, and reports looked upon as matters of major importance to teachers?
8. Are large numbers of students given an opportunity to participate in the government of the school community?

While all the questions above indicate some evaluation of democratic processes within the school, here are some further questions helpful in further evaluation.

LEVEL OF COMPLACENCY

1. Are children tested on what they have learned about democracy rather than on their own ways of living democratically?
2. Is there a tendency to say that you are "training for citizenship" without any attempt at real evaluation?
3. Is all the evaluation done by means of teacher-made paper-and-pencil tests and by subjective teacher judgments?
4. Do your grades and reports show results only in civic information and not growth in civic competency?

LEVEL OF ADAPTATION

1. Do you evaluate the results of pupils' activities and then give them your evaluation for further discussion?
2. Do you seek ways of testing civic competency without knowing exactly what you want as outcomes?
3. On report cards, do you give a grade in "Citizenship"?
4. Have you made checklists, anecdotal records, systematic observations, and so on, and then not known how to use the results?

LEVEL OF PRODUCTIVE ACTION

1. Do the pupils initiate and analyze their own activities to find out what qualities are needed for effective cooperation?
2. Are pupils developing their own criteria for standards of achievement as citizens?
3. Are the pupils constantly brought face to face with the necessity for judging their own experiences?
4. Have you overt evidence that the pupils respect the rights and opinions of others, no matter what their origins or creeds?
5. Have pupils observed, analyzed, and evaluated the benefits of democratic action in a specific experience of school and community life?

Building materials

Good teachers want good materials to help the students clarify the values they hold. There are books and other media that will aid in value clarification sessions. It is also possible for good teachers who are willing to commit time and effort to the task to create materials as they need them. The following is an example of a product designed by an experienced teacher who felt a need for special teaching aids in dealing with cooperation, a facet of democracy.

Working with Others. We have stressed the fact that the individual in a democracy is of great importance. While this is true, there are also "significant others" in each person's sphere. It is necessary to maintain balance between the self-expression of the free individual and the coercion of the organized group. This is more important as population increases. Helping others and learning to work together takes on real significance. Cooperation becomes an important goal. Teaching abstract democratic terminology, even ideology, to children may be virtually impossible. Teaching students to listen to others, to work together to solve problems is an approachable task.

Because Phillips[7] felt that students needed an opportunity to explore the dimensions of cooperation and to practice cooperating, he designed a study to examine this concept carefully. Each child was asked to tell or write "as many ways as you can in which people cooperate." (First graders responded orally and third and fifth graders responded in writing). Following is a small sample of the student answers:

First Grade

By doing things together
By playing together
Some person uses something, another person uses something, then they trade
By doing things right
Someone is in the sun eating ice cream and has a sweater on. It is too hot, someone holds the ice cream while she takes her sweater off

Third Grade

By listening to the teacher
By doing things together
By talking about things together
Marrying for love, kissing, hugging, squeezing
Building a puzzle together

Fifth Grade

Standing still when someone is hemming your slacks
To adjust to each other and help one another
Pay attention in class
Listen to what is said
When there is a blackout everybody starts helping everyone else

7. Wayne Phillips, "A Study of the Concept of Cooperation of First, Third and Fifth Grade Children in Public Elementary School" (Doctoral dissertation, Boston University, 1973).

A large number of the students defined cooperation in terms of authority, for example, "Doing what you're told." To help broaden their understanding of cooperation, a series of lessons were designed to explore tasks that should be done cooperatively. One activity shows the importance of cooperation in an assembly line task. Teams of five children each are used for the activity. One team divides the labor while the other team does not.

1. Children are first shown a pattern that is an 8½" × 5½" piece of white construction paper with five 2" × 2" pieces of different colored construction paper pasted on it. The objective of each of the teams is to duplicate as many of these patterns as possible within the given time period of five minutes.
2. On team one, each child receives enough construction paper and paste to duplicate the pattern as many times as possible within the given time period. The children of team two shall specialize, i.e., one takes the white paper and pastes on the red square, the following child pastes on the blue square, and so on until the fifth child pastes on the fifth square and stacks the finished product.
3. Both teams work for the same length of time and at the end of the demonstration, the group doing the individual construction totals their finished products while the assembly line does the same.
4. The class then discusses the advantages and disadvantages of the assembly line. (Each worker in the line had to develop only one skill; fewer tools for each person; less space is needed for each person; greater need for cooperation, for if one worker slows down or refuses to cooperate, the entire production will, in all likelihood, suffer.)

FOR FURTHER READING

Constitution of the United States. Community Relations Department, John Hancock Mutual Life Insurance Company, 200 Berkeley St., Boston, Mass. 02117. Text of the Constitution. Free.

How to Respect and Display Our Flag. Commandant of the Marine Corps, Headquarters, U.S. Marine Corps, Washington, D.C. 20380. This book tells the story of our flag. Free.

Kavett, Hyman. "How Do We Stand with the Pledge of Allegiance Today?" *Social Education* 40 (March 1976):135-140.

Preston, Ralph, C., and Wayne L. Herman, Jr. *Teaching Social Studies in the Elementary School.* New York: Holt, Rinehart and Winston, 1974. Chapter 11, "Government and Citizenship."

Shaftel, Fannie R. *Role Playing for Social Values.* Englewood Cliffs, N.J.: Prentice-Hall, 1967. Chapter 3, "Education for Citizenship."

Law-focused education

The laws under which we live and the willingness with which we obey them are basic constituents of the ways of democracy. During the past decade there has been increasing attention given to what has been termed law-focused education. "Since young children tend to readily accept the need for rules in their lives," says one writer, "the elementary school becomes an ideal place for children to begin asking questions about why we have laws and what purposes they serve."

Four articles were published in *Social Education* under the heading "Kids, Teachers, and the Law." The editor says that these articles have a threefold purpose: (1) to present a rationale for teaching elementary pupils about the law and one's rights and obligations under the law; (2) to demonstrate how teachers can incorporate law-focused education into the social studies curriculum; and (3) to help teachers understand and reduce their anxieties in teaching about value-laden law-related topics.

The first article, Arlene Gallagher's "Premises for Law," is an excellent introduction for the teacher who has never heard or read about law-focused education. To show students law in our daily lives she suggests an interesting activity, "The Sign Walk."

> The purpose of the sign walk (or ride) is to have pupils observe how many laws and rules regulate their *daily* lives. The task is to make extensive lists of signs that govern human behavior. When the lists are brought into the classroom they should first be classified according to these, or your own categories:
>
> Signs that regulate your behavior with respect to the environment
> Signs that regulate behavior between people
> Signs that protect the environment
> Signs that protect people

Some signs, of course, will fall into more than one category. No problem. It is hoped that there will be some arguments about the purposes of some of these signs. Which signs are most important; which are least important?

There is more to law-focused education than the factual content of governmental organization and the methods the system uses. It is essential that students develop an understanding of and be able to use such concepts as justice, authority, privacy, fairness, responsibility, tolerance, participation, freedom, and honesty. Leon Jaworski pleads for "a vitalized curriculum of education in the real meaning of citizenship."

The major curriculum materials now available for elementary students include *Law in a New Land* and its *Teacher's Guide* (Houghton Mifflin); *Law in a Free Society* (Law in a Free Society, 606 Wilshire Blvd., Santa Monica, Calif. 90401); *Law in Action Series* (West Publishing Company, 170 Old Country Road, Mineola, Minn., 11501). The best parts of these materials present open-ended problems that students must carefully reason through to make difficult decisions. Also valuable are a mimeographed compilation of *Law-Related Audio-Visual Materials for the Elementary Grades* (Special Committee on Youth Education for Citizenship, American Bar Association, 1155 East 60th Street, Chicago, Ill. 60637), and *Law-Focused Education in the Elementary School* (National Center for Law-Focused Education, 33 North LaSalle Street, Chicago, Ill. 60602).

ECONOMIC VALUES

Economics deals with more than money. It encompasses the production, distribution, and consumption of goods and services. Even given this broader definition of economics, an individual may need help in establishing priorities about the way in which he invests his time and energy and the exchange he gets for this investment. The establishment of priorities, deciding what is economically important, and arranging one's life so that the most important items can be acquired requires considerable skill even when there are few distractions. In an age when technology has made communication available to all, deciding what is important has become clouded by a multitude of messages from the media that are designed to influence your thinking. The messages are planned to make you want what the seller has to sell, and, in fact, to persuade you to rearrange your hierarchy of economic values so that the item for sale is high on your list of importance.

All of us are consumers, and nearly everyone seeks help at one time or another in deciding how to spend his earnings most profitably. Even young children spend money, and by the time students reach intermediate grades they are influencing the spending of millions of dollars on the national market. Because this is so, it seems imperative that we begin to train students in this area of economic values. Consumer education programs have attempted to do just this.

Consumer education

Each year billions of dollars are spent by companies in extolling the qualities of their particular products or services. Persuasion strategies have been developed to a high level of sophistication, and they can be so subtle that the buyer is hardly aware of them at all. With the availability of television advertising, along with other communication media now available to us, the opportunities for influencing the consumer are legion.

As a result, propaganda is used to *make* us accept products, ideas, and people. In our society, it is the responsibility of every citizen to make decisions about the consumption of goods and services after he has carefully evaluated many ideas. It is important that students learn to distinguish between the emotional overtones of propaganda and the actual content of the information. Consumer education deals with this need as well as a number of other objectives.

Objectives for consumer education will be presented followed by some worksheets and activities you may wish to use with students.

CONSUMER EDUCATION OBJECTIVES*

1. Present background information on the role of the consumer and consumer problems.
2. Identify techniques of advertising; learn how to evaluate products being advertised.
3. Examine the methods used in influencing people to believe certain ideas and to follow certain courses of action.
4. Present fraudulent practices (false packaging, unreliable vendors and merchandise, etc.)
5. Identify city and federal agencies whose role it is to protect the consumer and establish laws and guidelines to prevent these and other problems.
6. Present situations in which advertising is not nefarious—techniques can be used to move persons to acts of warmth and kindness.

*Examine the *Special Section on Consumer Education* in the October 1974 issue of *Social Education*, pp. 498-532.

FACT AND OPINION

A student researcher has to decide when he is told something, or when he reads something, whether it is a *Fact* or an *Opinion*.

Put *O* in front of the statements below that you think are *Opinions*, not *Facts*.

______ Swimming is more fun than bicycling.

______ I cannot run a mile in five minutes.

______ It is better to live in a small town than in a city.

______ The fifth graders in our school are smarter than the fourth graders.

Put *F* in front of the statements below that you think are *Facts*, not *Opinions*.

______ New York is larger than Boston.

______ To advertise means "to tell people about a product in order to sell it."

______ Ships from all over the world come into New York Harbor.

______ The United States is located in North America.

______ Paris is a more beautiful city than Washington, D.C.

Here are some words and phrases that describe or define a *Fact* or an *Opinion*. If you think the word or phrase best describes a *Fact* put an *F* in front of it; if it best describes an *Opinion* put an *O* in front of it.

______ believed to be true

______ a person's view

______ known to be true

______ often shows our likes or dislikes

______ known to have happened

______ it really exists

______ someone's idea about something

______ has been proven

PROPAGANDA

Propaganda is information that is used to convince people—either to buy a product or to believe in the information. You need to know that tactics are used to convince, and carefully examine the information given you.

A number of propaganda techniques will be given to you. Then sample statements that would be an example of this kind of propaganda appeal will follow. You may wish to list additional samples at home as you watch TV or you may use magazines or newspapers.

Appeal to you to be one of the group, to be important (social appeal)
1. Everybody is . . .
2. The latest rage with the jet set is . . .

Appeals to your love of nature (environmental appeal)
1. Natural look . . .
2. Mother nature . . .

Appeal to intelligence
1. A brilliant man has chosen . . .
2. Scholars say . . .

Appeal to interest in science
1. Statistics show that . . .
2. Scientists say that . . .

Appeal to your fondness for old times—tradition
1. In a world of increasing technology . . . this one thing remains
2. Remember when Grandma used to . . .

Appeal to your love of ease—you can get all this with great ease
1. ______________ has everything

Appeal to love of youth and beauty
1. Natural look . . .

ACTIVITIES FOR CONSUMER EDUCATION

1. Select a commercial and question a sample of other students to see if:
   a. they remember the product
   b. they can identify the manufacturer
   c. they use the product.

Once your survey is complete, compute, graph, and discuss your results.

2. Read the history of the Bell Telephone trademark in an encyclopedia. What is the purpose of a trademark? Create a trademark for a product you wish to sell.
3. Write a paragraph description of the product for which you made a trademark. Select a small sample of your classmates to check their ideas about the appropriateness of the trademark for your product.
4. Write an ad about your neighborhood as though you were a tourist agent trying to get someone to visit the area. Tell about the following attractions: natural features, landmarks, educational opportunities, entertainment, and other outstanding factors.
5. Watch TV for an hour. Count the number of commercials there are and time them. Summarize the content of the commercials. Indicate the number of minutes per hour spent in advertising.
6. Bring in a picture of someone you know well. Write an article telling why this person is "the greatest."

FOR FURTHER READING

Calderwood, James D.; Lawrence, John D.; and Maher, John E. *Economics in the Curriculum: Developmental Economic Education Program*. New York: Joint Council on Economic Education, 1970.

Hautzig, Esther. *Life with Working Parents*. New York: Macmillan Publishing Co., 1976.

Nappi, Andrew T.; Moran, R. Allen; and Berdan, Mary Jo. *Learning Economics Through Children's Stories*. New York: Joint Council on Economic Education, 1973.

"The Consumer: Another Forgotten American." In *Social Education*, 38 (October 1974). Six articles focus on consumer education.

MORAL AND ETHICAL VALUES

Moral and ethical values concern the individual's actions, attitudes, and behaviors as they affect other people. A moral value is one that responds to the rights of another person. Ethical values would raise the question, "Is this just for the person concerned?" or "Does this give Jim and Jane an equal chance to develop their skills?" Moral and ethical behavior are essential in a governmental system in which the people make the decisions that direct the government. There are some generally accepted moral values such as honesty and truth that people recognize as needed for the maintenance of the society in which they live. These moral imperatives are a requisite for group survival, but the behaviors must be implemented on an individual basis. Thomas Jefferson saw this individual behavior and the collective behavior of the group as subject to the same moral code, interrelated in an extricable fashion. "The man who is dishonest as a statesman would be a dishonest man in any station. It is strangely absurd to suppose that a million of human beings collected together are not under the same moral laws which bind each of them separately."[8]

Moral development

One expert has developed a way of identifying and increasing the adequacy of the way in which people deal with values. Kohlberg has delineated a six-stage hierarchy of moral development and has produced materials in the form of dilemma situations that will help individuals examine their values. The stages he suggests range from a young child's conviction that it is all right to do something as long as your parents give you permission (Stage One) to an abstract kind of morality that concerns itself with and commits the individual to high-level principles (Stage Six).

8. Thomas Jefferson in a letter to Dr. G. Logan, reported in Saul K. Padover, *Thomas Jefferson on Democracy* (New York: Mentor Books, 1939).

Stage I. Punishment and Obedience. Doing right means following the rules and being careful not to antagonize the authorities.

Stage II. Morality of "Exchange of Favors." Moral behavior here means giving the other guy a fair deal in a pragmatic way. You are not doing it because of any universal principle involved, but rather because you are protecting your own interests—"if I scratch his back, he'll scratch mine."

Stage III. "Good Boy—Nice Girl" Orientation. Doing right means doing what will win you the approval of your friends, your parents, and others. Good intentions are a part of what is right for the first time at this stage. Here the individual is very vulnerable to group pressure.

Stage IV. Law and Order. Right behavior means doing one's duty, showing respect for authority, and maintaining the social system. At this stage it is not punishment that must be avoided as in Stage I, but order and systematic procedure that must be maintained for personal integrity.

Stage V. Individual Rights and Standards. A morality of democratically accepted laws and ethical principles that determine the individual's decisions is the kind that operates at this stage. Individual rights that have been critically examined and agreed upon by the individual operate here.

Stage VI. Universal Ethical Principle Orientation. This stage reflects a total commitment to the principles of justice. It is not justice as determined by any one code or series of rules. Justice here is concerned with an unwavering, uncompromising respect for the dignity of human beings.

Kohlberg's theory of moral development is a fascinating one, and there are many questions and comments that could be raised about the ideas presented here. The entire April 1976 issue of *Social Education* deals with the pros and cons of accepting this structure. Many references for extended development of this topic can be found in this issue.

The question for the elementary social studies teacher seems to be how to get children to think about the consequences of their behavior. This is an initial step for raising one's moral consciousness.

It is difficult to see how children will develop the moral and ethical behavior that is a social essential unless there is some planning for such learning. We will suggest strategies for dealing with values and examine ethical values in the sections that follow.

Prejudice/discrimination

Many people affect the growth and development of each individual, and a child interacts with a variety of persons as he matures. However, interaction does not always occur on a one-to-one basis; groups often influence the growing child's impression of his world. Sometimes whole groups interact with other groups and patterns of response are set up that may then be applied to a single individual who fits the group category. In our own culture some groups of people have been valued less than other groups, or at least some groups have not had access to certain opportunities and have been recipients of unequal treatment by the larger group over long periods of time.

Individuals who differ markedly in language usage, skin color, or ethnic background, and cannot or will not be "like" the majority are assigned a status and frequently receive discriminatory treatment because of this. The treatment is overt enough that children can distinguish it at an early age. "There is a considerable amount of research available on the child's awareness of his position in the social stratification and his ethnic group membership. . . . . Awareness of ethnic group membership appears to begin during the nursery school years, perhaps as part of the process through which the child's self-concept is established. Studies of [black] and white nursery school children attending either interracial or segregated schools have shown that racial awareness appears as early as the age of four and increases with age, irrespective of the kind of school the child attends."[9] Those individuals who differ from the majority and are treated so are aware of the differential treatment they receive.

Either the group that is giving or the one that is receiving discriminatory treatment may come to believe that the status ascribed to the group by society is fixed and that the qualities perceived in a given situation are inherent qualities. Racism is an example of such a fixed belief. It is the belief that race is the primary determinant of human traits and capacities, and that racial differences produce an inherent superiority in a particular race. Sexism, then, can be defined as the belief that sex is the primary determinant of human traits and capacities, and that sexual differences produce an inherent superiority in a particular sex. Such prejudicial thinking and the resultant behavior stemming from this thinking created a massive blot on the pages of our history and the ensuing stain remains with us still. In the early days of this country when slavery existed, thinking individuals began to see the problems such behavior created for both the slave and the individual who was exercising his prejudicial beliefs. Jefferson said, "The whole commerce between master and slave is a perpetual exercise of the most boisterous passions, the most unremitting despotism on the one part, and degrading submissions on the other. Our children see this and learn to imitate it; for man is an imitative animal. This quality is the germ of all education in him. From his cradle to his grave he is learning to do what he sees others do. If a parent could find no motive either in his philanthropy or his self-love, for restraining the intemperance of passions towards his slave it should always be a sufficient one that his child is present."[10]

9. Robert D. Hess, "Social Class and Ethnic Influences on Socialization," in Paul H. Mussen, ed., *Carmichael's Manual of Child Psychology*, 3rd ed. (New York: John Wiley & Sons, 1970), 2:482.

10. Padover, *Thomas Jefferson*.

Prejudice and the discriminatory behavior that stems from it is hurtful to both parties involved. It is important that we begin to explore the areas of prejudice and discriminatory behaviors. "The school serves an important function by providing children with experiences necessary to revise their concepts about other racial and national groups. . . . . "[11] The school can provide opportunities for the students to learn about other groups of people and to explore feelings about being different. "The process of changing an individual's prejudices toward a particular group is not simply an intellectual process. Many children's concepts of people and events have developed in a haphazard manner."[12] Teachers can organize information and can help children develop strategies for clarifying their thinking. They also can design experiences that will involve the student emotionally as well as intellectually. Such planning is much needed.

Activities dealing with prejudice. It seems wise to confront children of the majority with the problems of minority groups and the results of discrimination. Since prejudice and discrimination are often based on half-truths and a lack of good information, some specific experiences exposing children to group problems may be necessary. It is also important for minority children to have an opportunity to deal with their impressions of the treatment they have received in our culture. Children develop attitudes early and should begin to explore their feelings in the elementary school. A sample of activities is provided here and a bibliography that may help to stimulate the teacher's thinking.

1. Play "Right On." Have students guess the occupation of a famous black American, Native American, or other minority person being studied. Provide a collection of cards on which a sequence of hints are collected. A student reads one hint, and when another student guesses who the person is the teacher says "Right On." A chart is kept of the winners.

   Example: George Washington Carver
   1. Professor
   2. Worked in laboratory
   3. Peanuts made him famous

2. Play "Winner Take All." Divide the class into two academic groups that are roughly equal. Each group will be given twenty minutes to draw up a series of questions dealing with the minority group being studied. The captain of one team will ask questions of the opposite team. One point is scored for each correct answer. A small reward is planned for the winning team.

11. Frederick McDonald, *Educational Psychology*, 2nd ed. (Belmont, Calif.: Wadsworth Publishing, 1966), p. 171.

12. *Ibid.*

3. Put the names of black Americans (or of other people who are subjected to prejudicial treatment—e.g., women, Mexican Americans, or Oriental Americans) on Bingo cards. Call out the achievements of the various persons and the student will place a chip on the name of the person who performed the deed. Be sure to check the winner's card for accuracy. Read the entire question and answer sequence again. This will provide a good review.
4. On a large bulletin board place the title "Traveler for Freedom." Provide a highway and divide it into periods of history dealing with the advancements of a minority group. Have partners do a brief report and a sketch for a period of time they select. Have the pictures mounted colorfully and placed on the board. After the reports are read to the class, post them near the sketch.
5. Make a paper train engine and twenty or thirty cars. Have students research people who have joined the *Freedom Train* and place a brief summary of the comments on a 3″ × 5″ card. Paste each card on a train car and discuss the people who have provided fuel for the train, who have fought against prejudice and discrimination.
6. Make a list of the organizations that are active in liberation campaigns in your community. Volunteer your time for one day to the one of your choice. The following day make a list of the things you learned there. Note especially any instances of discrimination that come to your attention.
7. Have the students in small groups discuss the following: You have been on a trip to a distant part of the world. The thing you liked most about the place was the way people treated each other. They were fair and treated all people with equal consideration. Discuss this with the group and then list several things you saw that convinced you this was so.
8. Read *"Only the Names Remain: The Cherokee and the Trail of Tears"*[13] or part of it to the class. Ask the students in teams or small groups to decide on an alternative plan of action—what could have been done instead of the forced march. Make a list of the suggestions on the chalkboard. How does the treatment given indicate the values of the majority?

Minority group emphasis. Numerous efforts have been made to provide adequate education for culturally different minority populations. A study by Pecoraro reflects one such effort.[14] "The two Passamaquoddy Indian reservations located in eastern Washington County in Maine are islands of extreme poverty in one of the most economically depressed counties in New England and the nation. . . . Evidence indicates a high incidence of negative self-image and anticipated rejection and failure on the part of Passamaquoddy youngsters. . . . Long-term educational efforts must, therefore, be aimed at improving the self-image of Indian youngsters while reducing

13. Alex W. Bealer, *Only the Names Remain* (Boston: Little, Brown, 1972).

14. Joseph Pecararo, "The Effect of a Series of Special Lessons on Indian History and Culture upon the Attitudes of Indian and Non-Indian Students" (Doctoral dissertation, Boston University, 1971).

the prejudices of youngsters in surrounding communities." The materials and ideas suggested here deal with a small minority population at a limited age level, but they might provide some ideas for you when you deal with others who are socioeconomically or culturally different. "Many Indian problems are identical to those of other groups: the problems of the poor are Indian problems, because poverty is a fact of Indian life in Maine."[15] Pecoraro reports,

> Substantial evidence exists concerning the attitudes and personalities of school-age youngsters living on the Pleasant Point and Peter Dana Point Indian Reservations. . . . The Indian student is caught in a trap. He comes from a different cultural background, and he requires a certain amount of understanding. There's not much evidence that the white community is making any effort. Beyond that there is a certain amount of overt discrimination.[16]

A series of specially prepared lessons on Native American history and culture were prepared dealing with the following concepts:

Arts and Crafts
The Reservation
Children
History and Culture
Employment
Successful Native Americans

"The major influence in deciding what areas to concentrate upon in the developing of lessons was the concern for the negative self-image of the Indians. Various Indians on the two reservations were consulted to see which areas they felt should be emphasized in the lessons. In addition, the Indian governors and the tribal council gave advice to the direction of the special lessons."[17] The first part of the lessons developed were intended to provide the children with a clear and vivid history of their own people.

Lessons were developed to show a range of possibilities for Native Americans. Slide/tapes and 8 mm. sound films were the primary teaching tools. Nine 8 mm. movies were made: *Passamaquoddy Indian Heritage, Project Description, Songs of the Passamaquoddy and Other American Indians, Passamaquoddy Indian Dancing, Passamaquoddy Basket Making Displays, Basket Making, Pie Basket, Ash Pounding, and Bermuda North.*

15. Ibid.
16. Ibid.
17. Ibid.

The success of Native Americans in the off-reservation world is shown on slide/tapes. We see them involved in various occupations in surrounding communities, such as:

Employment Office Worker
Forester
Waitress
Nurse
Trucker
Mechanic
Teacher
Barber
Registered Guide
Fisherman
Factory Worker
Secretary
Executive

Besides these materials some few select commercial materials were used, one of which was *The Magic Wigwam*, a filmstrip of an authentic legend collected over half a century ago by Gilbert H. Wilson (originally published by Ginn & Company in book form).

Overall, the attitudes of the Indian and non-Indian in the experimental groups did become more positive. The reactions of the Native American community were generally positive.

One instrument used to check attitude changes asked pupils in both Native American and public school classes to respond in writing to *sentence stems* like these:

1. The best thing about being an Indian is:
2. The worst thing about being an Indian is:
3. I'd like to be non-Indian because:
4. I'm glad I am an Indian because:
5. I'm glad I am not Indian because:

An excellent bibliography of sources and materials for teaching about Native Americans may be found in the May 1972 issue of *Social Education*. A copy of this bibliography may be obtained free of charge from the Association on American Indian Affairs, Inc., 432 Park Avenue South, New York, N.Y. 10016. There are other articles well worth exploring in that same issue.

Free materials are available. Write to: Indian Rights Association, 1505 Race Street, Philadelphia, Pa. 19102. Ask for *American Indians Today* or an *Indian Reservation Map*—a black-and-white map showing where the tribes, reservations, and settlements in the United States are located.

FOR FURTHER READING

Black Americans

See the bibliography in the Black American Unit, p. 114.

Native Americans

Conklin, Paul. *Choctaw Boy*. New York: Dodd, Mead, 1975.

Felton, Harold W. *Nancy Ward, Cherokee*. New York: Dodd, Mead, 1975.

Goble, Dorothy, and Paul Goble. *Brave Eagle's Account of the Fetterman Fight 21 December 1866*. New York: Pantheon, 1972.

Gridley, Marion L. *The Story of the Seminole*. New York: G. P. Putnam's Sons, 1973.

Keegan, Marcia. *The Taos Indians and their Sacred Blue Lake*. New York: Julian Messner, 1972.

McDermott, Gerald. *Arrow to the Sun*. New York: Viking Press, 1974.

Spanish Americans

Acuna, Rudolfo. *Occupied American: The Chicano's Struggle Toward Liberation*. New York: Canfield Press, Harper & Row, 1972.

Blue, Rose. *We Are Chicano*. New York: Watts, 1973.

Day, Mark. *Forty Acres: Cesar Chavez and the Farm Workers*. New York: Praegar, 1971.

Gamio, Manuel. *The Life Story of the Mexican Immigrant*. New York: Dover Publications, 1972.

Garcia, Ernest F., and George Shaftel. *Mexican-American Heritage*. Belmont, Calif.: Fearon, 1972.

Jones, Edward H., Jr., and Margaret S. Jones. *Arts and Crafts of the Mexican People*. Ritchie, 1971.

Meier, Matthew, and Feliciano Rivera. *The Chicanos: A History of Mexican Americans*. New York: Hill and Wang, 1972.

Politi, Leo. *The Nicest Gift*. New York: Charles Scribner's Sons, 1973.

Valdez, Luis, and Stan Steiner (eds.) *Aztlan: An Anthology of Mexican Americans*. New York: Alfred A. Knopf, 1972.

General References

Banks, James A., ed. *Teaching Ethnic Studies: Concepts and Strategies*, 43rd Yearbook. Arlington, Va.: National Council for the Social Studies, 1973.

______ et al. *Curriculum Guidelines for Multiethnic Education (A position statement)*. Arlington, Va.: National Council for the Social Studies, 1976.

Children and Intercultural Education. Washington, D.C.: Association for Childhood Education International, 1974. Three pamphlets.

Dunfee, Maxine. *Eliminating Ethnic Bias in Instructional Materials*. Washington, D.C.: Association for Supervision and Curriculum Development, 1974.

Ethnic Heritage Project, Social Science Education Consortium (SSEC), 855 Broadway, Boulder, Colorado 80303 will provide information about materials and teacher resources available for elementary teachers.

"Focus on the Culturally Different." *Social Education* (January 1969).

UNDERSTANDING PEOPLE IN OUR WORLD

It is not adequate for our young citizenry to be concerned with their country and internal issues alone. People all over the world are rising up to be counted as people. People make events. People are poor and hungry. People decide to make war. People are friendly, indifferent, or hostile. Some people in a country run its government, not always representing the majority, but dealing with people running other governments. Teaching our children about the world means building images of real people living in a real country who are like themselves in many ways and different in others. Teaching children about other cultures also helps clarify some of the elements within one's own.

Charles Mitsakos, social studies coordinator in Chelmsford, Mass., writes in an unpublished curriculum report, "One of the main purposes of the program is to teach children to understand *why* people act differently than we do, why they believe and value different things, and to understand that to these people such behavior seems natural and right. Children should learn to accept diversity in a nation and in a world in which they must live with diverse people. They should learn that our ways are not the only possible ways to live and that we can learn from other peoples of the world."

Certainly a primary goal in a program concerned with world affairs is the development of world-mindedness in the young American citizens we are educating. It was well stated in a publication, no longer in print, of the committee on International Relations of the National Education Association:

1. The world-minded American realizes that civilization may be imperiled by another world war.
2. The world-minded American wants a world at peace in which liberty and justice are assured for all.
3. The world-minded American knows that nothing in human nature makes war inevitable.

4. The world-minded American believes that education can become a powerful force for achieving international understanding and world peace.
5. The world-minded American knows and understands how people in other lands live and recognizes the common humanity which underlies all differences of culture.
6. The world-minded American knows that unlimited national sovereignty is a threat to world peace and that nations must cooperate to achieve peace and human progress.
7. The world-minded American knows that modern technology holds promise of solving the problem of economic security and that international cooperation can contribute to the increase of well-being for all men.
8. The world-minded American has a deep concern for the well-being of humanity.
9. The world-minded American has a continuing interest in world affairs and he devotes himself seriously to the analysis of international problems with all the skill and judgment he can command.

We live in a world of change; a crowded, urbanized world; a world dominated by bigness—big business, big labor unions, big pressure groups; a world of machines, electronics, increasing automation; a world made smaller by the speed of air travel and instant communication; a world in many ways not dominated by the West. Christensen has listed twelve key points as a basis for understanding a large portion of the world of the 1960s, from which the world of the 1970s and 1980s will emerge. These twelve facts offer a highly generalized but essentially accurate portrait of the way of life of about two-thirds of the human family and some of the forces that are remolding the world in our time.[18]

Fact One: Even when the vast Soviet area of Siberia is excluded, over half of the human family lives in Asia.

Fact Two: Most of the world's people are nonwhite.

Fact Three: Most of the world's people are non-Christian.

Fact Four: Most people live in rapid population growth areas and are members of large families.

Fact Five: Most of the world's people make their precarious living as farmers and craftsmen and depend heavily on hand and animal labor.

Fact Six: Most of the world's people are very poorly fed.

Fact Seven: Most of the world's people are poor in terms of money income.

18. David E. Christensen, "Two-thirds of the World," *Social Education* 31 (March 1967): 212-217. Reprinted with permission.

Fact Eight: Most of the world's people are sick and in need of medical care.

Fact Nine: Despite the high priority that school development programs now receive in the technologically less-advanced nations, the fact remains that about one adult in three in the world is illiterate. And about one in three knows only the bare rudiments of reading and writing.

Fact Ten: Countries in which most people live depend very little on trade and many of them depend on only a few specialized exports.

Fact Eleven: Most of the world's people live under new and relatively inexperienced and, in many cases, unstable governments.

Fact Twelve: The final fact in our brief primer is about the dynamics of change. In most technologically less-advanced countries, the "revolution of rising expectations" stems from a dissatisfied, educated minority. There is a ferment underway and there can be no turning back. In these countries they are, in fact, caught in the middle between the older culture which they have chosen to abandon and a Western culture which is not suited fully to their situation or needs.

The Glens Falls Project is a "total school program" to improve the teaching of world affairs from kindergarten through the twelfth grade. It states its primary goals as:

1. *Increasing* the understanding of world affairs.
2. *Developing* an appreciation of other peoples and cultures.
3. *Inculcating* an attitude of respect toward foreign peoples.
4. *Promoting* a sense of responsibility for furthering better understanding of foreign peoples and cultures.[19]

The activities below were taken from the Glens Falls program and other sources. They have been classified under primary grades and intermediate grades, but their value is not necessarily restricted to a particular grade. Teachers will find it possible to adapt many activities to other grade levels. These activities have not only stimulated an interest in but have also developed an understanding of world affairs. Once involved in a program like this, teachers will develop many more activities of their own.

19. Harold M. Long, and Robert N. King, *Improving the Teaching of World Affairs: The Glens Falls Story* (Washington, D.C.: National Council for the Social Studies, National Education Association, 1964). $2.00.

Activities in the primary grades

1. Filmstrips of life in China, Japan, and other countries.
2. Studying the Chinese—construction of kites, lanterns, a globe of papier-mâché.
3. Cultural comparisons between our ways and their ways in nursery rhymes, games, songs, and simple dances.
4. A visiting teacher from Japan teaches paper-folding to make birds and the like (you can buy books on Japanese paper-folding, which is called origami).
5. Artifacts of Japanese life (or any other culture) brought from home—stamps, money, toys, dolls, articles of clothing, dishes, or chopsticks, to point out similarities and differences in ways of living. Include pictures and postcards.
6. A tape-recording exchange program with a class at the same level in a foreign school to include songs, games, and other topics of mutual interest.
7. A Japanese-American art exchange.
8. An exchange of children's hand-drawn Christmas cards with a school in France.
9. Teachers develop a catalogue of stories in reading books—grades three through six—classified by country of cultural origin.
10. Finding out different ways of eating (fingers, forks, chopsticks), dressing, working, playing, traveling, and going to school.
11. Studying the influence of climate and natural resources on the food, clothing, and shelter of people in other lands.
12. Learning dances and music of foreign lands; learning a few foreign words.
13. Studying the family backgrounds of the class, tracing ancestors to other lands.
14. Constructing puppets to act out situations involving attitudes of respect toward different people.
15. Comparing various celebrations of holidays and festivals.
16. Finding out about the Halloween UNICEF project (write to UNICEF, United Nations, New York).
17. Finding answers to questions through interviews, field trips, and reading:
    a. Which animals are pets of children of other lands?
    b. What kinds of foods come from other lands?
    c. Which of our foods go to other lands?
    d. What recipes come from other countries?
    e. What candies—or candy ingredients—come from other lands?
    f. What places do people come from and go to on airplanes?
18. Inviting someone who has traveled extensively to show some slides he has taken of activities of children and grown-ups, and a few scenes (very carefully chosen) of the country. Answer children's questions.

Activities in the intermediate grades

1. Where do the needy people of the world live? Why are they in need? How can they be helped?
2. Read, maybe learn, poems that children in other lands enjoy.
3. Write letters to a pen pal in another country. You may experience some delay before getting an assignment of a foreign correspondent.

    International Friendship League, Mount Vernon St., Boston, Mass. 02108. Enclose self-addressed envelope and note with full name, full address (with zip), birth date, and $2 registration.

    League of Friendship, Inc., P.O. Box 509, Mount Vernon, Ohio 43050. Age twelve minimum. Send $.50 per name, age, and stamped self-addressed envelope.

    Afro-Asian Pen Pal Center, C.P.O. Box 871, Kingston, N.Y. 12401. Intended only for students under the guidance of teachers. Pen friends from specified nations cannot be guaranteed but replies, in English, are unconditionally guaranteed. Sixty cents per student. A teacher can get full information by writing to the address above stating the class grade.

4. Plan a puppet show to demonstrate customs, dress, and modes of life in another country.
5. Dramatize a legend from another land.
6. Plan a weekly World Bulletin Board. Determine what will go on it. Will it be a mixture of things from many countries? Will it be on one country each week? Will it display one subject each week such as sports, art, or current events?
7. What countries have television? Or make a chart of those countries that do not have television.
8. Is there any country in the world that cannot be reached by a commercial airline? Find out by sending a letter of inquiry to the public relations departments of all overseas airlines in the United States.
9. Find out some individuals in foreign countries, now living, who have made contributions to better ways of living in today's world?
10. What people now prominent in this country were born in foreign countries?
11. Perhaps an individual or a small committee would like to do a specialty report on the Nobel Prize.
12. Have the school glee club learn songs of a cultural area and explain their significance at the performance.
13. Learn folk dances of various nations and their significance.
14. Continue support of overseas projects such as UNICEF, Red Cross, and CARE.
15. Collaborate with other teachers in your building to develop a systematic program for teaching current world affairs. Stated aims:

    a. To acquaint pupils with news magazines and newspapers.

b. To develop some knowledge of special situations in the world which receive headline attention.

c. To distinguish between fact and opinion.

d. To sustain interest in continued reading about the topics discussed in class.

e. To produce individual reports, committee reports, and bulletin board displays based on news stories.

16. Emphasize the study of world affairs through some intensive library reading programs. Assign a different country to each group. Let each group decide in what form it will make its presentation to the whole class.
17. Trace the dependence of the United States on other countries for such items as foods, natural resources, and trained minds. If we had to be completely dependent upon our own resources, with no imports whatever, what would we have to go without that we now have? What changes would it make in the way *you* live?
18. Study the flags of foreign countries, along with our own, and their histories.
19. Arrange for overseas visitors to our schools and homes; learn to ask questions that reflect our concern for other peoples.
20. Use appropriate activities from those suggested for the primary grades above.
21. Continue study of the United Nations.
22. Study an overseas country in depth. Consider basic problems such as food, health, soil and resource conservation, education, and industrialization. Compare with the United States.
23. Study the world in terms of geographical and cultural regions, relating climate and geography to the lives of the people.
24. List and learn something about a number of world leaders.
25. Make a scrapbook of a country and send it to the nearest children's hospital in a large city in that country.
26. Before studying a country the class can write stories about the children there. After the study has been completed write again, and each pupil can compare his own two stories. Have some report to the class on the differences.
27. At the beginning of the year complete this sentence, "Of all the countries in the world I think I would care least about knowing any children my age in________, because. . . ." If you study that country in the school year, see if your attitudes change. Why did they change?

FOR FURTHER READING

We would call your attention to an article in the November/December 1974 issue of *Social Education* by Donald L. Morris, Director of School Services, U.S. Committee for UNICEF, titled "Teaching Global Interdependence in Elementary Social Studies: Old Concept—New Crisis." Interdependence is a concept widely accepted but unfortunately not widely developed in the depth its importance deserves and requires.

Kenworthy, Leonard S. *The International Dimension of Education.* Washington, D.C.: Association for Supervision and Curriculum Development, 1970.

Remy, Richard C., et al. *International Learning and International Education in a Global Age.* Bulletin 47. Arlington, Va.: National Council for the Social Studies, 1975.

Renaud, Mary, ed. *Bringing the World into Your Classroom.* Arlington, Va.: National Council for the Social Studies, 1968.

Teaching Toward Global Perspectives. INTERCOM Series, no. 73. The Center for War/Peace Studies of the New York Friends Group, 218 East 18th Street, New York, N.Y. 10003, 1973. Thirty pp., $1.50. There are nine teaching suggestions, each geared to a particular grade level. Some suggestions include several plans. Teachers will be impressed by the variety of methods and materials that can be used.

STRATEGIES FOR DEALING WITH ATTITUDES AND VALUES

"The goal of moral education should be to equip students with a method for deriving and clarifying their values in a reflective manner, and not to force them to accept what teachers consider the 'right' values. Values usually considered the right ones are those verbally endorsed by the dominant groups, but often contradicted in their actions."[20] Methods that help students reflect and allow them to make their own decisions could be termed "open" strategies.

In general such procedures provide a sequence of steps and sometimes include a question sequence, to be covered by the teacher and student in a period of interaction. A composite of these systems might look like the following sequence. Some variations of this model exist, and this is to be expected since there is an attempt to stress similarities between models, not differences between them.

1. Examine an issue: e.g., What was the problem that really concerned the people who were involved in the Boston Tea Party?
2. Look at the multiple facets of the background problem: What factors led up to this or contributed to the problem?
3. Look for possible behavioral responses to the problem. In what different ways could the people have responded to the problem?
4. Examine the consequences of the various possibilities. What would happen if a line of behavior suggested in #3 were pursued?
5. Choose the alternative you would be most willing to live with. What behavior would you have chosen in the light of the consequences?
6. Examine the reasons for choosing the action you selected. Why did you select this solution to the problem?

20. James A. Banks, *Teaching Strategies for Ethnic Studies* (Boston: Allyn and Bacon, 1975), p. 105.

This procedure is designed to help students judge responsibly while dealing with topics that involve values, the hope being that a process will be established in a minimum feeling situation that will carry over to a maximum feeling situation. The problem is that many classrooms never get past the names, dates, places, or events to the things that really mean something to the students. It may even seem to students that as teachers talk about values they are somewhat "phony" because they use the term to refer to a low level of valuing.

Think of something you value highly—something or someone you hold dear. Do you as a highly trained rational being always behave in a rational manner toward this, or at some point has the affective superceded the cognitive? It seems only fair that we allow the students to see the intensity of emotion we feel for something we value highly.

In dealing with the development of positive attitudes some emotion involvement seems essential. Information alone may affect the cognitive component, which may eventually temper the attitude, but an affective response deals directly with the other variables—the emotional and action components in the attitude.

How can one obtain emotional involvement in the classroom? Simulation exercises involve children intellectually and emotionally and can be used to help students reflect and become involved in decision making.

Simulation

Simulation is a process in which the element assumes the form without the reality. There is a need for using strategies that are similar to the real in the area of moral education where feelings as well as information are determinants of behavior. This allows and encourages student involvement in the situation, more nearly guaranteeing that the emotion of the participants will be forthcoming. There are five kinds of simulation strategies that we will examine here; role playing, dramatic play, pantomime, puppetry, and gaming. Each of these techniques has a particular emphasis, and thus will fulfill a somewhat different objective.

Role playing. Role playing is a form of simulation in which the individual involved is primary. What the person is like, and his personality, immediate problems, and feelings are all central to the operation. The event and setting are secondary in importance.

The most vivid, detailed, and directive presentation of role playing in elementary school situations has been developed by Fannie Shaftel.[21] She calls role play-

21. Fannie R. Shaftel and George Shaftel, *Role-Playing for Social Values* (Englewood Cliffs, N.J.: Prentice-Hall, 1967), Chap. 5.

ing a kind of "reality practice," which enables groups to relive critical incidents, to explore what happened in them, and to consider what might have happened if different choices had been made in the effort to resolve the problems involved.

While role playing is used in reliving situations in history and in other cultures to help children understand how people felt in certain circumstances (how the colonists felt under regulations imposed by the English government or how the people in Colombia reacted to Peace Corps workers), it finds its greatest use in reproducing typical group situations on the playground or in the classroom, or in decision-making problem situations outside of school—"getting even," responsibility for others, the letter of the law, honesty, etc.

Role playing as presented by Shaftel employs the following steps (the descriptions have been abbreviated):[22]

1. *Warming up" the group* (problem confrontation). Acquaints the group with the problem at hand, expressed often in a *problem story* that stops at the dilemma point. What do you think will happen now?
2. *Selecting participants* (role players). Teacher may ask the group to describe the various characters. Important to use individuals who have identified with the role or who have strong feelings about the behavior of specific characters.
3. *Setting the stage*. Each child is reminded of the role he is to take. A simple line of action is selected for exploration.
4. *Preparing the audience to be participating observers*. "Listening" is discussed with the observers. Think about alternative solutions, which you will have an opportunity to try out after the first idea has been explored.
5. *Role playing* (the enactment). Each player must think and feel on his feet, spontaneously reacting to the developing situation. No role player is evaluated for his acting. The test: is the portrayal true to life?
6. *Discussion and evaluation*. Discussion is usually vigorous. Alternative ideas are given. The teacher's questions look ahead to the consequences of the behavior that has been enacted.
7. *The re-enactment* (further role playing). Replaying revised roles, playing suggested next steps, or exploring alternative possibilities. Moving back and forth from acting to discussing to acting again can be a most effective learning sequence.
8. *Sharing experience and generalizing*. A period of general discussion—exploration of the consequences of behavior. Some role-playing sessions do not reach the level of generalization, but go no further than numerous attempts to solve the problem-story situation itself.

Research done on role playing indicates that students can propose more solutions to problems and develop more antecedent/consequent relations as a result of participating in role-playing sessions. Practice in the solution of open-ended prob-

22. *Ibid.*, pp. 203-418, problem stories for role playing.

lem stories allows students to decenter—and see the situation from another point of view—the consequences for several persons in the problem situation.

As a result of role-playing sessions students also become able to make long-range predictions of consequences. For example, when asked "What will happen next? the student could say, "She will hand him the money." Or, "She will return the money and will have to tell her parents what happened and ask for help." The second response is a kind of answer built upon a response. It shows a more thorough definition of the consequences of an act. This is the kind of examination of behavior we hope children will learn to make.

Team role playing. There are several variations on the Shaftel strategy for effective role playing. For example, team role playing is nonthreatening and permits a large number of participants to explore a problem simultaneously. Let us take a specific example. The students are studying about Alaska and the Eskimos from a particular part of Alaska. Some attempt to involve the students in the problems of the Eskimo people seems advisable.

1. Type the following descriptions on separate slips of paper (provide enough copies so that each member of the class will have one of the descriptions):

   a. You are Niko, an Eskimo from King Island. You climb steep, sharp cliffs to gather wild birds' eggs. The island is a great place to run and play and has many hiding places that make it interesting. Every fall your family moves to the mainland to attend school there and you miss the island life. You have just moved and are now meeting the teacher and a boy who will be in your classroom this year. You say. . . .

   b. You are the best baseball player in your class. The boys almost always choose you for the captain of one side at recess. The teacher has just called you to introduce you to a new boy. He is an Eskimo from King Island. The teacher asks you to be responsible for him at recess. You say. . . .

   Note: It is clear that the Eskimo boy is athletic, but can he play baseball? The student he is being introduced to is very good at this sport. Will he take the risk of including the Eskimo or will he avoid this possible difficulty? In a team role-playing vignette, it is advisable that a possible conflict or distress exists so that a range of responses exist.

2. Give each student in a team one of the two descriptions. Every student in the class should have a partner and one slip of paper with the role description needed to carry out this vignette.

   a. Instruct each student to read only his own description.

   b. Allow each student to talk to his partner, but all teams talk simultaneously about the problem presented. Ask them to have the answer to the following question ready when they conclude their discussion: "What will Niko *do* at recess?"

3. When the students have concluded their discussion, collect from each team their answer to the action problem presented. Get each person to verbalize at least once. Say to a team, "What will Niko do during recess?" If Niko answers, ask the other participant if he agreed to this or if he suggested this or some other related question that includes him in the verbal exchange.

   Role playing requires both physical and verbal involvement. This simple team role playing involves only one of the variables, verbal involvement. It is important therefore to have each student participate in a verbal exchange before the larger group. This is a skill-training or confidence-gaining session that precedes the Shaftel role-playing problem situations.
4. Note with the class the number of different solutions to the problem. Now look in the textbooks for other problems faced by the Eskimo people. Think of several possible solutions to at least one of them.

Student-initiated dilemma situations. It is possible for students who are familiar with open-ended problems to propose problems that they feel are of significance for role playing in the classroom. The students suggest the problems and then enact them. The teacher provides the follow-up questions and the activities that move the simple problem into a more generic one.[23]

One group of fifth graders was asked to make a list of problems that it felt were important. The problems may seem like relatively minor dilemmas, but they are nonetheless real problems that the children feel are significant.

One group of problems they listed dealt with respect for property:

> A student plays with Sally's science project and accidentally damages it, but does not tell anyone. When Sally presents her project she is embarrassed and cannot demonstrate her work satisfactorily.
>
> A student borrows a pencil from Brian's desk without telling him. This eventually gets Brian in trouble with the teacher.

Students acted out the situations, and the teacher raised questions that made the ideas involved more generally applicable. For example, who is really responsible for the research project, the student? all the students? What is the difference between petty theft and grand larceny?

A second group of problems dealt with consideration of other people's problems:

> Joan comes to class in a good mood but her fellow students make callous, unthinking remarks, and by lunch time she is becoming most unhappy.
>
> A group of students are working with paints and clay for a school project. They don't allow time enough for clean-up. In a few days, when other students need the supplies, they cannot find usable materials and their project idea is ruined.

23. These dilemma situations were developed by Dorothy A. Gill, a teacher in Dade County, Florida.

Again, the students act out the situations and provide several different possible endings. The teacher makes the situations more generic by raising questions about the effects of good or bad manners on others, and about neatness and how this affects people's feelings of well-being.

The students in the class also listed problems that dealt with sex discrimination and with cheating in school. It would be interesting for any teacher to discover the problems his students feel are worth discussing or role playing. In the specifics they suggest are the germs of age-old problems that human beings have had to work to resolve. Much can be gained by exploring alternative solutions while they are young.

Dramatic play. Children's dramatic play simulates the real. They love to imitate their parents, their teachers, friends, animals, workers, and professional people. Dramatic play is a technique that allows the students to demonstrate what they know about a topic, and allows the teacher and students to raise questions that will stimulate them to want to know more about it. Dramatic play at home or at school is fun, but there is a difference,

Dramatic play at home:

1. is a hit-or-miss "follow-that-new-idea game"
2. is based on ideas and impressions gathered at random
3. is make-believe, keeps children busy

Dramatic play at school

1. is guided so that children reach significant outcomes
2. is based on background information that is gathered and shared
3. develops definite concepts, skills, and attitudes

In dramatic play the situation or event is central and the roles are proposed and carried out as they are needed by the children. The event is primary and provides information about the complex interactions both human and material in the setting.

A situation should not be selected for dramatization until the class has studied the content relating to that situation. Have the dramatizations performed where all may easily observe the action. A specially designated area of the room is recommended for discussion use by those who are to play the dramatization. A time allotment of five or ten minutes should be given to a person or group to formulate plans for presenting the play and to decide upon the general plans, the beginning, climax, and culmination. Do not allow the use of too much time here, or extensive argument, but allow one quick practice, if desirable. Selection of the person or group to present the dramatization might be left to the teacher. In the earlier stages of this dramatic experience it might be a good idea to rely considerably upon volunteers. Relatively free interpretations of ideas and emotions should be encouraged. Undue criticism may stifle creative expression and discourage originality and naturalness in performance.

Evaluations and appraisals should be conducted immediately following each dramatization. They should be impersonal, with appraisal directed to the character role rather than to the pupil playing the role. The responsibility for appraisal should be shared by all—performers, audience, and teacher. Use a positive approach. In evaluation and appraisal you are concerned with:

1. Development of dramatization in a logical, sensible, and systematic fashion.
2. Convincing dialogue, avoiding unnecessary and trivial conversation.
3. Effective vocal expression and body movements.
4. Spontaneous action and dialogue.
5. Audible speech, using proper enunciation, grammar, articulation and emphasis.
6. Posture, gesture, and facial expression appropriate to the character and situation.
7. A smooth tempo and rate appropriate to the theme or mood of the situation.
8. The proper mood of the situation (e.g., humor, tragedy, adventure, fantasy, or pathos).
9. Cooperation in development and presentation.
10. Audience responsibilities of attentiveness, courtesy, and constructive appraisals.

Pantomime. Pantomime may focus on a fantasy situation, but may also simulate a real situation. However, it is different from reality in that it takes away one much-used human trait, the voice. An individual says and does many things in a normal interaction. Now he can only *do* things to communicate, and so he exaggerates them. He does things, moves about, overacts to assure communication.

Some helpful hints to get you started thinking about and using pantomime in your classroom are:

1. How many things can you say without using your voice or even moving your lips? Try "Yes," "No," "Come here," "Hello," "Go away," "I don't know." Or, pantomime something, saying, "If I do it well you should be able to guess what each movement means." Try to be enthusiastic. It is contagious.
2. Suggest some types of activities that the students have done or might do. For example, walking: an old man walking into a room and sitting down in a chair, or a boy going to dancing school who doesn't like it. Suggest gesturing with hands and arms like a person giving directions to a lost traveler or an English-speaking person in Mexico trying to order a meal with gestures. Have the pupils do exercises using only head movement and facial expression: a girl showing fright when

a lion gets loose at the circus, or a boy expecting ice cream for dessert and showing disappointment when served gingerbread.

3. With five to ten participants seated in a circle on the floor:

   The first person makes a gesture.

   The second person makes the first person's gesture plus his own.

   The third person makes the gestures of the first two people plus his own.

   . . . . and so on . . . .

   The last person makes the gestures of all the other players and everyone in the circle plays follow the leader and imitates in a final pantomime.

Now have two or three people go over the pantomime ideas mentally and rearrange them to make a more effective sequence, and allow time for them to demonstrate the sequence to the class.

4. Have students pair up with friends. Tell them:

   As you talk about an assignment, or a recent recess, watch the friend very closely. Try to "match" your friend's gestures. Observe eye movements as well as larger body movements. Note the amount of time it takes for your friend to notice the matching behavior. Try this with two or three friends. You will note that some people are more conscious of body position and movement than others.

5. Stress naturalness—seeing, feeling, and thinking the character from the inside. Suggest that the children begin to observe carefully how people around them behave in different situations. Gradually direct activities toward social studies situations or categories. Let students act out the reactions of the crew when Columbus refused to turn around and return to Spain, or Balboa climbing the last few feet in Darien and seeing the Pacific Ocean, or the arrival of the news to a Lexington family in 1775 that the British are coming from Boston.[24]

In the social studies classroom pantomime might be effectively used to demonstrate the problems encountered when one culture meets another, such as Columbus meeting the natives of North America. It might also be used to reinforce learning about a specific event. For example, the students could select a part of a larger problem, act out their choice, and have the rest of the students guess what the pantomime represented. This would provide a review and an emphasis on details that is helpful.

Puppetry. Puppets offer an opportunity for a child to express both his creativity and his feelings. There is an artistic experience involved in creating the puppet and a dramatic experience in making the puppets come to life. In both of these expressive areas, the student can explore attitudes and values.

Puppets may be used to simulate a real interaction or to explore the fantastic,

24. Items 1, 2, and 5 are taken from Vincent A. Cristiani, "Informal Dramatizations in Social Studies" (Ed.D. dissertation, Boston University, 1960).

but the strategy differs from some other simulation techniques in that it takes away one much needed, very expressive human element, the body. Because of this, the voice is frequently exaggerated and given all the unusual quality the puppet director can command.

There are several books that provide descriptions of puppets and instructions for making them. Puppets can be elaborate or simple, large or small, and made from a variety of materials. Finger puppets are simple paper cutouts or elaborately decorated cloth creations, designed to fit on a single finger. Hand puppets are often made from sacks or old socks or can be purchased from commercial sources. Stick puppets can be made by fastening a small figure on a short stick or by carving pieces or bits of wood and connecting them with wire. Papier-mâché or sawdust are frequently used for constructing puppet heads, to which the student adds a costume.*

Begin dialogues in social studies with casual conversations between two characters. Then move to more complex situations. Throughout social studies there will continue to be informal situations, but children should also be urged to think up story situations that follow a logical pattern, such as:

1. Opening lines that, through conversation, reveal the main characters, the location, and the approximate time.
2. Continuing dialogue that establishes the situation or incident around which the story is built.
3. A climax or high point wherein a decision or turning point is reached.
4. A closing that ends the incident or possibly looks into the future to predict its significance.

Gaming. Games can be used to simulate real situations. Frequently they combine a situation with specific roles for a more direct involvement in promoting an idea or product. There are rules spelled out for most games and competition is built up as the players strive to convince each other of a point or play to win. The term *simulation gaming* is sometimes used to differentiate between games that are designed for recreation and those that are problem centered and involve real-life situations.

Some new curriculum materials include games to involve the students more directly in the problem situations that face the people concerned. For example, the seal hunt is made real through a game and the student becomes involved in the dilemma the Netsilik Eskimo faces and the alternatives open to him as he participates in this survival hunt. The reality of the situation is further expanded by using films that bring out the details of the setting. Many games are available commercially, but teachers can invent simple games to enhance learning. Some game sources are:

*See M. Jagendorf, *Penny Puppets, Penny Theatre and Penny Plays*. Boston: Plays, Inc., 1966; and Shari Lewis, *Making Easy Puppets*. New York: E. F. Dutton, Inc., 1967.

The Seal Hunt and *The Caribou Hunt* are games that are part of MACOS (Man, A Course of Study). Curriculum developed by Educational Development Center, 15 Mifflin Place, Cambridge, Mass. 02138.

Abt Associates, 55 Wheeler Street, Cambridge, Mass. 02138. Game titles: *Post Office, Help! Transportation, Neighborhood, Pollution, Supermarket.*

Ghetto. Western Publishing, School and Library Dept., 850 Third Avenue, New York, N.Y. 10022.

Oxfam Education Department, 274 Banbury Road, Oxford, England. This company produces games that develop intercultural understanding; for example, *Botswana Game* and *Adivasi Game.*

FOR FURTHER READING

Benson, John. *Games Students Like to Play*. Belmont, Calif.: Fearon, 1973.

Dunfee, Maxine, and Claudia Crump. *Teaching for Social Values in Social Studies.* Washington, D.C.: Association for Childhood Education International, 1974.

Galbraith, Ronald, and Thomas H. Jones. "Teaching Strategies for Moral Dilemmas." *Social Education* 39: (January 1975): 16-39.

Hanna, Lavone A.; Potter, Gladys L.; and Robert W. Reynolds. *Dynamic Elementary Social Studies*. 3rd ed. New York: Holt, Rinehart and Winston, 1973. (Democratic values.)

Heinig, Ruth B., and Lydia Stillwell. *Creative Dramatics for the Classroom Teacher.* Englewood Cliffs, N.J.: Prentice-Hall, 1974.

Heyman, Mark. *Simulation Games for the Classroom.* Bloomington, Ind.: Phi Delta Kappa Educational Foundation, 1975.

Keach, Everett, Jr., et al. "Simulation Games and the Elementary School." *Social Education* 38: (March 1974): 284-295. Five articles.

Livingston, Samuel, and Stoll, Clarice. *Simulation Games: An Introduction for the Social Studies Teacher.* New York: Free Press, 1973.

Maidment, Robert. *Simulation Games: Design and Execution*. Columbus, Ohio: Charles E. Merrill, 1973.

McCaslin, Nellie. *Creative Dramatics in the Classroom*. New York: McKay, 1974.

Metcalf, Lawrence E., ed. *Values Education*, 41st Yearbook. Arlington, Va.: National Council for the Social Studies, 1971.

Nesbet, William A. *Simulation Games for the Social Studies Classroom.* New York: Foreign Policy Association, 1971.

Shaftel, Fannie R. "Role-Playing: An Approach to Meaningful Social Learning." *Social Education* 34 (May 1970): 556-559.

______ and George Shaftel. *Values in Action: Role-Playing Problem Situations for the Intermediate Grades.* New York: Holt, Rinehart and Winston, 1970.

Shelly, Ann C. "Total Class Development of Simulation Games." *Social Education* 37 (November 1973): 687-689.

Superka, Douglas, and Patricia Johnson. *Values Education: Approaches and Materials.* Boulder, Col.: Social Science Education Consortium, 1975.

Younger, John C., and John F. Aceti. *Simulation Games and Activities for Social Studies.* Dansville, N.Y.: Instructor Publications.

IMPROVING INSTRUCTION THROUGH THE USE OF RESOURCES

Chapter eight

There should be basic guidelines available to both teacher and student for the selection and use of a particular learning resource, be it equipment or material. Students as well as teachers should be aware of the potential of all of these instructional tools, and they should be encouraged to use these tools in creative ways to further their individual learning and to enhance their communication with their peers in class sharing sessions.

Any instructional material should be used to achieve a specific goal or purpose. There are understandings, skills, attitudes, and appreciations set up for each unit. If a film is used, it is used because it will make a contribution to a specific purpose in a particular unit. This is true of filmstrips, textbooks, or any other instructional resources.

It should be appropriate to the educational levels present in the class. It should be able to serve them effectively. With the same instructional material, different tasks can be set commensurate with levels represented. It is quite likely that the quality of the task is more important than any method used.

There should be variety and balance through a multimedia approach. Reading techniques alone, often in just one or two textbooks, predominate in too many classrooms. Several different instructional materials are frequently needed. While one would not necessarily want to develop a unit without using written materials, it would be possible to do so. In a given situation some learning resources will be used by the total class, some by one or more small groups, and others by one or more individuals.

Evaluate before, during, and after the use of specific resource materials. This evaluation occurs at the time of preplanning by the teacher, in pupil-teacher planning, during the use of the materials if questions are raised about what it is providing, and in retrospect when assessment is made of its contribution. The evaluation is made in terms of the particular material, the purpose or purposes it is supposed to serve, who uses it, and when.

The material should have a proper place in a sequence in order to be of greatest value. Proper planning might provide that certain things be done before using the particular resource and certain outcomes would naturally follow its use in proper sequence.

The values derived from the use of instructional resources depend, to a great extent, upon the skills of the teacher. It is the teacher who decides, or who helps children to decide, what, when, how, and how much. The beginning teacher grows through increasing experience if he constantly evaluates himself, the children he teaches, and the instructional tools he uses.

It has been said that planning for media and planning for optimal learning are essentially parts of the same process. First-rate planning has materials, equipment, and learning activities functioning together in the instructional process. Materials do not possess educative values in and of themselves; their values depend on the why, when, and how.

Each teacher must become a collector and an inventor of instructional materials. Watch out for the price tag on *free materials*. Many have value but must be carefully scrutinized. Such material must make a contribution to an ongoing enterprise—not direct or control it.

Some teachers ask about another teacher, "How does he do it and how does he know how?"—and want to know the secret prescription. There is none. Hard work, analysis of learning difficulties, constant search for new ways and new materials, experimentation, willingness to innovate, abundant enthusiasm, and a highly active imagination are some of the ingredients.

BULLETIN BOARDS

Good bulletin boards give that lived-in, worked-in feeling to a room, and are a visible display of what is happening there. They speak of a teacher who sees the bulletin board as an educational ally: a vehicle for reporting, clarifying concepts, arousing interest in new materials, serving as a source of information, provoking thought, developing individual and group responsibility, helping pupils learn to communicate ideas visually, and opportunities for working, planning, organizing, and evaluating together.

To make a good bulletin board, develop: *dramatic interest*, to catch and hold the viewer's attention; *organization* to make it easier for the viewer to "read" the board; and *educational significance*, to help the viewer understand the purpose of the display and to learn something from it. Dramatic interest can be achieved in these ways:

1. Use a variety of materials:
   Paper—corrugated, metallic, crepe, wallpaper, newspapers, sandpaper, aluminum foil, colored cellophane.

   Color—water color, tempera paint, finger paint, paper, chalk, crayons.

   Miscellaneous—yarn and string, cotton batting, crinoline, burlap, wire mesh, leather, branches, ribbon, pipe cleaners, soft wire, rope, cellophane straws, paper plates and trays.
2. Create three-dimensional effects by using:
   Paper sculpture—rolling it over a pencil, scoring, tearing, slitting and notching, cutting and threading through, curling or twisting, or punching holes.

   Letters raised from the surface of the board on pins.
3. Create a center, or area of interest, through an illustration, caption, cartoon, or unusual statement, color, or use of material. Use a large spot of color, an arrow, a large hand, string, or yarn to join ideas together, or diagonal lines to draw attention.
4. Provide basic equipment: hand stapler, paper cutter, large shears, yardstick, rubber cement, mucilage, thumbtacks, masking tape, cellophane tape, straight pins, bead-headed pins, stencil knife (or mat knife or razor), felt tip and nylon tip pens in a variety of colors and sizes.

Kinds of displays

These ideas may suggest further possibilities:

1. Current affairs under certain headings, such as
   a. People in the news: United States and foreign countries.
   b. "Hot Spots" on a world map.
   c. Last week's important events, printed in boxes around a world map with strings leading to the locations where they happened.
   d. Headlines in our town.
   e. The front page of a metropolitan newspaper, with all place names underlined and strings leading from them to a map.

2. Displays to commemorate holidays or "special weeks."
3. Summary of a field trip or preparation for a field trip.
4. Test purposes, when material cannot be duplicated, e.g., to recognize the countries or regions represented by pictures.
5. Display in connection with a specialty report.
6. One bulletin board for a work-type board:
   a. Post directions or show samples of work to be done.
   b. Committee assignments.
   c. Announcements.
7. All kinds of pupil work. Make choices so that there are not a dozen or more similar papers or drawings.
8. A display that develops from day to day as the unit develops.
9. Display themes of contrast: Then and Now, Here and There, Homes Around the World; show growth of territory, transportation, communication.
10. Show a production process—stages in making a particular object, with samples in various stages on nearby table. Analysis through pictures, drawings, captions, explanations of a complex process, e.g., from sheep to finished dress in pioneer days.
11. Development of a topic apart from a current unit, with additions every time it is discussed. "We Met Government Today"—policeman, fireman, street lights, sidewalks, garbage collection, the mayor, traffic regulations.
12. "Where were you this summer?" or "Where are you going?"—books, pictures, maps, realia.
13. Display a collection of maps collected by pupils from current magazines, newspapers, advertising material, etc., each captioned to indicate the specific type of map and why it is used there.

Sources of materials outside the classroom

Use *Elementary Teachers Guide to Free Curriculum Materials*, Educators Progress Service, Randolph, Wis. Revised annually. Look in *Free and Inexpensive Learning Materials*, Division of Surveys and Field Services, George Peabody College for Teachers, Nashville, Tenn. Revised biennially.

Be constantly on the lookout for posters, pictures, and objects used for advertising by merchants in your town, who may give you the material when they are finished with it. Watch for cut-outs from newspapers and magazines and for advertisements that offer materials.

Sometimes full-page pictures in large books are good in number and quality, and of more value cut out and displayed than kept in the book. Seek them in supermarkets, inexpensive department stores, and sales at bookstores. See "Using Pictures," p. 296.

How to make bulletin board space

1. Buy plywood or soft masonite and have it installed or hung from a molding, or rest it on a chalkboard tray. Or mount burlap on unused walls or chalkboards.
2. Cover heavy cardboard (from very large flat boxes discarded by stores) with flannel.
3. Corrugated bulletin board cover paper, available in several colors, can be rolled onto a soiled or otherwise unattractive area and taped or tacked in place. Write for information to The Bemiss-Jason Corporation, 49-20 Van Dam Street, Long Island City, N.Y.
4. Spaces away from walls can be made by mounting a board on an easel, fitting an old-fashioned folding screen with suitable material, hinging two or three sections of plywood together, or fastening a single piece of plywood along one edge at a right angle to a wall.

FOR FURTHER READING

Bulletin Boards and Other Displays. Belmont, Calif.: Fearon Publishers, Inc. A series of practical booklets. Ask for titles with descriptions and cost.

Involvement Bulletin Boards. Washington, D.C.: Association for Childhood Education, 1970.

Minor, Ed, and Harvey R. Fry. *Techniques for Producing Visual Instructional Media*. New York: McGraw-Hill, 1970.

Randall, Reino, and Edward C. Haines. *Bulletin Boards and Displays*. Worcester, Mass.: Davis Publications, 1971.

USING THE CHALKBOARD

The chalkboard has several useful qualities. It is ready at all times. Action at the board holds attention. Errors in performance are easily corrected.

There are many uses for the chalkboard:

1. Prior preparation for the in-school hours:
   a. Today's date.

b. Announcements.
c. Social studies work schedule as planned yesterday.
d. Guide questions for viewing a film or filmstrip.
e. Specific directions.
f. Outline of a plan.
g. An assignment not found in duplicated material.
h. Listing words in new vocabulary.

2. During in-school hours:

   a. Demonstration in teaching, through graphs, diagrams, or charts; a time line; summaries; a correct bibliographical form; an outline; demonstration of form and arrangement; enlarging a map; recording elements in explanation, point by point, as they are made.
   b. Sketching for an explanation, for example, making a community map; interpreting a cartoon; demonstrating position, size, or shape; showing relative locations.
   c. For emphasis during discussion or reporting, to emphasize a name, word, or date, spell a new word, point up key ideas, cite a book.
   d. For recording, by teacher or pupil, so that the whole class can see: suggestions in pupil-teacher planning; a master list from team secretaries' reports; impromptu ideas; voting tally; tabulation of opinions; progress of work; suggestions for further research; any suggestion that occurs as you teach.

TEACHING WITH FILMS

Films have value only if the students become involved. Films offer a real opportunity for involvement since they are colorful and moving, and provide auditory stimulation as well. In today's TV age, children are very much accustomed to this kind of stimulation and may very well get more from such an experience than adults do.

One first grade teacher was interested in using a film on Africa that had a high-school-level vocabulary. She decided to use it without the sound. As she watched it she began to think that this had been a mistake because it did not seem nearly as informative without the speaking voice. However, she found that her first graders had seen an unbelievable number of things that had fascinated them. She concluded that young children in today's world are very much attuned to moving pictures and interpret more readily than adults do.

This is just one way to use films creatively. Other teachers use only part of a film. Still others use only the sound track and have children draw pictures to go with some of the description in the film. A second or even a third showing of the film or a variation of the first showing often provides additional learning. The uses of film are many and the limit of uses is usually bounded only by the imagination of the user.

A. Films are useful instructional aids.

1. They make foreign countries and peoples real, bring periods of history to life, and bring new experiences into the classroom.
2. They are effective tools in giving factual information, and provide poor readers with a source of information.
3. They have been found helpful in developing desirable attitudes, and in providing informational backgrounds for elaborative and critical thinking.
4. They offer opportunities for focused discussion.
5. They offer a common denominator of experience to pupil viewers, making an impact on the total range of individual differences.
6. They hold the attention of pupils better than many other instructional aids, and have been found effective in increasing retention in learning.

B. Films are useful at particular times.

1. To set the stage as a starter or initiatory activity for a unit.
2. To add information and understanding during the development of a unit.
3. To summarize, reinforce, or use as a check-off of information and understandings as one of the concluding activities in a unit.
4. To give variety in activities—even when reading could give the same information, a film offers a change.

C. Preparation is the key to effective use of films.

1. Select the film to serve a particular purpose, and know clearly what that purpose is, *e.g.*, specific concepts, generalizations, skills, insights, or appreciations the film will assist.
2. Preview always—with pencil in hand—two days ahead if possible. If a film guide is available, read it before preview.
   a. Note vocabulary that must be explained before the children view the film.
   b. Determine what scenes you will call particular attention to.
   c. Decide how to connect the film with previous learning experiences.
   d. Make up guide questions.
   e. Decide on the likelihood of showing film more than once. For what purpose? Difficult concepts? Unanswered questions? Reinforcing learning? When? Tests have shown that an individual learns about a third more from a second showing of most films.
   f. Plan activities to follow viewing; in succeeding films, seek variety in activities.
   g. Have one or two pupils preview with you:
      1. For the pupils' point of view.
      2. For their suggestions on needed explanations to class.
      3. For preparation to participate in the discussion.
      4. For possible posing of guide questions for the class in viewing.

3. Prepare the classroom, taking care of:

    a. Technical details of darkening, seating, placement of projector, and ventilation. Write on the chalkboard the title of the film, vocabulary, and guide questions.
    b. Have available other instructional materials you plan to use—maps, flat pictures, books, filmstrip, etc.

4. Prepare the class.

    a. Establish with class the purposes of viewing. Learning from an educational film is a skill that has to be developed.
    b. Study the selected vocabulary.
    c. Do some map study if it is applicable to the film.
    d. Sometimes, a day ahead, the teacher may wish to use flat pictures or a filmstrip concerned with some of the basic ideas contained in the film. If desirable, indicate two or three particular scenes to watch for.
    e. Read over the guide questions on the chalkboard; possibly make assignments to specific individuals. Some teachers like to tell enough about the film so that children can raise questions they want answered.
    f. Tell the class to watch the first scenes carefully, for these often provide the key to a better understanding of the whole film. Tell them that if they observe closely, they will see more than the narrator or the characters talking refer to.
    g. Some films give "signposts" that help in recognizing *major* points:

        (1) When the picture fades out and fades in, this indicates a new point in the film's "outline."
        (2) Words printed on the screen usually indicate key ideas.
        (3) Dates, maps, and animated drawings present important information.
        (4) A partial summary of content so far indicates that a new point is coming up.

D. Follow-up after the presentation.

1. Sometimes desirable to allow two or three minutes for children to make notes, since none should be taken during the film.
2. In addition to guide questions concerned with content contributing to the unit, there are others:

    a. What were the major points in the film?
    b. How does the information fit into our unit?
    c. Do we need to get additional information somewhere to add to that of the film?

3. Divide the class into team discussion groups (three to five in each) to answer some of the guide questions.

4. Review and use the new vocabulary.
5. Some of the small groups at work on unit activities might make a report to the class on any extension of the ideas presented in the film. The ability to learn from films improves with practice.

Some further ideas are worth considering. Scheduling can be a serious problem as some school systems require films to be scheduled months in advance of use. If a film comes when it can not fulfill the purpose in the original plans, either find a new purpose for showing (which may be quite possible) or do not use the film. Keep a card file or record with your unit plans on each film used, showing the title, a summary of the content, strengths and weaknesses, and the source. A duplicate file should be in the office of the principal or audiovisual director.

The film-loop

Do investigate this fine instructional tool if you have not already done so. It usually requires a film-loop viewer. Some loops fit a regular 8 mm. projector and others require an 8 mm. super projector. Check with the librarian or media specialist to see if the projector can be adapted. Some can be used with either type of film by a simple knob switchover. The two to four minute 8 mm silent film, usually without captions, comes in a sealed plastic cartridge, which is pushed into the viewer.

The film-loop possesses these attributes:

1. It deals with a single concept or topic (e.g., Life Aboard a Sampan, Market Day in a Mexican Town, Eskimo Seal Hunt) and is often called a single-concept film.
2. It is a self-instructional tool, which can be used by individual or small group.
3. Without sound, and usually without captions, it forces a pupil to take an active role in viewing.
4. It provides motion that the filmstrip lacks.
5. Motion can be stopped to make a still picture for close study.
6. Most film-loops come with study guides.
7. The teacher can make Quest Cards to serve a specific purpose for students to use with the films.

Read the article "Innovations in the Social Studies: The 8mm Single Concept Film," by Leonard W. Ingraham, in *Social Education* 30 (February 1966): 91-92.

More single concept film-loops have been produced in the area of science than in the social studies, but there is an ever-increasing production in the latter. The single best source for a list of all of the producers is: *Silent Film-Loop Source Directory*, Technicolor Audiovisual Systems, 299 Kalmus Drive, Costa Mesa, Cal. 92626.

It lists worldwide sources in all subject areas, classified by subject matter and educational level. Two of the producers are: The Ealing Corporation, 2225 Massachusetts Avenue, Cambridge, Mass. 02140; and Society for Visual Education, Inc., 1345 Diversey Parkway, Chicago, Ill. 60614.

TEACHING WITH FILMSTRIPS

The filmstrip can be used for individual, small-group, or whole-class viewing, depending upon the purpose for which it was chosen. Its purchase cost is not much greater than the rental fee on some films. If motion is not important to learning, consideration should be given to using a filmstrip rather than a movie. It is a far more flexible instrument for teaching and learning purposes. Sometimes audio tapes or written scripts accompany the filmstrip and help to explain the data to the students.

Values of the filmstrip

The filmstrip can serve one or more of these purposes:

1. To introduce, enrich, review, or summarize a topic or unit.
2. To provide a good source of information.
3. To show steps or process in detail (e.g., building a log cabin, making butter, making a book).
4. To encourage further research.
5. To develop one or more skills.
6. To provide a basis for testing or other evaluation exercise.

The filmstrip can provide much detail on a subject, and it can be used to reinforce or supplement other experiences, such as field trips, textbooks, or films. Filmstrips are available on an extensive array of subjects. Sometimes the teacher wants very much to teach a topic that does not have filmstrips or media developed for use with it. One group of teachers in Brunswick, Maine, developed their own packet of filmstrips on "Maine" so that they could use these sources of input as research stimuli for the students.

Effective use can be made of only part of a filmstrip, and that part can be reshown at any time. Pace of presentation can be controlled and the filmstrip can be turned backward or forward. A single frame (picture) can be viewed as long as desired. Discussion can take place during viewing. The use of a filmstrip can be easily adjusted to a time schedule by showing a few frames or many frames. All pupils can focus attention on the same picture, and specific features can be pointed out.

Preparation is the key to effective use of filmstrips. Suggestions in the teacher's guide can be most helpful. Most of the suggestions mentioned above for teaching with films can be used also with filmstrips.

The whole class can view a film or filmstrip, but tasks in connection with a showing can be assigned commensurate with the learning levels of the children. Teams (three to five children) at each of the three levels below could discuss the questions suggested, which range from simple reactions at the lowest level to critical thinking through comparison and contrast at the highest level.

What did you like best in the filmstrip? Would you like to see it again? Why or why not?

If you were going to plan a dramatization on the subject, what in the filmstrip could you use in the planning? Be specific.

What did the filmstrip give you that you did not get from your textbook or from your reading? Does this mean it did a better or poorer job? Would you want to receive all your information from a textbook? Give reasons for your answers.

Most teachers seem to use filmstrips only in whole-class viewing. There are other possibilities:

1. Many filmstrips are excellent for independent study by an individual. (The individual, nonmechanical, nonprojective, inexpensive viewer is most useful).
2. Children in pairs or threes can use it in material for a report, in selecting certain frames for class viewing for specific purposes, in previewing to set questions for the class, in building a picture test.
3. Have an individual, pair, or three-group study a certain number of frames, then do research to determine a series of frames that should follow. Compare their choices with the frames in the actual filmstrip.

As an instructional tool the filmstrip has several advantages:

1. The projector can be operated by children.
2. The filmstrip is easily stored and transported.
3. It is not as easily damaged as movie film.
4. Projector equipment is less expensive than movie equipment.
5. A filmstrip library in a school is more possible than a motion picture library in a school system because filmstrips are less expensive.

Filmstrips usually have from forty-five to sixty-five or more frames. Most producers will send filmstrips to schools on approval. It is good to have the judgments of two or three teachers at the same grade level in deciding what to purchase.

Evaluating a filmstrip for purchase

1. Rate the value of the filmstrip for each of the following purposes. Circle the appropriate letter for *Excellent, Good, Fair,* or *Poor.*

a. To introduce a new topic or unit	E G F P
b. To provide a good source of information	E G F P
c. To enrich a topic or unit	E G F P
d. To encourage further pupil research	E G F P
e. To review a topic or unit	E G F P
f. To develop one or more skills	E G F P

2. Is the quality of the photography good?
3. Are the captions effective?
4. At what level would the vocabulary be appropriate—primary, intermediate, or upper?
5. Were too many ideas presented per frame?
6. Is the topic covered adequately?
7. Is the material up-to-date and accurate?
8. Is the material presented in a logical sequence?
9. Does it answer curricular needs?
10. Will it hold the interest of the pupils?
11. Can the content be just as, or more, effectively and efficiently presented in some other way? Can the filmstrip be used profitably without teacher guidance? Finally, do you recommend purchase? For which one or more of these groups is it suitable: slow learner, average, or superior?

The use of 2-by-2-inch color slides

Slides have the same advantages as frames in filmstrips. In addition, they offer great flexibility in adding or discarding. Two sources of slides are the teacher and the class. Also get descriptive literature and catalogs from:

Clay-Adams
299 Webro Road
Parsippany, N.J. 07054

Eastman Kodak Company
Dept. 412L
Rochester, N.Y. 14650
(Ask for Kodak Pamphlet No. S-2, "Some Sources of Color Slides")

Prothman Associates, Inc.
650 Thomas Avenue
Baldwin, N.Y. 11510

Society for Visual Education
Division of Singer Company
1345 Diversey Parkway
Chicago, Ill. 60614

THE USE OF REALIA

People are great collectors and enjoy seeing "the real thing." A picture of an African mask is interesting to look at, but handling one and holding it over your face is infinitely more thought provoking. When you feel it and try it on for size, you raise innumerable questions. How do the people who make these use them? Do they fasten them on their faces? How do they do that? Are there different sizes for different people? Do the eyes match better for some than for others? Perhaps the answer to any one of these questions is unimportant, but the questions so generated can carry over into an involvement with a people and a culture that is different from your own.

The collection of realia for a culture serves the same purposes as a filmstrip and adds to this list the generation of a curiosity that is information seeking.

The following list will give the teacher some idea of the different realia that might be used in a classroom.

- Masks
- Candles
- Artwork
  - Drawings
  - Sketches
  - Sculpture
- Cloth
  - Items of clothing
  - Swatches of weaving
  - Screen printing
  - Tie-dye products
- Beads
- Belts
- Moccasins
- Head-dresses
- Necklaces or jewelry
- Drums
- Food products
  - Processed canned items
  - Dried materials
  - Grains
- Musical instruments

USING THE FLANNELBOARD

The flannelboard, or felt board, is frequently used in the primary grades, especially in arithmetic and reading. It probably has greater possibilities in social studies in all grades than most teachers have yet realized. This teaching device is simply a board covered with flannel or felt-like material. Paper, pictures, and other light materials with sensitized backing may be made to adhere to the flannelboard by merely pressing them on.

How to make a flannelboard

Use a backing board made of Masonite, Celotex, plywood, or heavy cardboard, approximately 24″ × 30″, for one much larger is apt to be cumbersome. Use long fibred flannel (a good grade of outing flannel works well), felt, or suede. Cut the flannel four inches longer and wider than the backing. Stretch flannel tightly over the board, folding it over the edges. Have it smooth, for wrinkles will cause material to fall off. Attach the cloth on the back with adhesive or wide masking tape, thumbtacks, or staples.

Lightweight or flat material can be made to adhere to a flannelboard by attaching material to the back of it such as rough sand paper, flocked paper, strips of rayon flock, or flannel, which will provide friction. Depending on the weight of the material, it is not usually necessary to cover all of it; strips should be sufficient. Some materials will adhere to the flannel without any sensitized backing. These include:

1. wool
2. yarn
3. string
4. sponge
5. steel wool
6. corduroy
7. balsa wood
8. emery paper
9. suede
10. velvet
11. rough blotting paper
12. construction paper
13. embroidery floss
14. pipe cleaners

Test each kind of material you plan to use.

Reminders

1. To be educationally effective, each presentation must have a definite purpose.
2. Present a single idea, using a minimum of items on the flannelboard.
3. Make sure that printing is large enough to be read at a distance.
4. Tilt the top back a little, on an easel, on a table against the wall, or resting on the chalk tray.
5. Apply material with pressure on a slight downward movement.
6. Use contrasting colors.
7. Brush the flannel surface often to keep it working and looking like new.
8. In making a presentation on the flannelboard:
   a. Arrange cut-outs or strips in sequence, face down with the first one on top.
   b. Work from one side of the board.
   c. Talk to the class, not to the board.
   d. Place each cut-out carefully, but quickly and deftly, for "showmanship."
9. Store the material in large manila envelopes, properly marked, for later use. Cross-reference it in your own unit outline.

Suggestions for use

These ideas may stimulate others. Once the board is in use, the children will also probably see more possibilities.

1. The board can be used as a simple display or bulletin board; if so, it should be changed every day, for the flannelboard should not be static; it is for adding to, subtracting from, changing.
   a. A lettered sign can say "This Day in History." The daily newspaper often lists events in history that happened on that day's date.
   b. A big headline from today's paper can be posted, without any details. Or use a silhouette of a state, country, or continent, not always right side up, with a sign saying, "Recognize this?"
   c. Post a single, striking picture, with a "thinking" question.

The suggestions below are for a "presentation" by the teacher in teaching, by a pupil in reporting, or by a pupil using packaged learning exercises that he can correct himself after mounting on the flannelboard.

2. Anything in sequential order can be used: travels of a letter, from writing to delivery; steps in a process—making a candle, getting out a newspaper; an outline for research, or for note-taking.
3. New vocabulary coming in a film or filmstrip can be placed on the board word by word as each one is discussed.
4. Circle graphs, each percent or proportion in a different color, are effective.
5. Statistical material can be displayed, with cut-out symbols to illustrate date, for example, different numbers of silhouettes of men to illustrate the populations in the United States, Russia, India, and China.
6. Map possibilities include placing name cards (countries, oceans, other continents) on and around a large cut-out of a continent; making a map of a community, with streets, houses, stores, a river, a bridge; maps outlined in yarn; an overlay of maps drawn to the same scale for comparative size—Italy on the United States, or Holland on your home state; putting one continent in place in relation to another continent already there.
7. Build a simple bulletin board as a brief report is given on a historical character.

The board can be used for learning exercises, for an individual or a pair to do. Package each exercise in a large manila envelope. Make cards to place on the flannelboard. Have the answers in a small envelope for later self-correction. Examples of learning exercises are:

1. Arrange countries in order of size (area).
2. Place the correct word under right picture—Holland, Norway, and France, for

example, with small pictures of those countries. More than one picture of a country can be used.

3. A wide variety of classification exercises, like classifying *names* under *headings* of rivers, countries, and islands; classifying words ("crops," "sidewalk," "tractor") under *farm* and *city*; classifying *countries* and *conditions* (six months' darkness) under *high*, *low*, and *middle latitudes*.
4. Make cards with the names of many "helpers." Choose those that belong under *Helpers Who Come to Our House*.
5. Many kinds of matching exercises: dates and events; inventors and inventions; famous people and accomplishments; explorers and territories.

The teacher must be careful that time is not being used inefficiently by having only a single performer, with the rest of the class acting as nonparticipating spectators. The flannelboard certainly has possibilities for the teacher working with a group of slow learners on skills and on the content of a unit.

Source list for flannelboards and accessories

Creative Visuals
Snyder Highway
Box 1911
Big Spring, Texas 79720

Demco Educational Corporation
2120 Fordem Avenue
Madison, Wis., 53701

The Instructro Corporation
Paoli, Pa. 19301

Oravisual Company, Inc.
P.O. Box 11150
St. Petersburg, Fla. 33733

GRAPHICS

Graphs, tables, charts, cartoons, and diagrams are being used increasingly in textbooks for the middle grades to tell the kind of story each can tell best. All are commonly used in newspapers and current affairs magazines and children's current affairs periodicals. These graphic representations are much easier to read than if the information were in sentences and paragraphs. Comparisons are more easily made, relationships more easily seen, and understandings more quickly developed when expressed graphically. But they have to be taught and they have to be learned.

Helpful material for children has been published recently in four workbooks for grades 3,4,5, and 6 in a series called "Table and Graph Skills."[1] We quote from the *Teacher's Guide:*

> Children need to understand the purposes of and reasons for tables and graphs—what a table or graph *is* and *does.* Children must realize that tables and graphs provide an orderly shortcut to communication:
>
> Tables are a systematic arrangement of data.
>
> Tables contain certain standard components.
>
> Tables can be studied at the literal, interpretive, and critical levels of reading and thinking.
>
> Tables can be used as a source of data for graphs.
>
> Graphs present a collection of facts or data in a concise and organized manner.
>
> Graphs are visual interpretations of numerical relationships.
>
> Graphs vary in type and purpose.
>
> Graphs contain both standard and varying components.
>
> Graphs, too, may be studied at the literal, interpretive levels of reading and thinking.
>
> Children need to learn to read tables and graphs on three levels. The first level is the *literal level.* The child reads to remember the facts and data presented. We should ask, "What data is presented? What quantities are shown?"
>
> Second, we need to teach the reading of tables and graphs on the *interpretive level.* This is the level where the child compares facts and data. (This is the most important because graphs show changes, trends, parts, and comparisons.) We should ask, "Which is more? Which is less? How much more? How much less?"
>
> Third, we need to teach the reading of tables and graphs on the *critical level.* This level is a "must" because the child must read and evaluate the data and the graph. We should ask "Is the data complete? Are the data and source accurate and reliable? Is the presentation distorted? Is the presentation being used to sway public opinion or for propaganda purposes? Is there evidence of bias? What is the trend? Why do you think so? Is the graph form appropriate to the data?"[2]

Just as we introduce maps in the early grades at the children's level of understanding, we can also introduce graphs concerned with something they know. The number of boys in the room can be represented by pictographs of boys in a row. In a row below we can represent girls. The two rows make a bar graph. Or, a series of bars can represent the temperature outdoors each morning as school begins. As

1. Xerox Education Publications, Education Center, Columbus, Ohio 43216. Minimum order ten per title; $.50 each. Free thirty-two page Teacher's Guide.

2. Special permission granted by *Teacher's Guide, Table and Graph Skills Series,* published by Xerox Education Publications. © Xerox Corp. 1968.

we move through the primary grades, there are other opportunities: school savings collections, number of books read, and spelling scores, for example. Arithmetic and social studies should be correlated, for arithmetic texts at the middle grade level make excellent presentations. Graphs should always be used functionally, not developed apart from specific application of the knowledge. Whenever you come across graphs in material that the children are using, attention should be given to them and their meanings developed. Graphs show numerical data in a form that is easy to comprehend. There are several types of graphs, including those described below.

Tables

Quantitative information presented in a table is usually more easily understood than that written in paragraph form. Informational material for graphs often comes from tables. Both Table 8.1 and Table 8.2 provide the answers to many questions. Either can furnish considerable information. The teacher shows this by the questions he asks. Pupils will learn through such questions how to ask their own and find the answers in the table until "reading and interpreting" a table is done directly without invented questions.

TABLE 8.1 9 A.M. OUTDOOR TEMPERATURE READINGS AT OUR SCHOOL

DATE	TEMPERATURE
Dec. 6	44
Dec. 7	32
Dec. 8	27
Dec. 9	36
Dec. 10	49
Dec. 11	42
Dec. 12	27
Dec. 13	27
Dec. 14	22
Dec. 15	22
Dec. 16	47
Dec. 17	42

TABLE 8.2 AREA, POPULATION, AND POPULATION PER SQUARE MILE OF COUNTRIES IN SOUTH AMERICA

COUNTRY	AREA (SQUARE MILES)	POPULATION	POP. PER SQUARE MILES
Argentina	1,079,520	23,920,000	22
Bolivia	424,163	5,190,000	12
Brazil	3,286,473	100,100,000	30
Chile	292,257	10,000,000	34
Colombia	455,335	23,000,000	50
Ecuador	116,270	6,598,300	57
Fr. Guiana	37,740	60,000	2
Guyana	83,000	750,000	9
Paraguay	157,047	2,580,000	16
Peru	496,222	14,460,000	29
Surinam	62,000	385,000	6
Uruguay	72,172	2,960,000	41
Venezuela	352,148	10,970,000	31

Graphs

Pictorial graphs. In this type of representation, sometimes a symbol is repeated enough times to represent amount (one automobile for every 10,000 automobiles). Sometimes a picture is drawn at the end of each bar in a bar graph to show a type of item or commodity. Pictures are used as "Area" symbols (different size cotton bales to represent cotton grown in United States, Egypt, and India); or barrels of petroleum as in Figure 8.1.

PICTURE GRAPHS[3]

ADVANTAGES	LIMITATIONS
Eye-catching symbols	Necessitate counting symbols
Visual simplicity	Inexactness with partial symbols
Retention of facts superior over other graphs showing same data	Difficult to picture some data
	Time-consuming construction
	May necessitate computation

3. Ibid.

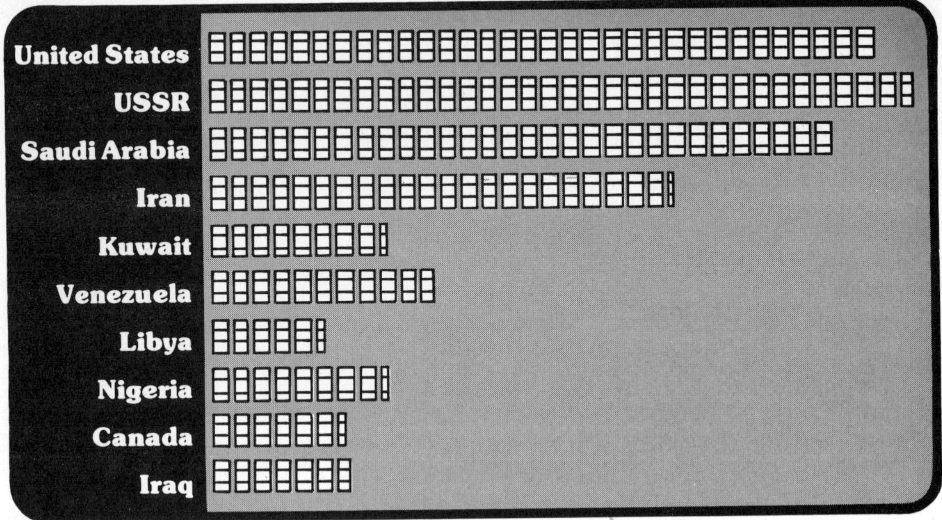

FIGURE 8.1 Leading producers of petroleum in 1974

Bar graphs are useful in comparing five to ten items. The amount of each item is shown by length of the bar. Each bar should be drawn the same width, and can be shown horizontally or vertically. Figure 8.2 shows the use of bar graphs.

BAR GRAPHS[4]

ADVANTAGES	LIMITATIONS
Visual simplicity	Trends not readily seen
Comparisons readily seen	Less effective with more than six or seven items
Bar connects grid point to axis for ease of reading	May necessitate interpolation
Multiple bar useful for comparisons	
Direction of bars (horizontal and vertical) helps give visual image to type of data.	

4. Ibid.

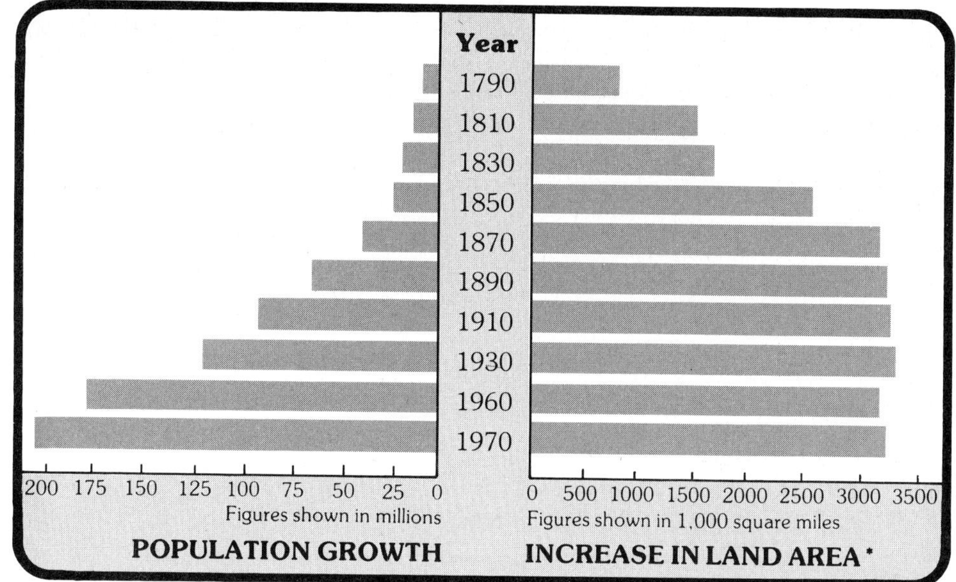

FIGURE 8.2 Increase in population and land area of the United States, 1790-1960

Circle, pie, or area graphs show best how a total amount was divided into parts (how a tax dollar is spent, how U.S. production compares with the world total). They are easy for children to interpret, but difficult to draw accurately. Construction of circle graphs is done in the upper grades. Figure 8.3 shows a pie graph on populations.

AREA GRAPHS[5]

ADVANTAGES	LIMITATIONS
Show parts of a whole	Show only the whole and its parts
Show fractions	Less effective with more than six or seven items
Show percentages	Trends not shown
May permit labeling of integral parts	Difficult to construct
Comparisons readily seen	Size of "slice" may affect labeling and readability

5. Ibid.

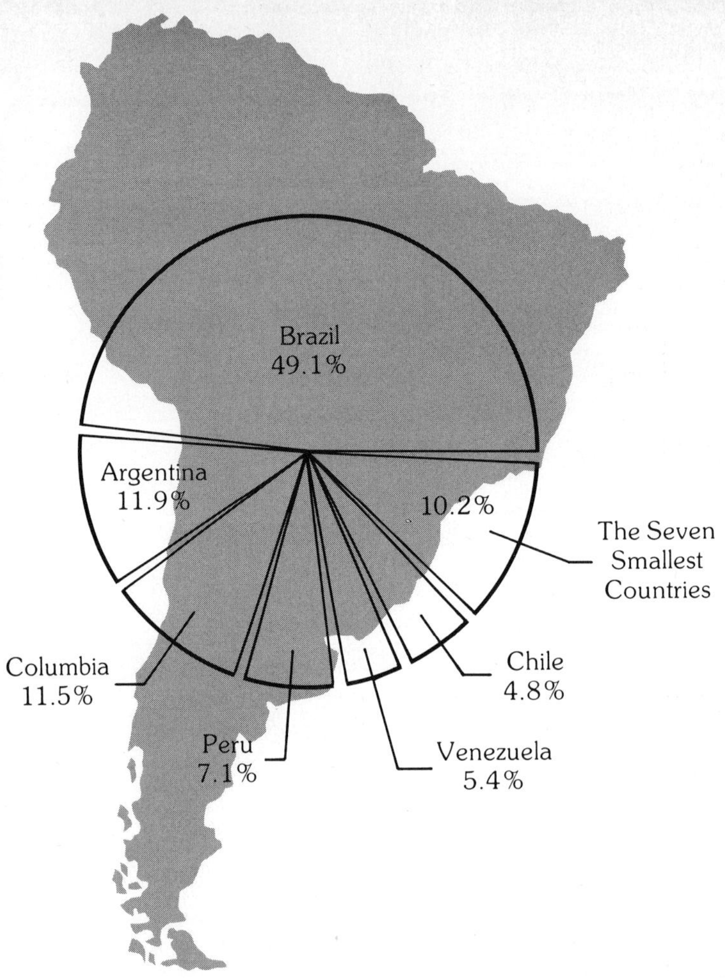

FIGURE 8.3 Population of South America

LINE GRAPHS[6]	
ADVANTAGES	LIMITATIONS
Show trends, changes, growth patterns	Most abstract of graph forms
Effective with many items	Not effective with just a few points plotted
Easy to plot, once constructed	Item comparisons not easily seen
Allow for highest degree of accuracy of all graph forms	May necessitate interpolation
Multiple line most useful for trend comparisons	Line pattern of close, irregular movements or sharp changes may cause readability problems

6. Ibid.

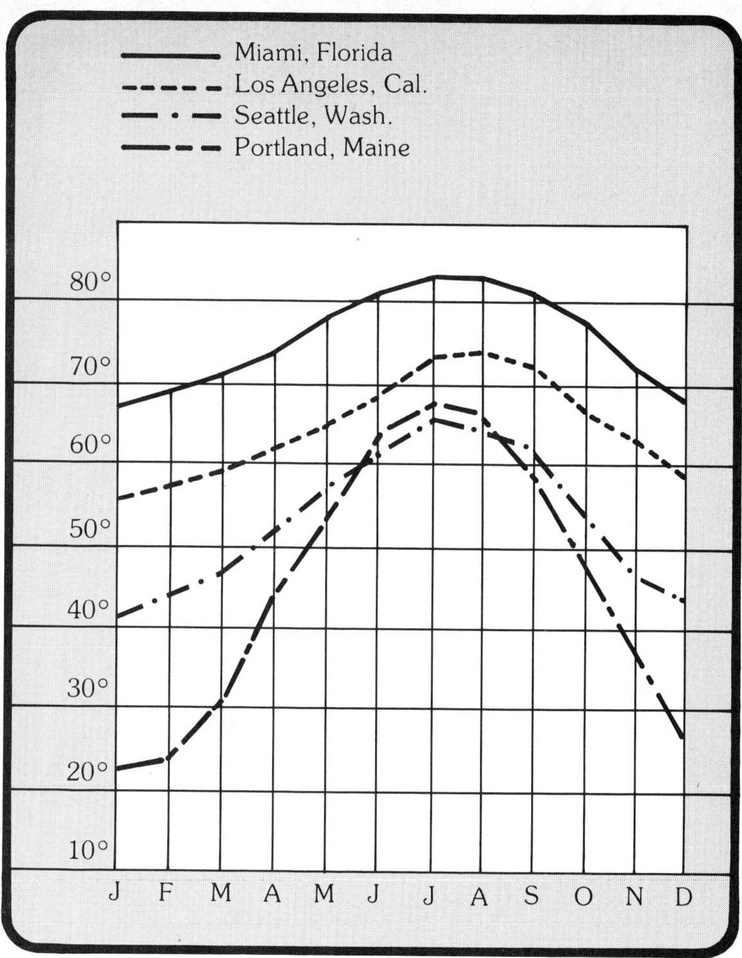

FIGURE 8.4. Monthly normal temperature in four corners of conterminous United States

Line graphs are used to show trends in amounts over a period of time (rainfall, population, production of automobiles). Figure 8.4 is a typical line graph. They are the most accurate of the various types of graphs.

Summary of suggestions. The abilities we seek to develop in reading and making graphs—reading and marking of rank, using a key, interpretation of significant data—involve much questioning as checks on understanding. It is better that these questions be on worksheets on specific graphs (multiple-choice test form is a good method) than that time be wasted in oral questioning by the teacher. Questions will be involved with such ideas as:

1. Comprehending the title to determine the topic on which the graph gives information.
2. Recognizing from subtitles and row or column headings what is shown by each part of the graph.
3. Reading amounts from a graph by using scales, by interpreting sectors in a circle graph, by using special symbols and a key.
4. Comparing two or more values from a graph.
5. Determining trends.
6. Realizing that percentages and proportions do not give absolute amounts.
7. Grasping one or more outstanding conclusions that can be interpreted from the graph concept.

Frequent, not sporadic, attention must be given to graphs if genuine understanding is to be developed. Reporting on a topic by pupils often offers opportunity to present information through a graph. Research shows that children can interpret pictorial graphs most easily, followed in order by circle, bar, and line graphs.

Charts, diagrams, and posters

In the literature, there is some overlapping of meaning in describing charts, diagrams, and posters.

Charts. The main function of charts is to show relationships, such as:

1. Comparisons (tools on the colonial farm and today's farm).
2. Developments (dates and events of territorial expansion of the United States).
3. Processes (churning butter or making candles).
4. Classification (vegetables that grow in the ground and above the ground, types of homes).
5. Organization (population chart).

On the other hand, charts are also used for telling a story, or merely listing, in:

1. Directions—how-to-do-it, making an oral report.
2. Reference—reading list, steps in note taking.
3. Vocabulary—new words learned on a field trip.
4. Record—contributions in the sharing period, questions, major learnings.
5. Planning—activities for school civic organization, a field trip.
6. Standards—the good citizen, behavior on the school bus.

7. Tabulation—admission of states to the union, date of inventions in sequential order.

Posters. There are advertising billboard posters, travel posters, Book Week, Education Week, and Fire Prevention Week posters, as well as posters which we make and which the children make. They all have pretty much the same things in common. Each of them

1. is attention-getting, often through color, lines, spacing.
2. has one specific purpose.
3. gives you the idea in a matter of seconds.

Sometimes a poster may have several scenes or sections, or it may be a combination of pictures, maps, and graphs, with few words. However, it fails in its purpose if it does not catch and hold the viewer's attention and get its message across quickly.

Diagrams. A diagram might be considered as a special kind of chart. Perhaps it shows with connecting lines and boxes the organizational pattern of the United Nations or the three branches of the U.S. government, or pictures the flow of money from its sources into a state government or the pathway of electricity from the power plant to a home.

Cartoons

Cartoons now appear in children's current affairs periodicals. Children often look at and interpret those that they come across in newspapers and magazines. A few textbooks have cartoons. The abler children should be encouraged to draw cartoons, with the emphasis on the idea, not the quality of art work. Cartoons characteristically

1. contain one central idea.
2. criticize, appraise, or interpret.
3. make use of exaggeration, satire, and caricature.
4. stress an outstanding physical feature of a person.
5. present *only one point of view.*
6. make use of common symbols such as Uncle Sam, the Republican elephant, the Democratic donkey, John Bull, the eagle, the Russian hammer and sickle, the dove of peace.

The next time your student periodical uses a cartoon, see how many of these characteristics the children can point out. Continue to do this with cartoons until the children have a correct concept of the medium.

FOR FURTHER READING

Jarolimek, John. *Social Studies in Elementary Education*. 4th ed. New York: Macmillan, 1971. Chapter 14.

McCune, George H., and Neville Pearson. "*Interpreting Materials Presented in Graphic Form*," in *Skill Development in Social Studies*, 33rd Yearbook. Washington, D.C.: National Council for the Social Studies, 1963. Chapter 11.

THE OVERHEAD PROJECTOR

To be most useful, the overhead projector should be a permanent fixture in a classroom; the teacher should have the projector at his fingertips when he needs it. It is possible, however, and reasonably convenient for one to serve several classrooms. The full surface that can be projected is an area 10″ by 10″. Let's look at some of the advantages of the projector.

1. Operation is extremely simple.
2. The teacher always faces the class and thus maintains direct eye contact with his pupils. Since no darkening facilities are needed with this type of projector, you have only to turn on the switch.
3. Inexpensive acetate sheets (used X-ray film, clear) or 100 foot rolls of acetate film may be prepared ahead of time and later stored for further use.
4. Several materials may be used for writing and illustrating. Magic markers, grease pencils, India ink, and crayons can be used for writing. Several varieties of colored transparent and opaque tapes and shading films can be used for illustrating.
5. Opaque objects, such as silhouettes, may be used for direct projection.
6. Thermofax films now make it possible to copy illustrations directly from textbooks, magazines, or newspapers, for immediate projection. Copying takes approximately four seconds.
7. Transparencies (sheets of plastic or film) can be mounted on a cardboard frame to be more rigid and for ease in filing. The frame provides space for writing labels and notes.
8. Teachers can explain, question, and instruct—before, during, and after projection.
9. Transparencies may be shown in any desired sequence.
10. Images may be projected on a white or off-white wall as well as on a screen.
11. Some colored magazine pictures (e.g., *National Geographic*) can be transferred to a transparency by a special process (original is destroyed in the process).
12. It provides opportunities for student participation in the instructional process.

Uses of the overhead projector seem to be limited only by the imagination of the teacher. Technical production of some kinds of transparencies has to be learned. Instructions are given by the companies selling the copying equipment, the audio-visual people in a school system, fellow teachers, and articles in magazines. Here are some ideas to consider in using transparencies and acetate sheets:

1. Three kinds of transparencies:
   a. Original composition pre-written by the teacher or written as the lesson proceeds.
   b. Made from printed materials discovered by the teacher (magazines, newspapers, books, current events papers).
   c. Pre-printed—commerically developed and listed in catalogs of social studies materials.
2. Use of maps in the three kinds of transparencies:
   a. Use an outline map of state, region, country to locate or draw in geographical phenomena given in response to query or class discussion.
   b. Compare size of one country with another by an overlay (a transparency laid over another transparency).
   c. Combine the outline map base transparency with overlay transparencies showing rainfall, population density, and land use of the same area.
3. Analyze and interpret cartoons (including those from today's paper).
4. Supplement talk with concrete illustrations that everyone can see.
5. In making points a teacher can write while he talks and is facing the class.
6. Lyrics of songs on records can be read while the record is playing.
7. Teach note taking, outlining, etc.
8. The "progressive disclosure" or "revelation" technique can be used.
   a. With the use of overlays show relationships or build up presentations, step by step, in logical sequence (territorial expansion of the United States).
   b. Sometimes you want to reveal the material part by part on a transparency. Use a piece of cardboard or paper to mask all but what you wish to show. Open up additional portions by sliding the mask. (Columns in a table; steps in note taking; the answer to a question.) Sometimes you want to exclude extraneous material in a transparency.

FOR FURTHER READING

"101 Teaching Ideas from Beseler." Charles Beseler Company, 8 Fernwood Road, Florham, N.J. 07932. Free. Good suggestions on use of both opaque and overhead projectors.

Schultz, Morton J. *The Teacher and the Overhead Projector.* Englewood Cliffs, N.J.: Prentice-Hall, 1965.

THE OPAQUE PROJECTOR

The opaque projector, because it requires a darkened room and is not easily portable unless on a table with wheels, is not as much used by teachers as its worth as an instructional device warrants. It projects nontransparent material. (For use with the overhead projector, such material must be made into transparencies.)

We see it used profitably in classrooms to project pictures, drawings, graphs, charts, diagrams, maps, statistical tables, music, illustrations from newspapers, photographs, postcards, cartoons, textiles, coins and paper money (useful in a first showing of foreign money), printed pages from textbooks, reference books, workbooks. Children can prepare materials to use in reports, other work can be shared. Maps in their enlargement through the projector can be traced on large sheets of paper; some portions of pictures and drawings can be traced for murals or scenery. Care should be taken not to overheat materials. Teachers who have neglected the use of the opaque projector now see it and use it as part of the instructional materials system.

USING PICTURES

In spite of the popularity of picture magazines, the use of the flat picture in social studies teaching seems to have been neglected. It is often forgotten that a few carefully chosen pictures, highly pertinent to the immediate subject, can be an excellent vehicle for teaching and learning. This includes pictures in the textbook.

The teacher will have to rely upon his evaluation and growing experience for always getting the right time and the right picture together. Many school libraries and many public libraries have good picture files. However, in addition, each classroom teacher should be building his own picture file, as a resource at hand or for a small group researching a particular topic.

As an instructional aid pictures can:

1. Illustrate steps in a process—how the Pilgrims built their houses, for example.
2. Raise questions and present problems—uncaptioned pictures often serve best.
3. Publicize events—new space flights for astronauts, urban renewal, recreational planning.
4. Prevent and correct misconceptions—dress, homes, and villages of people beyond the Arctic Circle in Norway.
5. Introduce a unit or topic—not all African homes are alike.
6. Create an emotional climate—floods, ravages of war, slums.
7. Illustrate a new concept—dike, irrigation, mountain, desert.
8. Provide authoritative reference—mural, costumes, scenery for a play.

9. Show relative size—men, camel, and pyramids; the Mayflower II with other boats.
10. Serve as a basis of comparison—our town, then and now.
11. Visualize a new environment—life along the Amazon.
12. Create reality in history—by showing people, objects, and events as they really were.
13. Illustrate important points in oral reports—locks on the St. Lawrence Seaway.
14. Supply detail through close-ups and cut-aways—the atomic-powered submarine.
15. Give directions for building a new experience—how to make a candle.
16. Develop critical judgment—the teacher can guide an individual or a committee in selecting pictures highly pertinent to a unit.

Remember in using pictures for instructional purposes that between immaturity and maturity in reading pictures there are different levels of proficiency. A pupil at the low level names objects; he merely lists and enumerates. One at the middle level develops details of meaning and describes what is happening. The students with the highest proficiency draw inferences, see relationships, interpret, and show critical thinking.

One should be aware of the fact that more children tend to pay more attention to the upper left hand quadrant of a picture than to any other area, until they learn differently.

Students need to be taught how to read a picture. Questions help guide them to look for those things that caused you to choose the picture. They can learn to recognize clues to interpretation, such as similarities and differences in what they see compared to what they know from experience; signs of the way people live, work, play, and travel (What are they doing? Why?); conditions of nature that help to explain what you see.

Children are conditioned in what they "see" (the meaning behind the observation) by their cultural background, past experience, personal feelings, and maturity. The teacher should recognize this and make an attempt to provide pictures that will have real meaning for the students he is teaching.

Experts in the field tell us that a picture selected for study should have sufficient, clear detail for information; should focus on one main idea with a definite center of interest; should be adequately captioned; and, if in color, should be faithfully reproduced. Obsolete, worn, and tired pictures should be discarded. If pictures are to be used for instruction, the teacher should see to it that the pictures are large enough to be seen clearly by all class members.

The teacher should check on pictorial as well as textual comprehension and understanding.

Pictures can be used for testing purposes. One might place several sets of four or five pictures, numbered individually, on the chalk rail. Each set contains one picture that does not belong there, and the pupil is to indicate in writing which one is the misfit in each case. In another kind of test, a single picture can have one or more multiple choice items written about it. Arrange a series of pictures in order historically (e.g., inventions, carrying the mail, means of communication). Ask students to find a picture, among several in an envelope, which illustrates a valley, or an island, or a cliff.

Pictures can often be more meaningful than words in learning about terrain, uses of land, kinds of vegetation, climate, clothing, tools and machinery, buildings, occupations, ways of travel and transportation, and recreation.

Making notes on the back of a picture or mount preserves the ideas you had when you selected it and the ones you add as you use it. File pictures in folders or manila envelopes under headings most appropriate to your curriculum so that they can be located easily.

Sources of pictures

The magazine sections of large city Sunday newspapers are often good sources of pictures. The *New York Times* frequently has a complete magazine put out by a foreign country as advertising. Send a notice to parents that you would like donations of magazines to be cut up for usable pictures: *Holiday* and *National Geographic* are good sources, as are occasional individual issues of other magazines.

Discarded textbooks often contain useful pictures. So do displays and advertisements in store windows; ask if it is possible to have material which interests you when the display is dismantled. Look carefully at displays of pictures wherever you see them. You may find a source to which you can write.

Some other sources include (prices are approximate):

American Association for the United Nations, 345 East 45th Street, New York, N.Y. 10017. Posters of flags of the United Nations, 10″ × 15″, $.20 each.

British Information Service, 845 Third Avenue, New York, N.Y. 10022. Picture sets, eleven or twelve panels with captions, and photo-posters on life in the United Kingdom and dependent territories. Picture sets, $.50. Posters free. List of titles available on request.

Detroit Institute of Art, 5200 Woodward Avenue, Detroit, Mich. Picture packets: Egypt, Land of Pharaohs, Greece and Rome, Age of Chivalry. Fifteen sheets, $.20 each.

Documentary Photo Aids, P.O. Box 956, Mt. Dora, Fla. 32757. Pictures of United States history, unretouched, 11″ x 14″. Printed on sturdy, glossy stock. Photos organized by topics. Write for circular.

Graph and Picture Study Skills Kit, Science Research Associates, Inc., 259 E. Erie Street, Chicago, Ill. 60611. Organization of material similar to SRA's *Map and Globe Skills Kit.* Study cards give children an introduction to the concepts, and skill cards offer the necessary practice to become familiar with graphs, pictures, cartoons, etc. Write for further detail.

Ideal School Supply Co., 8312 Birkholf Avenue, Chicago, Ill. Six picture sets on industries, cattle, cotton, fishery, glass, lumber, rubber. Sixteen pictures to a set, 8½″ by 11″.

Jackdaws. A *Jackdaw* is a packet filled with a wealth of original source material. Since each item in the packet is separate, it offers the teacher full freedom in the method of presentation used for a class, a group, or an individual. There are facsimile reproductions of original documents—letters, maps, cartoons, paintings, newspaper accounts, poster, broadsides, telegrams—virtually any document of significance pertaining to the topic. Among the topics are Columbus, and the Discovery of America; Immigration in Colonial Times; The American Revolution; The California Gold Rush; and many more. $3.95 each, 25 percent on a school order. Ask Grossman Publishers, 625 Madison Avenue, New York, N.Y. 10022 for their brochure on *Jackdaws*.

Metropolitan Museum of Art, 5th Avenue and 82nd Street, New York, N.Y. 10028. School picture sets on ancient Egypt, ancient Rome, colonial America, medieval life, 6¾″ by 3¾″. Fifteen cents per set of eighteen pages, four sets for $.50.

Realistic Visual Aids, Box 278, Highland, Calif., 92346. *Across Early America*, set of twenty-four photos with explanations illustrating the voyage of the Mayflower, building of the colonies, trails west, and the westward movement. Heavy poster board, 11″ x 14″, $2.98 per set.

Visual Geography Series, Sterling Publishing Co., 419 Park Avenue S., New York, N.Y. 10016. Volumes on ninety-five countries, over one hundred photos in each. Sixty-four pp. paperback. $1.50.

Study prints

A number of publishers have organized sets of pictures around major ideas or topics. Most of them are sold only in sets; some have teacher's guides in separate booklets or on the backs of the pictures. To know what values these study prints might have for your social studies program, it is worthwhile to have catalogs or circulars available for perusal and school system arrangements made for previewing them. There is variety in sizes, numbers in a set, prices, colors, and qualities. Here are sources and illustrative samples.

Bailey Films, 6509 De Longpre Avenue, Hollywood, Calif., 90028. Color, 11″ by 14″. "Colonial Living with Paul Revere," "Early Explorers of North America."

Denoyer-Geppert Company, 5235 Ravenswood Avenue, Chicago, Ill. 60640. Color, 21″ by 30″. Latin America, Europe, Middle East and India, and others.

Fideler Visual Teaching, 31 Ottawa Avenue, N.W., Grand Rapids, Mich. Life in America (eight portfolios), Life in Europe (ten portfolios), Story of America (ten portfolios). Twenty to forty-eight prints per folio, 9¼″ by 12⅜″, with accompanying text on reverse.

Harper & Row, Publishers, 49 East 33rd Street, New York, N.Y. 10016. *American Heritage Picture Cards,* color, 14″ by 10″. Settling the New World—The Spanish, French and Dutch; Settling the New World—The English; Life in the New Nation; The New Nation Moves West. Also, *Discussion Pictures for Beginning Social Studies,* ninety large pictures on eighteen social studies themes (dependence and interdependence of man, man's need for association and expression in groups, etc.).

Holt, Rinehart and Winston, Inc., 383 Madison Ave., New York, N.Y. 10017. *Words and Action,* a program of role-playing photo problems that stimulate verbal and action responses from young children.

A.J. Nystrom & Co., 3333 Elston Ave., Chicago, Ill. 60618. Primary grades, color, 9¾″ by 12¾″ on "Community Helpers," and a "Child's Life in Japan"; geography pictures, 30″ by 21″, color, Europe, Africa, North America, Australia and New Zealand.

Rand, McNally & Co., 8255 Central Park Ave., Skokie, Ill. 60076. UNESCO Geography Wall Charts—Denmark, France, Hungary, Netherlands, Spain, Switzerland, United Kingdom, U.S.S.R. Also UNESCO Study Prints.

Scholastic Magazines, Inc. 900 Sylvan Avenue, Englewood Cliffs, N.J. 07632. Multi-racial materials in Picture Collections I and II, early primary.

Silver Burdett Company, Morristown, N.J. 07960. A primary social studies program with textbooks and color Picture Packets for Kindergarten through Grade 3; also other Picture Packets, color, 19″ by 23″, on "Families Around the World" (India, Italy, Mexico, Soviet Union, and many more).

Society for Visual Education, Inc., 1345 Diversey Parkway, Chicago, Ill. 60614. Color, 18″ by 13″. South America, Mexico, Urban Life, Children Around the World. Indians, Community Helpers, Ecology. Sets of eight pictures.

UNESCO Publications Center, United Nations, New York, N.Y. A set of black and white photographs on Africa, 11½″ by 11½″, with a discussion guide. $1.

Superintendent of Documents, U.S. Government Printing Office, Washington, D.C. 20402. *America the Beautiful.* Set of 52 pictures.

Coronet, 65 E. South Water Street, Chicago, Ill. 60601. *Climates of the World* and *Family Life Around the World.*

Harcourt, Brace Jovanovich, Inc., 757 Third Avenue, New York, N.Y. 10017. *Beginning Level Study Prints* (K). Demonstrates interaction of people and environment.

Laidlaw Brothers, River Forest, Ill. 60305. *People and Their Needs,* (K-1). Twenty-four color readiness study prints to develop social science concepts.

Rand McNally and Co., P.O. Box 7600. Chicago, Ill. 60680. *Interaction Study Prints* (K-4). Four sets of color and black and white prints stressing man's interaction with his environment; teacher's guides.

Silver Burdett Co., 200 James St., Morristown, N.J. 07960. *Families Around the World* Picture Packets (1-3). Sets of study prints about seven countries, holidays, and *Earth, the Home of People.*

Society for Visual Education, Inc., 1345 W. Diversey Parkway, Chicago, Ill. 60614. *Indians of the United States and Canada* (2-6). Forty-eight study prints in six sets devoted to different regional Indians.

David C. Cook, Publisher, 850 North Grove Ave., Elgin, Ill. 60120. *Teaching Pictures.* Sets of twenty each with a teacher's guide. Native Americans, Ecology, Living Together in America, Ethnic Groups.

Charles Merrill Publishing Company, 1300 Alum Creek Drive, Columbus, Ohio 43216. *Visual Experience for Creative Youth.*

FOR FURTHER READING

James, Linnie B., and La Monte Crape. *Geography for Today's Children*. New York: Appleton-Century-Crofts, 1968. Pp. 129-139.

Miller, Bruce. *So You Want to Start a Picture File*. 24 pp. 60 cents; *Sources of Free and Inexpensive Pictures*. Twenty-nine pp. $1.10. Bruce Miller Publications, P.O. Box 369, Riverside, Calif. 92502.

Williams, Catherine M. *Learning from Pictures*. Association for Educational Communications and Technology, 1201 Sixteenth St., N.W., Washington, D.C. 20036.

PROGRAMMED MATERIALS

Using programmed materials to facilitate factual and skills types of learning is usually referred to as programmed learning. The author's emphasis on factual and skills types of learning is intentional. There are certain social studies objectives dealing with problem solving and attitudes that would seem to require social interaction as an integral part of the learning process.

The hardware (teaching machines) of programmed learning is not essential in social studies, and the programs for such machinery have not been developed yet. Some of the same benefits—at least in skills areas—can be gained in the use of programmed textual materials.

One publisher has a programmed booklet on *Reading Latitude from Maps*. (See sample page). On some fifty pages it contains 266 questions, each one requiring a written answer (on a piece of paper, not in the booklet). Down the left hand side of the page the correct answer appears opposite each question. These answers are covered with a piece of cardboard called an answer mask, or "tongue." As soon as the pupil writes his answer, he slides his answer mask down to reveal the correct answer, and so is able to check his answer immediately for correctness. There are five parts to the booklet, with a test at the end of each, for which he does not have the answers. Thus the curriculum material on lattitude is broken down into very small steps, with carefully planned repetition so that the majority of children get most of the answers right the first time and are learning as they move through the questions. The programming makes provision for able pupils to skip some of the questions so that they actually work through only 127 selected questions out of the 266.

Sample material from a programmed booklet[7]

• **80.** A short form for writing north latitude is this:

N. lat.

Notice that for the short form of north we use a capital letter followed by a period. Remember, the short form of latitude ends with a period, too. Write the short form for north latitude.

N. lat. ____________________

• **81.** What would the short form for south latitude be?

S. lat. ____________________

○ **82.** Look at the globe map at your right. Is Australia in the north latitudes?

no ____________________

○ **83.** Is Europe in the north or south latitudes?

north ____________________ latitudes

• **84.** Write the short forms for either north latitude or south latitude to show where Europe and Australia are located.

N. lat. Europe ____________________

S. lat. Australia ____________________

• **85.** If your home is in the United States, it is in the __________ latitudes, which we write in the following short form:

north

N. lat. ____________________

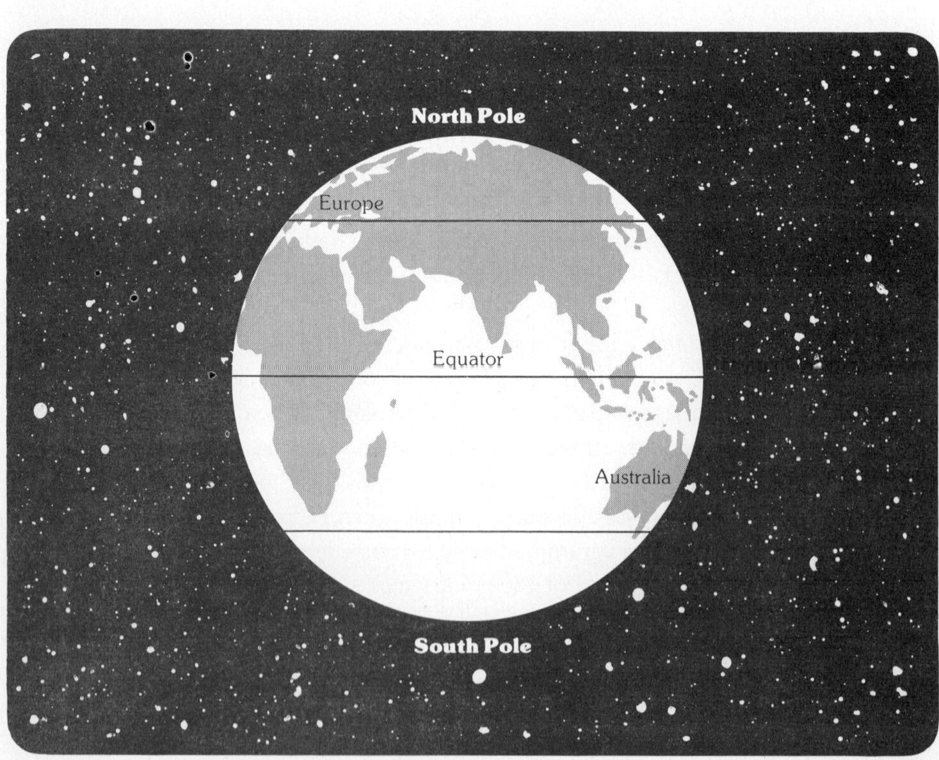

7. Source: From Glenn H. Koehrer, Dorothy Peterson, and Richard J. Paul, *Reading Latitude from Maps* (St. Louis, Mo.: Webster Division, McGraw-Hill Book Co., Inc. 1964), p. 15. Reprinted by permission.

The chief features of programmed instruction have been well stated by Trow:[8]

1. division of material into small sequential steps (frames)
2. overt learner response to each item (most usually by writing an answer)
3. self-pacing (rate of learning may be varied by the individual)
4. immediate feedback regarding correctness of response (self-correcting after each answer)
5. continuous reinforcement through knowledge of progress (learner gets personal satisfaction because he knows he is learning, therefore, highly motivational)
6. evaluation based on written record of performance (progress tests taken at intervals; some teachers use the tests for diagnostic purposes, apart from the program, to determine next steps in the learning process)

If too much of the substantive content of social studies, as contrasted with the development of skills, is put into commercially prepared programmed materials, there is grave danger of substituting printed materials for the teacher in the matter of drill on factual materials, a situation for which the teacher is already being criticized. It is quite possible to develop useful and necessary concepts through programmed learning, but children must use or apply the skills, facts, and concepts in the education aspect of schooling.

Some teachers in a kind of self-programming, laboratory-type, individualized instruction for gaining skill have used materials from workbooks and textbooks, disassembled and reassembled by hand into laboratory kits for individual use, or use by pairs.

Samples of programmed materials

Allyn and Bacon, Inc., 470 Atlantic Avenue, Boston, Mass. 02210. *Understanding Maps* (6-9). Teacher's Manual.

Center for Programmed Instruction of the Institute of Educational Technology, Teachers College, Columbia University, New York, N.Y. 10027.

Coronet Instructional Media, 65 E. South Water Street, Chicago, Ill. 60601. *Latitude and Longitude* (4-8); *Maps: How to Read Them* (5-7); *Westward Expansion of Our Nation* (4-6).

The Macmillan Company, 866 Third Avenue, New York, N.Y. 10022. Parry et al. *Elementary Map Reading* (4). Two volumes, teacher's manual, test booklet.

8. William Clark Trow, *Teacher and Technology: New Designs for Learning.* (New York: Appleton-Century-Crofts, 1963), pp. 93-96. Parenthetical notes have been added.

Behavioral Research Laboratories, Ladera Center, Box 577, Palo Alto, Calif. 94302. MacGraw, Frank, and Joseph E. Williams. Three volumes: *East; Central; West* (5-9).

Webster Division, McGraw-Hill Book Co., Inc., Manchester Road, Manchester, Mo 63011. Glen H. Koehrer, Dorothy Peterson, Richard J. Paul. *Reading Latitude from Maps; Reading Longitude from Maps.*

FOR FURTHER READING

Association for Educational Communications and Technology. *Teaching Machines and Programmed Learning II.* Washington D.C.: National Education Association, 1965.

Estvan, Frank J. *Social Studies in a Changing World.* New York: Harcourt, Brace & World, 1968. Pp. 218-222.

RECORDINGS—DISK AND TAPE

The tape recorder is a more versatile instrument than the record player, in that users can do recordings of their own. Neither instrument has been used as frequently in social studies as its value warrants, although the use of the tape recorder in the classroom has been increasing. Tape is a flexible extension of the disk. The small cassette and the cartridge tapes are easy to use and can be operated by young children. Through the use of tape and disk recordings a pupil can:

1. Have a feeling of "I was there" at some important event.
2. Feel that he is becoming acquainted with some well-known personality.
3. Gain a richer, broader background for understanding an event.
4. Increase the quality of his listening skills.
5. Evaluate himself in various activities when his performance is recorded on tape.

The tape recorder, the record player, tapes, and records are relatively inexpensive and have certain advantages. They can be quite easily transported from place to place. There is a rather good library of records and tapes available. Tapes can be erased and used again and again when what has been recorded does not need to be preserved. Recordings are in the control of the teacher, to be used when he wishes. Sounds and voices can even be transmitted to foreign correspondents.

The uses of tape are as limitless as the ideas of creative teachers and children. The suggestions that follow indicate lines for further development:

1. Discussing news items which have been taped from radio or a television sound track; comparing two or more newscasters recorded on the same evening.

2. Preserving for later use important comments and talks made by school visitors.
3. Presenting a foreign language in connection with a foreign country being studied—recorded by a native of the country living in the community.
4. Recording interviews with community resource people, perhaps developed from questions given in advance to them, with the student interviewer using a prepared script or outline.
5. Recording a first-hand description of a historical event by a local inhabitant, or stories of the past in the community.
6. Bringing sounds into the classroom—the sounds in "Our Town," and sounds from other lands.
7. Presenting a teacher-prepared or pupil-prepared script to accompany slides or filmstrips, with a tapping signal for changing the picture.
8. Analyzing for its strengths and weaknesses a lesson you have taught.
9. Recording class activities to be used for playback to absentees or for purposes of later review.
10. Recording free discussion of plans for an assembly or other activity to be rerun for study and planning by a committee, or for purposes of evaluating group work.
11. Listening to supplementary material useful in the unit being studied.
12. Recording the important points made by a guide on a field trip.
13. Recording a simulated radio program prepared by pupils, then using it in another classroom or over the public address system.
14. Making drills, exercises, and study guides, directing reading of the textbook with suitable explanations for students using earphones to follow the tape. Taped lessons can be highly directed by the teacher. This technique is as useful with first graders as it is with eighth graders. Students enjoy being "plugged in" to the learning center.
15. Recording a prepared or an informal historical dramatization by pupils, or the reading of an historical play.
16. Playing music of a historical period or of a foreign country.
17. Recording a special music program (Christmas in other lands, songs of colonial days, etc.) done in the school, which could be preserved in a tape library to be used again.

Some suggestions will help you make better use of records and tapes:

1. Do not make a tape recording too long.
2. Do not pack too much information into a few minutes; good readers can get more from reading than listening, and poor readers cannot absorb too much in a short period.
3. Be fully acquainted with the mechanics of recording and playback (not at all difficult but just be sure of yourself). Check equipment before class to see that all functions well.

4. Be careful not to erase valuable material.
5. Use a record or tape only when it provides the best teaching and/or learning that can be done at the time for a particular individual, or group, or the whole class. Ask yourself if it could be presented more effectively by some other available means.
6. A recording can be used to introduce a unit, or merely a bit of it for an illustration, or sometimes as the main focus for discussion and further development.
7. Pre-audit any tape or recording before using it with a class.
8. Set the stage—orient the class—make it quite clear to the class why the recording is being used.

You will find it worthwhile to:

1. Seek your nearest audiovisual center for information on recordings (tape and disk), the local or county audiovisual director, the audiovisual instructional materials center of the nearest university, and the state department of education.
2. Write World Tapes for Education, P.O. Box 15703, Dallas, Texas for full information about exchanging tapes with other schools in the United States and foreign countries.
3. Write to Enrichment Teaching Materials, 246 Fifth Avenue, New York, N.Y. 10001 for folder on records based on the Landmark Books. Each record presents two exciting dramatizations (for example, "Pocahontas and Captain John Smith" and "The Winter at Valley Forge") with music and songs.
4. Mincom Division, 3-M Company, 2401 Hudson Road, St. Paul, Minn. 55119. Ask for the free booklet, "Creative Teaching with Tape."

Audiovisual references

Unless the teacher has taken an audiovisual course he is frequently unaware of the amount of specific and very helpful material found in audiovisual texts. Sample these and you will discover many ways of improving the quality of your service to students.

Brown, James W.; Lewis, Richard B.; and Fred F. Harcleroad. *A-V Instruction: Technology Media and Methods*. 4th ed. New York: McGraw-Hill, 1973.

Erickson, Carleton W. H., and David C. Curl. *Fundamentals of Teaching with Audiovisual Technology*. 2d ed. New York: Macmillan, 1972.

Kemp, Jerrold. *Planning and Producing Audiovisual Materials*. 2nd ed. New York: McGraw-Hill, 1970.

Kinder, James S. *Using Instructional Media*. New York: D. Van Nostrand, 1973. Paperback; 271 pp.

Wittich, Walter A., and Charles F. Schuller. *Instructional Technology: Its Nature and Use*. 5th ed. New York: Harper & Row, 1973.

DUPLICATING MASTERS

Within the last few years a number of teachers have begun to use ready-made duplicating masters or dittos of many kinds published by many different companies. Such masters can provide much assistance for the teacher. There are several reasons for using these materials.

1. They provide clear readable copies of the information.
2. The variety in print and in sketches of pictures is eye catching.
3. The skills areas such as mapping and graphing have accurately drawn illustrations.
4. The masters have been submitted to a number of judges or editors before publication and thus have passed at least a beginning test of correct English construction.
5. The sequence used in the materials has a logic that can assist the student in developing skill along the content lines prescribed.

Duplicating masters should never be used to "take up time," or "to keep them quiet." They have a special purpose and are designed to provide help along a certain line. Use them if the purpose described in the material is the same as the one you have in mind for the class today. Do not feel compelled to use all the dittos because they are there. Assess each one carefully. The materials when they are being used are claiming the student's most valuable resource—time. Be sure they are making effective, productive use of that time.

THE TEXTBOOK

In the multimaterials approach to social studies, which is the most fruitful one, reading is a highly important instructional tool. The textbook has been and still is the universal instructional tool. Teachers must recognize and avoid questionable practices in its use.

There are certain things which the textbook does very well. It:

1. Gives an overview or general survey of a topic or unit for an information base.
2. Furnishes a point of departure for further exploration and new ventures—offers a basis for planning.
3. Provides a common body of knowledge, which usually represents a minimum.
4. Provides for study of specific maps, graphs, pictures, and charts under the direction of the teacher.
5. Provides one organized frame of reference.

6. Gives a degree of guidance from authors who are considered experts in the selection of subject matter, choice of learning experiences, and using the results of research.
7. Often has good bibliographical material for sources of additional information.

On the other side, there are things that the textbook does not seem to do well, which limits its value. The textbook:

1. Cannot furnish vivid detail consistently for lack of space.
2. Does not provide local and community implications and applications.
3. Develops the tendency to formalize instruction.
4. Tends to develop in some teachers the faulty belief that "covering the text" is the aim of education.
5. Encourages acceptance of the textbook as *the curriculum*, which it should not be.
6. Does not provide for individual differences in rate of learning or in enrichment.
7. Does not meet the reading needs of individuals.
8. Encourages the question-and-answer recitation if pages are assigned for study.
9. Cannot be up-to-date where timeliness is important.

Points to remember

Any teacher who uses a basic textbook, but does not know and hold in mind the overall purposes or objectives of social studies for the year as well as the ultimate in the school curriculum, can easily become concerned only with how well the pupils are learning factual information.

Some teachers mistakenly think that they have become more than just textbook teachers when they explain difficult points in the book, make or seek local applications, and give some assistance to the slow learner and the superior learner for whom the text is not really suitable. A textbook is an inanimate thing. To it the superior teacher brings creativity and ingenuity. Even an author using his own text would use it as a base, a jumping-off place—a launching pad. The textbook suggests activities but the teacher must aid the pupil in translating them into the kind of action for him which results in learning.

Individual interests, pupil initiative, abilities in thinking and expression, and the development of social responsibility and desirable social-personal qualities are objectives attained by methods of the teacher, not by the textbook. The author of your textbook did not know the children you have this year in your room, with their differences in ability, reading achievement, rate of learning, background experiences, attitudes, interest, and success in social studies.

Using a textbook

Once the textbook is seen as one of many useful sources, there are numerous effective uses that can be made of it. Note the suggestions above and the further ones that follow.

The teacher designs his own teaching unit, for he, not the teacher's manual or the textbook, makes the major decisions concerning learning tasks and their timing in his classroom. The material on a unit in a teacher's guide serves the same purpose as a good curriculum guide developed and used in a school system. It is like a resource unit, preplanned, from which the teaching unit is planned by the teacher.

Planning the teaching unit means that the teacher reads all of the material in the textbook, and then starts planning for his class. (See Chapter 2, "Improving Instruction Through the Unit Procedure.") The teacher's guide is not written as a prescription, but as an aid.

The teacher must feel that the organization of the teaching unit is his, not that of the textbook author. This means that he writes it out much in the form used in Chapter 3. Obviously, he can refer in his own outline to exercises in the text and materials in the teacher's guide by pages and numbers without copying all of the material.

Introductory activities for a unit can lead into some purposeful reading in the textbook, to give some general background information on a new topic. This is reading, not "studying facts for reciting," for which the teacher has anticipated any difficult words or concepts the students may meet by prior discussion and teaching.

On the basis of this reading, some questions or problems are formulated through teacher-pupil cooperative planning. The search for information to answer the questions or problems carries pupils back to the textbook and as great a variety of other sources as possible.

The teacher will want to do direct teaching of skills, sometimes with the whole class, often with groups, using the textbook for its charts, graphs, pictures, maps, and cartoons, and the text material for teaching note taking, outlining, and summarizing.

Toward the end of a unit the textbook is often returned to for the purpose of pulling together what has been done and steering toward statements of basic generalizations, or the big ideas, in answering the implications of "We know that. . . ."

The use of a textbook does not relieve the teacher from overall planning of a unit, or from short-term weekly planning, or from the necessary daily planning that is so intimately connected with the specific status of an individual and his progress.

Someone has said that a good textbook "should cause mental and attitudinal itches." However, "itches" are usually stimulated by what the teacher does with a textbook.

In developing a *concept*, different texts may provide different emphases. Here is the way six different texts discussed the cotton gin. None had specific activities to help in understanding the concept.

Book 1. One page. Large, specific pictures of how the cotton gin worked and how cotton is separated today. Brief mention of effect of the machine on cotton growers.

Book 2. A short paragraph. Effect on cotton-growing mentioned. "But cotton did not become an important crop until after the invention of the cotton gin."

Book 3. One page. Cotton gin discussed in frame of industrial revolution, along with other inventions. Treated in context of the idea that "Machines could do work that had always been done by hand."

Book 4. Three pages. Broad effects discussed: "How was Whitney to know it would increase the use of slaves? How was he to know it would plunge his country into a tragic and costly war?"

Book 5. Two-and-a-half paragraphs in a geography text. Effect of cotton growing on the soil discussed. Need for more land to grow cotton caused settlement of new lands—because cotton wore out the soil.

Book 6. Two paragraphs in a history text. Cotton gin discussed within the context of the Civil War. Implication is that cotton gin caused increased slavery and slavery was a major issue in the war.

Advantages of the multi-text approach

You will note from reading the advantages of the multi-text approach below that some items suggest and others explicitly indicate the use of other books of a nontextbook nature.

A. Advantages for Teacher

1. Provides the teacher with a variety of viewpoints and information.
2. Makes it easier to provide for ability and interest differences.
3. Provides material at a wide range of reading levels.
4. Gives wider listing of resources, references, creative ideas, project suggestions, etc.

B. Advantages for Children

1. Exposes children to a variety of approaches to problems and events in social studies.
2. Shows children (and teacher) that there is more than one cause-and-effect relationship that can be used to examine various historical events.
3. Gives greater opportunity for easy access to in-depth studies.

4. Gives children opportunity to unite material from several sources into one cohesive picture with all its possibilities.
5. With several texts, it is more likely to engender critical thinking and comparisons.
6. Helps reduce the possibility that the class will be stuck with a "bad" text for the year.

These statements of advantages in no way imply that "the textbook method" is herewith commended. We simply believe that textbooks are important resource material but so are library books, films and filmstrips, recordings, tapes, resource visitors, maps and globes, etc.

IMPROVING THE SKILLS PROGRAM

Chapter nine

Whether objectives of the social studies are classified in the three categories of understandings, problem solving skills, and attitudes, or stated as cognitive (content and process) and affective (attitudes and values) outcomes, the development of skills is essential in a social studies program. There should be nothing casual or incidental about teaching social studies skills, or nothing but disaster will result. Students' ability to investigate topics of their choosing will be severely limited if they lack skills to interpret social science materials.

The teacher's skill is the dominating element in a quality program of skills development. He does not take a group of pupils with no skill at all, step by small step in close-order fashion to final achievement of the skill, and then duplicate the same process, skill by separate skill. The total skills process is much more complicated.

1. Organize the skills program in the classroom. The suggestions in this chapter comprise the elements with which you work and plan with individual differences and different degrees of skills of your class members in mind.
2. Plan for the effective use of your teaching time and a pupil's learning time. Much time is wasted by whole-class activities, *e.g.*, the question-answer recitation technique, which leaves many pupils doing nothing most of the time.
3. Develop self-instructional, self-checking skills activity learning packages for completely independent study by individuals or pairs (map and globe skills, locating information, etc.).
4. With your grade-level colleagues develop dittoed or mimeographed exercises, which may serve not only as learning experiences but also as evaluating checks for excusing some pupils from further practice.

5. Pupils in any class, from Grade One on, present a broken front in skills attainments.
6. Make a check-off skills chart to show you and the pupil what he has accomplished. Obviously, it is under constant review. (We do not like such a chart on a bulletin board for public inspection and comparison.)
7. If teaching does not result in the pupils learning a skill, it is likely that the pace is too fast, the level of instruction too difficult, or the method of instruction wrong.

Throughout the National Council for Social Studies 1963 Yearbook, *Skill Development in Social Studies*, the point is made that pupils develop skills most effectively when there is systematic instruction and continuing application of the skills. The following principles of learning and teaching are emphasized as a basis for the social studies skills program.[1]

1. The skill should be taught functionally, in the context of a topic of study, rather than as a separate exercise.
2. The learner must understand the meaning and purpose of the skill, and he must have motivation for developing it.
3. The learner should be carefully supervised in his first attempts to apply the skill, so that he will form correct habits from the beginning.
4. The learner needs repeated opportunities to practice the skill, with immediate evaluation so that he knows where he has succeeded or failed in his performance.
5. The learner needs individual help, through diagnostic measures and follow-up exercises, since not all members of any group learn at exactly the same rate or retain equal amounts of what they have learned.
6. Skill instruction should be presented at increasing levels of difficulty, moving from the simple to the more complex; the resulting growth in skills should be cumulative as the learner moves through school, with each level of instruction building on and reinforcing what has been taught previously.
7. Students should be helped, at each stage, to generalize the skills, by applying them in many and varied situations; in this way, maximum transfer of learning can be achieved.
8. The program of instruction should be sufficiently flexible to allow skills to be taught as they are needed by the learner; many skills should be developed concurrently.

In applying these principles, the teacher should keep in mind the fact that, although it is possible to make a general plan for continuity in skill development, *it is impossible to set a particular place in the school program where it is always best to*

1. From Eunice Johns and Dorothy McClure Fraser, Appendix, in *Skill Development in Social Studies*, 33rd Yearbook (Arlington, Va.: National Council for the Social Studies, 1963). Reprinted with permission of the National Council for the Social Studies and Eunice Johns and Dorothy McClure Fraser.

introduce a specific skill. Many factors enter into the final decision of the teacher, as he works with a specific class, and the general plan can serve only as a guide to what seems to be good practice. True continuity in skill development is that which is developed within the learner, not that which can be blocked out in general plan. It can never be blocked out in a general plan. Furthermore, it can never be assumed that a child has gained command of a particular skill merely because he has been exposed to it. Review and reteaching of skills that have been stressed at an earlier grade level are often necessary, even with the most capable students.

INSTRUCTION IN RESEARCH SKILLS

It seems clear that research is a skill or a series of learned, interrelated subskills, but it is more than a mere routine application of skills. Research requires skill in the implementation of certain ordered steps or the utilization of a process that produces a product.

Students can be helped to develop a questioning research stance. It is fairly simple to describe steps in a basic research process, but making decisions within a particular step is more difficult. For example, in the "Collecting Data" step:

1. Do I have enough data?
2. Where else might I find information?
3. Have I located enough research?
4. Have I located pertinent research?
5. Is the data balanced for counter-biases of writers?

These are but a few of the decisions one must make before going on to the next research step. The responses to these questions are not really simple "yes" or "no" objective responses. The answers to the questions listed and others like them are subjective, and thus a basis for argument and decision making.

Research has become an increasingly important emphasis in a modern world that is concerned with growing numbers of people and voluminous amounts of data. It is necessary to expose students to research processes early in their school careers, in nonthreatening surroundings. Early exposure to research in the normal classroom may develop a positive disposition toward research. Some research skills can be dealt with in a simple form in elementary schools, and can be expanded and dealt with in more sophisticated form in high school, college, and graduate school.

Some facets of the research process are dealt with in the section on the pupil specialty (pp. 163–173). The authors have also developed three books of duplicating masters to be used in the intermediate and upper grades. Each book has twenty-four duplicating masters at duplicating levels.[2] *Practice in Research and Study Skills* will assist the student in a research project from the beginning through the evaluation stage. These masters aid the student in making an oral report, or a written report, or a combined report in which surveys, tallying, and charting and graphing are part of the training. These dittos are inductively designed to help guide the student from the free selection of a topic to the final phase of self-evaluation some twenty-four pages later. The skills practice in using an index, a card catalog file, or special map are provided as the student proceeds through the materials.

The ERIC/CHESS has the most complete listing of research findings for the teacher on any particular facet of social studies (e.g., learning map skills). Reviews from this resource are found in nearly every issue of *Social Education*, the magazine of the National Council for the Social Studies.

FOR FURTHER READING

Chapin, June R., and Richard E. Gross. *Teaching Social Studies Skills*. Boston: Little, Brown, 1973.

Hanna, Paul R. et al. *Geography in the Teaching of the Social Studies: Concepts and Skills*. Boston: Houghton Mifflin, 1966.

Joyce, Bruce R. *New Strategies for Social Education*. Chicago: Science Research Associates, 1972.

LISTENING SKILLS

Children learn to listen, to recognize and interpret the spoken word, gradually. There are several aspects of this listening skill.

There is *subconscious listening* in which you hear, but are not intent on hearing. For example, a student may have a radio on while he does his homework, and while he is aware of the song being sung, he is actually concentrating on the mathematics problem at hand.

Another type of listening is *enjoyment listening*. When one is listening for enjoyment, he is consciously attending, but not with the intent of reproducing nor reorganizing the sounds he has heard. Listening to music, to poetry being read, or to a story record would be examples of situations that would allow for enjoyment listening.

2. Martha Tyler John and W. Linwood Chase, *Practice in Research and Study Skills*, Books A, B, and C (Dansville, N.Y.: Instructor Publications, 1974). See also three workbooks for grades 4, 5, and 6 by Donald L. Barnes and Arlene Burgdorf, *The Study Skills for Information Retrieval Series* (Boston: Allyn and Bacon, 1969).

Still another kind of listening might be called *memory listening*. One listens carefully so that he can repeat or give back certain bits of information, a quotation, or an ordered sequence of points in a speech. There is no intent to alter or change the structure provided; quite the opposite—an exact replica is desired.

Perhaps the listening that requires the most extensive application of cognitive skills is *analytical listening*. With this type of listening, one must attend carefully so that the message is clear and detailed. He must then mentally organize the ideas that are being presented, and compare and contrast them to the ideas he already has gathered on the topic. He must consider the need to modify or change his own mental picture so that the new information is incorporated. He may decide to reject the new information or idea because it is not in accord with his established ideas.

One other kind of listening is perhaps the most difficult to describe in terms of precise skills; yet it is much needed in a productive society. Let us call this *selective creative listening*. Some people have the ability to listen to the ideas of others and pick up certain fragments of ideas on which they build new systems of their own. Sometimes the response of this type of listener may be downright discouraging. He seems to be listening carefully, but in response to the stated ideas is off on a tangent showing how the idea applies in a wholly different context. One wonders how the listener got from here to there. When such a break occurs, it has probably come about because the listener had already set up some priorities or was already working on an idea. This tends to make him single focused in his thinking for the time being. It is a creative kind of selective listening that is often productive, and therefore much to be desired.

Ways to promote listening skills

Subconscious listening

1. Play a musical piece during a map practice session.
2. Play a tape of sea sounds when you begin to study exploration.
3. Have a selection about Australia on the record player as students come in from recess or lunch. Do not study it—just allow them to hear it incidentally as they settle down.

Enjoyment listening

1. Listen to a folk tale record before studying about a like culture in Africa.
2. Play a tape of a story based on the country or group of people you are studying now.

3. Play some folk songs of the United States when you are studying about this country.

Memory listening

1. Have students follow simple directions that are repeated only once. This can be readily applied in mapping and graphing training sessions.
2. Warn the students that they are going to be asked to identify a key word in each sentence. Read the sentence, then read it again, and have the students fill in the missing word.
3. Have the students memorize some item of information from a tape about a president.

Analytical listening

1. Have the students develop a rough outline for a brief lecture presented by the teacher.
2. Have the students listen to a paragraph on tape, and then state the main idea in a single sentence—or even a single word.
3. Provide students with the music of two countries (one of which you are currently studying). Ask them to compare the two types of music. How are they different? How are they alike?

Selective creative listening

1. Play a record of Dylan Thomas poetry—"Christmas in Wales," for example. Have the students use the technique for description in a portion of a report they are writing.
2. Have the students listen to two or three open-ended problem stories. Then have them write a short problem story that has to do with the content they are considering.
3. Present several two person role playing skits to the class. Suggest that they write one that would be appropriate for two people in the setting they are studying.

FOR FURTHER READING

Burns, Paul C., and Betty L. Broman. *The Language Arts in Childhood Education.* Chicago: Rand McNally College Publishing, 1975.

Greene, Harry A., and Walter T. Petty. *Developing Language Skills in the Elementary School.* Boston: Allyn and Bacon, 1975.

Sebesta, Sam L., and William J. Iverson, Jr. *Literature for Thursday's Child.* Palo Alto, Calif.: Science Research Associates, 1975.

SKILL IN INTERPRETING CURRENT AFFAIRS

Public opinion analysts over the years have reported that the majority of our citizens are ill-informed on foreign affairs and little realize how events anywhere in the world may affect the individual family. As elementary teachers we have an obligation to build a growing basis of concern and understanding. Practice and skills are needed to prepare the student for effective participation in current issues.

Purposes for current affairs instruction

Among the ends in view for planned current issues instruction are to:

1. Introduce some of the social conditions of our times (poverty, pollution, overpopulation, ideological differences) and examine in world context as well as local and national.
2. Demonstrate the interdependence of nations.
3. See similarities and differences in other people's lives and cultures.
4. Develop the habit of reading newspapers with understanding—quite different from simply reading newspapers.
5. Combine a view of the world in the present with history and geography.
6. Understand how lives can be changed by decisions made by people anywhere on the globe.
7. Close the gap between the content of a unit and the current news about it.
8. Begin to understand who wields the power that builds the world in which we live.
9. Provide a basis for developing value judgments.
10. Challenge students to understand something of the fast changing pattern of the contemporary world.

Programming for current affairs

Current affairs discussion in the elementary classroom varies from none through the casual to the highly organized. Varieties of programming show:

1. A sharing period each morning separate from the social studies period.
    a. Events reported may or may not be related to the social studies unit being studied.

b. Most teachers put reporting on a voluntary basis.
c. Children are encouraged to bring in items related to class work.
d. Collections of reports of unrelated, unselective items are open to serious question at the middle grade level.

2. Beginning a social studies class with any reports on news articles related to unit.

3. Scheduling a period once a week based on a pupil periodical—a weekly classroom newspaper—is the most common method. Utilization of the period is dependent on the teacher's ingenuity, enthusiasm, knowledge, and planning.

   a. Oral reading—typical of lack of planning by the teacher.
   b. Silent reading with differentiated guide questions based on reading ability of pupils in class.
   c. Class discussion on one major topic assigned in advance.
   d. Class divided on basis of major topics with report to class and discussion.
   e. General discussion on any topics in classroom periodical, sometimes classified as local, national, and international.
   f. Functional use of maps and globes.

4. Short current affairs units, each based on a single topic, coming between the longer, regular units—developed from the viewpoint of what do we need and want to know about it. Allows variety of materials and activities as in any unit.

5. The "continuing unit" or continuing committee approach.

   a. "Continuing unit" similar to #4 above, except taken up weekly or periodically instead of on successive days.
   b. Continuing committee follows the news on some persistent problem and reports to class periodically.
   c. Individuals or committees, assigned at beginning of the year as "experts" on unit topics to be covered, report periodically on current news on their topic.

6. A combination of the patterns indicated above may well be carried on during the course of a school year. Based on his particular situation, each teacher should make the decision how to handle current affairs in his classroom. One thing is certain: teaching current affairs is imperative!

Geographic skills in current affairs

Geographic tools such as maps, charts, tables, graphs, and pictures accompany many articles in newspapers, news magazines, and the classroom weekly. Skills must be developed in using these tools. This skills learning should begin in the first grade, for development must be cumulative and habit-forming.

1. *Globes and maps.* Globes are the only true representation of the earth. Maps are visual representations of geographic, historical, political, and socioeconomic facts from which inferences may be drawn.
2. *Charts.* Record and classify information and illustrate processes.
3. *Graphs.* Graphs are one symbolic way to show comparisons of relationships between numerical facts.
4. *Tables.* Another way to present statistical facts and best for exact numerical facts; graphs are best for quick comparisons.
5. *Pictures.* Substitutes for the real thing, they help to develop accurate concepts of landscapes, people, and activities.

Every event has a time and place. The geography behind most important events brings out the interrelationships of communities, countries, and peoples. Here is where geographic facts, relationships, and understandings are functionally real. "Current events put man in the role of the principal actor with the contemporary world as a stage." An event cannot really be understood unless it is examined and evaluated geographically.

Depending on the nature and the importance of the event, considerable background of its locale can be developed through answers to questions like these:[3]

1. Where did the news event take place? What direction is it from where you live? How far away is the place and how would you travel in order to reach it? About how much time would it take you to reach the place via commercial travel?
2. On what continent is the place found? Where on the continent? Who are the neighbors? How are they involved in the news event if they are? Are any countries involved besides neighbors? Why and how?
3. What are the landforms of the area where the event took place? What about the slope of the land? In which direction do the rivers flow? Does a map suggest ways in which the rivers are used? If so, in what way?
4. What is the general climate of the area? What season is taking place there at this time? What is the length of the growing season? Does this area have adequate rainfall for agriculture? What generalizations can be made about the types of agriculture carried on in this area?
5. What do the people do to make a living in the area involved? Does this work touch you in any way? If so, in what way?
6. What are the major resources of the area? How are they adapted and used? Do we use any of the resources of this area? Which ones? How well can we get along without them?
7. What are the major items of international exchange stemming from the area of the news event?

3. Kennamer, Lorrin. From a leaflet, *The Place of Maps in Current Events* (Chicago: Denoyer Geppert Co., 1964). Reprinted by permission.

There are any number of activities that can be used by either the teacher or the student to communicate interest and enthusiasm for a topic to other persons. Bulletin boards, cartoons, news programs, scrapbooks, and general discussions can all be used effectively to convey information.

Materials for current affairs

Xerox Education Publications, Education Center, Columbus, Ohio 43216. *My Weekly Reader, Surprise,* Kindergarten; *My Weekly Reader,* at each grade level, Grades 1 through 6; *Current Events,* Grades 7 and 8.

Scholastic Magazines, Inc., 902 Sylvan Ave., Englewood Cliffs, N.J. 07632. *News Pilot* (Grade 1); *News Ranger* (Grade 2); *News Trail* (Grade 3); *News Explorer* (Grade 4); *Young Citizen* (Grade 5); *Newstime* (Grades 5 and 6); *Junior Scholastic* (Grades 6, 7, and 8).

Your high school may be subscribing to the *New York Times* filmstrips on current affairs. Explore them. Some filmstrips (or many of the frames) might be useful for your class or a special group.

About five hundred newspapers in the United States are working with the school systems in their area on a *Newspaper in the Classroom* program. This is worth exploration. To find out if any newspaper serving your community is conducting such a program, write for information to the American Newspaper Publishers Association Foundation, P.O. Box 17407, Dulles International Airport, Washington, D.C. 20041. The ANPA Foundation also distributes, for minimal charge, teacher guides on using the newspaper as a teaching tool in the elementary school.

The *Materials Order Catalog* available from Chicago Tribune Educational Services, 654 Tribune Tower, Chicago, Ill. 60611 describes three teacher guides concerned with a comprehensive reading program, an inquiry-based plan of teaching, and the development of a skills program in current affairs teaching. The catalog lists many inexpensive Background Reports.

In addition to keeping a file of pupil current affairs newspapers, many teachers who have a resource file clip articles, pictures, and other pertinent material and file them under the appropriate headings for future reference.

Evaluation of current affairs learning

While we will test factual information we should remember that this usually involves only one area of accomplishment. Consideration should also be given to:

1. Appraising the pupil's ability to recognize significant current problems.
2. Appraising his skill in skimming a news story to locate major facts.
3. Appraising his ability to locate accurate information.
4. Appraising his ability to use various sources for news and to evaluate them in relation to each other.
5. Judging the growth of a student's ability and willingness to discuss ideas and opinions with others.
6. Appraising his ability to form valid judgments.
7. Determining generalizations developed and growth in concept learning.
8. Using questionnaires, interviews, checklists, and similar devices.

The teacher's part

The key to success in current affairs instruction is careful planning and organization coupled with enthusiasm and understanding. It involves much more than picking up the classroom weekly and looking at it with the children. You cannot be any more casual about this preparation than you would be in any other phase of social studies learning.

Keep up to date yourself by reading newspapers and magazines, watching news and documentary programs on television, and having discussions with other people. The teacher is justly expected to be better informed and to have a better grasp of what is happening that the average citizen. Scholarship, or lack of it, is more quickly evident in current affairs than in geography and history.

The teacher must fully comprehend the goals of current affairs if he is to teach the area effectively. He has the knowledge and the understanding to integrate the discussion with the content of the social studies program. The current affairs period is not the time for a pupil to be in charge while the teacher does clerical work at his desk.

FOR FURTHER READING

Fraser, Dorothy M. "Current Affairs, Special Events, and Civic Participation." In *Social Studies in Elementary Schools*, 32nd Yearbook. Arlington, Va.: National Council for the Social Studies, 1962. Pp. 131-149.

Jarolimek, John. *Social Studies in Elementary Education*. New York: Macmillan, 1976. Chapter 8. "Current Affairs in the Social Studies."

Michaelis, John U. *Social Studies for Children in a Democracy*. Englewood Cliffs, N.J.: Prentice-Hall, 1976. Chapter 8, "Investigating Current Affairs and Special Events."

Ploghoft, Milton E., and Albert H. Shuster. *Social Science Education in the Elementary School.* Columbus, Ohio: Charles E. Merrill, 1971. Chapter 12.

"The Need to Know Starts Young." *Instructor* (March 1974). An excellent series of articles concerned with television and newspapers, focus on human beings, and a series of reports telling you how a number of teachers are working with their children and the news.

DEVELOPING TIME RELATIONSHIPS

This is a skill that is most important to the social scientist. There are some things teachers can do to help develop this skill. Although merely growing older improves time understanding and time relationships, time sense can and should be cultivated from kindergarten through every grade level. Beginning with primary children:

1. Check understanding of time concepts in reading. The most common are, in order: then, now, day, soon, time, morning, when, again, night, old, year, winter, first, tomorrow.
2. Enrich time concepts in reading as you enrich other concepts in vocabulary development.
3. Use brief systematic exercises frequently
   a. in telling time by the clock.
   b. with a large calendar. How many days in this month? Show us what week it is; name the days of the week, the months of the year; name the last month, the next month; and so on.
4. Build exercises for pairs or threes to use and check each other.

As children continue through the grades, embrace every opportunity to clarify time concepts and increase understanding.

1. Teach years in relation to a child's birthday, the year he was in Mrs. Smith's room, the ages of his brothers and sisters compared with his own.
2. Develop such terms as "my lifetime," "my father's lifetime," "my grandfather's lifetime."
3. Arrange events in the life of the child in order of happening, without dates.
4. Arrange events from a story in order of happening.
5. Begin to work with materials from social studies concerned with time.

For further help, two excellent references are: *How to Develop Time and Chronological Concepts,* by Kopple C. Friedman from the National Council for the Social Studies (25 cents); and Chapter 10, "Developing a Sense of Time and Chronology," in *Skill Development in Social Studies,* 33rd Yearbook (Arlington, Va.: National Council for the Social Studies, 1963).

Time lines

In general, fifth grade children cannot draw time lines to scale. There is no reason, however, for the teacher not to make use of a time line. Grade six children can definitely be taught this skill. One method of approach is to ask some of the children in the class their ages. Draw a time line indicating the age in years of one child, with one inch representing one year. Ask the child what year he had the measles. Indicate the "measles" date. Ask when he started school. Mark that on the time line. You now have four dates on the time line—birth year at one end, "measles" year, school entrance year, and at the other end, the present year. Have each child who can do so draw his own life line, or time line, and put two events in his life on it (*e.g.*, the birth of a younger sister or brother). The development of an historical time line can follow this. The teacher should not be at all concerned if he frequently has to "tell" rather than draw information from the children.

Depending on the subject matter in your class, all kinds of time lines may be developed and constructed:

1. One showing the life of an individual with two or three historical events inserted.
2. One showing famous inventions.
3. One showing a few important events in the Space Age.
4. One showing events in different parts of the world on opposite sides of the same line.

A few samples of other time sense exercises are:

1. Here are two lists of events. Place the number of each event in the first list in front of the event in the second list which occurred about the same time.
2. Here is a list of five persons. Put the letter "B" in front of those who lived *before* Abraham Lincoln. Put the letter "A" in front of those who lived *after* Abraham Lincoln.
3. Here is a list of four persons. Put the figure 1 before the name of the man who lived first, put the figure 2 before the one who lived second, and so on.
4. Put a group of three to five pictures in order of time sequence (pictures of modes of transportation or communication, or pictures of a city at different periods of time, or pictures of famous men and women).
5. Make a class list of things you are able to do that boys and girls could not do one hundred years ago.
6. Suppose that a ten-year-old boy living in Palos, who saw Columbus leave on his great voyage in 1492, lived to the age of eighty. On his eightiefh birthday he told the story to his ten-year-old grandson. The grandson told the story on his eightieth birthday to his ten-year-old grandson, etc. How many men have learned this story this way?

Test items

Perhaps you would like to try making a time sense test. The sample items below range from easy to difficult.

1. Wednesday is the day after:

   *a. Tuesday c. Thursday
   b. Friday d. Monday

2. Draw a calendar with thirty-one days on it. The calendar must be for:

   a. June c. February
   b. October *d. No month

3. By using the word *sometime*, when do we say something has happened?

   a. in the past *c. no particular time
   b. in the present d. in the future

4. Three words which all have to do with things that have *not* happened yet are:

   a. future, before, now c. before, now, tell
   *b. next, future, soon d. before, ago, last

5. Which list of words is in the correct order from past to present?

   *a. ago, last, today, next c. next, today, last, ago
   b. ago, today, last, next d. today, last, next, ago

6. The amount of time from the dawn of one day until dawn of the next day is:

   a. eight hours c. sixteen hours
   b. twelve hours *d. twenty-four hours

7. When the sun is rising in New York City, on the Atlantic Ocean, what is the sun doing in San Francisco, on the Pacific Ocean?

   a. The sun has been up for about three hours.
   *b. The sun will rise in about three hours.
   c. The sun set about three hours ago.
   d. The sun will set in about three hours.

8. The things which we see in a museum that were used in 1930 could have been used at that time by:

   a. you c. your grandfather, as a boy
   *b. your father, as a boy d. your great-grandfather as a boy

9. Today you are enjoying a happy family life. Below are some events in the lives of your family that led up to the present time. Number them in the order in which

they happened, using number 1 for the event which happened the longest time ago.

______a. Your grandfather and grandmother were married. (1)
______b. Your father and mother met each other. (3)
______c. You started school (5)
______d. Your father was ten years old. (2)
______e. You were born. (4)

INSTRUCTION IN MAPS AND GLOBES

The thread of map and globe instruction and use is a continuous one through the whole fabric of the social studies program from kindergarten to twelfth grade. While maps provide information for us, they have changed in appearance over the centuries, and continue to change. In the process of changing they provide us with new data. The child of the 1980s and beyond will be more and more comfortable with space travel and the use of satellite maps. (*See* the July 1976 *National Geographic,* "A Satellite Makes a Coast-to-Coast Picture.") The scientific invention of rockets and spacecraft have changed the quality and quantity of information available to us. This is a good example of the interaction between the social sciences and the physical sciences in the real world.

Developing map and globe skills requires careful planning by the teacher throughout all the elementary school years. We cannot say, nor should we, "Here is step 1, now 2, 3, and so on to 153," or whatever. Progress of children in a class in achieving map and globe skills is along a broken front, as it is in other learning skills.

The major skills[4]

In this *Guide* we have chosen a scheme of presentation that we think is the best we know. Special skills are needed to use maps and globes as sources of information, as tools for developing spatial concepts, as records of experiences, and as materials for making inferences. To acquire these skills, children need definite instruction. Each skill has a developmental aspect; although the suggestions which follow give a general grade placement, the reader should realize that these are tentative suggestions. Bright students and others with a degree of competence in these skills may be ready for more advanced work than is suggested at a given grade level. Conversely, slow learners or

4. From Lorrin Kennamer "Developing a Sense of Place and Space." in *Skill Development in Social Studies.* 33rd Yearbook (Arlington, Va.: National Council for the Social Studies, 1963), pp. 157-168. Reprinted with permission of the National Council for the Social Studies and Lorrin Kennamer.

young people with little or no previous training in map skills may not be ready for the activities in the grade for which they are suggested. Adaptation of any suggested program of skill and activity sequence must depend on each teacher in his classroom.

Since many abilities are involved in the development of skill in map and globe interpretation, it is necessary to categorize them. The following set of six skills has proven to be comprehensive and is offered as basic to a program in map reading and interpretation.[5]

1. Ability to orient the map and to note directions.
2. Ability to recognize the scale of a map and to compute distances.
3. Ability to locate places on maps and globes by means of grid systems.
4. Ability to express relative locations.
5. Ability to read map symbols.
6. Ability to compare maps and make inferences.

It is most important to note that teachers at *all* grade levels have a responsibility to aid in the development of these six basic skills. Each teacher, from the primary grades through the college years, should build upon the work and experiences that have gone before.

Skill I: Ability to orient the map and to note directions. Developing a sense of direction is basic to map interpretation. Activities directed toward this goal are often referred to as readiness activities. The children must learn to orient themselves in their immediate environment and then to relate to other directions. This skill needs repetition and review if the high school and the college student are to orient maps properly and readily.

PRIMARY (K—3) ACTIVITIES:

1. Use cardinal directions with direction signs located on classroom walls.
2. Practice cardinal directions by noting sun's shadow at noon.
3. Practice giving directions. Take walks around the neighborhood.
4. Use relative terms of orientation and direction: over here, over there; this way, that way; under, over; below, above; up and down as differentiated from top and bottom; near, far; nearer, farther; blocks, steps; uptown, downtown; here, there.
5. Use the symbols N, E, S, W and place them correctly around the room.
6. Use a floor map oriented to north.

5. Clyde F. Kohn, "Interpreting Maps and Globes," in *Skills in Social Studies*, 24th Yearbook (Washington, D.C.: National Council for the Social Studies, National Education Association, 1953), pp. 146-147.

7. Draw an appropriate map and use it for a trip into the community.
8. Make a trip map after the class returns. Show the routes taken.
9. Construct a large floor map of the community. Orient the map correctly. Hang it on a wall. Hang it on the north wall if possible so that E and W are correct. Remove the map from the wall and place it on the floor from time to time to remind the class of the relation of the map to reality.
10. Study a community street map. Examine sundials and weather vanes.
11. Introduce large simplified globes to see north-south lines and east-west lines, the shape of the earth, and the existence of land and water bodies.
12. Relate community street map with a community aerial photgraph.

INTERMEDIATE (4—6) ACTIVITIES:

1. Conduct simple experiments with the compass.
2. Construct neighborhood and community maps.
3. Study road maps of the state. Discuss directions of trips taken.
4. Introduce and use the terms "parallels" for east-west lines and "meridians" for north-south lines. Spin a coin to illustrate concepts of "axis," "North Pole," and "South Pole."
5. Note directions as regional study units move to different parts of the world.
6. Orient maps correctly to north and hang them on the wall.
7. Review the meanings of "up" and "down" to counteract the tendency to use these words for "north" and "south."
8. Review the concept that north is toward the North Pole and south is toward the South Pole.
9. Practice finding and identifying direction by using a shadow stick and by observing weather conditions, wind drection, the sun, etc.
10. Review the use of "northeast," "northwest," "southeast," and "southwest."
11. Use the north arrow on a map as a directional finder. Recognize and understand the use of a compass for direction.
12. Identify direction on a map or globe, using the cardinal and intermediate directions.
13. Orient desk outline and atlas maps.

Skill II: Ability to recognize the scale of a map and to compute distances. Maps are graphic representations of parts of the earth or of the entire earth. Children understand simple reduction in size, but have difficulty in visualizing the true area represented by the map. The abstraction of the map must be related to the reality being represented. To do this, the student must learn scale and its application. This begins with simple comparison of ground and map distances and leads to ways of expressing scale and finally to visualizing scales.

PRIMARY (K—3) ACTIVITIES:

1. Measure distance in the neighborhood by blocks from home to school, to the fire station, and to other landmarks.
2. Express time related to distance—relative time it takes to go from home to school, and to other places.
3. Illustrate that long distances in the neighborhood can be represented by short distances on the map.
4. Build a model community on a sand table or work table.
5. Take a walk to an open view to observe spatial distance.
6. Design and use maps (drawn to scale by the teacher) for a trip into the community. Make a trip map after the class returns. Discuss distance and time of trip.
7. Construct large floor maps to scale.
8. Compare the sizes of simple large-scale maps of the classroom, neighborhood, and community.
9. Compare snapshots of children in the class to actual size.
10. Display a series of progressively larger pictures of the same person to show different scales of measurement.
11. Use simple commercial maps of community area.
12. Develop a sense of ground distance. Observe relative lengths of blocks, a mile, ten miles, etc.

INTERMEDIATE (4—6) ACTIVITIES:

1. Study different-size maps of the same area.
2. Recognize and interpret scale of miles on map.
3. Practice the use of scale—one inch to a foot; one inch to a mile. Draw a scale map of the classroom, of the school yard.
4. View the globe as a model of the earth.
5. Estimate distances between points on maps and globes, using scale of miles. Estimate distances using latitude and longitude (possibly grade 6).
6. Estimate the time to take trips between two points.
7. Compute and estimate the distance between the same two points on maps of different scales.
8. Walk a mile to develop distance concept.
9. Note the scale of miles on every map used in grades 5 and 6.
10. Make maps of community to scale.

Skill III: Ability to locate places on maps and globes. Children learn first to locate places on the simple maps of their neighborhood. This experience is the basis for the study of globes to see location. This leads to knowledge of the earth's grid for location, followed later by the introduction of projections. The ability to express relative location is a further refinement of locational skills.

PRIMARY (K—3) ACTIVITIES:

1. Locate desks and seats on a classroom map.
2. Locate places around the school, such as the cafeteria and the auditorium.
3. Locate routes to neighborhood facilities, such as the post office.
4. Trace steps from home to school on a teacher-made map of the area.
5. Trace routes over which certain foods are brought to the town or city.
6. Locate places where classmates have visited and where they live.
7. Locate tunnels, bridges, etc., on a neighborhood map.
8. Locate land and water areas on a globe. (Some children will want to learn names of continents and oceans, although this need not be pressed.)
9. Locate the pupils' home area on a globe. Develop the idea that the earth is their home.

INTERMEDIATE (4—6) ACTIVITIES:

1. On a simplified map of the world and on a globe, locate, name, and identify: equator, tropics, and circles; continents, oceans, and large islands.
2. Locate places in relation to the poles, the equator, the tropics.
3. Use grid lines to locate places. Use atlas grids.
4. Use the number-and-key system for locating places on the home-state highway map.
5. Use maps, globes, and atlases to locate places mentioned in instructional units and in current events.
6. Introduce latitude (grade 5). Practice the use of latitude measurements and parallels.
7. Introduce longitude (grades 5 or 6). Locate all places by the use of latitude and longitude.
8. Plan a trip using a highway map; include distance, direction, locations.
9. Identify the time belts on a U.S. map and relate them to longitude.
10. Examine the relationship of longitude to time and of latitude to miles.
11. Introduce terminology of "low latitude," "middle latitude," and "high latitude."

Skill IV: Ability to express relative location. Each place on the earth's surface has, in addition to its latitudinal and longitudinal location, a relative location or position to other items or places. Relative location is dependent not only upon the distance between any two or more places and the direction in which one lies with respect to the other, but also upon certain features which make one more accessible than another. For example, the character of the topography between two places may make them farther apart or nearer together in terms of the time needed to travel from one to the other. Mountains may impede access to one area, while natural waterways make another place accessible. Also, there are manmade barriers (such as boundaries, tariffs, and international tensions) to ease of movement. Thus, understanding relative location is basically a process of learning first to read exact locations as shown by maps and globes and then of interpreting the interrelatedness of these exact locations. This interrelatedness includes consideration of both physical phenomena and the ever-changing character of political, social, and economic conditions. It is especially this skill in map interpretation which develops a sense of place and space.

PRIMARY (K—3) ACTIVITIES:

1. Study a teacher-made map of the classroom.
2. Visit, discuss, and picture on a large teacher-made map the important places in and around the school.
3. Trace on a community and state map the routes over which certain foods are brought to the local market.
4. Locate the home community on a globe; on a map of the nation.
5. Find places mentioned in the news. Discuss their position and direction relative to the home community.
6. Design a map and use it for a trip into the community.
7. Examine the relation of a pupil's home to the school in direction and travel time; the relation of the community to major terrain features, to transportation routes.
8. Recognize land and water bodies on the globe.

INTERMEDIATE (4—6) ACTIVITIES:

1. Review the relation of the community's site to terrain features (lakes, rivers, mountains, valleys, etc.).
2. Use highway maps to describe trips taken by a pupil's family.
3. Locate places in relation to the equator; the poles.
4. Name important countries, continents, cities, regions, rivers, states, islands, oceans, mountains on a map or globe. Use those studied in the social studies units and those talked about in current affairs.
5. Be able to use simple sketch maps to illustrate a point in class presentation.
6. Relate low latitudes to the equator and high latitudes to the polar areas.
7. Use string or tape on the globe to find shortest distances and directions from the home town to such places as Tokyo and Copenhagen.
8. Stress terms of accessibility, such as coastal, continental, insular, peninsula, maritime.
9. Note the relation of major cities in the world to their physical setting.

Skill V: Ability to read map symbols. The four map skills discussed above have dealt with spatial aspects of places such as distance, direction, and exact and relative location. The ability to read map symbols furnishes another dimension to be gained from maps. Symbols represent the natural and cultural phenomena which occur in varying patterns and are the so-called language of maps. As the student understands the symbols used, so does the map come to life in what it represents.

PRIMARY (K—3) ACTIVITIES:

1. Provide real or vicarious contacts with the physical and man-made features for which symbols stand. The pupils' introduction should begin with reality.
2. Recognize the difference between land and water areas on a wall map or globe.
3. Identify well-known places in pictures and aerial photos of the city.
4. Identify familiar signs and symbols: stop sign, shelter, one-way street, etc.
5. After a trip into the community, make a map showing the routes taken. Use symbols to represent things observed.
6. Introduce the concept that real objects can be represented on a map by pictures or symbols.
7. Recognize the use of a line to represent a street on a map.
8. Design cut-out symbols to represent things and places on a large teacher-made floor map.

INTERMEDIATE (4—6) ACTIVITIES:

1. Use simple maps of the city to learn symbols for streets, rivers, etc.
2. Use pictorial, semi-pictorial, and abstract symbols.
3. Place great emphasis on the use of the map legend, beginning in grade 5.
4. Use desk outline maps for recording different types of data necessary for work in the social studies units. Actual tracing of maps may be of little value, but symbols placed on outline maps will aid map reading.
5. Study the meaning of color and shading on simple physical maps of the United States and of the world.
6. Continue to use pictures and stories to visualize real things which are expressed on maps by symbols.
7. Recognize more semi-pictorial symbols on a map—dots for cities, color and shading for elevation, physiographic symbols for land forms.
8. Understand color contour maps and visual relief maps. Look at photos of mountains and then at map symbols for mountains; visualize what the symbol represents.
9. Conduct regular practice of visual imagery for old as well as new symbols. Develop imagery for mountains, plains, rivers, and other features.
10. Understand and use comprehensive legends on a variety of maps.
11. Interpret abbreviations commonly found on maps.
12. Trace the course of a river from its source to its mouth. Identify the symbols used for water features.
13. Collect pictures to develop understandings of geographical terms and land forms. Pupils must visualize natural and man-made parts of the landscape; if an actual visit is impossible, they must study photographs and relate each phenomenon to (or with) the representative symbol for it.

Skill VI: Ability to compare maps and to make inferences. The skills discussed thus far deal with learning—either how to read and express location, or how to read the symbols. As these skills are developed the student should be taught to look for relationships: to seek correlations of things in space; and to make inferences concerning the distributions of things shown on maps. It is this skill of comparing maps and making inferences that serves as a capstone to all other skills developed. Yet, like that of all of the other skills, work on this skill must take place at all grade levels. As maturity develops, the level of sophistication of comparisons and inferences increases with the use of maps.

PRIMARY (K—3) ACTIVITIES:

1. Study simple community maps to draw conclusions: gas stations are generally located at street intersections; schools are generally located in residential sections; shopping centers are near routes of public transportation—bus lines, rail lines, subways, etc.
2. Discuss in a general way what globes and highway maps are used for.
3. Recognize that there are many kinds of maps for many uses.

INTERMEDIATE (4—6) ACTIVITIES:

1. Study the relationship between two maps of the same area which depict different phenomena; for example, a map of the corn belt showing distribution of hogs and one showing distribution of corn production.
2. Make simple inferences from globe study (by grade 4): the relationship of temperature and climate to the way people live; the relationship of temperature to distance north and south of the equator.
3. Use maps increasingly as a source of information. Use the globe and the world map increasingly to get specific information about places.
4. Recognize special-purpose maps—e.g., rainfall, climate, population, and land forms.
5. Relate historical events to the setting in which they took place.
6. Examine photos and maps of the same area and draw inferences about the terrain, climate (note the vegetation), and people's activities.
7. Understand and use a simple atlas.
8. Interpret altitude and draw inferences regarding it.
9. Illustrate events in history by sketch maps. Use maps and globes in giving reports.
10. Consult two or more maps to gather information about the same area.
11. Compare text descriptions with accompanying maps.
12. By the end of the sixth grade, pupils should realize that certain types of information can be read better and more quickly from maps. The habit of consulting maps and globes for information should be well developed.
13. Use maps in newspapers, magazines, books, in relation to social studies units.

Interpretation of maps

Skill in map interpretation is definitely a growth process requiring careful planning, adjusted to each child's maturity, experience, and achievement. A majority of adults have not built map habits. The teacher must not assume the interpretational and associational processes will be carried on by the pupil without stimulation or assignment. In school, turning to maps in search of information cannot be left to chance.

When you can ask map questions and find answers by studying different types of maps (political, physical, special-purpose) and the globe, you are making interpretations. You are making the map tell you a story much as words in a book tell a story.

1. Geographically, why did this event happen where it did?
2. Why did its happening influence people in one direction and not in the opposite direction?
3. Why is the population more dense in this area of the country or continent than in that area?
4. Why did Chicago develop as a rail center? Why is it an airlines center?
5. What part is played by high mountains and prevailing winds in determining weather patterns?
6. Make comparisons and inferences (interpret altitude; compare text descriptions with accompanying maps).
7. Look for relationships; temperature and climate, in relation to the way people live; relationship of temperature to distance north and south of the equator; recognize special-purpose maps and their relationships, e.g., rainfall, population, production.
8. Relationship of one concept to another.

Some understandings about map instruction

Most map skills normally used by people throughout their lives should have been experienced by the end of the sixth grade. However, ability to make inferences can continue to grow through practice.

Map and globe materials are just as much basic content to work on as a unit on Colonial life in America, or one on Inca civilization.

Reading in geography involves reading maps, graphs, pictures, and the landscape itself as well as verbal or textual materials. The map is not a picture, and it cannot be expected to convey a general impression to the child. Map symbols constitute a language that has to be learned like any other language, and is no easier for a beginner to learn to read than a foreign language.

The map is always a useful tool: note its constant use in magazines, newspapers, even advertisements.

A global world requires global thinking. Only statesmen and citizens who can do political and strategic thinking in terms of a round earth can keep their country safe and prosperous.

Since the textbook (and possibly its accompanying workbook) is going to be the major source of activity in map work, the teacher should become thoroughly acquainted with its manner of presentation and development before beginning the year's work, and then *determine his procedure* with it. The teacher—not the textbook—must take command of the map program. One textbook series has grouped the many questions and activities in one place in the teacher's manual for his convenience. This the teacher should do for his own text.

Even when map skills appropriate to the primary grades have been developed, many teachers prefer to teach a unit on maps for several weeks at the beginning of the fourth grade as a basis for continued practice and use. Research has shown that this results in high interest and better retention than presenting the material only in driblets through the middle grades.

Any places located on flat maps should also be located on the globe. The textbook map, the globe, and the wall map make three excellent sources for comparison. Different projections on different flat maps make for a valuable discussion of differences. The globe used should be the kind that can be lifted out of its holder with the freedom of a ball in space; any other seems inappropriate in this age when astronauts orbit the earth, and go to the moon.

In this scientific age it might be appropriate to call the classroom, or a place in it, "our map laboratory."

Never guess whether or not a child has particular information or understanding about maps and globes. Check him if you are not really sure. It is usually necessary to reteach many map skills at all grade levels.

Put a glossary of geographical terms (delta, isthmus, tributary, plateau) on a bulletin board chart if your text does not have a complete glossary in one place.

Stress the importance of making careful observations out of doors, "in the field." Relate these observations to a U.S. Geological Survey topographic map for your town. (See page 342.)

Have children *always* use an accurate and specific map vocabulary in reading maps and making maps. Make symbols on maps (dots for cities, lines for rivers, shadings for mountains), and locations all over the world real, meaningful, and concrete by giving them significance through:

1. Children's own experiences in country, city, mountains; on rivers and ocean; and through television.

2. Liberal use of pictures.
3. Oral description by teacher of his own travels or reading.
4. Reading of vivid description by teacher or pupil from library books and travel articles.
5. Filmstrips, films, slides, and photographs.

Translating symbols into realities is not enough. Rivers, mountains, rainfall, population, and other symbols must be interpreted in their relationship to each other.

The slated (markable) map and globe on which special crayon and tempera color can be used are especially valuable tools.

Good suggestions for the use of maps can often be found in the adult atlas and in manuals accompanying globes and wall maps. Have you ever spent time leafing through an atlas to find out what is there?

Without the established habit of consulting the map key or legend, one cannot really read maps, for the key unlocks the map. Keys for special types of maps—elevation, rainfall, and population—require explicit teaching of the specific type for most children.

Develop the habit of using a map to place any event in the news that warrants report or discussion. An event or the existing situation in a country cannot be correctly understood or evaluated unless the place is located on a map and looked at in its total relationship to adjacent areas and other parts of the world.

"The place where I live" is the most important place on any map for any child. It orients him to north, south, east, and west when he begins map learning. As he goes out into the world on maps and the globe, every part of his country and world has a relation to the place where he lives.

If work on an outline map is to have greater value, use physical outline maps frequently. They are only slightly more expensive than political maps. Have you ever used a large wall outline map (drawn from a projection on a large sheet of paper or purchased)?

Package materials in envelopes for independent study by individuals or by pairs. For example, pick up some road maps. Put one in an envelope with a list of questions about direction, distance, legend, population, longitude, latitude, etc. Some teachers put in a list of answers so the exercise can be self-correcting; others furnish the list when students are ready. Packaging for independent study can be used with other types of work: map skills tests, maps clipped from old map catalogs, textbooks, etc.

Put on a bulletin board a present-day map of a region or area of the world. Place beside it an old map of the same area. Without comment by the teacher, these maps will raise questions among some pupils that will lead into inquiry demanding solutions. Use the *National Geographic* Index to locate issues of magazines of different dates having maps of the same territory—Europe, Asia, Africa, and others.

Suggestions for making maps

Carefully planned opportunities for pupils to make maps can be good learning experiences. Freehand maps are of questionable value because of the great inaccuracies and the pupils' time involved. Mere reproduction of an existing map contributes little. But deriving information from the use of one or more maps for the purpose of developing a map directly related to a problem or understanding in a unit is working as a geographer works.

The following list suggests types of maps that children can make:[6]

1. *Floor* maps using blocks, boxes, and models, or chalk, tempera, and crayon on linoleum, paper, or oilcloth; simple line maps in the schoolyard.
2. *Pictorial* maps of community buildings, harbors, products, types of housing, food, clothing, plant and animal life, minerals and other resources, birthplaces of famous people, arts and crafts, modes of travel, methods of communication, raw materials.
3. *Specimen* maps using real items such as wheat, corn, cotton, and rocks.
4. *Relief* maps of papier-mâché, salt and flour, plaster of paris, clay or moistened sand; large relief maps on a section of the school yard.
5. *Mural* maps with strips of paper for streets, pictures or silhouettes for buildings, and so forth.
6. *Wall outline* maps made by using an opaque projector or a pantograph.
7. *Jigsaw puzzle* maps of states and countries.
8. *Slated* maps and globes or individual and wall outline maps to show air routes, famous flights, early explorations, trade routes, physical features, boundaries, rivers, and so forth.
9. *Political and physical* maps using colors to show various features.
10. *Transportation* maps using various line and dot patterns to show railroad lines, airplane routes, steamship lines, and major highways.
11. *Progressive or developmental* maps of a region or topic such as the westward movement, colonization, or industrial America.
12. *Communication* maps using symbols to show telephone lines, cable crossings, radio networks, and television networks.
13. *Special interest* maps, such as those of national parks, state parks, major imports, major cities, seaports, and river systems.
14. *Historical* maps of the Colonies, early travel routes, and early settlements.
15. *Transparent* maps of resources, transportation networks, and other distributions to project or to place over other maps in order to show relationships.

6. John V. Michaelis. *Social Studies for Children in a Democracy: Recent Trends and Developments*, 6th ed. Copyright © 1976. Reprinted by permission of Prentice-Hall, Inc., Englewood Cliffs, New Jersey.

Challenging map activities

These activities are for students who are developing considerable skill in reading and interpreting maps. As a teacher, begin to collect ideas for such activities from any reading that you do.

1. Boundaries separate states or countries politically, but they do not change the climate, physical features, agricultural production, or other activities of men in adjoining states or countries. Illustrate this.
2. Put dots on an outline map (preferably a relief map) of the United States to locate all cities of more than 100,000 population. Make interpretations or deductions and prove them.
3. Even if one does not use the map himself someone else has done the map reading for him. Who, and for what purpose?
4. It is possible, through air travel, to be in New York at breakfast time and in Los Angeles at lunchtime but not vice versa.
5. Prove the following:

   San Francisco is closer to Asia than to South America.

   The north polar sea is essentially the center of our world.

   The air route from New York to Chungking passes over the North Pole.

   The capital of Nevada is farther west than Los Angeles.

6. What do the map symbols and legend on a globe and on a flat map tell you about the region five hundred miles in every direction from the place where you live? This might be an interesting map to construct and display.
7. If you follow the equator, or the Tropic of Cancer, or the Tropic of Capricorn, or the 45 N. parallel, or the latitude of your home town around the world, first on the globe and then on a flat map, what do you find out about mountains, oceans, climate, agriculture, population, and other geographical ideas along that parallel of latitude?
8. Find the degree of longitude nearest your home. Follow it along from pole to pole listing the names of places on or near that meridian (these places are directly north or south of where you live).
9. There are no heavily populated areas along the equator.
10. On many maps and globes, the scale—in addition to the usual way of stating it as one inch to 4 miles, etc.—is shown as a representative fraction. For example, 1:250,000 or 1/250,000, meaning one inch to 250,000 inches works out to about one inch to 4 miles. Many of the Geological Survey quadrangles are marked 1:24,000, meaning one inch to 2,000 feet. A 12-inch globe may say 1:41,817,600 or 660 miles to an inch. Find the R.F. (representative fraction) on other maps and globes. Maybe you will want to prove the scale of miles mathematically.
11. There have been many changes in boundaries and territories in the last thirty

years. Can you find any maps published about 1940 and compare them with the newest maps? What brought about the changes?

12. Do you truly realize how large Africa is? A signpost at Nairobi airport (country?), almost on the equator, helps to emphasize the size of the world's second largest continent. Among the mileages posted are: Cairo, 2,250; Cape Town, 2,548; Accra, 2,602; and Timbuktu, 2,973. Where would you land if you flew those distances from your airport?
13. Skatro, a mythical island, is located 10 degrees South latitude and 30 degrees West longitude, with a mountain 9,000 feet high on it. Speculate about the island's natural features, describe its climate and growing season. What crops might grow there? (It would be interesting to have two pairs work on this problem, then compare results.)

Films and filmstrips

Films and filmstrips as teaching tools for maps and globes *must be used very carefully*. All *must be previewed* before use. The range and quantity of concepts presented in a single film or filmstrip varies greatly. The film—because it is motion—presents usage problems not inherent in the filmstrip. The chief learning problem in use of both is too much material in too little time. Probably no filmstrip should be shown in its entirety to a total-class group in the first viewing, unless previewing indicates that it constitutes a review for that group. Planning should result in selecting frames for total group or small groups suitable to the map and globe skills achievement status. Having pupils working in pairs with a filmstrip has proven a good technique. A few producers of filmstrips on maps and globes are: Eyegate House, Inc.; Jim Handy Organization; McGraw-Hill Book Co., Inc.; Society for Visual Education; Stanbow Productions; and H.M. Elkins Co.

FOR FURTHER READING

For Children

Carlisle, Norman, and Madelyn Carlisle. *True Book of Maps*. Chicago: Children's Press, 1969.
Hackler, David. *How Maps and Globes Help Us*. Westchester, Ill.: Benefic Press, 1964.
Matkin, R. B. *Your Book of Maps and Map Reading*. Levittown, N.Y.: Transatlantic, 1970.
Oliver, John E. *What We Find When We Look at Maps*. New York: McGraw-Hill, 1970.
Riggs, Robert, and William Deters. *Language of Maps*. Birmingham, Mich.: Midwest, 1970.
Tannenbaum, Beulah, and Myra Stillman. *Understanding Maps: Charting the Land, Sea, and Sky*. New York: McGraw-Hill, 1969.

For Teachers

Anderzhon, Mamie L. *Steps in Map Reading.* Skokie, Ill.: Rand McNally, 1970.

Brown, James W.; Lewis, Richard B., and Fred F. Harcleroad. *A-V Instruction: Materials and Methods.* 4th ed. New York: McGraw-Hill, 1973.

Preston, Ralph C., and Wayne L. Herman, Jr. *Teaching Social Studies in the Elementary School.* New York: Holt, Rinehart & Winston, 1974.

Whipple, Gertrude. *How to Introduce Maps and Globes: Grades One Through Six.* Arlington, Va.: National Council for the Social Studies. The How To series.

SOURCES OF MAPS AND TEACHING AIDS

1. *Where and Why: A Map and Globe Study Skills Program.* A. J. Nystrom & Co., 3333 Elston Avenue, Chicago, Ill. 60618. A multimedia sequential map and globe program. Learning activities are presented through audio-tutorial cassettes that require active student involvement. In addition to the twenty-three cassettes, the *Where and Why* program includes a teacher's guide, twenty spirit master test sheets, and a number of maps, globes, and charts that must be used in conjunction with the cassette lessons. Well worth examining.
2. *Map and Globe Skills Kit.* Science Research Associates, Inc., 259 East Erie Street, Chicago, Ill. 60611. An expensive investment but teachers have found it highly useful. Designed for grades 4, 5, and 6. Highly adaptable to the present achievements of individual children because it is self-teaching. The *Kit* contains Study Cards, Skill Cards, Key Cards, Pupil Booklets, and a Teacher's Handbook. Write for further details.
3. Other pupil materials for developing map reading skills:
   a. Xerox Education Publications, Education Center, Columbus, Ohio 43216. "Map Skills for Today." Five booklets, grades 2 through 6. Thirty-two pp., $.50 each. Minimum order: any ten books.
   b. Scholastic Book Services, 904 Sylvan Ave., Englewood Cliffs, N. J. 07632. "Map Skills Project Books." I for primary grades, II for middle grades, III for upper elementary. Pupil and teacher editions, each $.60.
   c. Nystrom (see address above). Booklet I, "Learning to Use a Globe"; Booklet II, "Learning to Use a Map." $2.95 per set.
   d. Follett Publishing Company, 1010 West Washington Blvd., Chicago, Ill. 60607. "Study Lessons in Map Reading." Fourth grade. Interest level: 5th through the 9th. Approximately one hundred pp. $1.86. Teacher's Guide
   e. Rand McNally & Co., P.O. Box 7800, Chicago, Ill. 60680. *Going Places Series*—classroom tested to teach children directions, measurements, and location; *Which Way?* —a guide to direction; *How Far?*—how far one place or point is from another; *Where?*—presents location systems such as time zones, parallels, meridians, etc. Each book has a student's test, an activity book, and a teacher's edition.

f. W. H. Sadlier, Inc., 11 Park Place, New York, N.Y. 10007. MAP MAKS. Suitable for use with any program based on culture-area studies. Constructed on a multilevel capability basis, they provide for the wide range of abilities found in any classroom. Produced for nine culture areas: the United States and Canada, Latin America, Middle East and North Africa, and others. About $.40 each. The student, or a team of students, is led through a variety of activities.

4. Washington Distribution Section, U. S. Geological Survey, 1200 South Eads St., Arlington, Va. 22202.

   a. Request "Index to Topographic Maps of (your home state)." These maps are topographic sheets, or quadrangles, which use contour lines to show relief and elevations. Some of the United States is mapped at 2,000 feet to the inch showing farmhouses, wooded areas, swamps, roads, etc., in detail. Middle grade pupils find these maps of their own areas fascinating. Some large bookstores stock them (approximately $.60). If you do not know these maps you should become acquainted with them.
   b. *Elevations and Distances in the United States.* This brochure presents a series of tables of geographic statistics of the fifty states, including elevations of mountains, distances between various map points, etc. Price $.30.
   c. The new six-color map of the conterminous United States with insets of Alaska and Hawaii, in two 54″ x 41″ sections. Scale one inch to nearly forty miles and shows state boundaries and capitals, county boundaries and seats, major metropolitan areas, swamp areas and water features, and the continental shelf. (Check cost.)

5. National Ocean Survey, Distribution Division C 44, Riverdale, Md., 20840. Item #3068, Outline Map of the United States, shows conterminous United States, indicates major cities. Black and white, 22″ × 28″, $.20. Item #3090, World Map, shows political boundaries and major cities. Size 35″ × 47″, $.40. *Free materials:* (a) Map of "Coastline of the United States," lengths in statute miles of each coastal state; (b) "Principal Rivers and Lakes of the World" (includes a list of rivers and lakes by depth, size, etc.); (c) "List of Free and Inexpensive Educational Materials."
6. Defense Mapping Agency Depot, 5801 Tabor Ave., Philadelphia, Pa. "Standard Time Chart of the World," No. 76, $1.50. "Chart of the World," No. 68, shows countries, major cities, islands. Uncolored, 36″ x 50″, $1.50.
7. Scholastic Book Services, 904 Sylvan Ave., Englewood Cliffs, N. J. 07632. "How to Be a Map Explorer"—a chart, 28″ x 42″, designed to help children read maps. Explanations of different kinds of maps and map terms under a map of the United States, Canada, and part of Mexico. Send payment with order, $1.50 less 25 percent educator's discount.
8. Instructor Publications, Dansville, N. Y., 14437. Send for price list of outline maps prepared for the spirit duplicator to run off pupil copies. Other companies also have duplicating masters.

9. National Geographic Society, Washington, D.C. 20036. Write for their list of maps. Maps are excellent; too detailed for most teaching purposes, but some children will devour them. Nearly every issue of the National Geographic now has a loose inserted map; there may be subscribers in your community who would give the maps to the school.
10. *Motel-Motor Inn Journal,* Attn. Advertising Director, Box 769, Temple, Texas, 76501. *Time Zone Map.* A map of the United States showing its various time zones. Free.
11. Ginn and Company, 191 Spring St., Lexington, Mass. 02173. *Map Slides.* Set 1—United States and Canada (ten slides); Set 2—Latin America, Africa, and Australia (eleven slides); Set 3—Eurasia (twelve slides). 2″ x 2″ cardboard mounted. May be projected at a much larger size than the conventional wall map.
12. The George F. Cram Company, Inc., School and Library Division, 301 South Lasalle St., Indianapolis, Ind. 46206. Seven-color outline desk maps, 12″ x 17¼″, on special mapboard; plastic surface can be marked with wax crayon. Maps of United States and all continents. $.60 each (minimum order six maps).
13. The American Waterways Operators, Inc., 1250 Connecticut Ave., N.W., Washington, D.C. 20036. A map of "Commercially Navigable Inland Waterways of the United States." Free.
14. Chicago: Denoyer-Geppert. Paper wall outline maps, 46″ x 35″. Political boundaries, principal rivers, lines of latitude and longitude shown. United States, continents, world, and some individual countries. $.90 each. The map can be developed in many different ways as a class works on a unit, or even a small group on a special report.
15. *Publishers' Catalogs.* One way to learn about the variety of different types of maps is to go through publishers' catalogs. A copy of each should be made available in the principal's office or school library. Many teachers are unaware of the kinds and variety of helpful teaching materials available. Some schools designate a volunteer middle-grade teacher as the "expert" to be knowledgeable about what publishers have to offer. Major publishers are: George F. Cram Co., Inc., 301 LaSalle St., Indianapolis, Ind. 46206; Denoyer-Geppert Company, 5235 Ravenswood Ave., Chicago, Ill. 60640; Nystrom, 3333 Elston Ave., Chicago, Ill. 60618; Rand McNally & Co., P.O. Box 7800, Chicago, Ill., 60680; Hammond, Inc., 515 Valley St., Maplewood, N. J. 07040; Weber Costello, 1900 North Narragansett, Chicago, Ill. 60639.

IMPROVING EVALUATION

Chapter ten

Evaluation in social studies is the process of gathering, interpreting, and using evidence to determine changes in a learner's behavior as a result of his classroom experiences in the social studies. Facts and information can be measured by a test and are easiest to evaluate. Map skills and the study skills also lend themselves well to testing, but other skills are evaluated with varying degrees of success. Understandings and generalizations, along with attitudes and social behaviors, are difficult to assess, for less objective appraisal techniques must be used.

Every teacher needs to know what happens to the boys and girls because of his instruction. How are they different because he was their teacher? There once was a time when subject matter mastery was the objective of learning in the elementary school. Paper-and-pencil tests told the teacher how well the pupils had achieved. Now that many other, and different, kinds of learning goals have been added, many types of outcomes are expected and must be evaluated. Evaluation is only a process, not an end-product or a goal in itself.

GUIDELINES IN THE EVALUATIVE PROCESS

1. *Good evaluation is directly related to the goals of instruction*. There are the overall goals for the total social studies program; the goals for the year, sometimes expressed as concepts, generalizations, or main ideas; and the goals for a unit, usually in the form of understandings, skills, attitudes, and appreciations. Most often the goals being evaluated are those that come within the scope of a unit and other concurrent social studies activities, but other long-term goals should not be neglected.

Plan the evaluation techniques for your teaching unit when you design it. This means that you will provide many opportunities and activities that will contribute to each of the goals. Turn your understandings for the unit into questions: Do your third grade children understand that:

a. The Pilgrims wanted to live in ways that were not possible in their old homes in England and Holland?
b. The Pilgrims built board houses because they did not know how to build log cabins?
c. The Indians were helpful to the Pilgrims?

Take the problem-solving skills listed for the unit and ask questions in like fashion. Have the children grown in:

a. Ability to make simple comparisons between long ago and now?
b. Ability to use pictures to help them to develop new meanings and understandings?
c. Ability to learn through an interview?

Appreciation and attitudes listed for the unit can be put in this form also. Have the children developed:

a. An appreciation of cooperation among neighbors in a community?
b. An interest in what maps and globes can show?

These are some of the questions. The techniques for obtaining answers are discussed later.

2. *Good evaluation is a continuous process.* Here are some points to consider:

   a. Some evaluation procedures are a part of instructional procedures: observation of group discussions to determine needs for materials or change of plans, phases of teacher-pupil planning, use of checklists, quality of contributions in problem-solving, and need for further research.
   b. Accumulated judgments become evaluations.
   c. Be able to identify the objectives to which the daily activities are directly related and check progress.
   d. Evaluate the contribution of out-of-school experiences to children's learning.
   e. Explore what the children already know before proceeding with further instruction.
   f. At the close of each period, or at the beginning of a new period, when the children are asked to tell what has been accomplished and what needs to be done, evaluation is taking place.
   g. The teacher must understand and practice the integration of a great variety of evaluation techniques with activities and teaching objectives if evaluation is to make its needed contribution.

3. *Good evaluation must be a cooperative endeavor.* Once evaluation was wholly teacher oriented. Now it is known that to be most effective it must be a cooperative affair.

   a. Any activities carried on by a group should be evaluated by the group. What did we do? How well did we do? How could we have gained more? Why did certain activities lack value? Which activities planned were not needed? What did we have to add after we got started? What did we learn?
   b. What opportunities did this unit give for pupil-teacher evaluation? Did I take advantage of all of the opportunities? Would it be wise to plan even more opportunities in a unit?
   c. A purpose jointly assumed usually encourages group response to its demands.
   d. Involvement of pupils in gathering evidence about the group in which they were participants and about themselves as members of groups makes for more effective learning.

4. *Self-evaluation by pupils is necessary.*

   a. The evaluation a child makes of his own growth or status can be more revealing to him than any single comment made or mark given by the teacher.
   b. The points to be evaluated by the pupil put into one or more checklists, which might be made by the teacher and/or by the teacher and children cooperatively, will help the child cover the most important areas.
   c. The pupil should keep a record of his own progress. (Sometimes part of the record is in the form of a profile.) He should see the direction in which he is moving.
   d. In this self-evaluation, and in a teacher-pupil conference, the emphasis must be on "results as products," not on any marks given by the teacher or a group. *Never use the symbol marks of a report card for this evaluation.* (See the checklist items in the following section.)

5. *Good evaluation is concerned with individual growth,* not with comparative status of children in a class. Concern for growth is not shown by merely looking at a child as a statistic.

   a. It should provide the kind of information that will help the teacher guide the individual learner.
   b. It informs each pupil of his own progress.
   c. In looking at a group the teacher is asking himself questions. Who was active? Who gained little? Why? How can I involve this child?
   d. The concern is with how well a child did in relation to an objective, not simply with what grade he got in an examination (although achievement in an examination is *one* part of evaluation).
   e. The teacher must recognize that there are weaknesses in every kind of device used in evaluation and give any benefit of a doubt to the child.
   f. The teacher's goal is the maximum development of each child.

6. *Good evaluation reexamines all planning in retrospect.* It is one of the three stages of good planning: (1) pre-planning; (2) planning in process; (3) evaluation in retrospect. This would apply not only to a unit but also to the total social studies program for the year. Let us look at a unit just completed.

   a. Any evaluation should be systematically recorded so that it can be interpreted and can result in action.
   b. Evaluation should suggest modifications in teaching plans before using them again. These should be recorded, or they will not be remembered.
   c. The teacher appraises his participation in the unit planning and instruction. Curriculum guides published by school systems raise questions such as these for the teacher to ask himself:

      1. Did all of the children know exactly what they were to do and how they were to do it?
      2. Were provisions made for those who had difficulty reading the books that were available?
      3. Did the period provide opportunity for children to develop some of the social skills needed?
      4. Did the children get enough facts to develop the generalization I hoped they would make?
      5. Did the children have experiences that gave meaning to the concepts involved?
      6. Did every child have an opportunity to realize success?
      7. Were all the children involved?
      8. Did the period provide opportunity for the use and development of skills such as reading, writing, and speaking?
      9. Were provisions made in materials and in tasks for individual differences?
      10. Did pupils participate in any of the decisions that were made to move an activity along in the desired direction?
      11. Was use made of the local community?
      12. Did I notice definite instances of a change in the attitudes and appreciations of the pupils?
      13. Did I continue to learn along with the children?
      14. How many books did I read on the various pupil levels in order to acquaint myself with the types of information contained in them?
      15. How many books on an adult level did I read to prepare myself for this unit?
      16. Am I keeping abreast of current affairs connected with the unit?

7. *Good evaluation is comprehensive.* There is a considerable variety of evaluation techniques available for the wide range of social studies goals and purposes.

TECHNIQUES OF EVALUATION

Observation

Observation is more widely used than any other evaluative technique except for teacher-made tests, which will be discussed later. A third grade teacher, recording the outcomes of a unit on clothing, listed the items below almost wholly from observation. Parents played a part in this observation.

1. Some children become more interested in their personal appearance and develop desirable habits in the care and selection of their clothing and in the way they dress.
2. Events in the community that relate to clothing, such as museum displays of textiles or of historical costume, catch the interest of some of the children.
3. The child shows considerable improvement in his ability to use the information found in his reading. The child's reading interests are extended to include materials on history and development of our country.
4. The child is interested in home furnishings that have been made with great care and skill, such as quilts, counterpanes, rugs, and the like.
5. An extension of interest is noted with respect to the work that people do.
6. There seems to be greater understanding for the need for getting good values for money spent on clothing.
7. A greater appreciation for things made by hand is evident, as is an increased interest in making things and sharing with others.
8. Interest arises in developing a hobby, such as weaving or collecting samples of cloth and design.

Teachers make behavior rating scales, listing as many items as they wish (from only six or eight up to eighteen or twenty) for rating children. It will not be possible to make a separate scale for each child. Make some choices. To be most valuable it should be done for the children selected two or three times during the year to show growth. Rating scales can also be designed for self-evaluation by a child. A sample rating scale is shown on page 350.

Another kind of checklist has its items running down the side, as in the list above, and its columns at the right for children's names. Here a check mark in the column opposite an item could represent satisfactory achievement of the child, or a symbol could be used to indicate the child's status of accomplishment.

Perhaps you want a checklist on map skills for your second grade. Use items like this:

DESCRIPTIVE RATING SCALE

Name______________________________

BEHAVIOR	ALL OF THE TIME	MOST OF THE TIME	OCCASION-ALLY	NEVER
1. Waits his turn to talk				
2. Listens to the suggestions of others				
3. Abides by majority decisions				
4. Doesn't get resentful if his suggestions aren't carried out				
5. Takes his share of responsibility				
6. Once he starts a task carries it to completion				
7. Carries his share of work load in a small group				
8. Respects the feelings of his classmates				

1. Knows cardinal directions.
2. Has sense of ground distance.
3. Knows land and water areas on globe.
4. Can find some places mentioned in the news.
5. Understands time related to distance.

At the middle grade level, written test items can be used to check many map skills. There are map skills, also, that can be checked by observation. (See pp. 327-334 for map skills.)

A simple plan for developing a checklist would be to:

1. Check the objectives and needs of the group when making up the check sheet.
2. Decide what behavior, skill, or attitude is to be developed and checked.
3. Work out the method of checking that seems most satisfactory.
4. Allow for more than one check so that growth can be noted.
5. Note where emphasis is needed after first check.
6. Select only a few children to check during any one period.

The teacher who is an alert observer and knows what he is looking for can do some important evaluation through observation. Two things, however, must be emphasized strongly: (1) Avoid the shotgun approach of spraying a large area in attempting evaluation observations. Choose only one or two items in any one day; (2) Record your observations. Do not rely on your memory, for it will not serve you well.

Phases of other techniques described here are also based on observation.

Total class generalizing session

In social studies the amount and variety of data is sometimes overwhelming. Because of this fact, social scientists attempt to collect information, develop certain ideas, and generalize about a topic. It is difficult to teach children to generalize but not to overgeneralize. In many classrooms some attempt is made to encourage the students to make generalizations and provide practice. The teacher may say, "Who can tell us in one sentence what we have been talking about?" Often a few students finalize or summarize the ideas for the "silent majority."

It is necessary for all students to learn how to make good generalizations. In order for them to do so, a strategy for written participation is needed. It would take an excessive amount of time for all students to verbalize generalizations following a given research emphasis. Besides practice in writing general statements, the students need practice is assessing statements for qualitative differences. The following sequence is one that was designed to provide some practice verbally as well as extensive practice in writing statements. Practice in assessing the relative worth of statements made by other students is also an objective in this lesson.

Materials

Pictures for opaque projector review
Packets of small stapled papers (roughly 8″ x 4″—one packet for each student)
One retrieval chart of butcher paper— divided into categories
Quarter sheets of manila drawing paper

Procedure

1. The teacher may use the opaque projector and with pictures he has collected review some of the basic areas the children have researched. No comment is to be made with the pictures.
2. The teacher places headings on the board (e.g., homes, transportation, food, cities, problems) that involve the major areas of research. The technique used in this portion of the lesson is as follows:

   a. "Look at these headings and decide which is the easiest one to discuss. Raise your hand when you can make a nice full sentence about it." "Did someone else pick the same one?" (A number of responses are verbalized about a given category.)
   b. "Did someone else choose a different heading as the easiest?" (Proceed as in 2. a.) Three or four categories are reviewed, and then the instructions change.
   c. "Listen carefully to your new instructions. I want you to look at the board and see if there are headings that you think are too difficult to discuss." Several responses and arguments ensue because some children think it possible to say something about these headings, and the remaining items are reviewed.
   d. "Are there categories you would like to leave out?" Several pupils respond. "Are there any you feel must be added?" Again several students respond.

3. The teacher calls the students' attention to a small clipped pad of paper on the corner of each desk. She now has them write one general statement about the first category on the first slip of paper. The children read one or two statements to be sure they have the idea and then the teacher has them do the remaining category statements, each on a separate slip of paper. (This procedure requires about fifteen minutes.)
4. When a large percentage of the class is finished, the teacher calls for statement #1 to be torn off and held high. Someone collects all of these. The same procedure is followed with all categories. Now the students are arranged in small groups. Each group will consider one category.

5. A chairman for each group is quickly identified. The chairman deals out the slips of paper, on which the students have written a general statement, to the team members. (Each group considers only one category, and a sufficient number of groups are formed to deal with all the categories.)
6. The teacher instructs the class. He says that each student should read the statements he has in his hand and place the best one on top.
7. Each child in the group now reads the statement he has selected as the best statement to the group, and the group decides which one is the best of all the statements from this sample. The children are told at this point that if no statement suits them, they must revise the statements. Suggestions for revision are sought from the group. (For example, you might put two statements together, or you might write a new one using words from a good one, etc.)
8. Each group chairman reads his group's choice to the class and writes it on a large retrieval chart. Each member of the group sketches a miniature (3″ x 4″) manila drawing of his interpretation of the statement. These are taped up under the generalization on the chart.
9. A final effort to collect the statements and to judge generalizations is made. The chairmen line up across the front of the room and the teacher says, "These statements are all about different things, but see if you can tell us which one is the very best of all the statements regardless of the topic. Which one tells the most about its topic?" The class members decide on the one they like best and tell why they like it. They give such reasons as: it is based on facts; it is true (accurate); it is compared with something else; it tells why or explains why. All of the criteria presented by class members are discussed by the entire class, and an agreement on the best statement is reached.

Over four hundred statements produced in fifty minutes, with every child involved every minute! The task of locating the best statement is almost a game. The evaluation of statements is nonpersonal and nonthreatening (no names appeared on statements), but all children can begin to see what is needed to produce a good statement. It is a technique you might try in your classroom.[1]

Group discussion

Class discussion serves two main purposes. It contributes to getting and giving information, offering opportunities for children to evaluate together what has been done and decide what needs to be done, exploring various possibilities prior to decision making. Secondly, it provides the teacher a favorable time for evaluating the group process as well as the individual pupil.

1. The lesson procedure above is adapted from a lesson developed in a fourth grade taught by Donna LaPierre, Brunswick, Maine.

The teacher needs to examine critically how much actual participation there is in a discussion of a total class group. Even a lively give-and-take discussion usually involves only eight or ten out of a class of twenty-five. An alternative is small-group discussion (four or five) all on the same question, reporting back to the class through secretaries, which will occasion further discussion. The teacher moves among the small discussion groups and this, with the total group discussion, provides more data on more people. It is obvious that the question-answer recitation based on regurgitating facts does not provide discussion. Questions calling for organizational, elaborative, or critical thinking in small groups can provoke lively discussion.

Sometimes the stage is set for discussion in the whole class; then the class adjourns to small groups and reconvenes for group reports. Perhaps the occasion is the development of a chart on regulations for a field trip or a checklist on pupil behavior as a good citizen, appraisal of a film, or a summary of what has been learned in a unit. Sometimes group (usually small) discussions are taped, which enables the teacher to analyze later. Hearing its own recording may well spark further appraisal by the group.

Questionnaires and inventories

Questionnaires and inventories get at special interests, hobbies, after-school activities, home resources for study materials, and the like. In questionnaires the children usually write short answers, whereas in inventories they are more likely to circle or mark responses provided.

Anecdotal records

Anecdotal records are actual brief descriptions, without interpretation, of behavior the teacher feels significant for a particular child. They can be recorded in a notebook, or, better yet, merely noted on a small piece of paper, dated, and dropped into the pupil's dossier folder. (There should be a folder for each child, in which are collected work samples and any other information pertinent to making evaluations on him.)

The brief descriptions might be concerned with a child's self-initiated activities such as: voluntarily bringing contributions for school activities; submitting, voluntarily and orally, data or information based on observations or trips; presenting a report on a self-directed investigation; or suggesting methods, materials, activities, etc., for developing a project.

The record might also be concerned with a pupil's cooperative activities, especially if he were one who needed to develop cooperation, such as: helping pupils or teacher with their problems or projects; offering objects or materials to teacher, pupil, or visitor; or responding quickly to requests for quiet, materials, help, etc.

Other items can be concerned with work habits, reading, personal relationships, or improvement in personality characteristics.

Charts and checklists

Charts and checklists can be developed for self-evaluation and group evaluation. There can be short checklists of only half a dozen items where the child checks under the *Yes* or *No* column the answers to questions such as: How do I listen?; Am I helpful?; Making an oral report; Watching a film; or Using a map. We call it a checklist when items are actually checked with pen or pencil, and a chart when it is posted and occasionally called to the attention of the class or an individual.

Other checklists to be marked by the pupil could be developed in formats like this:

WORKING WELL WITH OTHERS

HOW OFTEN DO YOU DO EACH ITEM LISTED BELOW?	ALWAYS	USUALLY	SOME-TIMES	NEVER	?
1. I suggest ways of working.					
2. I consider carefully suggestions of others.					
3. I offer to help when my work is done.					
4. I take my share of the responsibility.					

In another type of checklist, preferences in social studies activities are shown by circling one of three designations after each activity: *L* for like, *I* for indifferent to, *D* for dislike.

1. See filmstrips about the unit	L I D
2. Use many different books	L I D
3. Draw pictures to illustrate unit	L I D

A series of statements can be used to check beliefs or attitudes by putting an *A* in front for *Agree*, a *D* in front for *Disagree*.

______Japanese people are strange.
______I should choose an occupation at which I can make the most money.
______Everyone should learn to speak a foreign language.

In addition to checklists, the teacher may wish to have some measure of children's social relationships and the changes that occur in them as a result of group work. See Chapter 2, pages 65-67, for sample sociometric measurement suggestions.

A daily progress checklist can provide both a number of suggestions for developing and organizing information and a stimulus to the student to think about accounting for his use of time. Table 10.1 is one such progress sheet that you might use. You will note that the date is recorded at the top and the student records initials on the checksheet each day.

TABLE 10.1 PROGRESS REPORT

	2/1	2/2	2/3	2/4	2/7
Map					
Graphs					
Report writing					
Play writing					
Making display	MJ	MJ	MJ		
Drawing picture					
Locating information				MJ	MJ
Charts					
Survey					
Interview					
Viewing films					
Making overheads					
Discussing					
Sharing information					
Evaluating					

Work samples

Samples of the paperwork done by a pupil should be kept in his dossier (cumulative folder), each item dated, as a basis for judgment of progress. All production—pictures, murals, items constructed, diaries, booklets, scrapbooks—should be evaluated from the viewpoint of the evidence it gives about progress toward objectives, not the symbol grade it was given.

This is a particularly valuable technique in dealing with the evaluation of problem-solving processes. It is possible to set up criteria for judging general statements, for example, and then use these criteria in looking at the student's products at several points during the year. One can detect changes over time readily this way.

If the unit of work that has been covered dealt with broad understandings, and the students have developed general statements as a part of the summary of the unit, the teacher may be interested in saving samples of these statements for comparative puposes. The student's first statements might be compared with some of the generalizations he makes later in the year.

To determine whether or not the children were aware of the elements that make up a good general statement, the following question was asked of a sample of over two hundred fourth and fifth graders.

> If you were given two statements about Antarctica, how would you decide which one is the better statement? List the things you would think about as you decide.

The types of things suggested by over half the students could be categorized as follows:

Based on fact: "What kind of animals live there?"
Relevance: "That it sticks to the subject." "Which tells about the topic?"
Accurate: "Which one was true?" "True words."
Broad: "Which one told more about it?"
Dynamic: "Which sentence is more up-to-date than the other one?"
Good Structure: "I would look to see if you used correct English."
Cause/Effect: "Why it is the way it is."

It seems clear that students who have been involved in the problem-solving process and have developed general statements as a concluding activity do recognize levels of sophistication in statements. Perhaps some of these ideas might be useful to a teacher in looking at students' work samples.

Work samples can also be used as a basis for comments during parent-teacher conferences. Parents want specific information about their children's progress.

The day of "Your son isn't doing so well" as a lead-in to a parent conference is past. Such an approach is unacceptable, and the need for data and definitive, helpful suggestions is clear.

Dramatization

The sociodrama, role playing, and creative dramatization are all means of revealing attitudes and understandings. They are performed either without any rehearsal except for a brief conference among the players in order to establish the general situation and the place of the characters in it, or spontaneously, with no conference, if the stage has been set by the teacher. The teacher does not find it difficult to evaluate the depth of understanding or identification of the child with his role. We have seen spontaneous dramatizations of the relationship between a serf and a feudal lord, of social life in the conversation room of a Roman bath, and of women shopping in a Roman market place, which showed real understanding and keen insight into the situations portrayed.

Mini-situations can be developed and used for evaluation. When this is done one can look for a particular criterion such as "sensitivity to the feelings of others" in one situation, and a different criterion in connection with another mini-situation.

In order to assess dramatization it is necessary to delineate clearly the quality of learning that such a technique most effectively develops.

The simulation techniques presented on pages 260-265 promote

1. verbal involvement
2. physical involvement
3. an understanding that problems often have more than one solution
4. an opportunity to engage in analyzing or extending characters in the situation.
5. antecedent/consequent thinking or causal thinking
6. sensitivity to other people's feelings

To evaluate these sessions, then:

1. and 2. Use participation checklists[2]
3. Count the number of solutions in sentence stems
4. Have students extend the character in a one-paragraph description
5. Use #2 of the sentence stems
6. Use #7 of the sentence stems

2. It is important that the teacher have some knowledge of the extent of pupil participation. It is easy to forget that a pupil discussed an idea or had a minor role in an enactment. If participation is an objective, then an ongoing record should be kept like in Figure 10.1.

FIGURE 10.1 PARTICIPATION CHECKLIST

	SESSION I		SESSION II		SESSION III	
	DISCUSSION	ENACTMENT	DISCUSSION	ENACTMENT	DISCUSSION	ENACTMENT
Ann Jameson						
George Willoby						
Marvin Shapiro						

Sentence stem possibilities

1. Tommy said ____.
2. If Tommy ____________________then ____________________.
3. The boat (object in story) ____________________________.
4. The owner of the wallet (offended person) ______________.
5. The main problem in the story is ______________________.
6. The problem could have been avoided if________________.
7. Eddie feels (peer) _____________________________________.
8. Eddie's uncle (adult authority figure) __________________.
9. Some different ways the problem might be solved are _____________.

Logs and diaries

The daily class log is an excellent way to keep a class in touch with what they have done in a unit. Teachers who have used it tell us that their pupils frequently refer to it to check on places and decisions made when evaluating a unit in progress or making ready to conclude it. A diary is one of the easiest ways for a child to record his growth, since the record is kept daily while accomplishments are still fresh in the child's mind. Even first graders can keep simple diaries, dictating their sentences to their teacher until they are able to write and express themselves with more ease.

Open-ended questions

Many teachers have found using open-ended questions very helpful in evaluating the needs of children. This technique can be used as soon as children are able to do any response writing, probably in the second grade. Questions such as "What is the best thing that could happen to my family?" "What things do I like most about my neighborhood?" "What do I like best in school?" (or "in social studies") or "The boy (girl) I like best is" (describe but do not name) are good.

Conferences

The conference is one of the best methods of evaluating what children feel and know. The child should have the opportunity to talk about what he considers his progress and growth. Through talking with the teacher he may gain a better insight into the ways in which he is improving and obtain specific suggestions on how to make further improvement. Sometimes a checklist prepared by the pupil may direct some, but not all, of the conversation.

If the teacher is planning a parent-teacher conference, it is wise to have a child-teacher conference first. Tell the child exactly and honestly what will be discussed, and share with the student the remedial steps you plan, if such steps are in order.

Some school systems use the report card as a form of written conference. The teacher writes a comment about the child's present level of achievement in a subject, and what he perceives the next steps to be. The child also has a space and does the same thing. The parent signs and adds remarks in a third space. This written conference should not eliminate the face-to-face conference when the latter is needed.

Teacher-made tests

Teacher-made tests in the elementary school are usually of the informal objective type, based largely on factual information and to some degree on work-study and other skills. As the teacher grows increasingly skillful they can be applied to other aspects of the social studies.

From the very beginning of test item construction, the teacher should make a practice of building a reservoir file. In it he will place all items he builds, *one item only* to a 3″ by 5″ card. This kind of filing allows him to:

1. Add an item at any time.
2. Throw out an item easily.
3. Rewrite an item to improve the form.
4. Comment on the card about the item, based on test experience with it.
5. File items under any subject heading desired.
6. Pull items, and place them in any order needed on a ditto stencil.

A valuable reference on evaluation in social studies is a yearbook of the National Council for the Social Studies on that subject. In it, Dunfee has made some excellent suggestions on types of items for tests of factual information, other types of items to test children's grasp of important understandings, and ways for evaluating attitudes. These types of items are representative of those that test for factual information in desirable ways. The pupil may be asked to engage in such activities as the following:

1. To arrange in order the steps in a process.
2. To match events with periods of time.
3. To supply key words missing in statements of fact essential to the unit.
4. To match vocabulary and definitions.
5. To select from a collection of facts those related in some designated way.
6. To support a generalization with essential facts.
7. To match objects or agencies with their functions, principles with their applications, etc.
8. To support response to true-false items with confirming data.
9. To distinquish between facts that are subject to change and those that will not vary with time.
10. To make statements of fact derived from charts, diagrams, and graphs.
11. To select from a list of facts those that are useful in solving a given problem.
12. To place events or persons on a time line.
13. In a multiple-choice item, to support responses with data.
14. In true-false items, to alter false items to make them true.

Children's grasp of important understandings that have been developed may be tested in some ways that are practical and helpful. Admittedly, such tests are more difficult to devise than tests of information, but the following suggestions may encourage the creative teacher to try for more significant evaluation techniques. In these test situations pupils are required to respond to a variety of demands:

1. To match statements of cause and effect.
2. To distinguish between facts and generalizations in a given list of statements.
3. To supply the generalization to be drawn from a given set of facts.
4. To select the conclusion to be drawn from a chart, diagram, or graph.
5. To support a given generalization with facts.
6. To state the generalizations that can be drawn from a field trip or other project.
7. To match a generalization with its supporting data.
8. To select the generalization that may explain why a given situation exists.
9. To draw conclusions from an imaginary dialogue in which an issue is discussed, i.e., what person has inaccurate information, what person's comments reveal prejudice, etc.
10. To state the most important ideas learned from the unit of work.
11. To state an opinion about why a particular unit of work was chosen for study.
12. To select responses to multiple-choice items that emphasize why something happened or why a condition exists.
13. To match pictures with the generalizations they represent.

Attitudes are not easily tested. But it is possible to determine whether or not a child recognizes a socially desirable attitude. Perhaps this is all that can be hoped for. Attitudes are subject to change, and we can know only what the child reveals in a test situation. The following suggestions may be helpful to teachers seeking an insight into the attitudes of their pupils. It is often revealing to ask pupils to perform evaluative tasks such as these:

1. To select, from a teacher-prepared dialogue, comments that reveal desirable or undesirable attitudes.
2. To respond yes or no to questions that ask, "Do you think . . . ?
3. To respond to a list of statements of belief, feeling, or opinion by indicating degree—always, sometimes, never.
4. To respond to statements that imply prejudice or lack of prejudice by indicating statement of agreement—I agree, I disagree, I am uncertain.
5. To match attitudes with likely resultant actions.
6. To state what one liked best about the unit of work being developed.
7. To give opinions about described situations that reveal the attitudes of the characters.
8. To give reasons to support the action that should be taken in a described problem situation.
9. To write the ending to a story that describes a problem situation.
10. To complete an unfinished sentence such as, "Our unit of work has changed my ideas about. . . ."[3]

General suggestions for constructing objective tests

The forms of objective test items most commonly used in the elementary school are simple recall and completion, alternative response, matching, and multiple-choice. There are some general rules that should normally be observed in the construction of all objective tests:

1. The language should be clear, with only one way in which a statement or term could be interpreted.
2. Difficult or technical words should be avoided unless they are part of the material being tested.
3. Textbook wording should be avoided, for it puts a premium on memorization.

3. From Maxine Dunfee, "Evaluating Understandings, Attitudes, Skills and Behaviors in Elementary School Social Studies," in *Evaluation in Social Studies*, 35th Yearbook (Arlington, Va.: National Council for the Social Studies, 1965). Reprinted with permission of the National Council for the Social Studies and Maxine Dunfee.

4. Items having obvious answers should not usually be used.
5. "Give-away" clues and suggestions should be avoided: having the right answer longer, the use of "a" and "an," etc.
6. Items that can be answered by intelligence or reason alone should not be included in an achievement-type test.
7. Quantitative rather than qualitative words should be used where possible.
8. "Catch" questions should be avoided.
9. Avoid items that help pupils to answer other questions.
10. Avoid items that depend on preceding ones.
11. The placement of answer blanks should preferably be aligned for ease in marking.
12. Avoid trivial details in objective tests; emphasize important facts and generalizations.
13. Make clear-cut directions for each part of the test (each type of objective test items) and if necessary show a correct answer in a sample item.
14. In the complete test arrange items according to type (multiple-choice together, etc.) with answer blanks placed for scoring, and not crowded together.
15. Items should be written in pupil language.
16. Do not penalize pupils for spelling errors.
17. Do not penalize pupils for poor handwriting or reward them for good handwriting.

Simple recall and completion. Directions: What are the names of the places described below?

Write the answers in the space provided.

1. The country in which the first experiments were carried on with wireless, or radio. ______________________________

2. The country from which the United States secured land through which to build a canal. ______________________________

Complete the sentences by filling in the correct word on the blank at the right.

1. The Italian who made his adventures in Cathay into a book was ______________
2. The fiftieth state in our Union is ______________________________

The following are rules applicable primarily to simple recall and completion tests:

1. Lines for responses should be about the same (but of adequate length) so as to give no clue to the length of the answer.

2. Any correct answer should receive credit.
3. Desired responses should be important, not trivial.
4. Spelling errors probably should not be penalized.
5. "A" or "an" should not immediately precede a blank.
6. The omitted word or phrase should ordinarily be at the end of the sentence.
7. It is best to omit only one key word or phrase.
8. Use recall items only when the correct response is a simple word or brief phrase.

Alternative-response (true-false). Directions: Some of these statements are true. Some are false. Put a plus sign (+) in front of those you think are true. Put a zero sign (0) in front of those you think are false.

____1. Rubber trees grow in Mexico.
____2. Brazil is the largest country in South America.
____3. Rio de Janeiro is nearer Africa than New York is.

Another way of using false statements is this. Directions: Something is wrong with each of the following statements. Correct each one so that it is true.

1. Among the heroes of South America are Bolívar, Miranda, Júarez, and San Martín.
2. Canada celebrates July 1 as a holiday because on that day in 1867 it elected a president and became a Dominion within the British empire.

The following are some suggestions to consider when devising alternative-response items (primarily true-false questions) in which the answer calls for the items to be marked true or false:

1. Avoid using statements containing double negatives.
2. Avoid statements that are partly true and partly false.
3. Avoid the use of specific determinators. Such words as "no," "never," "always," "very," "none," and the like are usually associated with false statements; while "may," "some," "generally," "often," and the like are usually in true statements.
4. Answers should be required in easily scorable form.
5. An approximately equal number of true and false statements should be employed.
6. Random occurrence of true and false statements should be employed.
7. Avoid making true statements consistently longer than false ones.

Matching. Directions: Put the letter in front of the name in Column I in the space before the item in Column II with which it belongs. There are more names in Column I than you will use.

I	II
A. Sacajawea	____Author of "The Star-Spangled Banner"
B. Fremont	____A guide for Lewis and Clark
C. Houston	____Mapmaker and geographer of the West
D. Jefferson	____First American Explorer of the Southwest
E. Carson	____Most famous of the "Mountain Men"
F. Key	
G. Serra	
H. Pike	

Another type of matching test is a very good form for testing concepts or other items which can be placed in categories. Directions: Put the number of the word in the first column in front of the words in the other columns with which you associate it.

1. city	____Adriatic	____Moscow	____United States
2. state	____Africa	____Pittsburgh	____Asia
3. country	____Potomac	____Florida	____Indian
4. continent	____Argentina	____Paris	____Chile
5. river	____Duluth	____Norway	____Cleveland
6. ocean	____Volga	____Cairo	____Utah
7. lake	____Ireland	____Europe	____Pacific

In preparing matching items, the following rules should normally be observed for the usual form, which is the first of the two illustrations above.

1. Usually there should be only one possible correct matching response for each item.
2. Consistency of grammatical form should be used.
3. The shorter of the two lists should contain no more than five to eight items.
4. The answers should be given in a highly objective form, such as a letter or a number.
5. The column of responses should usually contain more items than are used—two or three more—but all should appear to be good possibilities for an answer.
6. Do not mix items that are dissimilar or inconsistent; e.g., in the same exercise matching inventors and inventions, and matching events with dates.
7. Directions should clearly state which column is to be matched with which, and what is to be written in, letters, numbers, or words.
8. Pupils may be given a map on which certain locations are assigned numbers or letters. These numbers or letters can then be matched with a list of cities, islands, rivers, and the like.

Multiple choice. Directions: Pick out the word or phrase that makes the sentence most nearly correct, and put the letter in the blank.

____1. In the United States, the Argentine Pampas are most like

a. the Appalachian Mountains
b. the Great Plains
c. The Western Deserts
d. the Forest Lands of the Northwest

____2. The United States became a separate nation when

a. the battle of Lexington and Concord was fought
b. the Declaration of Independence was signed
c. the treaty of peace was signed
d. the people refused to pay the taxes England demanded.

In the construction of multiple-choice questions, the following rules should normally be observed:

1. As much of the item as possible should occur in the introductory portion (or stem); thus the alternative choices which follow may be made brief.
2. Alternative answers should be stated in a grammatical style consistent with the stem.
3. Incorrect alternatives, the distractors or options, should be plausible.
4. "A" or "an" should not ordinarily be used to introduce the alternative answers.
5. All items should ordinarily have four or five alternative answers: sometimes it is only possible to get three alternative answers. Putting alternatives that are obviously false have no value in measurement.
6. Alternative answers should ordinarily occur at the end of the statement.
7. Answers should be required in a highly objective form, such as a letter or number.
8. Random occurrence of the position of correct responses should be employed throughout the test.
9. Make all responses plausible.
10. The correct answer should not be consistently longer than the incorrect ones.

Most frequently the multiple-choice question is designed to have only one correct answer in the alternatives. But, there are variations: (1) selecting the *best answer* when the responses vary in degree of acceptability; (2) selecting two or more correct answers from the responses; (3) selecting the incorrect response when all responses but one are correct.

Standardized tests

There are few standardized tests available for elementary grades. The basic reference for the test user is the *Mental Measurement Yearbook series*, which publishes detailed information about each test with one or more critical reviews. *The Seventh Mental Measurement Yearbook* was published in 1972 (Highland Park, N. J.: Gryphon Press).

Only those that are available in separate-booklet form and have been favorably reviewed are listed here. Grade range, number of forms, and publisher are given. Write the publisher for information and cost.

Iowa Tests of Basic Skills. Houghton Mifflin. For grades 3 through 9, work-study skills including map reading.

Metropolitan Achievement Tests: Social Studies. Harcourt Brace Jovanovich. Grades 5-9. Two scores: information (geography, history, civics) and study skills (maps, tables, charts, and graphs readings). Essentially factual but insignificant facts are generally avoided.

Preston, Ralph C., and Robert V. Duffey. *The Primary Social Studies Test*. Houghton Mifflin. Grades 1 to 3. Requires no reading by children.

Sequential Tests of Educational Progress: Social Studies. Cooperative Test Division, Educational Testing Service, Princeton, N. J. Grades 4-6. Most items are said to require both skill to deal with the material and understandings in the social studies.

Stanford Achievement Test: Intermediate and Advanced Social Studies. Harcourt Brace Jovanovich. Grades 5-9. Content is essentially factual, about equally distributed among history, geography, and "civics or social problems," but few teachers are likely to find unimportant items.

FOR FURTHER READING

Banks, James A., and Ambrose A. Clegg, Jr. *Teaching Strategies for the Social Studies*. 2nd ed. Reading, Mass.: Addison-Wesley, 1977. Chapter 15.

Dunfee, Maxine. "Evaluating Understandings, Attitudes, Skills, and Behaviors in Elementary School Social Studies." In *Evaluation in Social Studies*, 35th Yearbook, Arlington, Va.: National Council for the Social Studies, 1965. Chapter 8.

Estvan, Frank J. *Social Studies in a Changing World*. New York: Harcourt Brace Jovanovich, 1962.

Jarolimek, John. *Social Studies in Elementary Education*. New York: Macmillan, 1976. Chapter 13.

Kurfman, Dana, and Robert J. Solomon. *Skill Development in Social Studies*, 33rd Yearbook. Arlington, Va.: National Council for the Social Studies, 1963. Chapter 14, "Measurement of Growth in Skills."

Michaelis, John U. *Social Studies for Children in a Democracy*. 6th ed. Englewood Cliffs, N. J.: Prentice-Hall, 1976.

Ploghoft, Milton E., and Albert H. Schuster. *Social Science Education in the Elementary School*. Columbus, Ohio: Charles E. Merrill, 1971. Chapter 14.

Preston, Ralph C., and Wayne L. Herman, Jr. *Teaching Social Studies in the Elementary School*. 4th ed. New York: Holt, Rinehart and Winston, 1974. Chapter 22.

Wrightstone, J. Wayne. "Evaluation of Learning in the Social Studies." In *Social Studies in Elementary Schools*, 32nd Yearbook. Arlington, Va.: National Council for the Social Studies, 1962.

TenBrink, Terry D. *Evaluation: A Practical Guide for Teachers*. New York: McGraw-Hill, 1974.

RESOURCE MATERIALS FOR THE SOCIAL STUDIES TEACHER

Chapter eleven

There are at least three areas of reading that have direct relationships to the social studies teacher's work in the classroom: (1) adult background material and children's books for the unit being taught; (2) current affairs materials; and (3) professional social studies publications.

THE TEACHER'S READING

Bibliographies of children's books will be found in textbooks, teacher's manuals, courses of study, and other sources. Reading reviews of new children's books in magazines and newspapers and keeping in close touch with your school and public libraries (even making special requests) will keep you up to date. Reading reviews and skimming children's books are really not too time consuming and can be richly rewarding.

Adult books concerned with the subject matter of your units are frequently listed in unit materials. Often you will have to do your own research in the public library. Don't hesitate to ask a librarian if he knows of books or other materials on a particular subject. Librarians are usually happy to be of assistance and often welcome suggestions on the purchase of books (as long as they have the funds).

Keeping informed on local, national, and world affairs through daily newspapers, television news and documentary television programs, and newsmagazines

(*Newsweek, Time, U.S. News and World Report*) is a minimum for the well-informed citizen. Surely every teacher should plan to be a well-informed citizen.

Reading professional social studies publications serves three main purposes: (1) it gives you a background that your teacher education program may not have included; (2) it provides you with ideas and suggestions to improve the quality of your instruction; and (3) it keeps you up to date on what is going on in an area that is dynamic in these days.

Every school system that is attempting to keep abreast of what is going on in social studies should have one or more institutional memberships in The National Council for the Social Studies (1515 Wilson Blvd., Arlington, Va. 22209). This includes a subscription to *Social Education* (eight issues a year), a clothbound copy of the *Yearbook*, and a copy of each publication during the year of membership.

A Special Elementary Section appears in *Social Education* four times a year with five or six articles on the special topic. Since the first one appeared in November, 1966, there have been special issues geared to elementary teachers on these topics: Concepts, Values, Skills, Individualizing Instruction, Geography, Economics, Anthropology, History, Inservice Education, the Culturally Different, Inquiry, Teacher Education, the Humanities, Teaching About Latin America, and others.

Professional magazines are a fine source for keeping up with what is happening in the social studies. Examine these magazines whenever possible.

Audiovisual Instruction, Journal of the Association for Educational Communications and Technology, National Education Association, Washington, D. C., 20036. (Published monthly except in July and August.) Latest news and professional developments including reviews of teaching materials, equipment, and audiovisual literature.

Journal of Geography, Journal of National Council for Geographic Education, A. J. Nystrom and Company, 3333 Elston Avenue, Chicago, Ill. (Published monthly except July and August.) For teachers of elementary, secondary, and college geography. Articles combine content and method, often on some current topic.

The Social Studies. McKinley Publishing Co., 112 S. New Broadway, Brooklawn, N.J. (Published monthly October through April.) Articles of general interest to the teacher and administrator. Includes regular sections on teaching materials and book reviews.

Social Education, Journal of the National Council for the Social Studies, 1515 Wilson Blvd., Arlington, Va. 22209 (Published monthly October through May.) A general treatment for all levels, including content articles, curriculum developments, and methods. Regular departments for audiovisual materials and book reviews. A special Elementary Section appears four times a year with five or six articles on a special topic.

Today's Education. Journal of the National Education Association. Look at the "Reader Service" columns, and the "Free or Inexpensive" listings for materials available.

Check other magazines when you can, such as *Elementary School Journal, Learning, Early Years, Childhood Education*, and the professional articles in *The Instructor* and *Teacher*. The "Materials" columns of the latter two often provide detailed information about the content, availability, cost, and usefulness of various kinds of free or inexpensive instructional materials. Do you read the advertisements in professional magazines?

Throughout this *Guide* we have given bibliographies and references in connection with the specific topics in each chapter. We are not repeating them here. Many of them have excellent material in areas of teaching the social studies other than the chapter topics under which they were listed. We are listing here, however, some special-purpose materials.

Books for Children. Chicago, Ill.: American Library Association. As selected and reviewed by *The Booklist* and *Subscription Books Bulletin*. Five-year compilations with annual supplements.

Christensen, Erwin O., ed. *Museums Directory of the United States and Canada*. American Association of Museums, 2306 Massachusetts Ave., N. W., Washington, D. C. 20008. A valuable reference to use in finding all the museums in your area that can make a contribution to the teaching of social studies.

Fay, Leo; Horn, Thomas; and Constance McCullough. *Improving Reading in the Elementary Social Studies*. Bulletin No. 33. Washington, D.C.: National Council for the Social Studies, 1961. Paper, $1.50. Many helpful suggestions built around the nine questions commonly raised by teachers about reading in the social studies.

How-To-Do-It Series. Arlington, Va.: National Council for the Social Studies. Paper, $.25 each. Designed for a loose-leaf binder, each 6- or 8-page pamphlet provides a practical and useful source of classroom techniques for the teacher. New titles published from time to time; all are periodically revised. Present titles especially pertinent for the elementary teacher are: No. 1, "How to Use a Motion Picture"; No. 3, "How to Use Local History"; No. 4, "How to Use a Bulletin Board"; No. 8, "How to Use Recordings"; No. 12, "How to Conduct a Field Trip"; No. 13, "How to Utilize Community Resources"; No. 15, "How to Introduce Maps and Globes"; No. 16, "How to Use Multiple Books"; No. 20, "How to Use Sociodrama"; No. 22, "How to Develop Time and Chronological Concepts"; No. 24, "How to Ask Questions"; No. 25, "How to Use Folksongs."

Simmons, Beatrice, ed. *Paperbacks for Children*. Compiled by a committee of the American Association of School Librarians, American Library Association. Englewood Cliffs, N. J.: Citation Press. Describes more than seven hundred books for grades K-6, widely recommended in hardcover editions, which are now available in paperback. Books are arranged by subject area. Each entry is annotated and includes publisher, price, suggested grade levels, and (where appropriate) illustrator. Author and title indexes.

Spache, G. D. *Good Reading for Poor Readers*. Champaign, Ill.: Garrard Publishing. Revised biennially. An important reference to hundreds of books under subject headings indicating reading level of each book.

Tolman, Lorraine E., and Thomas E. Culliton, Jr. *High-Interest-Low-Vocabulary Reading Materials*. Boston: Journal of Education, Boston University School of Education, 1967. $1. Several hundred books are evaluated for reading and interest level.

Tooze, Ruth, and Beatrice P. Krone. *Literature and Music as Resources for Social Studies*. Englewood Cliffs, N. J.: Prentice-Hall, Inc., 1955. In spite of its age, a reference that must be available to elementary teachers. For literature and music sources to enrich social studies units it has no equal. The music for many songs is in the text.

One could wish that the bibliographical books listed below could be brought up to date. High costs of publishing and somewhat limited sales probably discourage that possibility. However, many children's books in social studies areas have a long life, and are valuable both for their insights and, often, for their comparisons with today's living.

Eakin, Mary K. *Subject Index to Books for Intermediate Grades.* Chicago: American Library Association, 1963. $8.00. Organized in the same fashion as the Primary Index but its 1800 titles are mostly library books.

______and Eleanor Merritt. *Subject Index to Books for Primary Grades.* 3rd ed. Chicago: American Library Association, 1967. $4.00. Indexes the contents of nearly one thousand library and textbooks under sensible subject headings. Valuable for finding reading material for specific units.

Huus, Helen. *Children's Books to Enrich the Social Studies for the Elementary Grades.* Bulletin No. 32. Washington, D. C.: National Council for the Social Studies, 1966. Paper, $2.50. Over six hundred titles fully annotated and graded under many headings. Main headings: "Our World," "Times Past," "People Today," "The World's Work," and "Living Together." An author-and-title index increases its usefulness as an important reference bulletin.

A periodical for librarians, *The Booklist,* is published by the American Library Association twice monthly (once in August). We have always found it a fascinating publication to peruse for it makes us realize how much material is available. It does make the classroom teacher more knowledgeable about resources. It is an essential aid for selecting and buying currently produced books, 16mm films, filmstrips, and other nonprint media for use in public and school libraries. The items are selected by *The Booklist* staff and experienced librarians and media specialists in the field. Books and nonprint materials for all ages and a broad range of interests are described in concise, objective appraisals that summarize content; note point of view, style of presentation, and special features; and suggest audience or use. There are selective listings of such additional types of nonprint materials as slide sets, transparencies, videocassettes, tape cassettes, kits, simulations, games, 8mm filmloops, study prints, charts, maps, and globes, arranged by medium or in multimedia listings.

See "Notable Children's Trade Books in the Field of Social Studies" listed in *Social Education, Journal of the National Council for the Social Studies*—36 (December 1972): 858-864; 37 (December 1973): 784-792; 39 (March 1975): 172-176; and 40 (April 1976) 238-244. Look to future issues for further listings, probably in March each year. Books were evaluated by a special Book Review Committee appointed by the National Council for the Social Studies—Children's Book Council Joint Liaison Committee. In general, books selected for this bibliography met the following criteria: (1) they are primarily written for children (K to 8); (2) they emphasize human relations; (3) they present an original theme or fresh slant on a traditional topic; (4) they are highly readable; (5) they are accurate in fact an in interpretation; and (6) wherever appropriate, they include maps and illustrations. Not included were books judged basically inaccurate, lacking in originality, too limited in scope or too advanced for most readers in the K to 8 range. However, books were not rejected for using nonstandard English, or for raising provocative questions without supplying answers.

A number of authors have edited books of readings wherein articles from magazines and some other sources have been brought together. Thumbing through such books you will undoubtedly find some articles you will want to read.

Herman, Wayne L., Jr., ed. *Current Research in Elementary-School Social Studies*. New York: Crowell-Collier-Macmillan, 1969.

Jarolimek, John, and Huber M. Walsh, eds. *Readings for Social Studies in Elementary Education*. 3rd ed. New York: Macmillan, 1974.

Walsh, Huber M., ed. *An Anthology of Readings in Elementary School Social Studies*. Arlington, Va.: National Council for the Social Studies, 1971.

A different kind of valuable presentation is found in a paperback book, *Successful Models and Materials for Elementary Social Studies* by Barbara J. Capron and Charles L. Mitsakos, published in 1977 by Social Science Education Consortium, Inc., 855 Broadway, Boulder, Colorado 80302. The authors present a variety of materials which, from their own extensive experience in elementary education, they believe will be useful to elementary social studies teachers. They have selected, excerpted, and described models for teaching many of the major generalizations and concepts that are common in elementary programs. In addition, they present several approaches to values education and references to give perspective to (and go beyond) the particular models they have presented.

An elementary teacher who wants to dig into particular areas of social studies to see, among other things, the relationship between elementary and secondary school treatment in choice of content subject material and methodology will find perusal of the Yearbooks of the National Council for the Social Studies interesting and worthwhile. Many of the Yearbooks have specific chapters concerned with elementary social studies.

We begin with the 31st Yearbook, 1961, *Interpreting and Teaching American History;* 1962, *Social Studies in Elementary Schools;* 1963, *Skill Development in Social Studies;* 1964, *New Perspectives in World History;* 1965, *Evaluation in Social Studies;* 1966, *Political Science in the Social Studies;* 1967, *Effective Thinking in the Social Studies;* 1968, *International Dimensions in the Social Studies;* 1969,

Social Studies Curriculum Development; 1970, *Focus on Geography: Key Concepts and Teaching Strategies;* 1971, *Values Education: Rationale, Strategies, and Procedures;* 1972, *Teaching about Life in the City;* 1973, *Teaching Ethnic Studies: Concepts and Strategies;* 1974, *Teaching American History: The Quest for Relevancy;* 1975, *Controversial Issues in the Social Studies: A Contemporary Perspective;* 1976, *Values of the American Heritage: Challenges, Case Studies, and Teaching Strategies.*

In the future a variety of resource booklets and materials will be published by the National Council, and these will replace the yearbook publication.

For many years there have been publications listing free and inexpensive materials available to social studies teachers. At one time, one of the authors of this *Guide* had a large class in social studies methods divide the task of writing for every item in a publication of such materials. Brought together in an exhibition, in quantity it was an imposing sight. Members of the class soon learned that there was a wide variation in the quality of material and its usefulness in an elementary classroom. However, they did find useful material they could recommend to fellow teachers. Free and inexpensive materials can vary from rather obvious propaganda (label it for what it is) and direct advertising to productions by organizations and commercial enterprises that make a worthwhile contribution to the teacher and the learner.

We list below some of the sources listing available materials.

Educators' Guide to Free Curriculum Materials. Educators Progress Service, Randolph, Wisc. 53956. Many excellent materials, but all should be evaluated for the purpose for which they will be used. This company publishes three other guides: *Educators' Guide to Free Tapes, Scripts and Transcription; Educators' Guide to Free Films; Educators' Guide to Free Filmstrips.*

Free and Inexpensive Learning Materials. Division of Surveys and Field Services, George Peabody College for Teachers, Nashville, Tenn. 37203. An extensive guide to carefully evaluated educational materials. Entries are logically classified under ninety-six subject headings, cross-referenced, and indexed. Lists hundreds of free items; few cost more than one dollar. Complete ordering information given.

Miller, Bruce, ed. *Sources of Free and Inexpensive Teaching Aids.* Box 369, Riverside, Calif. 92502.

Selected Free Materials for Classroom Teachers. Fearon Publishers, 6 Davis Drive, Belmont, Calif. 94002.

Catalogs keep us informed of not only what is available but also what is new. In addition to the references made in this chapter, there are many companies that are distributors for publications of other companies. One of the largest is Social Studies School Service, 10,000 Culver Blvd., Culver City, Calif. 90230. Send for the elementary school catalog (a good introduction to all types of social studies resource materials).

SERIES BOOKS FOR CHILDREN

There is an increasing number of children's books about countries, regions, cities, rivers, historical events, etc., all over the world. Many publishers have developed books in a series. Given below are series titles, a representative book in the series, and the publisher. This information is provided to help you locate such books in a library or send to the publisher for a catalog. See publishers' addresses on page 395.

Series	Representative Book	Publisher
Adventures in Courage Series	*Pioneers of Freedom*	Reilly
Around the World Today Books	*Ali of Egypt*	Watts
Away to . . . . . . Series	*Venezuela*	Dodd
Big Cities of America Series	*Chicago*	McGraw-Hill
Children of Early America Series	*Children of the Mayflower*	Benefic Press
Children of the World Books	*Noriko, Girl of Japan*	Follett
Children of the World Series	*Marko Lives in Yugoslavia*	Macmillan
Cities of the World	*Rome*	Rand
*Colonial Americans Series	*The Architects*	Watts
*Colonial History Series	*Colonial South Carolina*	Nelson
*Come Along to	*Germany*	Dennison
*Cornerstones of Freedom Series	*The Story of the Supreme Court*	Children's Press
*Countries of Today Series	*Japan*	White
*Crossroads of America Series	*Enough Wise Men: The Story of Our Constitution*	Putnam
*Documents of Freedom Series	*The Emancipation Proclamation*	Grosset
*Enchantment of South America	*Bolivia*	Nelson
First Book Series	*Modern Egypt*	Watts
Freedom to Worship Series	*The Mormons*	McKay
*Frontiers of America Series	*Stalwart Men of Early Texas*	Children's Press
*Famous Museum Series	*Mystic Seaport: The Age of Sail*	Hastings
Getting to Know Books	*Getting to Know Iran and Iraq*	Coward
*Great Ideas Series	*Great Ideas in Communications*	White
*Historical Events Series	*D-Day*	McGraw-Hill
How People Live Books	*How People Live in the Middle East*	Benefic Press
In America Books	*The Mexicans in America*	McCormick
Keys to the City Series	*The Key to Tokyo*	Lippincott
Lands and People Series	*The Land and People of Iran*	Holiday
Let's Travel Series	*Let's Travel in Nigeria*	Children's Press

* Junior High Level

Of Black America Series	*Black and Brave*	McGraw-Hill
Let's Visit Series	*Let's Visit China Today*	Day
Life in Other Lands Series	*Life in the British Isles*	Fideler
Living in Today's World	*India: Old Land, New Nation*	Garrard
Looking at . . . . . . Series	*Looking at Brazil*	Lippincott
Made in . . . . . . Series	*Made in Japan*	Knopf
My Village Books	*My Village in Israel*	Pantheon
*Negro History Source Series	*Army Life in a Black Regiment*	Grosset
Picture Book of . . . . . . Series	*California*	Whitman
Picture Map Geography Series	*Picture Map Geography of Asia*	Lippincott
Picture Stories Series	*Picture Story of the Middle East*	McKay
Portraits of the Nation Series	*The Land and People of Burma*	Lippincott
Regions of America Books	*New England*	Harper
*Rivers of America Series	*The Sacramento*	Holt
Rivers of the World Series	*The Amazon: River Sea of Brazil*	Garrard
Stories from Many Lands Series	*Makato: A Story of Japan*	Crowell
They Helped Build America	*The Chinese Helped Build America*	Messner
*They Lived Like This Series	*In the Roman Empire*	Watts
This is . . . . . . Series	*This is Greece*	Macmillan
*Trade Routes Series	*Rival Cities: Venice and Genoa*	McGraw-Hill
Twins Series	*The Norwegian Twins*	Walker
*Two Worlds Books Series	*A Chinese Year*	Evans
Understanding Your World Series	*Understanding Ethiopia*	Laidlaw
Visual Geography Series	*Saudi Arabia*	Sterling
World Explorer	*Robert Falcon Scott*	Garrard
*World Neighbor Series	*Yugoslavia, Romania, Bulgaria*	Nelson
Young . . . . . . Series	*Young Israel*	Dodd
*Young Historian Series	*Modern China*	Day
Young Traveller Series	*Young Traveller in Germany*	Dutton

OBSERVATION GUIDE FOR FOREIGN TRAVEL

There are few teachers who would not like to travel. A teacher would anticipate a pleasant personal experience, but would also expect professional benefits. This observation guide does not mention museums, cathedrals, restaurants, or night clubs. It does direct your attention to the way in which people live and behave in the

*Junior High Level

countries you visit. It probably raises more questions than you can answer in one trip, but its use will assure you of greater understanding of a country than if you did not think of these things.

One of the major dangers any traveler faces in visiting a foreign nation is the tendency to generalize on the basis of an inadequate sampling. Each of us is prone to think that the few Frenchmen, Mexicans, or Egyptians whom we meet are typical of all others. On such hasty generalizations do we build invalid stereotypes.

The purpose of this observation guide is to direct your thinking and observation along certain specific lines. You should be able to reach conclusions that are based upon careful observation and wider sampling. In any event, an earnest search on your part for answers to some of these questions will certainly add depth and meaning to your travel experience.

Clothing

1. Compare clothing costs with those for similar items at home and elsewhere.
2. Are ready-made items of apparently good quality?
3. Can you tell a person's social or economic status by the manner in which he dresses?
4. Do school children wear uniforms? Why?
5. How much evidence do you see of picturesque and traditional costumes?
6. Are there any customs of dress that differ markedly from our own? What reasons can you find for such customs?

Sports and recreation

1. Are people as interested in sports as you expected? Which sports? Why?
2. What type of films seem to be popular? Prices?
3. How well attended are musical and dramatic events, and by what particular population groups?
4. How do most people seem to spend their leisure time?
5. What do you observe of the play activities of children?
6. Does "commercial" entertainment and recreation seem to be as important in this nation as in our own?

Family relationships

1. How would you describe family relationships?
2. Which parent seems to control the children?

3. Do most groups you observe seem to be age groups, sex groups, or family groups?
4. Compare observed behavior of children here with that of children of the same age in your country.
5. How much freedom do children seem to have?
6. What evidence do you see of working mothers, nursery schools, etc.?
7. What material possessions, if any, seem to dominate the family group?

Shopping

1. Is there much bargaining or is there a fixed price system?
2. Which member of the family shops for which types of items?
3. Compare the relative importance of small shops and department stores.
4. How do items being bought compare with similar items in our country?
5. What goods seem to be in greatest demand?
6. How would you characterize the efficiency of the local shopping habits?

Class and caste

1. On what does the upper class base its strength—industrial power, hereditary privilege, money, etc.?
2. Through what forms of conspicuous consumption is class displayed?
3. Do you see much evidence of class mobility?
4. Is there evidence of discrimination against minorities?
5. Would you say that this nation is more or less democratic than the United States? Why?
6. Compare the spread between classes here with that in our own country.
7. How large would you say the middle class is?

Foods and health

1. Do local foods differ markedly from your normal diet, and if so, why?
2. What are the local staples, particularly in winter?
3. Does the average person seem to be well fed and healthy?
4. How popular are canned and frozen foods?
5. Is there a public or private system of medical care and hospitals—and how does the system work?

Reading material

1. Analyze the newspapers most people read and compare them with your own.
2. What kinds of news stories get the biggest headlines?
3. What sections of the daily newspapers are read most avidly?
4. What kinds of books are for sale and who buys them?
5. Are U.S. books and magazines widely distributed and read?
6. Do you see many public libraries, newsstands, book stalls, etc.?

Public services and transportation

1. What, if any, services have been nationalized? How well do they operate?
2. How do people heat their homes, cook, and communicate with friends?
3. What is the normal means of family transportation?
4. How do manners displayed on public transportation compare with those in our own country?
5. What is the relative importance of such transportation means as bicycle, auto, bus, train, etc.?

Religion

1. Is there a state church, a dominant religion?
2. Can you find out what percentage of the people actively participate in the life of the church?
3. Does the church have any influence on public education?
4. Are the churches poor or wealthy? Why?
5. Does religion as a cultural force seem to be diminishing or increasing in importance?

General economy

1. Is there a housing shortage? How much new building do you observe?
2. Are there any price controls or rationed goods?
3. How many years of free education for each child? In what kind of a system?
4. Do women do more work in this economy than in our own?
5. Compare the amount and types of work done by hand with that done by machines. What is the respective importance of labor and capital?

Stereotypes

1. Before this trip, what words would you have used to describe the average resident of this nation?
2. What incidents and observations can you report to confirm or deny your previous stereotypes?
3. What words will you use in the future to describe these people? Why?
4. Do you feel that these people have an accurate and complete picture of the United States? What are the sources of their ideas? How can we correct misconceptions?

RESOURCE MATERIALS ON UNDERSTANDING OUR WORLD

Materials that concern more than one area of the world have been placed together under the heading *General Resources*. Further resources have been classified under *Africa, Asia, Canada, Europe, Middle East,* and *Latin America*. Even if you are interested in only one of these areas you should check the material under *General Resources*.

Embassies, Consulates General (in some large U.S. cities), and Information Offices of various countries are good sources of up-to-date materials. The teacher, not the children, should write. He should make known his interest in pictures, maps, and printed materials. The letter should indicate for what grade or age the material is wanted and some explanation of how the teacher expects to use it. It is not wise to give the impression that you want anything and all you can get if the material is free. Letters may be mailed to the Embassy in Washington, D.C. (without a specific street address). Travel advertisements in magazines and newspapers will give you the addresses of information offices of many countries.

General resources

1. *Background Notes* are short factual pamphlets about the countries and territories all over the world written by officers in the Department of State's geographic bureaus. Each *Background Note* includes information on the country's land, people, history, government, political conditions, economy, and foreign relations. Included also is a map and usually a brief bibliography. Obtained from the Superintendent of Documents, Government Printing Office, Washington, D.C. 20402. $.25 each. (Do not send stamps.)
2. *Family Holidays Around the World*. The American Home Economics Association, Washington, D.C. 20036. Eighty pp. $2.00.

3. The Fideler Company, 31 Ottawa Avenue, Grand Rapids, Mich. 49502. Get their brochure on Resource Books on eight regions of the world. Excellent illustrations and teacher guides.
4. American Red Cross Youth Service Programs, 17th and D Streets, N.W., Washington, D.C. 20006. Check with your local Red Cross chapter about intercultural and international youth programs. An elementary teacher's resource is the Red Cross *Youth News* magazine, a seven times yearly publication, available through subscriptions. Order direct from the above address for $3.00 per year or through your local Red Cross chapter for $1.25 per year.
5. Folkways/Scholastic Records, 906 Sylvan Avenue, Englewood Cliffs, N.J. 07632. Their catalog shows recordings of music from all over the world.
6. *Status of the World's Nations*. Pub. 8735. Prepared by the Geographer of the State Department. Superintendent of Documents, Washington, D.C. 20402. $1.05. (Stamps not accepted.) A twenty-page booklet containing the 148 sovereign states in the world recognized by the United States as being independent. Add Granada, February 7, 1974, and Guinea-Bissau, September 10, 1974, and you will have all of the world's independent nations. An excellent map of the world, 24″ x 36″, in color, with only the names of the countries and their capitals. A "must have" reference.
7. Goetz, Delia. *World Understanding Begins with Children*. Superintendent of Documents, Washington, D.C. 20402. 1960. Thirty-six pp. $.15. (No stamps.)
8. *Global Dimensions in U.S. Education: The Elementary School*. ISA Education Commission, 752 Comstock Ave., Syracuse University, Syracuse, N. Y. 13210. Fifty-two pp. $1.50. Describes several programs that have attempted to improve the international dimension of the curriculum.
9. *Understanding Your World Series* (4-8). Laidlaw Brothers, River Forest, Ill. 60305. Thirteen supplementary books, each dealing with a separate country.
10. National Council for Geographic Education, 115 North Marion St., Oak Park, Ill. 6030l. Get the one-page announcement of the Instructional Activities Series with the twelve items for elementary teachers. $.50 for each activity.
11. Kenworthy, Leonard S. *World Affairs Guides*. Teachers College Press, 1234 Amsterdam Ave., New York, N. Y. 10027. The general plan is the same in each booklet. Each contains an overview of the area, spotlights a few of the "big ideas" to stress in studies of that region, and pinpoints a wide variety of resources—including books, booklets, films, fimstrips, maps, and charts. Helpful content for the elementary teacher planning units.
    Studying Africa in Elementary and Secondary Schools, 1970. $1.95.
    Studying the Middle East in Elementary and Secondary Schools, 1965, $1.95.
    Studying South America in Elementary and Secondary Schools, 1965, $1.95.
    Studying the U.S.S.R. in Elementary and Secondary Schools, 1969, $1.95.
    Studying China in Elementary and Secondary Schools, 1975, $2.75.
    Studying Japan in Elementary and Secondary Schools, 1975, $2.75.
    Studying India in Elementary and Secondary Schools, 1975, $2.75.
12. Kenworthy, Leonard S. *Three Billion Neighbors*. Ginn, Lexington, Mass. 02173. 1965. 160 pp. School ed, $3.20. This pictorial story shows cultures,

nations, and peoples of the world. Families, houses, clothes, foods, schools, what they exchange and sell, how they earn their livings.

13. Lambert, Wallace, E., and Otto Klineberg. *Children's Views of Foreign Peoples*. New York: Appleton-Century-Crofts, 1967. 311 pp. A study of children's ideas about other peoples. Highly recommended for teacher's use.
14. Millen, Nina. *Children's Games from Many Lands*. New York: Friendship Press. 1958. Paperback and hardbound.
15. Monitor Recordings, Inc., 156 Fifth Avenue, New York, N.Y. 10010. The catalog is called "Monitor Music of the World."
16. National Geographic Educational Services, National Geographic Society, Dept. 1241, P.O. Box 1640. Washington, D.C. 20013. Request their catalog and any other materials for elementary teachers.
17. Representative of abundantly illustrated books for young students are these:

    a. *Visual Geography Series*. Sterling Publishing Company, 419 Park Avenue, New York, N.Y. 10016. Sixty-four pp. $1.50 each. Orders must be prepaid; include postage. Booklets discuss the land, history, people, government, and economy of one hundred countries. Black-and-white photographs.
    b. William H. Sadlier, Inc., 11 Park Place, New York, N.Y. 10007. Nine *World Culture Communities—The People of United States and Canada, Latin America, Western Europe, Eastern Europe, Middle East and North Africa, New Africa, South Asia, East Asia and the Ocean World*. One hundred pp. Color and black-and-white photos. Fine maps. Woven throughout each text are the basic themes and concepts appearing in a variety of ways. Excellent review questions at the end of each chapter.

18. *World Traveler*, P.O. Box 3618, Washington, D.C. 20007. This sixteen-page magazine, ten issues a year (September through June), is planned and written by teachers who use the publication in their own classrooms. Each article is illustrated with full-color National Geographic photographs. Each issue is developed around a central theme. Highly recommended by the *Journal of Geography*. $3.75 for individual subscriptions; $3.00 each when ten or more subscriptions are ordered for a classroom, at one address.
19. Information Center on Children's Cultures, U.S. Committee for UNICEF, 331 East 38th Street, New York, N.Y. 10016. Annotated lists of printed materials for children. Selective guides to help in choosing children's books, picture sets, and developing units. Other printed material on specific regions—*Africa, Near East, Latin America*, each $1.00. Teacher's kits, at $1.50, have been developed on *Teaching About Interdependence in a Peaceful World, Teaching About the Rights of the Child, Teaching About Spaceship Earth*.
20. *Songs of Many Nations*. Cooperative Recreation Service, Radnor Road, Delaware, Ohio 43015. 1962. One hundred pp. $.30. Pocket-size edition of folk songs, rounds, hymns, and spirituals.
21. *World Today Series*. Stryker-Post Publications, 888 17th Street, N.W., Wash-

ington, D.C. 20006. Annually revised and published each August. A valuable resource for the teacher. *Africa; Latin America; The Middle East and South Asia; The Far East and Southwest Pacific;* and *The Soviet Union and Eastern Europe*. From 90 to 102 pages each, 8½″ x 11″, each book presents concise and up-to-date information about the political and economic situation in the areas covered, plus the geography, history and culture of each nation. Illustrated with many useful maps. Paperbacks. $2.25 each.

22. United Nations Association—United States of America, 345 East 46th Street, New York, N.Y. 10017. *Annotated Bibliography of Teaching Materials on the UN*. This unique bibliography is a compilation of current and available selected materials recommended by educational authorities. It is divided into four categories for both the teacher and student. $.50.
23. *New Catalog of United Nations Publications*. Available free from UNIPUB, Inc., Box 433, Murray Hill Station, New York, N.Y. 10016. This thirty-three page catalog presents all in-print titles issued by the United Nations, including series publications, monographs, atlases, directories, annuals, conference proceedings, and statistical compilations.
24. *We the Americans*. Superintendent of Documents, U.S. Government Printing Office, Washington, D.C. 20402. A sixteen-page bulletin reporting in simple form with pictures, graphs, and tables the results of the 1970 census. $.35.
25. Many publishers produce paperbacks for high school students on different regions and countries of the world. Appropriate titles make good general background reading for the elementary teacher. Get catalogs or circulars from Ginn, Scholastic Publications, McCormick-Mathers, Laidlaw Brothers, Oxford Book, and others advertising in magazines such as *Social Education* and *Social Studies*.
26. *Area Handbook*. Superintendent of Documents, Government Printing Office, Washington, D.C. 20402. Studies of a country's social, economic, political, and military organization designed for the nonspecialist. Each *Handbook* describes a single country with a view toward depicting cultural and historical origins and the role these play in the country's present institutional organization and functioning. All volumes are clothbound. Available for more then ninety countries (send for list). Mostly priced between $4.50 and $8.00.
27. *National Geographic WORLD*. National Geographic Society, Washington, D.C. 20036. A new magazine (first issue September 1975) designed primarily for the eight through twelve year old. Each issue contains thirty-two pages with a folded 20″ x 31″ picture insert containing a wealth of related information and pictures on the reverse side. Liberally illustrated in color. Engrossing articles on history, science, nature, and geography and many other unusual features. $4.85 for one year. Send for a sample copy.
28. InterCulture Associates, Inc., Box 277, Thompson, Conn. 06277. Don't fail to examine the elementary catalog of cultural learning materials. You will be introduced to materials on and from Africa, Japan, and India, which will help make the world of other people from distant lands real for elementary students.

Resources on Africa

Africa today is not predominately the tribal Africa of the popular American stereotype. Modern Africa is highly diverse, and the materials used should help students comprehend this diversity.

1. Murphy, E. Jefferson, and Harry Stein. *Teaching Africa Today*. Citation Press, Englewood Cliffs, N.J. 07632. 1973. $3.85. Paperbound. Strongly recommended, interestingly written, and with excellent references. Valuable summaries of African history and geography of the developing nations with annotated listings of print and nonprint materials and extensive references on films and filmstrips. The authors were so concerned about the distorted views of Africa held by American students that they were exceedingly careful in their recommendations of materials to be used in the curriculum. Every teacher who teaches Africa should have access to this book.
2. The African-American Institute, School Services Division, 833 United Nations Plaza, New York, N.Y. 10017. The free annotated bibliographies are constantly being updated. They suggest background readings for teachers, audiovisual materials, text-and story books useful for activities on a wide range of African studies topics. (1) *Basic Bibliography;* (2) *Bibliography of Filmographies;* (3) *Bibliography for Elementary School Students*. The School Services Division is constantly developing supplementary classroom materials (e.g., *African Recipes* and a *Pronunciation Guide* to African countries and cities). The Division encourages teachers to write them. Ask about "Teaching about Africa: Effective Materials for Teachers."
3. African Travel Posters. African travel posters are available from various airlines; however, each one has its own procedures for distribution. TWA sells theirs for $1.25 each. Ethiopian Airlines gives theirs away but prefers that you ask for specific pictures; in this case you will have to write first and ask what they have. Most airlines have only limited supplies. Below are listed the names and addresses of airlines that generally have posters of African settings.

   Air Afrique, 683 Fifth Avenue, New York, N.Y. 10022
   Air France, 1350 Avenue of the Americas, New York, N.Y. 10019
   Air India, 345 Park Avenue, New York, N.Y. 10022
   Ethiopian Airlines, 200 East 42nd Street, New York, N.Y. 10017
   Pan American World Airways, Pan Am Building, New York, N.Y. 10036
   Trans World Airlines, 605 Third Avenue, New York, N.Y. 10022

4. *General Reference Maps of African Countries*. Superintendent of Documents, U.S. Government Printing Office, Washington, D.C. 20402. $.60-$1.00. Sizes range from 13" x 19" to 29" x 12". Write first for a price list.
5. In this *Guide*, see p. 380, General Resources; page 000, Study Prints.
6. *The New Africa*. Scholastic Book Services, 904 Sylvan Avenue, Englewood Cliffs, N. J. 07632. A chart that gives twenty-two columns of essential and up-to-date facts about thirty-six nations, with a large map and vivid illustrations.

$.70. Could be used as a model for students to construct their own information charts.

7. *African Song Sampler*. Cooperative Recreation Service, Radnor Road, Delaware, Ohio 43015. The best inexpensive collection of songs. $.30.
8. Kenworthy, Leonard S. *Studying Africa in Elementary and Secondary Schools*, New York: Teachers College Press, 1970. Has a wide variety of resources. See item 11, p. 381.
9. Quinn, Vernon. *Picture Map Geography of Africa*. Rev. ed. J.B. Lippincott Co., East Washington Square, Philadelphia, Pa. 19105. 1964. 119 pp.
10. Wright, Rose. *Fun and Festival from Africa*. Friendship Press, 475 Riverside Drive, New York, N.Y. 10027. 48 pp. $.95. Games, songs, poems, stories, recipes.
11. Allen, William D. *Africa*. Fideler, 31 Ottawa Avenue, N.W., Grand Rapids, Mich., 49052. 1962. 160 pp. Grades 5-8. Arranged by topics. Especially good for its 146 photographs and maps.
12. See *Social Education*, Special issue on Africa (February 1971).
13. Map publishers have excellent, large inexpensive maps. Look in their catalogs. See addresses on page 343, item 15.
14. *Africa*. UNICEF, 331 East 38th St., New York, N.Y. 10016. 1968. $1.00. An annotated list of printed materials suitable for children, selected by a joint committee of the American Library Association and the African-American Institute.
15. *World Today Series. Africa*, 1975. See 21.
16. *Ashanti Family of Ghana Kit*. Selective Educational Equipment, Inc., 3 Bridge Street, Newton, Mass. 02195. Some publishers have developed comprehensive kits; illustrative of these kits is this one. It contains a teacher resource guide, fifteen children's books produced in Ghana (in English), twenty study prints (11" x 14"), materials for duplication and handout, two filmstrips depicting Ashanti Life in Ghana, pre-recorded audio cassette containing songs and Ashanti legends, three magnetic compasses, cocoa beans, and six artifacts. These materials and their use are based on the *Family of Man Social Studies Project for the Elementary Grades* developed at the University of Minnesota. This is a major school purchase. It comes in a carrying-storage case and can be used in one classroom after another during the year.
17. Murphy, E. Jefferson. *History of African Civilization*. Dell Publishing Co., Inc., One Dag Hammarskjold Plaza, New York, N.Y. 10017. Paperback. Praised as the "best single survey of African history and civilization published to date," here is the story of all Africa from prehistoric times to the present.

Resources on Asia

1. *Focus On Asian Studies*. Service Center for Teachers of Asian Studies, Association for Asian Studies, Ohio State University, 29 West Woodruff Avenue, Columbus, Ohio 43210. This publication, three issues a year, $2.00, will keep

you in touch with new materials and helpful ideas. Make checks payable to Ohio State University.

2. *Giant Asia.* Scholastic Book Services, 904 Sylvan Avenue, Englewood Cliffs, N.J. 07632. An illustrated notebook chart containing a 5,000-year panorama of life on the world's largest continent, a map, and excerpts from a *World of Facts.* $.70.
3. The Asia Society, 112 East 64th Street, New York, N.Y. 10021. Write for a report on the evaluation of 306 elementary and secondary school social studies textbooks with Asian content.
4. Are you interested in getting books for children published in the Philippines, Malaysia, or India (in English) priced from $2.25 to $3.25, paperbacks? Send for a price list to The Cellar Book Shop, 18090 Wyoming, P.O. Box 6, College Park Station, Detroit, Mich. 48221.
5. The Japan Society, Inc., 250 Park Avenue, New York, N.Y. 10017, distributes free of charge various pamphlets pertaining to Japanese culture that teachers and pupils will find useful. One is "What Shall I Read on Japan?" Write for a complete listing.
6. Japan Information Service, Consulate General of Japan, 235 East 42nd Street, New York, N.Y. 10017. Write for a complete file of *Facts About Japan*, a series of excellent illustrated leaflets, each one treating a single topic. Two booklets with good information for the teacher are "The Japan of Today" and "A Nation Reborn." Charts, posters, maps, and slides are also available.
7. Write Charles E. Tuttle, Inc., Rutland, Vt. 05701, for their general catalog, which has much fine material on Japan.
8. *Fun and Festival from Japan;* also *Fun and Festival from India, Pakistan, Ceylon, Nepal.* Friendship Press, 475 Riverside Drive, New York, N.Y. 10027. $.95 each.
9. Kenworthy, Leonard S. *World Affairs Guides.* See p. 381, item 11.

   Studying China in Elementary and Secondary Schools. 1975, $2.75.
   Studying Japan in Elementary and Secondary Schools. 1975, $2.75.
   Studying India in Elementary and Secondary Schools. 1975, $2.75.

10. China Books and Periodicals, 95 Fifth Avenue, New York, N.Y. 10003. Their catalog also includes films, posters, and records.
11. *Social Education*, Special issue on China (January 1973). Up-to-date background for the teacher with many references to other sources.
12. *Publications and Resources.* This catalog is available from the National Committee on United States-China Relations, Inc., 777 United Nations Plaza, New York, N.Y. 10017. In addition to an extensive and annotated list of "China Conversations" on tape and various publications, including curriculum guide references, it contains brief descriptions of the National Committee and its School Services Program.
13. Posner, Arlene, and Arne J. de Keijzer, eds. *China: A Resource and Curriculum Guide.* University of Chicago Press, 5801 Ellis Avenue, Chicago, Ill. 60637.

1973. 280 pp. Paper, $2.95. The main part of the *Guide*, "Resources and Curricula," is a critical annotated evaluation of curriculum units, audiovisual materials, books (including a recommended "basic bookshelf"), packets and miscellaneous materials, and periodicals on China. Put this book at the top of your list.

14. *Indian Study Prints*. InterCulture Associates, Box 277, Thompson, Conn. 06277. Seventeen black-and-white 8″ x 10″ prints designed to examine preconceptions of India before class study begins. Packet $1.50. Have groups of three or four examine the prints and decide whether or not the pictures are of India and why they think so. An exciting way to introduce India in the classroom.

Resources on the Middle East

1. Information Services, American Friends of the Middle East, Inc., 1717 Massachusetts Avenue, N.W., Washington, D.C. 20036. "Some Major Concepts to Stress in Studying the Middle East" and "Directory of Films on the Middle East" available free. Ask if there are other materials for the elementary school teacher.
2. "The Middle East," Special Issue of *Social Education* (February 1976). National Council for the Social Studies, 1515 Wilson Blvd., Arlington, Va. 22209. The special issue of January 1961 is also worth exploring.
3. Rowland, John. *Fun and Festival from the Middle East*. New York: Friendship Press. 1959. Includes games, recipes, songs, and other materials. 43 pp. $.95.
4. *The Near East and North Africa*. An annotated list of books for children. 1970. $1.00. UNICEF, 331 East 38th St., New York, N.Y. 10016.
5. The League of Arab States, Arab Information Center, 747 Third Avenue, New York, New York 10017.*

Resources on Europe

1. *Soviet Life*. Illustrated monthly. 1706 Eighteenth Street, N.W., Washington, D.C. 20009. $6.50 a year. Circulated in the United States by agreement of the governments of the United States and the U.S.S.R. Advertised as "firsthand information on the hopes, problems, aspirations, plans of the Soviet people." When you find propaganda in it, as you will, so label it. Its illustrations, many in color, and its variety of materials (including Children's Corner) provide some insight into everyday Soviet life.
2. On page 380 read the suggestions about writing to foreign embassies for information and materials on their countries.
3. Read through the items under *General Resources*, where you will find information about some other source materials which would be applicable to European nations.

*When publications deal with an area in which there are opposing cultural views, the teacher should use judgment in recommending a particular publication. Some balance in presenting the two positions should be sought by the teacher and provided for the students.

Resources on Latin America

1. Kenworthy, Leonard S. *Studying South America in Elementary and Secondary Schools*. New York: Teachers College Press. 1965. $1.95. A "must" as a teacher reference. Has a wide variety of resources. (See item #11, p. 381)
2. Scholastic Book Services, 904 Sylvan Avenue, Englewood Cliffs, N.J. 07632. Chart on Latin America. $.70. Presents up-to-date information on the Latin American republics. Illustrated with a large map and numerous photographs.
3. *Latin America*. An annotated list of books for children selected by a committee of librarians, teachers, and Latin American specialists in cooperation with the Center for Inter-American Relations. Some books not recommended. 1969. $1.00. Address UNICEF (see item #19, p. 382).
4. Charles E. Merrill Company, 1300 Alum Creek Drive, Columbus, Ohio 43216. Series of booklets on "Sports in Latin America"; "Peoples of Latin America"; "Foods from Latin America." Get listing and inexpensive prices.
5. Organization of American States, 19th Street and Constitution Avenue, Washington, D.C. 20006. Ask for the "Short List of Publications." Excellent illustrated booklets of the separate Latin American countries. Twenty-four to forty-eight pages, $.25 to $.50. Films available for small rental fee. Study Kit on Latin American countries (collection of booklets). $1.00.

Resources on Canada

1. *Canada—Land of Hope*. Canadian Chamber of Commerce, 300 Sacrament St., Montreal, Canada. Free.
2. Canadian National Railways, 630 Fifth Avenue, New York, N.Y. 10020. Sixteen-mm color and sound films available, without charge. Demand is heavy, so book as far in advance as possible. Send for catalog.
3. *A Conspectus of Canada*. The Royal Bank of Canada, P.O. Box 6001, Montreal, Quebec, Canada. As you travel from province to province, learning a little about its history, its people, its resources, and prospects, you will get an overall view of the natural grandeur of Canada. 186 pages. A map of Canada is also included. Free.
4. *Teacher's Kit on Canada*. This basic set of information materials, which has been prepared for use by U.S. teachers, includes an encyclopedic handbook on Canada, pamphlets, and a map. Inquire about the large selection of 16-mm films on a variety of subjects for free loan. Write the nearest Canadian Consul General.

   Suite 2000, 310 South Michigan Ave., Chicago, Ill. 60604
   Illuminating Building, 55 Public Square, Cleveland, Ohio 44113
   Suite 1600, 2001 Bryan Tower, Dallas, Texas
   1920 First Federal Building, 1001 Woodward Ave., Detroit, Mich. 48226
   510 West Sixth Street, Los Angeles, Calif. 90014
   Suite 2110, 2 Canal Street, New Orleans, La. 70130

Suite 2110, 2 Canal Street, New Orleans, La. 70130
3 Parkway Building, Philadelphia, Pa. 19102
One Maritime Plaza, Golden Gateway Center, San Francisco, Calif. 94111
412 Plaza 600, Sixth and Stewart Streets, Seattle, Wash. 98101
1251 Avenue of the Americas, New York, N.Y. 10020
500 Boylston Street, Boston, Mass. 02116
260 Peachtree Street, N.E., P.O. Box 56169, Atlanta, Ga. 30343
One Marine Midland Center, Buffalo, N.Y. 14203
15 South 15th Street, Minneapolis, Minn. 55402

5. Map Distribution Office, Surveys and Mapping Branch, Department of Mines and Technical Surveys, 601 Booth Street, Ottawa, Ontario, Canada. Request a list of maps for sale.
6. Canadian Government Travel Bureau, Ottawa, Ontario, Canada. "Highway Map of Canada," 24″ x 37¼″, in color.
7. Canadian Embassy, 1746 Massachusetts Ave., N.W., Washington, D.C. 20036. Map of Canada, 40″ by 36.″

CALENDAR OF NATIONAL HOLIDAYS

The national holidays listed below are those officially designated and celebrated by the member nations at United Nations headquarters. Usually these national holidays represent the anniversary of independence. In a few countries a different date represents the major national holiday celebrated in the country itself.

We suggest that the teacher make it possible for the students to hear something about many of these countries as their holidays come along. Why not assign several students to several countries, or ask for volunteers, in advance of the holidays coming up, to get interesting information on the country and present it to the class on or near the holiday date. Each one could make his own plan of presentation. He would use a globe, a map, even a large drawing of the flag (see flags in color in the World Almanac). He might use pictures, make a chart, draw a graph, get a partner and discuss the country, find out how to get there by plane (airline, cost, length of time), look for items about the country in newspapers and newsmagazines (parents could help here), and many other things. Three or four students could make a committee presentation.

JANUARY

1 Cameroon*
1 Haiti
1 Sudan*
1 Western Samoa*
1 Cuba
4 Burma*
11 Chad*
26 Australia
26 India*

FEBRUARY

6 New Zealand
18 Gambia*
23 Guyana*
25 Kuwait*
27 Dominican Republic

MARCH

3 Morocco*
6 Ghana*
12 Mauritius*
17 Ireland
23 Pakistan*
25 Greece

APRIL

4 Hungary
4 Senegal*
16 Denmark
16 Israel*
17 Syria*
19 Sierra Leone*
26 Tanzania*
27 Togo*
29 Japan
30 Netherlands

MAY

9 Czechoslovakia
11 Laos*
14 Paraguay
17 Norway
22 Sri Lanka (Ceylon)*
25 Argentina
25 Jordan*
27 Afghanistan
31 South Africa

JUNE

1 Tunisia*
2 Italy
6 Sweden
7 United Kingdom
10 Portugal
12 Philippines*
17 Iceland
17 Fed. Rep. Germany
23 Luxembourg
26 Malagasy
30 Zaire*

JULY

1 Burundi*
1 Canada
1 Rwanda*
1 Somalia*
4 U. S. A.
5 Venezuela
6 Malawi*
14 France
14 Iraq
18 Spain
20 Columbia
21 Belgium
21 Mongolian People's Rep.
22 Poland
23 Ethiopia
23 Egypt
26 Liberia
26 Maldive Islands
28 Peru

AUGUST

1 Dahomey*
1 Switzerland
6 Bolivia
6 Jamaica*
7 Ivory Coast*
9 Singapore*
10 Ecuador
15 Korea*
15 People's Republic of the Congo*
17 Gabon*
17 Indonesia*
23 Rumania
25 Uruguay
31 Malaysia*
31 Trinidad and Tobago*

SEPTEMBER

1 Libya*
2 Democratic Rep. of Vietnam (Hanoi)*
3 Qatar*
6 Swaziland*
7 Brazil
9 Bulgaria
15 Costa Rica
15 El Salvador
15 Guatemala
15 Honduras
15 Nicaragua
15 Rep. of Korea
16 Mexico
18 Chile
22 Mali*
23 Saudi Arabia
26 Yemen
30 Botswana*

OCTOBER

1 Nigeria*
1 Cyprus*
2 Guinea*
4 Lesotho*
7 German Dem. Republic (East Berlin)
9 Uganda
10 Taiwan*
10 Fiji*
12 Equatorial Guinea*
21 Somalia*
24 Zambia*
26 Austria
26 Iran
29 Turkey

NOVEMBER

1 Algeria*
1 Rep. of Vietnam (Saigon)
3 Panama
7 U.S.S.R.
9 Cambodia*
18 Oman
22 Lebanon*
28 Mauritania*
29 Yugoslavia
29 Albania
30 Barbados*

DECEMBER

1 Central African Republic*
5 Thailand
6 Finland
11 Upper Volta*
12 Kenya*
16 Bangladesh*
18 Niger*
28 Nepal

*New nation since 1943

SOURCES OF STATE INFORMATION*

Alabama Information and Education Section
Department of Conservation and Natural Resources
Administration Building
Montgomery, Alabama 36104

Alaska Travel Division
Pouch E
Juneau, Alaska 99801

American Samoa Office of Samoan Information
Pago Pago, American Samoa 96920

Arizona State Office of Economic Planning
and Development
1645 West Jefferson Street
Phoenix, Arizona 85007

Arkansas Department of Parks and Tourism
149 State Capitol
Little Rock, Arkansas 72201

California Office of Tourism
926 J Building, Room 812
Sacramento, California 95814

Colorado Division of Commerce and Development
600 State Capitol Annex
Denver, Colorado 80203

Connecticut Development Commission
Promotion and Public Relations Division
State Office Building, Box 865
Hartford, Connecticut 06115

Delaware State Development Department
Travel Division
45 The Green
Dover, Delaware 19901

District of Columbia
Washington Convention and Visitors Bureau
1616 K Street, N.W.
Washington, D.C. 20006

Florida Department of Commerce
Division of Tourism
107 West Gaines Street
Tallahassee, Florida 32304

Georgia Department of Community Development
Tourist Division
P.O. Box 38097
Atlanta, Georgia 30334

Guam Visitors Bureau
P.O. Box 3520
Agana, Guam 96910

Hawaii Visitors Bureau
2270 Kalakaua Avenue
Honolulu, Hawaii 96815

Idaho Division of Tourism and Industrial Development
108 Capitol Building
Boise, Idaho 83720

Illinois Department of Business
and Economic Development
Division of Tourism
222 South College Street
Springfield, Illinois 62704

Indiana Department of Commerce
Tourist Division
334 State House
Indianapolis, Indiana 46204

Iowa Development Commission
Tourism and Travel Division
250 Jewett Building
Des Moines, Iowa 50309

Kansas Department of Economic Development
Travel Division
State Office Building, Room 122S
Topeka, Kansas 66612

Kentucky Department of Public Information
Travel Division
New Capitol Annex
Frankfort, Kentucky 40601

Louisiana Tourist Development Commission
P.O. Box 44291
Baton Rouge, Louisiana 70804

*Includes Puerto Rico and the Virgin Islands, American Samoa, and Guam

Maine Department of Commerce and Industry
State House
Augusta, Maine 04330

Maryland Department of Economic Development
Tourist Division
State Office Building
Annapolis, Maryland 21401

Massachusetts Department of Commerce
and Development
State Office Building
100 Cambridge Street
Boston, Massachusetts 02202

Michigan Tourist Council
300 South Capitol Ave.
Lansing, Michigan 48926

Minnesota Tourist Information Center
480 Cedar Street
St. Paul, Minnesota 55101

Mississippi Agricultural and Industrial Board
P.O. Box 849
Jackson, Mississippi 39205

Missouri Division of Tourism
Box 1055
Jefferson City, Missouri 65101

Montana Travel Promotion Unit
Department of Highways
Helena, Montana 59601

Nebraska Economic Development Department
Travel and Tourism Division
P.O. Box 94666
State Capitol Building
Lincoln, Nebraska 68509

Nevada Department of Economic Development
State Capitol Building
Carson City, Nevada 89701

New Hampshire Division of Economic Development
Promotion Department
State House Annex
Concord, New Hampshire 03301

New Jersey Department of Labor and Industry
State Promotion Office
P.O. Box 400
Trenton, New Jersey 08625

New Mexico Department of Development
Tourist Division
113 Washington Avenue
Santa Fe, New Mexico 87503

New York State Department of Commerce
Public Information
99 Washington Avenue
Albany, New York 12245

North Carolina Information Project
Department of Cultural Resources
Division of the State Library
109 East Jones Street
Raleigh, North Carolina 27611

North Dakota Travel Department
State Capitol Grounds
Bismarck, North Dakota 58505

Ohio Development Department
Travel Promotion
65 South Front Street
Columbus, Ohio 43215

Oklahoma Tourism and Recreation
Tourist Promotion Division
504 Will Rogers Building
Oklahoma City, Oklahoma 73105

Oregon Highway Department
Travel Information Division
Salem, Oregon 97310

Pennsylvania Department of Commerce
Travel Development Bureau
Harrisburg, Pennsylvania 17120

Rhode Island Development Council
Publicity and Recreation Division
Roger Williams Building
Providence, Rhode Island 02908

South Carolina Development Board
Travel and Information Division
P.O. Box 1358
Columbia, South Carolina 29202

South Dakota Department of Highways
Publicity Department
Pierre, South Dakota 57501

Tennessee Economic and Community Development
1028 Andrew Jackson State Office Building
Nashville, Tennessee 37219

Texas Highway Department
Travel Information Division
P.O. Box TT, Capitol Station
Austin, Texas 78701

Utah Travel Council
Council Hall-Capitol Hill
Salt Lake City, Utah 84114

Vermont Teacher's Services Section
Agency of Development and Community Affairs
61 Elm Street
Montpelier, Vermont 05602

Virginia State Department of Education
History, Government, and Geography Service
Division of Secondary Education
Richmond, Virginia 23216

Washington Department of Commerce
and Economic Development
Tourist Promotion Division
General Administration Building
Olympia, Washington 98504

West Virginia Department of Commerce
Travel Development Division
State Capitol
Charleston, West Virginia 25305

Wisconsin Department of Natural Resources
Vacation and Travel Service
P.O. Box 450
Madison, Wisconsin 53701

Wyoming Travel Commission
2320 Capitol Avenue
Cheyenne, Wyoming 82001

Puerto Rico Tourism Development Company
Box BN
San Juan, Puerto Rico 00936

Virgin Islands Commerce Department
Travel Promotion
Box 1692
St. Thomas, Virgin Islands

APPENDIX

Directory of publishers

Addison-Wesley Publishing Company, Reading, Mass. 01867

Afro-American Publishing Co., 1727 S. Indiana Avenue, Chicago, Ill. 60616

Allyn and Bacon, Inc., 470 Atlantic Avenue, Boston, Mass. 02210

American Book Company, 450 West 33rd Street, New York, New York 10001

American Home Economic Association, 2010 Massachusetts Ave., N.W., Washington, D.C. 20036

American Library Association, 50 East Huron Street, Chicago, Ill. 60611

Appleton-Century-Crofts Inc., 440 Park Avenue South, New York, N.Y. 10016

Association for Childhood Education International, 3615 Wisconsin Ave., N.W., Washington, D.C. 20016

Association for Supervision and Curriculum Development, 1701 K Street, N.W., Suite 1100, Washington, D.C. 20006

Basic Books, Inc., 10 East 53rd Street, New York, N.Y. 10022

Beacon Press, Inc., 25 Beacon Street, Boston, Mass. 02108

Benefic Press, 10300 West Roosevelt Road, Westchester, Illinois 60153

Bobbs-Merrill Co., Inc., 4300 W. 62nd St., Indianapolis, Ind. 46268

Chandler Publishing Co., 124 Spear Street, San Francisco, Calif. 94105

Children's Press, 1224 West Van Buren Street, Chicago, Ill. 60607

Citation Press, 906 Sylvan Avenue, Englewood Cliffs, N.J. 07632

F. E. Compton Company, 1000 North Dearborn St., Chicago, Ill. 60610

Coward-McCann, Inc., 200 Madison Avenue, New York, N.Y. 10016

Crowell Collier and Macmillan, Inc., 866 Third Ave., New York, N.Y. 10022

Crown Publishers, Inc., 419 Park Avenue South, New York, N.Y. 10016

The John Day Company, Inc., 257 Park Avenue South, New York, N.Y. 10010

T. S. Denison & Co., Inc., 51 West 82nd. St., Minneapolis, Minn. 55437

Denoyer-Geppert, 5235 Ravenswood Avenue, Chicago, Ill. 60640

Dial Press, Inc., 245 East 47th Street, New York, N.Y. 10017

Dodd, Mead and Company, Inc., 79 Madison Ave., New York, N.Y. 10016

Doubleday & Company, Garden City, New York 11530

Dover Publications, Inc., 180 Varick St., New York, N.Y. 10014

E. P. Dutton and Company, Inc., 201 Park Avenue South, New York, N.Y. 10003

Educators Progress Service, Randolph, Wisconsin 53956

M. Evans & Co., Inc., 216 East 49th Street, New York, N.Y. 10017

Fearon Publishers, Inc., 6 Davis Drive, Belmont, Calif. 94002

The Fideler Company, 31 Ottawa Ave., N.W., Grand Rapids, Mich. 49502

Follett Publishing Company, 1010 W, Washington Blvd., Chicago, Ill. 60607

Foreign Policy Association, Inc., 345 East 46th St., New York, N.Y. 10017

Friendship Press, 475 Riverside Drive, New York, N.Y. 10027

Garrard Publishing Co., 1607 N. Market St., Champaign, Ill. 61821

Ginn and Company, 191 Spring Street, Lexington, Mass. 02173

Grosset & Dunlap, Inc., 51 Madison Avenue, New York, N.Y. 10010

Hammond, Inc., Maplewood, N.J. 07040

Harcourt Brace & Jovanovich, 757 Third Ave., New York, N.Y. 10017

Hart Publishing Co., 15 West 4th Street, New York, N.Y. 10012

Hastings House, Inc., 10 East 40th Street, New York, N.Y. 10016

Harper & Row, Publishers, 10 East 53rd Street, New York, N.Y. 10022

Hill and Wang, Inc., 72 Fifth Avenue, New York, N.Y. 10024

Holiday House, Inc., 8 West 13th Street, New York, N.Y. 10011

Holt, Rinehart & Winston, Inc., 383 Madison Ave., New York, N.Y. 10017

Houghton Mifflin Company, 2 Park Street, Boston, Mass. 02107

Intext Educational Publishers, 257 Park Avenue South, New York, N.Y. 10010

Joint Council on Economic Education, 1212 Avenue of the Americas, New York, N.Y. 10036

Alfred A. Knopf, Inc., 201 East 50th Street, New York, N.Y. 10022

Laidlaw Brothers, Thatcher and Madison, River Forest, Ill. 60305

J. B. Lippincott Co., East Washington Square, Philadelphia, Pa. 19105

Little, Brown and Company, 34 Beacon Street, Boston, Mass. 02106

Macmillan Publishing Co., Inc., 866 Third Avenue, New York, N.Y. 10022

McCormick-Mathers Publishing Co., Inc., 450 West 33rd St., New York, N.Y. 10001

McGraw-Hill Book Co., Inc., 1221 Avenue of the Americas, New York, N.Y. 10020

David McKay Company, Inc., 750 Third Avenue, New York, N.Y. 10017

Melmont Publishers, Inc., 1224 West Van Buren Street, Chicago, Ill. 60607

Charles E. Merrill Publishing Co., 1300 Alum Creek Drive, Columbus, Ohio 43216

Julian Messner, 1 West 39th Street, New York, N.Y. 10018

National Council for the Social Studies, 1515 Wilson Blvd., Arlington, Va. 22209

National Education Association, 1201 Sixteenth St., N.W., Washington, D.C. 20036

National Council for Geographic Education, 115 North Marion Street, Oak Park, Ill. 60301

National Geographic Society, 17th and M Sts., N.W., Washington, D. C. 20036

Natural History Press (See Doubleday & Co.)

New American Library, Inc., 1301 Avenue of the Americas, New York, N.Y. 10019

Thomas Nelson, Inc., 30 East 42nd Street, New York, N.Y. 10017

Nystrom, 3333 Elston Avenue, Chicago, Ill. 60618

Olympus Publishing Co., East 13th Street South, Salt Lake City, Utah 84105

Pantheon Books, Inc., (See Random House)

Paul S. Eriksson, Inc., 119 West 57th St., New York, N.Y. 10019

F. E. Peacock Publishers, 401 W. Irving Park Rd., Itasca, Ill. 60143

Pflaum Standard, 38 West Fifth Street, Dayton, Ohio 45403

Plays, Inc., 8 Arlington Street, Boston, Mass. 02116

Praeger Publishers, 111 Fourth Avenue, New York, N.Y. 10003

Prentice-Hall, Inc., Englewood Cliffs, N.J. 07632

G. P. Putnam's Sons, 200 Madison Avenue, New York, N.Y. 10016

Rand McNally & Company, 8255 Central Park Ave., Skokie, Ill. 60680

Random House, Inc. 201 East 50th Street, New York, N.Y. 10022

Reilly & Lee Company, 114 West Illinois Street, Chicago, Ill. 60610

The Ronald Press Company, 79 Madison Avenue, New York, N.Y. 10016

William H. Sadlier, Inc., 11 Park Place, New York, N.Y. 10007

W. B. Saunders Co., 218 West Washington Square, Philadelphia, Pa. 19105

Scholastic Publications, 906 Sylvan Ave., Englewood Cliffs, N.J. 07632

Science Research Associates, 259 East Erie Street, Chicago, Ill. 60611

Scott, Foresman & Co., 1900 East Lake Avenue, Glenview, Ill. 60025

Shocken Books, 200 Madison Avenue, New York, N.Y. 10016

Charles Scribner's Sons, 597 Fifth Avenue, New York, N.Y. 10017

Silver Burdett Company, Park Avenue and Columbia Road, Morristown, N.J. 07960

Simon and Schuster, Inc., 630 Fifth Avenue, New York, N.Y. 10020

Sterling Publishing Company, Inc., 419 Park Avenue South, New York, N.Y. 10016

Superintendent of Documents, U.S. Government Printing Office, Washington, D.C. 20402

Teachers College Press, 1234 Amsterdam Avenue, New York, N.Y. 10027.

Charles E. Tuttle Co., Inc., 28 South Main Street, Rutland, Vermont 05701

United Federation of Teachers, 260 Park Avenue, New York, N.Y. 10017

University of Chicago Press, 5801 Ellis Avenue, Chicago, Ill. 60637

D. Van Nostrand, 450 West 33rd Street, New York, N.Y. 10001

Wadsworth Publishing Co., Inc., 10 Davis Drive, Belmont, Calif. 94002

Walker and Company, 720 Fifth Avenue, New York, N.Y. 10019

Franklin Watts, Inc., 845 Third Avenue, New York, N.Y. 10022

Webster Division, McGraw-Hill Book Co., Manchester, Missouri 63011

Westinghouse Learning Press, 100 Park Avenue, New York, N.Y. 10017

David White, Inc., 66 East 55th Street, New York, N.Y. 10022

Albert Whitman & Co., 560 West Lake Street, Chicago, Ill. 60606

Whittlesey House (See McGraw-Hill)

John Wiley and Sons., Inc., 605 Third Avenue, New York, N.Y. 10016

The World Publishing Company, 110 East 59th Street, New York, N.Y. 10022

Xerox Education Publications, 245 Long Hill Road, Middletown, Conn. 06457

INDEX